KU-537-825

GARDENERS'

•DIARY•

GARDENERS'
•DIARY•

D

DEALERFIELD

This edition specially printed for Dealerfield Ltd in 1995
by Marshall Cavendish Books, London

ISBN 1 85927 057 3

Printed and bound in Spain

Some of this material has previously appeared in
the Marshall Cavendish partwork *MY GARDEN*

CONTENTS

foreword

Gardeners' Diary **is now a widely viewed weekly television programme, covering the activities of a calendar year. Looking at the year in this way is a good memory jogger, and this practical book, with its helpful advice and huge number of illustrations, will ensure you get the best from your garden.**

Enjoyment is what gardening is all about. Your garden is your domain; plants are inherently interesting and beautiful and should be enjoyed for their own sake. In this book I hope to exaplain the simple principles which lie behind other people's seemingly effortless success. Gardening shouldn't be a list of chores; for most of us it is far better that we feel relaxed in our own garden, surrounded by a few small successes. The *Gardeners' Diary* is designed to help you achieve this.

I have been gardening all my life; for the past 40 years as a nurseryman, I have been completely unable to rein in the enormous variety of plants I feel I must grow. Very fortunately, this enthusiasm is shared by over one and a half million people who visit the Bridgemere Garden World each year.

The nursery began in 1962 just growing a crop of roses. There was then huge enthusiasm in Britain for roses, a most exciting time! By the late 1960s, there developed a craze for heathers and other small evergreens. Eventually we rediscovered the wealth of herbaceous border and cottage garden plants which had been somewhat eclipsed by the vogue for roses and the inevitable neglect of nurseries during the war years. Another group of plants almost forgotten but, thanks to the efforts of plant breeders, now making an astonishing contribution to gardening are bedding plants whose reliability, colour range and variety seem endless.

It is happily true – and a source of much fascination – that the variety of plants we can grow in our climate is endless. In an age of standardization, gardening is one of the few areas where we can all give expression without interference to our own tastes and fancies. It is a marvellous hobby – even for those without a garden since houseplants are so versatile that there is something to suit almost all indoor conditions.

The *Gardeners' Diary* television programme is made in a part of our six-acre

Opposite: *The Cottage Garden, one of the show gardens at Bridgemere Garden World.*

Left: *Tulips, just one of the many plants grown at the Bridgemere nursery.*

show gardens which are known as The Garden Kingdom. It is not a television set which is later tidied away. Everything we do, with its subsequent success or partial failure, can be seen by visitors at any time. The rest of the gardens contain over 20 interlinked gardens in different styles whose aim is to show you some plant combinations and give you ideas to be used in your own gardens. It is very important that as many plants as possible are seen in their growing positions and not just in rows in pots. All these gardens are open all year round and our staff are happy to explain anything to do with the growing of plants.

I would like people to enjoy their gardens and the plants in them as I do. The television programme, this book and the gardens at Bridgemere are designed to help viewers, readers and visitors to achieve this. Gardening is not a mystery revealed only to a few experts and denied to the rest of us. Plants are most adaptable and seem to have almost an conscious urge to succeed. Over the years some of them can be almost like friends and I can understand the attachment earlier peoples had for trees – I share it.

I have mentioned several groups of plants. There are, of course, many others, including rock plants, bulbs, climbers, fruit trees and flowering trees. At Bridgemere we are involved in all of them. We grow a huge variety of plants in about a million pots a year. In fact, we believe we grow more plants, both indoors and out, in more varieties on one site than anywhere in Europe and we wouldn't wish to be without any one of them. When not growing plants, the staff at Bridgemere are busy looking for

Left: *John Ravenscroft at work in the* Gardeners' Diary *garden.*

them. We visit gardens and nurseries in Britain and Europe and look at plants in North America, Australia and China. Wherever we are in the world there are always fascinating plants to see. So it is hardly surprising that we have every intention of adding to the many thousand varieties of plants we grow. It is an obsession for which we have no desire to seek a cure. Gardening is a most enjoyable full-time occupation and hobby which we would like to share with as many people as possible. I hope that this book kindles or helps to increase your enthusiasm for plants and gardening and that your garden becomes a source of continued enjoyment.

JOHN RAVENSCROFT
Bridgemere Garden World

HOW TO USE THIS BOOK

Throughout the book, dates are given as seasons, as months will vary from country to country. As a guide, the seasons are taken to mean the following in the northern and southern hemispheres:

Season	Northern Hemisphere	Southern Hemisphere
Early Spring	March	September
Mid Spring	April	October
Late Spring	May	November
Early Summer	June	December
Mid Summer	July	January
Late Summer	August	February
Early Autumn	September	March
Mid Autumn	October	April
Late Autumn	November	May
Early Winter	December	June
Mid Winter	January	July
Late Winter	February	August

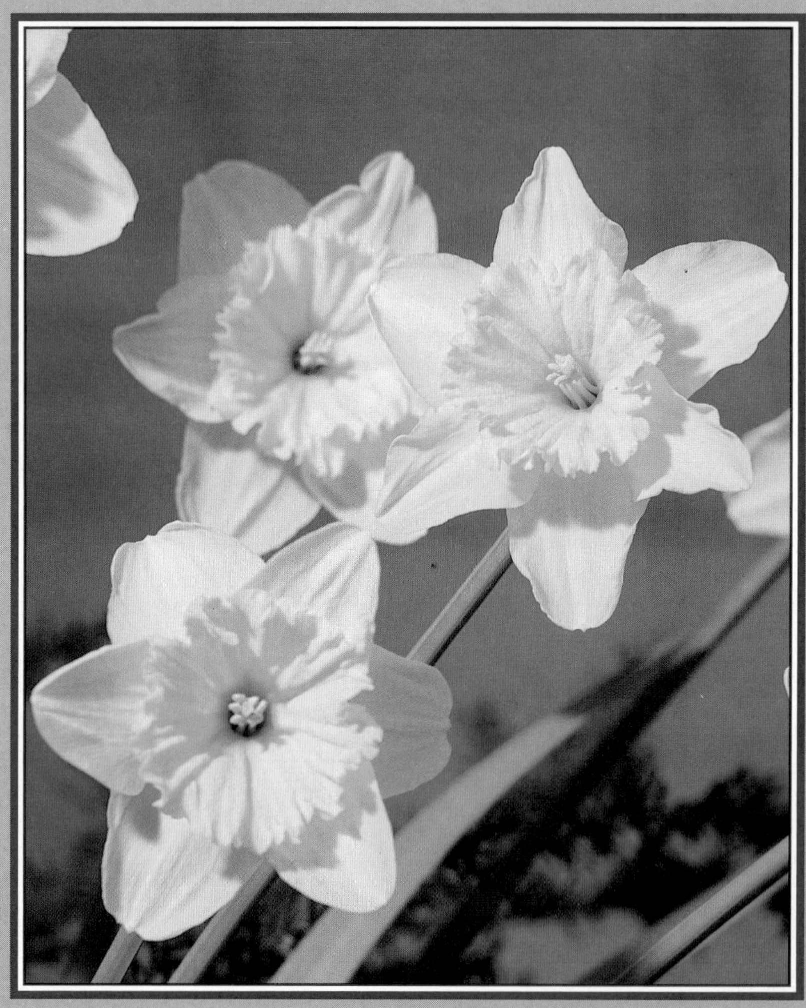

Daffodils herald in the spring with their sunshine-yellow flowers – vigorous new growth makes for a busy time in the garden.

SPRING

EARLY SPRING

MID SPRING

LATE SPRING

CHECKLIST

WHAT TO DO

BORDER PLANTS
Provide supports if necessary

CHRYSANTHEMUMS
Pot up rooted cuttings

SEEDLINGS
Prick out before they become crowded

SWEET PEAS
Plant out autumn-sown seedlings

LOOK AHEAD

ORDER
Summer-flowering bulbs

PROPAGATE
Heathers by layering, take dahlia cuttings

PLANT
Border plants, trees, shrubs and hedges, gladioli

SOW
Summer bedding plants, dahlia seeds

WHAT TO SEE

BULBS AND BORDER PLANTS
Crocuses, daffodils, *Iris reticulata*, Lenten rose (*Helleborus orientalis*), polyanthus, primroses, tulips (early species and hybrids)

SHRUBS AND TREES
Camellias, *Chaenomeles japonica*, corylopsis, *Daphne mezereum*, *Prunus cerasifera*

VISITORS

FRIENDS
Chaffinches, frogs, robins, wrens

FOES
Scale insects, slugs and snails

EARLY SPRING
WEEK 1

WHAT TO DO

In most areas spring has arrived, despite frequent cold days. More spring bulbs are in flower, and many early bedding plants are starting to show colour. Be cautious about sowing outdoors, but complete as much planting as possible.

Plant trees and shrubs
Container-grown plants can be planted at any time of the year, but this is a good time to plant all kinds of trees and shrubs. If you want to make a hedge, bare-root plants (or bundles of small plants potted up together) are the most economical way to buy plants in bulk. Plant now so they have a chance to become established before the dry summer months.

Buy summer-flowering bulbs
Gladioli can be planted from now on, and most of the more tender kinds within the next month or so. Order or buy them now, while there is still a good selection.

Plant herbaceous border plants
Try to finish planting new border perennials within the next couple of weeks.

If the weather is dry, be sure to water the plants in thoroughly, and, if necessary, mist them with water every few days. Although drought is uncommon at this time of year, drying winds may cause plants to wilt if they cannot take up water quickly enough from roots that have been disturbed by transplanting.

An ideal time to plant border perennials.

Remove winter protection
Remove protection from slightly tender shrubs and from tubs that have been insulated to prevent damage from severe freezing. These plants should have plenty of light now.

Plant autumn-sown sweet peas
Plant out sweet peas sown in the autumn and overwintered in a cold frame. Place slug pellets around the plants as a precaution. Tie plants firmly to supports.

Layer heathers
This is a good time to layer heathers. It is easier than taking cuttings as they need less attention. They will be ready for transplanting next spring.

WHAT TO SEE

Insight Picture Library

Polyanthus are good for massed bedding.

Primroses and polyanthus are synonymous with spring, although modern primrose hybrids are now sold in flower as pot plants right through the winter.

Modern primroses bear little resemblance to the wild version, in colour or size of flower. Some look almost like polyanthus from a distance. Those sold as pot plants need careful hardening off before you put them outdoors, and even then they are best used in window boxes or containers.

For a bold display in beds, it is better to grow your own and keep them in a cold frame without too much heat during the winter, then plant out in early spring. Better still, grow polyanthus, which have a similar colour range and are more dependable for massed bedding.

If the pale yellow, delicate blooms of the wild primrose appeal more, buy seeds or plants from a wild flower specialist. There is no need to raid the local hedgerows to enjoy them in your own garden.

Polyanthus can be treated as a perennial but they are far better grown as a biennial. They come in a bright range of colours that includes red, yellow, pink, blue and white, many with a contrasting eye.

LOOK AHEAD

Dahlias are popular as cut flowers, but they are also great for border decoration. Most flower from late summer well into autumn, just when most other herbaceous border plants have either died back or are beginning to look decidedly dejected.

You can wait until spring and simply plant tubers in unprepared ground to get a reasonable display, but the results will be better if you plan and prepare now.

Eric Crichton

The splendid dahlia 'Glorie van Heemstede'.

Choose a sunny site, and dig over the ground, making sure it is cleared of perennial and difficult weeds. There is no need to add a lot of compost or manure, but on a very light, sandy soil it helps to retain moisture. Rake in bone meal at about 280g per sq m/8oz per sq yd, which will release its nutrients over a long period.

If you already have tubers and want to take cuttings, start them into growth by planting in trays of compost and misting daily.

You can get earlier flowers from tubers by starting them off in pots in a greenhouse during the next few weeks, then planting them in the garden once there is no danger of frost.

It is not too late to sow the seed of bedding dahlias.

VISITORS

There are many kinds of scale insects, but all produce white, yellow or brown wax scales to cover their relatively featureless bodies. Although they are only a few millimetres long, you are unlikely to miss them because they generally occur in large clusters.

Soft scale is usually light brown with a darker centre, and you may find it on the undersides of leaves on bay (Laurus nobilis), *camellias, hollies and ivies, and other plants. Brown scale is dark brown and usually develops on the woody stems of plants such as cotoneasters, flowering currants and pyracanthas. Woolly scales, which may attack plants such as cotoneasters, grape vines and hawthorns, feed mainly on stems and produce conspicuous egg sacs of white wax wool in late spring.*

Scale insects are easiest to kill with a contact insecticide shortly after they hatch. Once they settle and become static, systemic insecticide such as dimethoate is more likely to be successful.

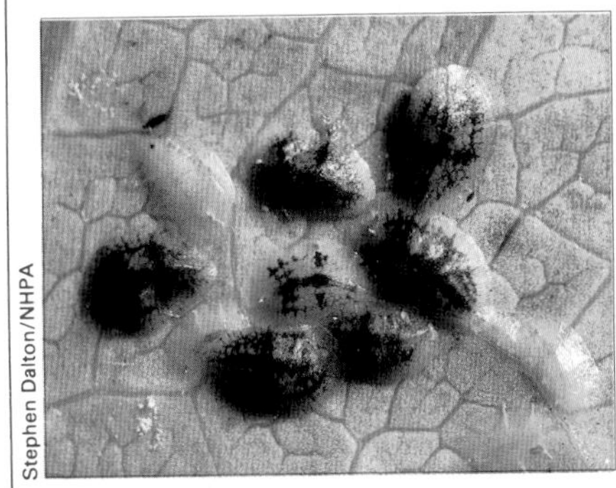

Stephen Dalton/NHPA

Scale insects cluster together on a leaf.

SUPPORT BORDER PLANTS

Tall border perennials, and compact ones with weak stems, are often spoiled by strong winds, especially if accompanied by heavy rain. Staking them after they have blown over, or once the centre of the clump has been opened out, is seldom satisfactory. It is better to provide the supports early, so that the plants can grow through them.

Vana Haggerty

1 *Twiggy sticks, popularly called pea sticks because they are often used to support pea plants, are ideal. Save suitable prunings for this.*

2 *Insert the sticks around the edge of the clump, inclining them slightly towards the centre. Trim off the tops of any that are too long.*

3 *Proprietary supports work well, and some link together so you can join them to suit the size of the clump. They are available in several heights.*

4 *A cheaper method is to use three or four garden canes staked around the plant, with garden string to support the shoots as they grow.*

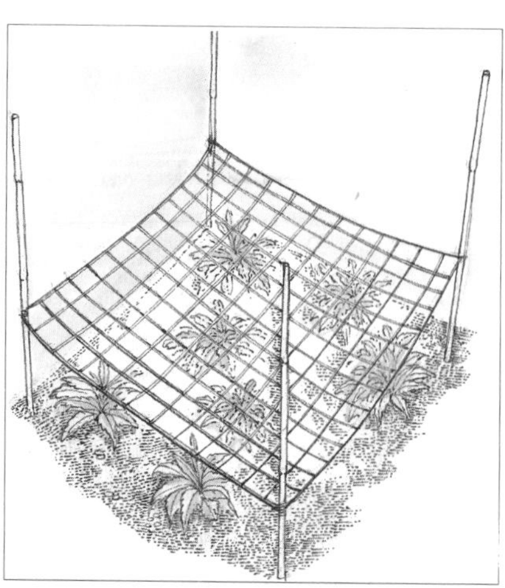

5 *A large mesh netting can be used to support a bed of similar plants, such as chrysanthemums. Support it on canes, and move it up as the plants grow.*

PLANT GLADIOLI

Gladioli are excellent for cutting, but they also make attractive plants for the herbaceous border if you plant them in groups to form bold clusters of spikes.

For a long flowering season, buy early, mid-season and late varieties of corm (good catalogues will give you this information), but plant one kind together in the same group for maximum impact.

Plant at 10-day intervals to extend the flowering period.

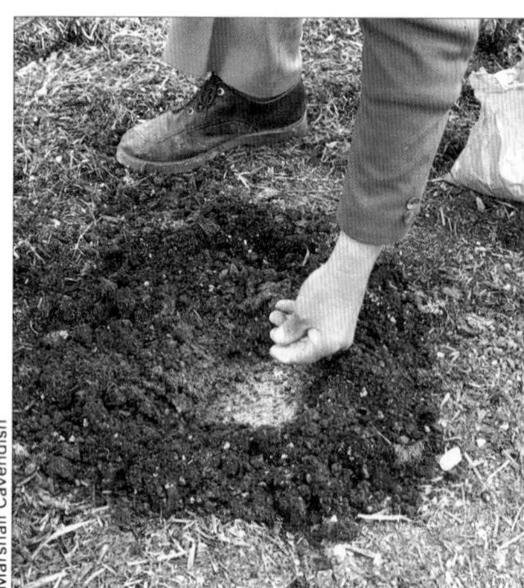

Marshall Cavendish

1 *Prepare the ground well, forking it deeply for good drainage. Work in bone meal or balanced fertilizer. Do not place corms directly on the fertilizer.*

Peter McHoy

2 *If drainage is poor, sprinkle a layer of sand or grit over the planting area. Plant in groups, and space the corms about 15cm/6in apart and 7.5cm/3in deep.*

TAKE WINTER CHERRY CUTTINGS

Winter or Christmas cherries (Solanum capsicastrum) are popular winter-interest plants, with red or orange berries that resemble small tomatoes. These are as bright as many flowers and last much longer. The plant is often discarded once the berries drop, but if you have saved one, take cuttings from it now. You will have a number of plants to enjoy next Christmas.

Peter McHoy

1 *Old winter cherry plants are difficult to keep for a second year, and results are often disappointing, but you can take cuttings now.*

Marshall Cavendish

2 *Fill a small pot with a peat-based seed compost, vermiculite or perlite. Tap the pot a few times to settle the compost.*

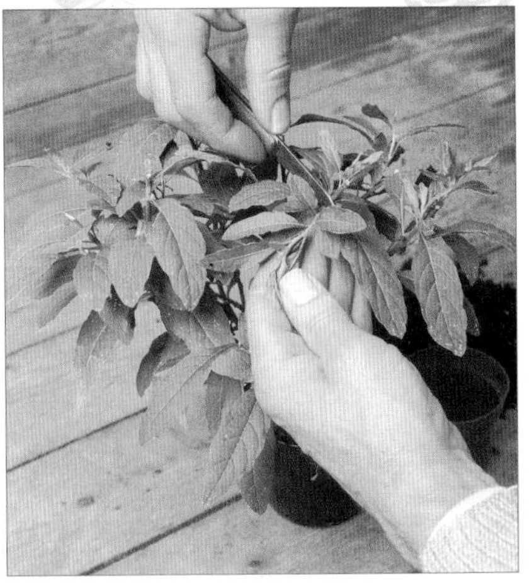

3 *Choose the tips of healthy shoots to take cuttings 5-7.5cm/2-3in long. Use a sharp knife or a razor-blade to avoid damaging the stems.*

4 *Carefully pull off the lower leaves, leaving about four on the tip of the cuttings. Leaves left below compost level will cause the cutting to rot.*

5 *Insert the cuttings around the edge of the pot, but do not overcrowd them. They will root more readily if you use a hormone rooting powder.*

POT UP CHRYSANTHEMUM CUTTINGS

Depending on when you took them, chrysanthemum cuttings will probably be ready for potting up.

Do not leave them in the cuttings compost for longer than necessary, but wait until they are well rooted, even if this means delaying for another few weeks.

Chrysanthemum cuttings can be taken from mid winter to early spring.

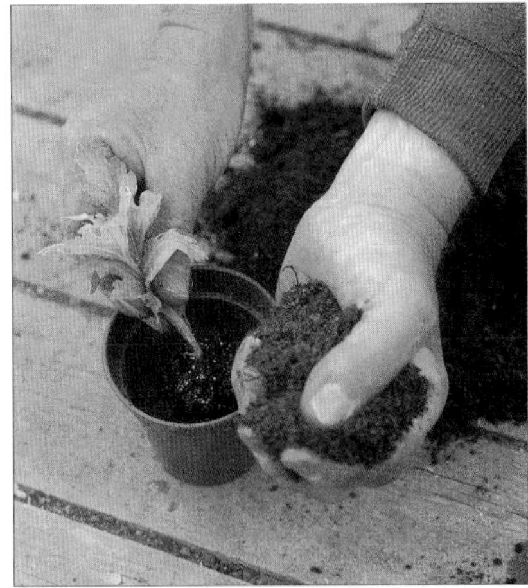

1 *If the cuttings are in a pot, knock the soil-ball out of the pot and separate the cuttings; if in trays, ease them out with a knife. They should be well rooted.*

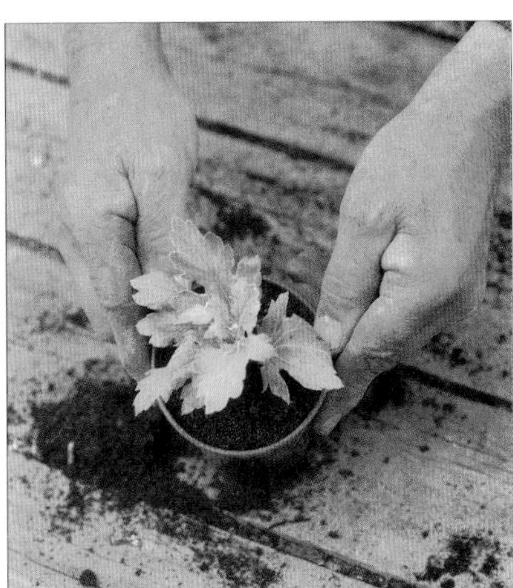

2 *Using a loam-based potting compost, put some in the bottom of the pot, then trickle more around the roots of the plant. Firm it gently, then water.*

CHECKLIST

WHAT TO DO

BORDER PLANTS
Move young plants from nursery bed
Divide *Iris unguicularis*

CONTAINERS
Make a clematis wigwam

COTTON LAVENDER
Trim with shears to maintain neat growth

HYDRANGEAS
Cut off old flower heads left on over winter

LAWNS
Feed grass

SEEDLINGS
Prick out before they become crowded

TREES AND SHRUBS
Plant evergreens
Prune butterfly bush

LOOK AHEAD

SOW
Annual herbs, summer bedding plants

PLANT
Border plants, trees, shrubs and hedges, gladioli

WHAT TO SEE

BULBS AND BORDER PLANTS
Daffodils, Lenten rose (*Helleborus orientalis*), polyanthus, primroses, tulips

SHRUBS AND TREES
Camellias, *Erica carnea, Prunus cerasifera*

VISITORS

FRIENDS
Frogs, newts

FOES
Slugs, snails

EARLY SPRING
WEEK 2

WHAT TO DO

Greenhouses and window-sills are now crowded with healthy young seedlings that will provide masses of colour in the garden and in containers during the summer. If you have not already done your sowing there is time to do it, but you can save weeks by purchasing small plantlets sold by some garden centres for potting up and growing on.

Make sure that all your seedlings have plenty of space and light.

Divide winter irises

Winter-flowering Iris unguicularis *(syn.* I. stylosa*), is best divided once the clump becomes very large and congested. This is the best time to divide* I. unguicularis *but spring and summer irises should not be touched. Lift the clump with a fork, then prize it into pieces with two forks back-to-back, or simply chop through it with a spade. Fork over the ground and remove any weeds, then sprinkle bone meal over the area. Trim the leaves back before replanting the smaller pieces.*

Move plants from nursery bed

Move border perennials that were raised from seed or cuttings last year and are now in a nursery bed, or in pots in a cold frame, to their flowering positions.

Plant evergreens

This is a good time to plant evergreens. They are often damaged by cold winds if planted in winter, and like other newly planted shrubs can suffer from drought in summer.

Planting now is the best compromise, but remember to water evergreens well if the weather is at all dry.

Plant evergreens now.

Prune the butterfly bush

If the butterfly bush (Buddleia davidii) *is left unpruned it will become tall and straggly with smallish flower heads on very long stems. If you prune it now, it will remain compact and produce bigger flowers on shorter stems. Cut last year's shoots right back to within 5-8cm/2-3in of the old wood.*

Trim cotton lavender

The beautiful silver foliage of cotton lavender (Santolina chamaecyparissus) *will become straggly if the plant is allowed to become leggy. Lightly trim established plants with shears to keep them compact.*

Cut hydrangea flower heads

Old flower heads are often left on hydrangeas in cold areas as winter protection for young buds. Cut them off now to tidy the plants and let in more light to promote new growth.

LOOK AHEAD

Some popular culinary herbs, especially the perennial ones, are available in garden centres now, but there is no point in buying annual herbs that you can raise easily by yourself.

Herbs that you can sow outdoors during the next few weeks, include borage, chervil, dill, fennel (if you treat it as an annual) and parsley.

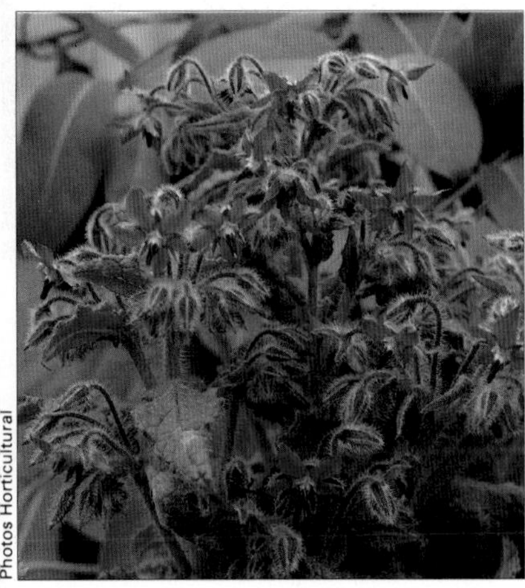

Photos Horticultural

Borage can be grown from seed.

If you have a greenhouse, it is worth starting some herbs, such as fennel and parsley, off in pots. They will transplant better if you sow a couple of seeds in each pot and thin to one plant if both happen to germinate, in order to reduce root disturbance.

Sow some basil as soon as possible in a greenhouse or on a light window-sill.

Whether you are creating a complete herb garden in a sunny corner or just growing a few in containers, the plants that you raise will mean fewer to buy later.

WHAT TO SEE

The tulip season lasts from early to late spring, but the early types are useful as garden brighteners when colour is still scarce.

Among the earliest of the widely grown tulips are the T. kaufmanniana *hybrids, often known as waterlily tulips. Many of these have leaves that are flecked or striped brown or purple, so they contribute to the garden even before they bloom. Because these tulips are low and compact, they do well even in exposed situations, and are good for window boxes and troughs.*

The group of hybrids based on T. greigii *follow* T. kaufmanniana *varieties into flower. Again, many have striped or mottled foliage, and the same compact habit.*

Derek Gould

Tulipa fosteriana *'Orange Emperor'.*

T. fosteriana *hybrids are a little taller at about 30-50cm/12-20in, but have a richness of colour that makes them especially bold. 'Red Emperor' (also sold as 'Mme Lefeber') is a bright pure scarlet, 'Orange Emperor' a clear orange. There is also a 'Yellow Emperor'.*

VISITORS

If you have a pond, newts are likely to be spring visitors. Like frogs they need an aquatic environment for the breeding season, though the rest of the year they live on the land, where they feed mainly on insects, worms and slugs.

The smooth newt, also known as the common newt, grows to about 10cm/4in, and is usually olive-brown with darker spots on the upper side and dark streaks on the head. The underside is flushed orange. During the mating period the male also develops a crest running along the back from head to tail.

The palmate newt is very similar to the smooth newt, but smaller at about 7.5cm/3in. In the breeding season, the male looks more rectangular in profile as a fold of skin develops along each side of the back. The name palmate refers to the black web that connects the toes.

The crested newt can reach 15cm/6in, and it has a warty skin. The upper parts are dark grey or blackish-brown, the underside yellow or orange. The male's nuptial crest is deep with big notches that give it a toothed appearance.

Stephan Dalton/NHPA

The smooth newt eats mainly insects.

PRICK OUT SUMMER BEDDING PLANTS

Prick out summer bedding plants before the seedlings become overcrowded. Because of the number of bedding plants required, it is usually impractical to prick them off into individual pots.

Plastic seed trays are adequate for the majority of seedlings, but modular systems give each seedling its own plug of compost, which means less root damage when you transplant them.

Peter McHoy

1 *Fill the tray or container with a 'universal' or multi-purpose peat-based or peat substitute compost, or use a loam-based compost.*

2 *Strike the compost off level, then firm it with your fingers and press it level. Do not over-fill the tray as you should leave space to water.*

3 *To prick off a seedling, loosen the compost and hold it by its seed leaves (the first that form) while gently levering it up with a small dibber or pencil.*

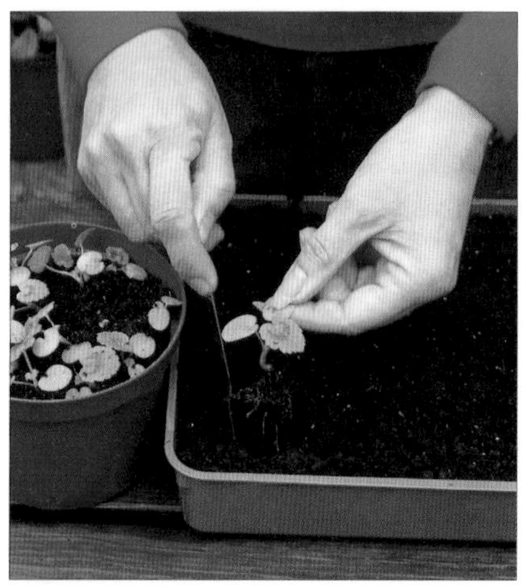

4 *Make a hole in the compost with a small dibber or pencil, deep enough to take most of the roots without curling them. Gently press the compost round.*

5 *To space the seedlings evenly, insert the end row first, then complete a row along one side. Use these rows as guides for even spacing for the rest.*

6 *Adjust the spacing to suit the size of the plant. Large ones need more spac than small ones. Forty seedlings is typical for a standard seed tray.*

7 *Modular systems are available in man sizes. Choose an appropriate size for the type of seedling and prick out one seedling into each cell.*

8 *To save pricking out, you can sow directly into modular trays. Sow two or three seeds into each cell, then pull out any surplus if more than one germinates*

FEED THE LAWN

Top quality lawns are fed regularly throughout the growing season, but this is not necessary for most utility lawns. You will only increase the spread of growth and, with it, the necessity of frequent mowing. Almost all grass benefits from at least one annual feed, however, and this is a good time to apply it.

For best results, choose a lawn fertilizer formulated for spring and summer use.

Marshall Cavendish

1 *A wheeled spreader is the quickest and easiest way to apply a lawn fertilizer. To check the delivery rate, roll it over a sheet of polythene then weigh the fertilizer.*

2 *To avoid missing some areas and over-dosing others, mark out the lawn with canes and string to provide guidelines as you walk along with the spreader.*

MAKE A CLEMATIS WIGWAM

Clematis can be grown up a wigwam of canes in a border, but if you try them in a half barrel or large tub they will make a really stunning patio feature for your patio.

Because the support is quite small, it will soon be covered. If you plant now you can expect a display of flowers this year, and next season it should make a really stunning display as the shoots climb and then cascade.

Vana Haggerty

1 *Plant three different large-flowered varieties – either different colours that flower at the same time, or varieties that bloom at different times.*

2 *Use a large container, such as a half-barrel, and fill it with a loam-based compost. Leave enough space at the top for watering.*

3 *Plant at an inward-facing angle. Tease out a few of the largest roots if they are curling around the inside of the pot, and spread them in the planting hole.*

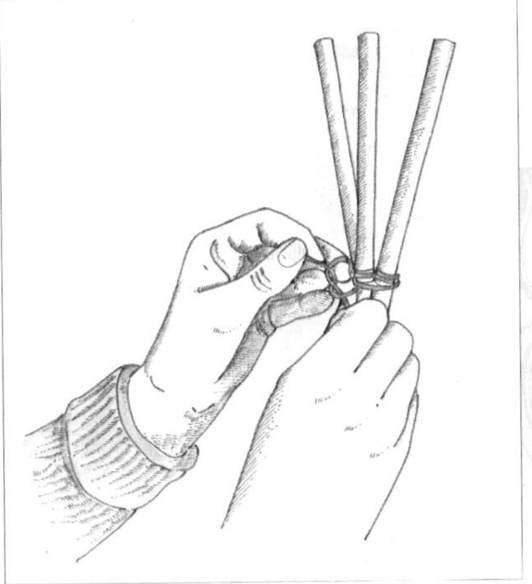

4 *Insert three long bamboo canes, and tie them close to the top. Alternatively, you may be able to use proprietary runner bean cane holders.*

5 *The plants may already have short canes when you buy them. Untie these and discard the small canes, then secure the plants to their new supports.*

CHECKLIST

WHAT TO DO

BEDS AND BORDERS
Feed shrubs and border plants

COLD FRAME
Ventilate on warm days; begin to harden off the hardiest bedding plants

PONDS
Stock with new plants and fish

SEEDLINGS
Prick out before they become crowded

TREES AND SHRUBS
Apply a balanced fertilizer, plant a bamboo

LOOK AHEAD

PLANT
Border plants, trees, shrubs and hedges, acidantheras, anemones, garden freesias, gladioli, *Nerine bowdenii*, ranunculus

SEVER
Layered shrubs and climbers ready for transplanting

SOW
Hardy annuals outdoors, summer bedding plants and outdoor tomatoes

WHAT TO SEE

BULBS AND BORDER PLANTS
Bergenias, daffodils, Lenten rose (*Helleborus orientalis*), polyanthus, primroses, tulips

SHRUBS AND TREES
Camellias, *Erica carnea*, *Mahonia aquifolium*

VISITORS

FRIENDS
Small tortoiseshell and brimstone butterflies, frogs, newts

FOES
Slugs, snails.

EARLY SPRING

WEEK 3

WHAT TO DO

Sowing can begin in earnest. Warmer days mean that greenhouses are less expensive to heat and the light is better for plants on window-sills. The soil is likely to be warm enough to sow many vegetables and hardy annuals in the open ground.

Feed for the future

Shrubs and herbaceous plants benefit from an annual feed. Apply a balanced fertilizer now if you want to reap the benefits later in the year. Few border plants and shrubs will die if you do not bother to feed them, but they will be more vigorous and healthy if you do. Rose enthusiasts should apply a good fertilizer now because the benefits will be obvious later with bigger blooms and stronger, healthier foliage. Vigorous plants are also more able to resist diseases and tolerate any pests.

For special plants such as roses, there are benefits in buying a specially formulated fertilizer, but it is cheaper and almost as good if you buy a larger bag of a general fertilizer, such as Growmore, for all your beds and borders. Follow the instructions on the bag.

Sow outdoor tomatoes

Outdoor tomatoes can be sown now, in a greenhouse or on a light window-sill. If you want a good crop of nicely flavoured tomatoes, sow a variety such as 'Gardener's Delight' or 'Tornado', but for a patio where appearance is important too, consider 'Tumbler' (it will cascade over the edge of a tub and can even be grown in a basket) or 'Totem', which was bred for pots and window boxes.

'Totem' tomatoes are bred for pots.

Use the cold frame

Use your cold frame to raise seedlings that do not require much heat, such as alyssum and French marigolds. If you can provide frost protection (simply covering the frame with an old carpet may provide enough insulation on a cold night at this time of year), many bedding plants can be raised. But do not sow too many – you need space to grow them after pricking out.

If you have a greenhouse, or have raised seedlings on a window-sill, move the most advanced plants into the cold frame to start hardening off and to create more space indoors. If there is a cold spell you may have to bring them indoors to protect them in the evening.

On warm, sunny days, a frame can heat up rapidly. Ventilate it whenever the weather is mild enough to do so.

LOOK AHEAD

It is easy to overlook the summer-flowering bulbs that need planting during the next month. Try to find a few gaps in borders that would benefit from a little extra colour. Most flower after the main flush of herbaceous plants has finished, which makes them especially useful.

Gladioli, florists' type anemones, ranunculus, freesias (choose an outdoor strain), and acidantheras can be planted now. Wait for a few more weeks before planting the more cold-sensitive types such as dahlias, the Peruvian daffodil (Ismene festalis) *and the tiger flower* (Tigridia pavonia), *but buy the bulbs now while stocks are still available.*

If you want to plant something that looks a little exotic, try the hardy orchid Bletilla hyacinthina, *which can be planted outdoors in mild areas. These unusual carmine-pink orchids, which grow to about 25cm/10in, can also be grown as a pot plant.*

Pat Brindley

Plant the exotic Bletilla hyacinthina.

Look even further ahead and plant for late autumn colour. Nerine bowdenii *is an outstanding late-flowering bulb to plant now, but it needs sun.*

WHAT TO SEE

Bergenias, popularly known as elephants' ears because of the shape of their large, thick leaves, are year-round plants worth growing as ground cover wherever a low block of evergreen 'texture' is required. The leaves often taken on a purplish colour in the winter, an effect more pronounced in some varieties.

Photos Horticultural

Bergenia *'Silberlicht' in bloom.*

Above this dense bed of weed-suppressing foliage rise bold spikes of cheerful, and often bright, bell-like flowers. These are usually at their best in early and mid spring, but a few extra spikes may be produced later in the year.

There are many fine hybrids, and good ones to look for include B. cordifolia *(deep pink) and its variety 'Purpurea' (good winter leaf colour, carmine-purple flowers), and hybrids 'Ballawley Hybrid' (bright rose-red), 'Silberlicht' syn. 'Silver Light' (white, tinged pink), and 'Abendglut' syn. 'Evening Glow' (purple-red flowers, maroon winter leaves).*

VISITORS

Two butterflies that you might see in the garden at this time of year are the small tortoiseshell and the brimstone.

The small tortoiseshell is a pretty tawny-brown, patterned with black markings and edged with a row of bright blue spots round the wings.

The brimstone is a beautiful clear yellow butterfly that will visit town and country gardens alike. The male is bright lemon yellow, the female a paler parchment shade.

If you want to encourage both butterflies to stay and breed in your garden, try to provide suitable food plants for the caterpillars. This is quite easy for the small tortoiseshell, which will be very happy with nettles. The brimstone is more difficult to provide for because it prefers buckthorn and alder.

Michael Leach/NHPA

A female brimstone butterfly.

PLANT A BAMBOO

Some bamboos make big bold screens, other provide compact and attractive ground cover, such as the dwarf **Arundinaria pygmaea** ***being planted here. They will add a touch of oriental charm to your patio, and you can even grow some of them in large containers as a focal point. It may be possible to lift a few paving slabs to provide a suitable place on the patio, but enrich the soil before planting.***

All photos Peter McHoy

1 *Do not be surprised if you find a few large, root-like rhizomes growing out of the bottom of the pot. Many species put out probing rhizomes.*

2 *Carefully remove the root-ball from the pot. Give a gentle pull first, especially if rhizomes have grown through the drainage holes.*

3 *If there are shoots around the edge of the root-ball, gently pull them out to expand the initial area covered, but do not disturb the mass of very fine roots.*

4 *Make the planting hole larger than the root-ball to leave space to pull out some of the new shoots that are developing around the edge.*

5 *Trickle good soil or potting compost around the roots, making sure the plant remains at its original level. Firm the soil well, then water thoroughly.*

SOW HARDY ANNUALS

There are dozens of good hardy annuals that you can sow now, and they are ideal for filling a piece of vacant ground with masses of colour very cheaply. If you want, you can economize still further by buying a packet of mixed annuals rather than several packets of different kinds. This is great if you like an element of surprise, but sorting out weed seedlings from the plants is a challenge!

1 *Fork over the ground, then rake it level. If planting drifts of several kinds, mark out the blocks with sand. Sowing in straight rows will make weeding easier.*

2 *If possible space the seeds individually, but with fine seeds you may have to sprinkle them into the drills. Label them if sowing several kinds.*

STOCK YOUR POND

Some aquatic plants will only just be producing new growth, but this is a good time to plant them. If you plant once they have grown a lot of leaf, it is difficult to avoid damaging them in some way.

It is a good time to stock your pond with fish. Water gardens and good garden centres usually sell a good range of hardy pond fish, but common goldfish are the best choice for beginners.

1 *Plastic planting baskets, which are lined with hessian, can be used for water plants. An old washing-up bowl, however, will do just as well.*

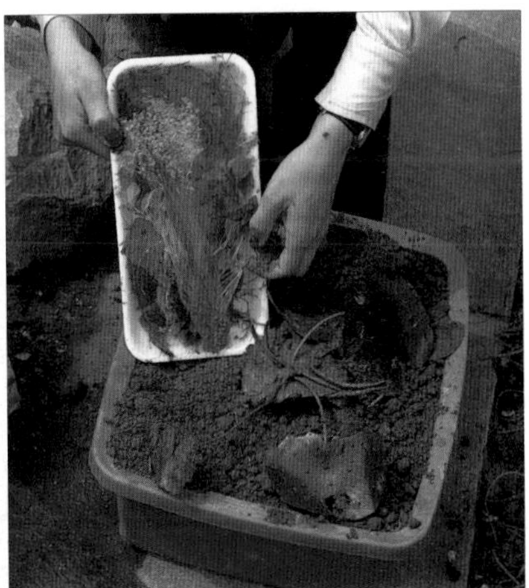

2 *It is a good idea to buy a collection of oxygenating plants. If using a large container, like a washing up bowl, insert them around the edge.*

3 *Add a thick layer of gravel or coarse grit to help prevent the compost clouding the water when you plunge the bowl. It will also stop fish stirring up mud.*

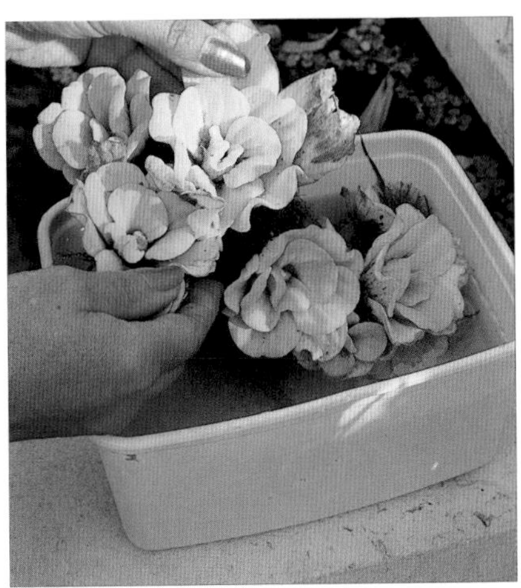

4 *Tender floating plants, like these water lettuce, that have been overwintered indoors, only have to be floated on the surface of the water.*

5 *If you buy fish, float the bag on the surface for an hour so that the water temperatures can equalize. Open the bag and let the fish swim out.*

SEVER ROOTED LAYERS

Shrubs and climbers layered last spring, or the previous autumn, will probably have rooted. Carefully draw away a little soil from around the stem to check whether roots have formed. If they have, this is a good time to prepare the new plant for an independent life.

If there are no roots, do not disturb the plants further. Leave them until autumn, then check again.

1 *Remove a little soil from around the layer to check for roots. If well rooted, replace the soil but sever the plant from its parent with secateurs.*

2 *When the rooted layer has been living off its own roots for a couple of weeks, and if it is not wilting, lift it carefully and plant or pot up immediately.*

CHECKLIST

WHAT TO DO

BEDS AND BORDERS
Feed shrubs and border plants; weed and mulch beds; dead-head bulbs

CONTAINERS
Plant agapanthus, lilies and border plants

LAWNS
Feed and weed

SEEDLINGS
Prick out before they become crowded

TREES AND SHRUBS
Prune shrubs

LOOK AHEAD

POT UP
Herb seedlings

TAKE CUTTINGS
Propagate delphiniums and lupins

SOW
Sweet peas and other hardy annuals, summer bedding plants and cucumbers

WHAT TO SEE

BULBS AND BORDER PLANTS
Arabis, aubrieta, bergenias, daffodils, polyanthus, primroses, saxifrages, tulips

SHRUBS AND TREES
Camellias, *Cytisus* × *praecox*, *Erica carnea*, *Magnolia stellata*, *Mahonia aquifolium*

VISITORS

FRIENDS
Brimstone and small tortoiseshell butterflies, chaffinches, frogs, newts

FOES
Slugs, snails

EARLY SPRING
WEEK 4

WHAT TO DO

This is a crucial time of the year. What you sow and plant now will determine how your garden looks for the rest of the summer.

If you make an effort to feed your beds and borders with a balanced fertilizer, the benefits will be reaped in the months that follow.

Weed and mulch

With the milder days of spring, weed seedlings will germinate rapidly, but even difficult perennial weeds are easy to control if you kill them while they are young seedlings.

Once you have weeded your beds and borders, apply a mulch at least 5cm/2in thick to control the weeds for the rest of the year. A mulch will also conserve moisture in the soil. Decorative mulches such as pulverized bark will improve the appearance of beds and borders.

Dead-head spring bulbs

Dead-head the early-flowering bulbs to prevent them forming seed, but let the leaves die down naturally. Do not tie daffodil leaves into knots to 'improve' their appearance.

Take lupin cuttings

Lupin cuttings can still be taken if the shoots are not more than 10-13cm/4-5in tall. Cut them off with a tiny portion of the woody base (they must not have a hollow stem), and treat like delphiniums.

Although lupins are easy to raise from seed, cuttings ensure the offspring will be the same as the parent plant.

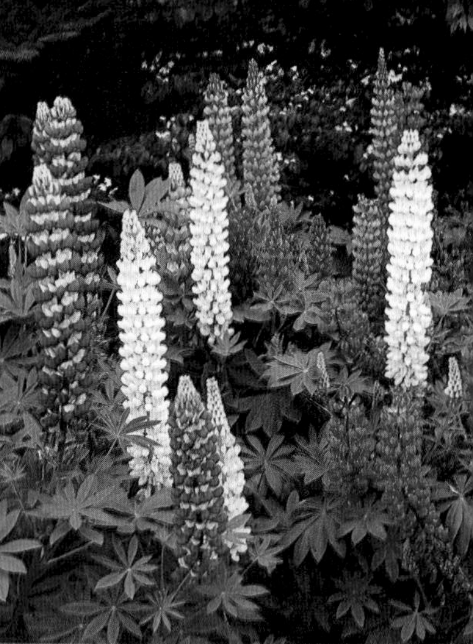

Propagate lupins now.

Plant or sow sweet peas

If you have raised seedlings under glass, plant them out now. Sweet pea seedlings can usually be bought in garden centres, but it is not too late to sow your own seeds. Soak them overnight then sow where they are to flower. Place three seeds every 23cm/9in, and thin to one at each position if more than one germinates.

Sow other hardy annuals

Sow other hardy annuals, such as cornflowers, clarkia, godetia, pot marigolds (calendulas) *and nasturtiums where they are to flower. They will germinate readily now that the soil has warmed up, but keep the ground watered if the weather is dry.*

Weed and feed grass

Feed the lawn with a spring or summer lawn feed if not already done. This is also a good time to use a selective lawn weedkiller if weeds are a problem. You can always combine weeding and feeding with a lawn feed-and-weed mixture.

LOOK AHEAD

Do not let your patio tubs become too predictable, there is plenty of scope to experiment with new arrangements. But do not abandon the tried and trusted plants entirely – they will almost certainly be attractive for a much longer period than some of the alternatives.

If you live in a mild area or can take the tubs into a greenhouse or conservatory for the winter, plant a bold group of African lilies (agapanthus). *Ordinary lilies are striking too, but these are best*

Derek Gould

Agapanthus ***is a perfect container plant.***

replaced each year. Choose compact types like the widely-available 'Enchantment', and plant plenty of them.

If you have some large clumps of hostas in the garden, lift one up (divide it if necessary) and put it in a large pot or tub. It will make a really super show, even if the variegation fades as the season advances.

Bold border plants with striking foliage and distinctive flowers, such as Acanthus spinosus *and* A. mollis *also make feature plants for a patio pot.*

All these can be planted now.

WHAT TO SEE

Aubrietas are among the most widely grown rock plants that perform reliably every year with the minimum of fuss or attention. To keep the plants compact and flowering prolifically, however, trim the dead flowers off with shears in early summer.

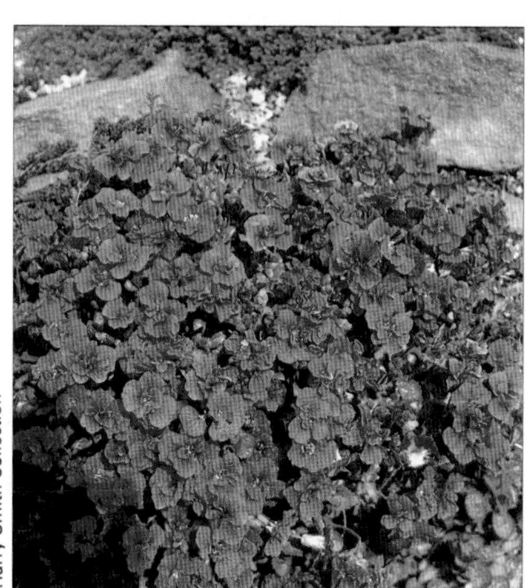

Harry Smith Collection

Aubrieta deltoidea *'Dr Mules'*.

Good varieties to look for include 'Alix Brett' (carmine), 'Bressingham Pink' (clear pink), 'Bressingham Red' (deep red), 'Dr Mules' (deep violet-purple) and 'Triumphant' (almost a true blue). Variegated varieties will hold interest when the plants are not in flower; these include A. deltoidea *'Variegata' (leaves edged white, purple flowers) and 'Aurea' (leaves edged gold, purple flowers).*

VISITORS

The cheeky chaffinch is one of our commonest birds, and one of the most friendly. Its plumage makes it instantly recognizable. Both male and female have white outer tail feathers and two broad white bars on the wings (especially noticeable in flight). In spring the male has bright orange-brown or pink underparts, a chestnut-brown back, and a blue-grey crown and nape, with a black forehead. The colouring becomes less colourful towards autumn, when it is more buff.

The female is drab by comparison: generally greyish-brown above and whitish below, but she has an attractive green rump.

Chaffinches eat mainly insects and seeds of weeds, so they are welcome visitors. During the breeding season many caterpillars will be caught to feed the young. In some areas, breeding has already started.

E.A. Janes/NHPA

The chaffinch feeds on insects and seeds.

SPRING PRUNE SHRUBS

Pruning is not essential, but it helps to keep shrubs compact and often more floriferous. Sometimes shrubs are pruned for a special effect: to provide a mass of colourful young winter stems on shrubs such as dogwoods, or to stimulate large or juvenile foliage.

Below are some shrubs that you can prune right now, but if you are in doubt about any, it is far better to leave them alone.

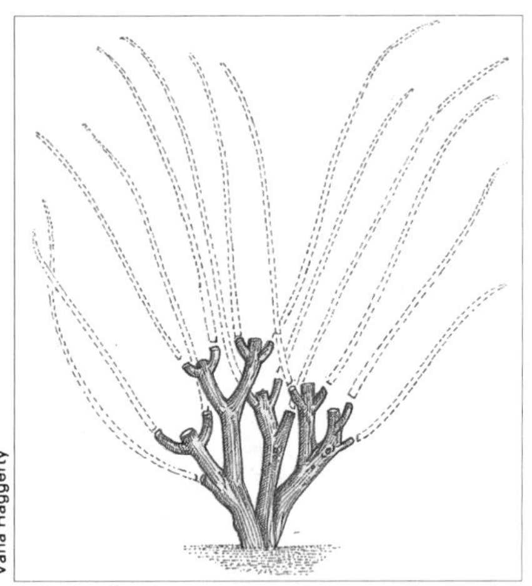

Vana Haggerty

1 *Cut back last season's shoots to within one or two buds on shrubs that flower on shoots produced this year such as* Buddleia davidii.

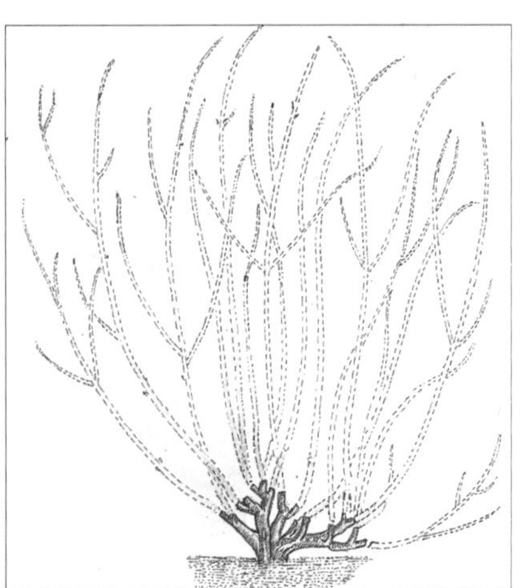

2 *Cut back shrubs grown for their stems or leaves, such as dogwoods, pheasant berry, and some willows, to within a few inches of the base.*

3 *Winter-flowering shrubs generally need little pruning, but clip over autumn and early winter heathers with shears to remove old flowers.*

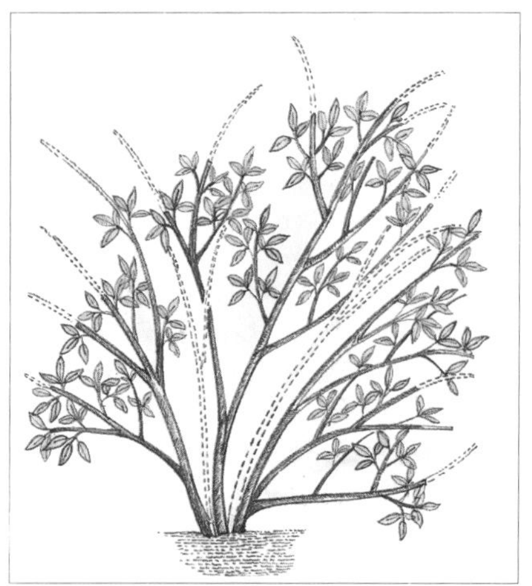

4 *Prune out a proportion of old wood from winter jasmine* (Jasminum nudiflorum) *to prevent the long, arching shoots becoming a tangled mass.*

5 *Cut out winter-damaged or diseased shoots on evergreens, and any all-green shoots on variegated plants, but be careful not to spoil the shape.*

PLANT CHEAP AND EASY HERBS

Supermarkets and some greengrocers sell trays of germinated herbs for cooks who want a supply of fresh cut herbs for the kitchen. They are not intended for growing on in the garden, but it is worth experimenting. If they have not become too thin and drawn while on display, you should be able to separate the seedlings and pot them up. This is much cheaper than buying plants.

Peter McHoy

1 *The seedlings will be growing on a special medium and not in compost. Prize them apart carefully, trying not to damage the roots. This is basil.*

2 *Pot up individual seedlings in small pots of compost, retaining any of the original growing medium attached to the roots.*

TAKE DELPHINIUM CUTTINGS

Delphiniums bring valuable height and welcome towers of colour to the back of a border. They are plants that you can always find a place for, or give them away to friends if you have any extra. As delphiniums tend to be short-lived or damaged by slugs, it is worth having a few replacement plants.

Cuttings are easy to take and will root readily at this time of year.

Marshall Cavendish

1 *You can use plants already growing in the border, or buy young pot-grown specimens to provide a supply of shoots for the cuttings.*

2 *Make the cuttings 8-10cm/3-4in long, removing them just above the soil or compost with a sharp knife. Make a clean cut across the end of each one.*

3 *Dip the ends into a hormone rooting powder first. Insert the cuttings into individual pots containing a peat/sand mix or a rooting compost.*

4 *Gently firm the compost down with your fingers to make sure there are no large pockets of air around the base of the cutting.*

5 *Water, then place in a propagator or put a polythene bag over the top of the pots and cuttings until rooted. Turn the bag daily so that the cuttings do not rot.*

GROW CUCUMBERS

You can grow cucumbers even if you do not have a greenhouse. Grow them in a cold frame or even in a tub.

The tall greenhouse climbing types are not so dependable outdoors, so choose a variety such as 'Bush Champion' for a cold frame or a container on the patio. 'Burpless Tasty Green' is a taller variety but produces outdoor cucumbers that compare well with those grown in a greenhouse.

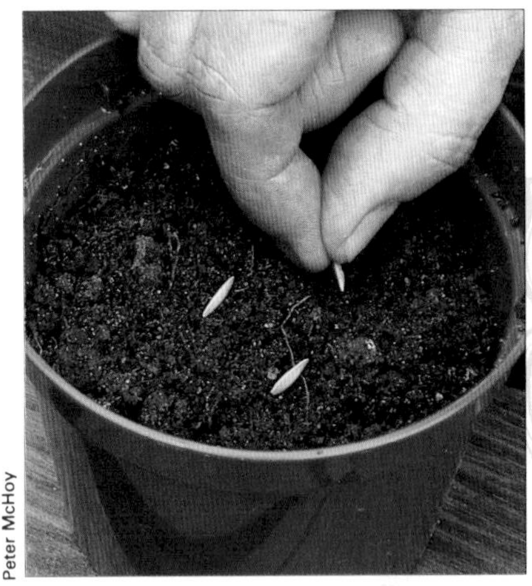

Peter McHoy

1 *Cucumber seeds are large and easy to handle, but they tend to rot if conditions are not right. Set the seeds on edge and germinate at about 21°C/70°F.*

2 *Pot on into larger pots and keep in a warm, light position. Plant out in a 30cm/12in pot, or in a large tub, once there is no risk of frost.*

CHECKLIST

WHAT TO DO

GENERAL TASKS
Prune winter-flowering jasmine
Feed and divide herbaceous perennials
Feed spring-flowering bulbs

COMBAT DISEASES
Mildew

MAKE LAWN REPAIRS
Rake up winter debris and feed grass
Destroy moss and weeds. Aerate soil

LOOK AHEAD

SOW HARDY ANNUALS
Marigolds, candytuft, clarkia, cornflowers and love-in-a-mist for flowering in July

WHAT TO SEE

BORDER PERENNIALS
Alyssum, aubrieta, bergenia, speedwell

TREES
Magnolia and snowy mespilus

SHRUBS
Camellia, viburnum, barberry, forsythia

BEDDING PLANTS
Wallflower, forget-me-not, double daisy polyanthus, winter-flowering pansy

BULBS
Windflower, glory of the snow, crocus, cyclamen, dog's-tooth violet, narcissus

VISITORS

FRIENDS
Ladybirds, bees and lacewings

FOES
Greenfly, blackfly, whitefly, slugs and snails

MID SPRING
WEEK 1

WHAT TO DO

Now that the weather is improving, it's time to start cleaning up winter debris and looking ahead to summer. Start to plan and sow your summer-flowering plants for a brilliant display and don't neglect those which you planted in the autumn as the new spring growth will benefit from constant care.

Prune for new growth

Prune early shrubs like forsythia to encourage new shoots to flower next year. Cut out flowered shoots to just above a healthy bud or shoot.

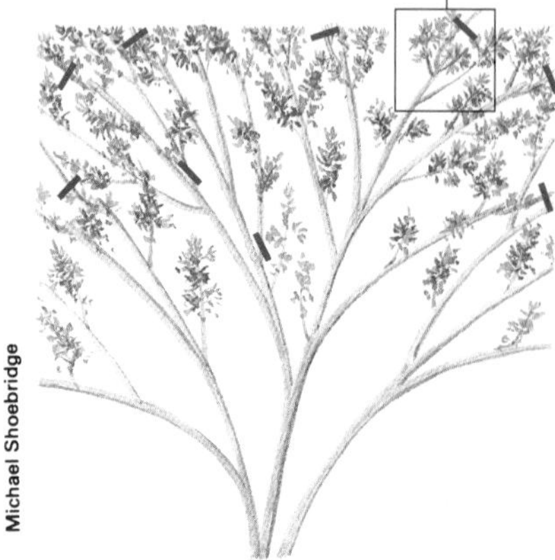

Michael Shoebridge

Shrubs that flower early, on shoots produced the previous year, such as forsythia, flowering currant, and spring-flowering spiraeas, should be pruned as soon as they finish flowering.

Divide border plants

Plants are waking up and need feeding. Boost sturdy new growth by sprinkling their root area with a balanced organic fertilizer such as blood, fish and bone. Lightly hoe or water in the fertilizer.

Some perennials can be pulled apart simply by using your hands.

Clumps with woody roots are levered apart with handforks.

Divide crowded clumps of herbaceous plants (perennials which die back to a crown of buds in autumn) into well-rooted portions. Use your hands or a pair of handforks to tease the roots apart, taking care not to damage them.

Tackle weeds
Control chickweed, creeping buttercup, dandelions, daisies, thistles and other newly emerging invaders with a total weedkiller. Products based on paraquat or glyphosate suit paths or borders. Use selective weedkiller on a lawn.

Feed spring-flowering bulbs
Feed daffodils, tulips, crocuses and other spring-flowering bulbs with a slow-acting balanced fertilizer such as bone meal to help plump them up for blooming well next year. Sprinkle a handful lightly onto the soil around the base of each plant and gently rake it in.

Combat diseases
Take action now against mildew, whose white felty covering cripples leaves, by spraying regularly with a suitable fungicide from your local garden centre.

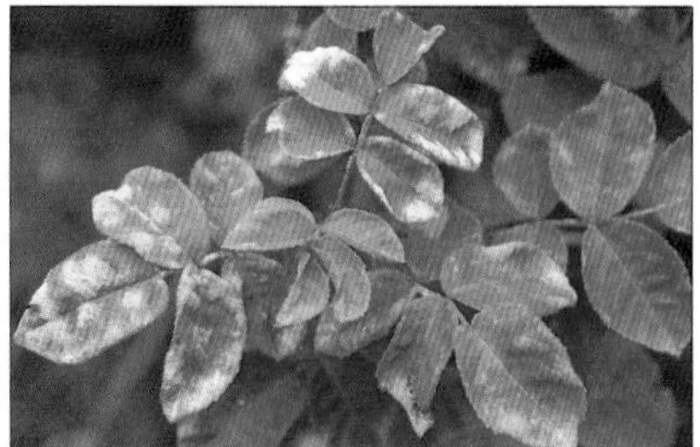

Powdery mildew on a rose.

LOOK AHEAD

Sow hardy annuals
Create a bright splash later by sowing hardy annuals now. Easy and reliable kinds include orange, yellow and cream calendula (pot marigold); stunning red candytuft; white, violet or rose clarkia; blue cornflower; pink lavatera (mallow) and blue nigella (love-in-a-mist).

WHAT TO SEE

Spring-flowering plants bring a profusion of colour. Perhaps you still need a bold splash of a certain hue to brighten up your existing display. Plan for next year with reference to the plants listed below.

S & O Mathews

Narcissus poeticus.

Whites
Amelanchier lamarckii *(snowy mespilus);* Magnolia stellata; *malus; narcissus;* Pieris japonica *'Scarlett O'Hara';* Prunus avium *'Plena' (wild cherry);* Spiraea × vanhouttei; *viburnum.*

Photos Horticultural

Chionodoxa luciliae.

Blues and violets
Chionodoxa (glory of the snow); Erythronium dens-canis *(dog's-tooth violet);* Iris reticulata; *myosotis (forget-me-not); pulmonaria (lungwort), especially* P. angustifolia *'Mawson's Blue';* Pulsatilla vulgaris *(pasque flower).*

Yellows
Alyssum saxatile; Berberis darwinii *(barberry);* Cytisus × praecox *(broom); daffodils; forsythia;* Jasminum mesnyi *(primrose jasmine);* Kerria japonica.

Harry Smith Collection

Camellia × *williamsii 'Donation'.*

Reds and pinks
Anemone fulgens *(windflower); aubrieta;* Bergenia cordifolia; *camellias; cyclamen (hardy varieties); malus (crab applies); prunus.*

Multihued
Cheiranthus (wallflower); Viola × wittrockiana *(pansy); primrose; polyanthus; crocus;* Bellis perennis *(double daisy).*

VISITORS

Ron & Christine Foord

Watch out for snails and slugs.

As the weather becomes milder, slugs and snails emerge to eat new shoots and leaves. Keep them at bay by sprinkling slug pellets around plants.

SPRING LAWN CARE

As temperatures rise in early spring and the grass begins to grow again, the lawn can look good in comparison to its lacklustre surroundings of empty borders and leafless trees. Take a closer look, however, at the state of your lawn at grass-root level. After a long, hard winter, problems can arise that may spoil the appearance of your lawn for the rest of the year. But a little work early in the season really pays dividends.

Worm activity *in the lawn is good for its general well-being but several species of worm have the annoying habit of producing spiral casts on the surface. No matter, simply brush them up and use the fine loamy soil produced for filling any shallow hollows in the lawn surface.*

Harry Smith Collection

Worm activity helps to aerate the lawn.

Brushing a lawn *removes any debris that has accumulated. If not removed, twigs and stones hidden among the growing grass will soon take the sharp edge off your mower blades.*

Rake the lawn, *using a wire or spring-tined rake (not a soil rake). The whole lawn should be raked using light but firm strokes. Pull the rake towards you to 'comb' out the matted clumps so that all the grass blades lie in roughly the same direction. This ensures a neat and even cut when you give the first mowing.*

If moss is present, *destroy it with a moss killer based on iron sulphate, dichlorophen or chloroxuron. Rake it out when it's black and dead.*

Make the first cut *with the mower blades set to leave utility lawns 3cm (1¼in) and luxury lawns 2cm (¾in) high.*

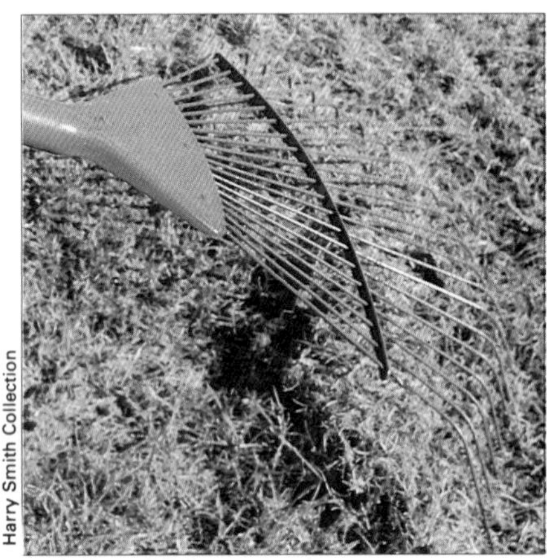

Harry Smith Collection

Use a spring-tined rake to remove debris.

To check the cutting height of your mower, first lay the machine on its back. Then lay a straight edge across the front and rear rollers and measure between the rule and the cutting edge of the fixed blade.

Signs of wear and tear *will show in areas that get used a lot, such as short cuts across the garden, play areas and patches underneath the washing-line. The soil will have compacted, producing a hardened surface. Not only is the grass physically worn, but the soil in which it roots has less air spaces, which reduces moisture and air content, and restricts root growth. The compacted layer can become impervious to water so that puddles will sit on the surface for hours after rain, encouraging damp-loving mosses. The remedy is aeration.*

Harry Smith Collection

Well-used areas of lawn may need some repair.

Aerate the soil *by spiking the surface of the lawn at about 10cm (4in) intervals with a garden fork wiggled in to its full depth. Then sprinkle on to the surface an equal part mix of sharp sand, moist peat and sifted top soil, and work it in with the back of a rake. This can be tiring, so try to do just a*

Harry Smith Collection

Aerate the lawn by spiking it with a fork.

little at a time – or get some help with the heavy work. It does provide effective draining channels to encourage root growth, prevent waterlogging and improve the overall health of the lawn.

Unless you are looking for a perfect 'bowling-green' type of finish to your lawn, a few weeds are normally tolerated. But they do multiply quickly and

Collections/Patrick Johns

Weedkiller can be applied in liquid form.

can soon get out of hand without some control.

There are basically two methods: hand weeding or chemical control.

Raking can help lift weeds ready to be trimmed back by the lawnmower. Core out tap-rooted weeds such as dandelions using a small, sharp tool such as an old knife if there are only a few invaders. You can also weaken the crowns of persistent weeds by slashing them with a knife.

Hormone selective weedkillers are best applied once weeds start to grow vigorously.

If you carry out these tasks your lawn will be set up for the summer. A healthy lawn will make a good garden even better so it is worth taking the time and trouble.

SOWING ANNUALS OUTDOORS

Choose a sunny, well-drained patch in your garden for sowing hardy annuals. The soil should have a good 'tilth' and appear loose and crumbly, but not be too dry. Prepare the seed bed by treading the soil down evenly and then gently raking over the surface. Follow the steps below for sowing the seeds successfully.

1 Rake in a fine sprinkling of fertilizer and then gently firm the soil with your feet by lightly treading it in – but don't stamp!

Ray Duns

2 Use the corner of a steel rake to make an evenly-spaced grid of sowing drills 1cm (½in) deep and 15cm (6in) apart in both directions.

3 Sow a pinch of two or three seeds where the drills intersect. Check with the seed packet instructions for distances.

4 Draw the soil back over the seeds using the back of the rake and lightly firm it in. Mark the boundary of each type of seed by pressing down the rake.

5 Finally water the seed bed well using a watering can with a fine rose. Insert a waterproof label at once, for future reference.

CHECKLIST

WHAT TO DO

GENERAL TASKS

Tidy up spring-flowering bulbs; dead-head daffodils to ensure good blooms next year

Divide border perennials (see Gardener's Diary, Spring/Week 1) and replant to increase stock

Clean out pond

Spray apple trees to protect this year's crop

PLANTING

Plan ahead: plant trees and shrubs

Plant gladioli corms and dahlia tubers to appear in late summer

WHAT TO SEE

BORDER PERENNIALS

Alyssum, aubrieta, bergenia, Lenten rose, pulmonaria

TREES

Magnolias, flowering cherries

SHRUBS

Camellia, Mexican orange, flowering currant, forsythia, rhododendron, viburnum

BEDDING PLANTS

Wallflower, forget-me-not, double daisy, polyanthus, primrose, winter-flowering pansy

BULBS

Anemones, crocus, cyclamen, daffodils, lily-of-the-valley, grape hyacinths, tulips

GARDEN VISITORS

FRIENDS

Ladybirds, bees and lacewings

FOES

Greenfly, blackfly, whitefly, slugs and snails

Beat aphids the garden-friendly way by encouraging ladybirds to your garden

WHAT TO DO

Clear weeds from beds and borders. Remove protection from tender and exposed plants during the day, but replace if cold winds or frosts are forecast. Tidy underneath hedges and remove debris caught between woody stems – a favourite hiding place for slugs and snails. Rake established lawns to remove any 'thatch' (dead grass) and moss, if not already done.

Plant gladioli

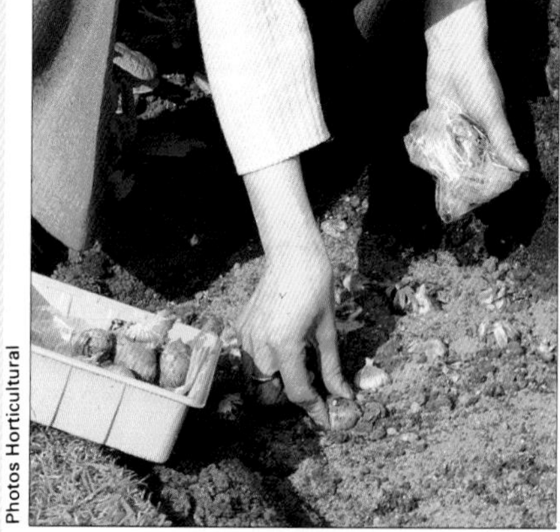

Photos Horticultural

Plant corms of gladioli for a late display. Prepare the soil by adding a balanced general fertilizer such as bone meal then plant each corm about 10cm/4in deep (add 5cm/2in more for light, sandy soils). This planting of a late batch will prolong the flowering display and liven up end-of-summer beds. Gladioli prefer well-drained soil in an open, sunny site.

Tidy spring-flowering bulbs

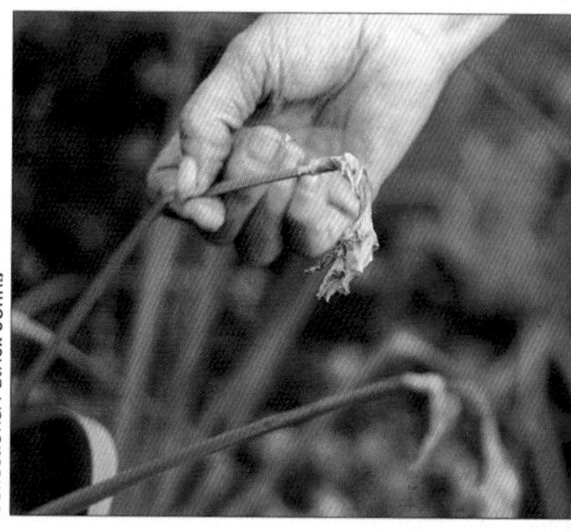

Collections/Patrick Johns

Dead-head spring-flowering bulbs such as daffodils and then let the foliage die down naturally. Do not tie up leaves because this restricts the nourishment which feeds the bulb for flowering next year.

Spray apples

Collections/Patrick Johns

You can now start a spraying programme for your apple tree against apple scab and mildew, but spraying is generally easier when trees are small. Timing can vary somewhat from season to season, but it should be carried out when the buds are just beginning to burst. Spray the tree

at fortnightly intervals until mid summer with either benomyl or carbendazim. Try to choose a still day so that the spray does not waft about in the air too much and do not spray when the apple blossoms are open and pollinating insects are on the wing.

Spray other kinds of small fruit trees with insecticide to kill pests that emerge now.

WHAT TO SEE

There are many shrubs and herbaceous perennials to fill your garden with early colour next year, so plan now.

Whites

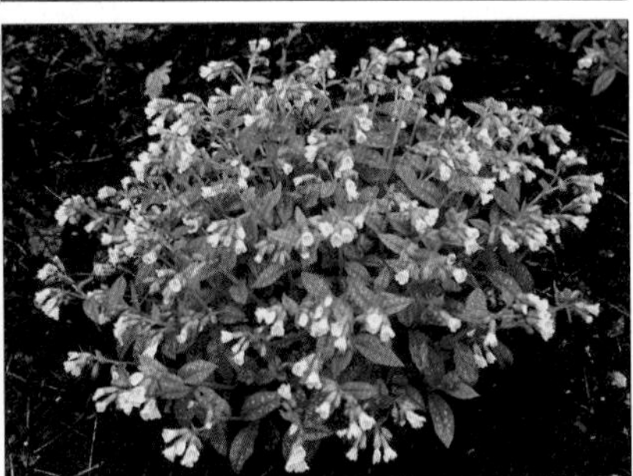

Pulmonaria *'White Wings': bright ground cover.*

Camellia; Christmas rose (Helleborus niger); Cyclamen creticum; *lily-of-the-valley; magnolia; Mexican orange* (Choisya ternata); *narcissus; viburnum; double wild cherry* Prunus avium *'Plena'.*

Yellows

Alyssum saxatile; *forsythia; narcissus.*

Alyssum saxatile 'Citrinum'.

Insight Picture Library

Delicate blue grape hyacinth.

Blues

*Forget-me-not (myosotis); grape hyacinth (*Muscari armeniacum*) 'Heavenly Blue'; iris; lungwort (pulmonaria): blue varieties;* Aubretia *'Cobalt Violet'.*

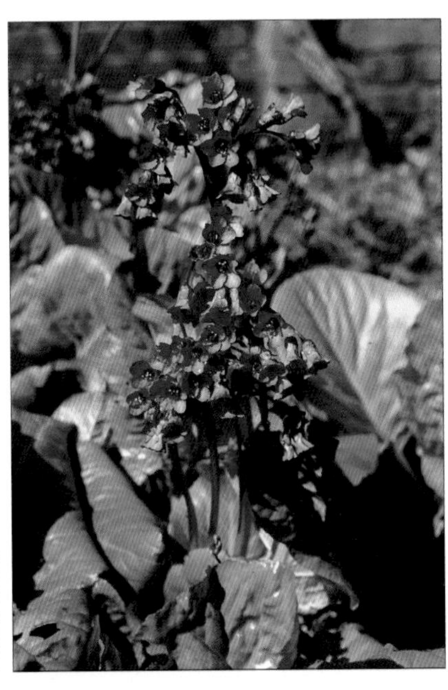

Andrew Lawson

Leafy elephant ears: Bergenia 'Ballawley'.

Reds and pinks

Anemone (windflower); apple blossom; Aubrieta *'Carnival'; bergenia; camellia; cyclamen; flowering currant; magnolia; pulmonaria; weigela.*

Multihued

Crocus; double daisy (Bellis perennis); *pansy* (Viola × wittrockiana); *polyanthus; primrose* (Primula vulgaris); *rhododendron; tulip; wallflower (cheiranthus).*

VISITORS

Greenfly, blackfly, whitefly – they are all common garden pests which multiply rapidly on plants and eventually destroy them.

Ron & Christine Foord

A plague of white aphids feeding on leaf sap.

Natural control

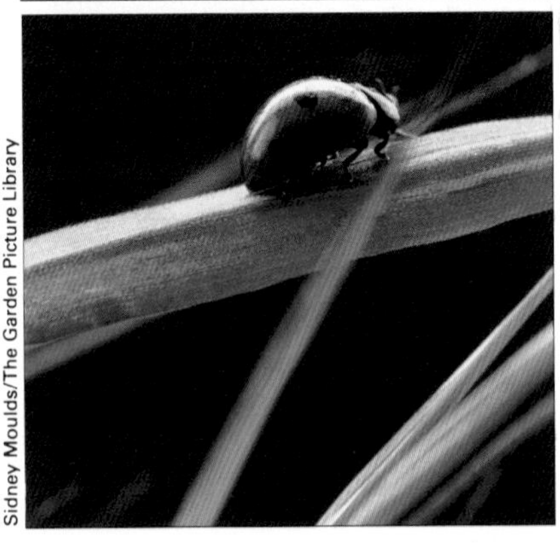

Sidney Moulds/The Garden Picture Library

Ladybirds – adults and larvae – eat aphids.

Ladybirds are the gardener's friend: they do no harm themselves but eat the aphids.

You can encourage ladybirds to your garden by growing a diversity of plants. They also like to hibernate under bits of tree bark and fallen leaves, so if you are less tidy in the autumn these useful insects may well choose your garden for a winter resting place (but bear in mind you may encourage other pests).

Ladybirds emerge when the weather warms up in spring, just as the aphids descend.

CLEANING A POND

After the long period of inactivity during the winter, the pond will be full of debris that has blown in as well as debris from pond dwellers.

Activity in the pond increases as the weather warms and a thorough spring clean is essential before the new growth starts.

Harry Smith

Trim back the dead foliage still remaining on last year's plants.

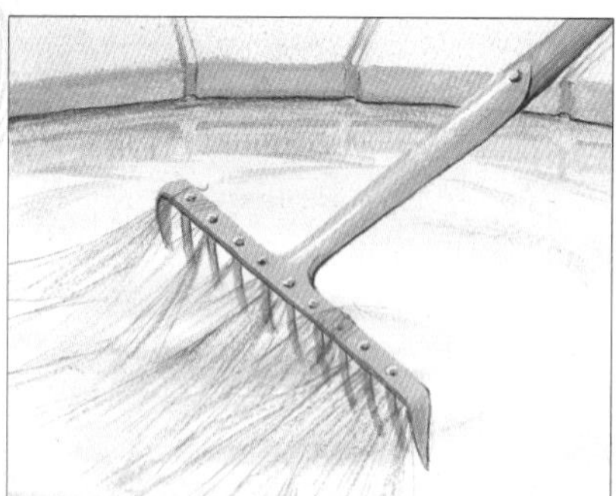

Clear out leaves and rubbish; rake out blanket weed (like green cotton wool).

Every few years the entire pond should be drained and thoroughly cleaned out (take care not to puncture liners). Having first removed the fish, bale out the water (if you have a pond pump it will do the job for you). Remove the dead leaves and debris but leave most of the mud which may house insects.

Fill the pond with fresh water, allowing several days for the chlorine to disappear before replacing the fish.

GROWING TOMATOES OUTDOORS

Why not grow your own tomatoes using young plants and growing bags!

Buy your bags and select plants ready for planting when all danger of frost has passed.

Varieties such as 'Alicante' or 'Moneymaker', whose growth is restricted to a single stem by pinching out side shoots, are recommended. Choose a sunny, sheltered position where you can water them easily.

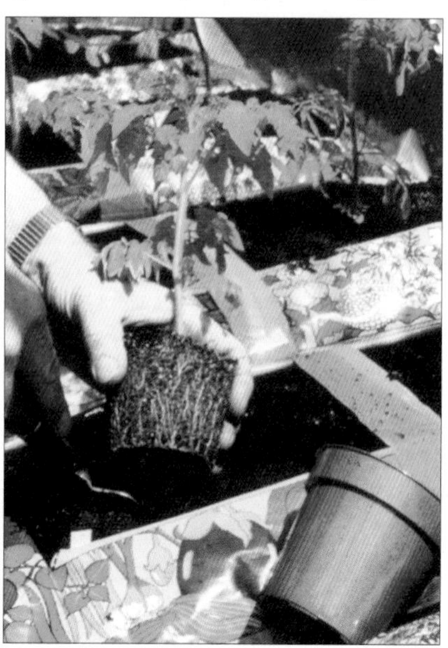

Photos Horticultural

1 Plant two to four plants in each growing bag, depending on the size of tomato you want – two plants will yield fewer but larger tomatoes.

Photos Horticultural

2 As the plants grow, tie their stems loosely to stakes at 30cm/12in intervals for support and pinch out side shoots regularly for sturdy growth.

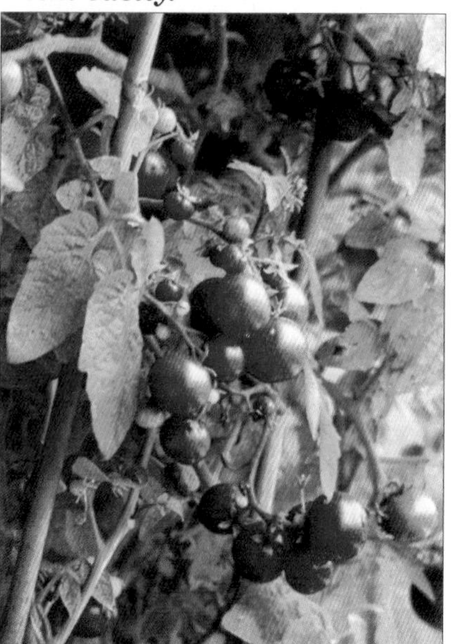

EWA

3 Water plants frequently and when small tomatoes start to appear, feed weekly with tomato fertilizer. Pinch out top shoots after fourth truss.

EWA

4 Your tomatoes should be ripe and ready for picking and enjoying in late summer or early autumn, depending on the weather conditions.

PLANTING A CELEBRATION ROSE

A rose bush makes a beautiful, lasting present, particularly if it is in celebration of a baby's birth or a special anniversary. Perhaps you will find one with a particularly appropriate name. Follow these easy steps to planting your rose or, indeed, any container-grown shrub, and you will be rewarded with many beautiful blooms for years to come.

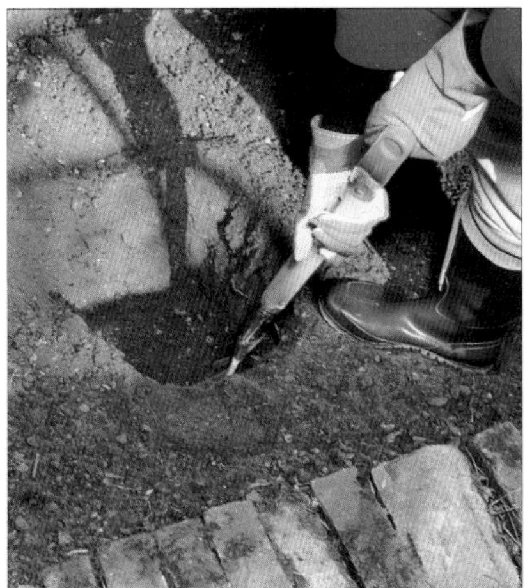

1 *Dig a hole about one-and-a-half times as deep and twice as wide as the container. Fork over the bottom of the hole to improve drainage.*

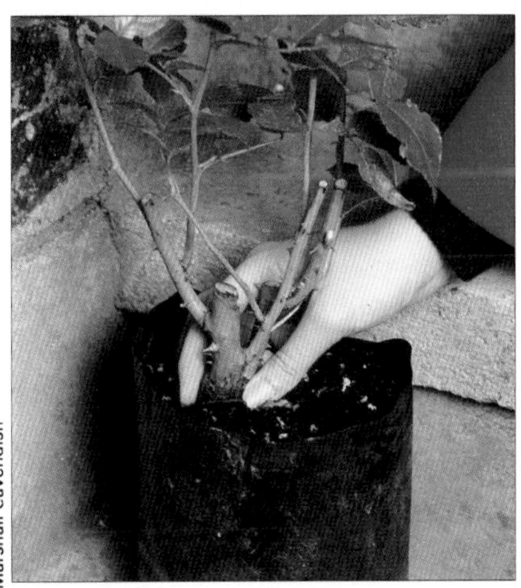

2 *Check the level of the graft (join) is not covered by soil. When planting your rose, make sure the soil does not rise any further above this level.*

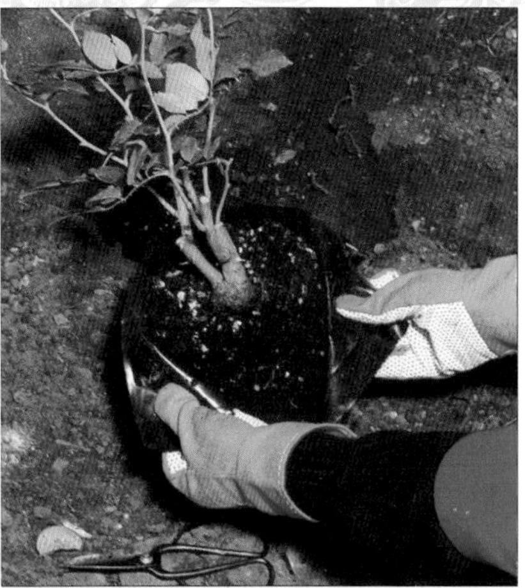

3 *Cut down the side of the polythene and through the base. Peel away carefully. With a rigid plastic container, gently tip out the rose.*

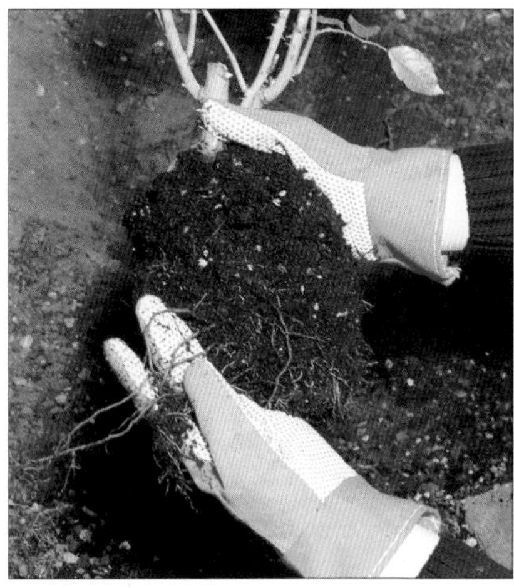

4 *Tease out any pot-bound roots in the soil ball and make sure that any extra long roots are spread out in the hole carefully when planting.*

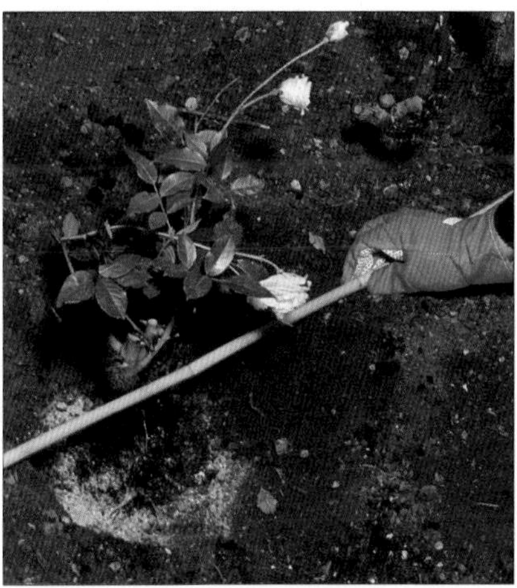

5 *Spread peat mixed with soil and a dusting of bone meal in the base of the hole. Place rose in position and check planting depth using a garden cane.*

6 *Put in more peat, soil and bone meal mixture around the roots. Firm down, pressing out air pockets. Shake rose gently to distribute soil.*

7 *Repeat the process again with the same soil mixture, firming down carefully each time until the hole is filled to the cane level.*

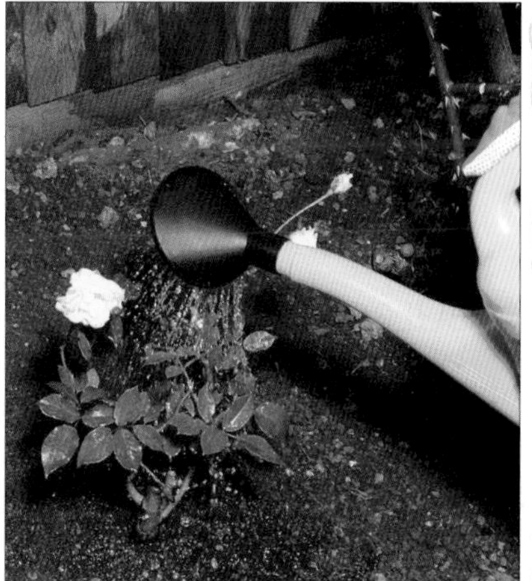

8 *Water the rose in well immediately, using a whole watering-can full of water. Keep moist during the first few weeks, particularly if weather is dry.*

CHECKLIST

WHAT TO DO

GENERAL TASKS
Prepare hanging baskets.
Prune summer flowering shrubs; hardy fuchsias, buddleias, hydrangeas, spiraea
Mulch fruit trees
Feed soil with fertilizer
Choose pond plants: oxygenating plants
Increase stock: divide snowdrops, perennials
Harden off bedding plants: geraniums, zinnias, lobelia, marigolds

LOOK AHEAD

NEW LAWNS
Plan and prepare the ground for making a lawn from seed

PLANTING OUT
Harden off chrysanthemums gradually for a long summer display

WHAT TO SEE

BORDER PERENNIALS
Alyssum, aubrieta, bergenia, hellebore, lungwort, primula

TREES
Amelanchier, magnolias, flowering cherry

SHRUBS
Camellia, choisya, flowering currant, forsythia, rhododendron, viburnum

BEDDING PLANTS
Forget-me-nots, double daisies, polyanthus, primroses, winter-flowering pansies

BULBS
Anemones, crocuses, cyclamen, daffodils, lily-of-the-valley, grape hyacinths, tulips

VISITORS

FRIENDS
Birds, ladybirds, bees and lacewings

FOES
Greenfly, blackfly, whitefly, slugs and snails.

WHAT TO DO

Spring is a busy time in the garden, so try to do a little work every day, if the weather allows. It pays dividends later on – and in the years to come – if you give some regular attention to it now.

Dividing snowdrops
Snowdrops in large clumps can be lifted and divided now. They establish much better when still in leaf. Specialist nurseries will also supply you with new stock in this condition.

Variegated plant care
Remove any green shoots that have developed on variegated plants, using a sharp knife or a pair of secateurs. These shoots are more vigorous than the established variegated leaves and if left unchecked they will eventually take over.

EWA

Prune out green shoots of elaeagnus to maintain the variegated leaves.

Mulching fruit trees
Suppress weed growth and conserve moisture by placing a mulch around established fruit trees. Spread an 8cm/3in deep covering of bark chippings, manure or well-rotted compost over the root area.

Collections/Patrick Johns

Mulch fruit trees with manure to retain moisture and suppress weeds.

Increase your stock
There is still time to lift and divide border perennials – a cheap and effective way of increasing your stock – if not already done. Make sure each division has several healthy, plump buds and a reasonable amount of roots. Set in new plants with peat.

Boost new growth
Give plants breaking into growth a spring boost with a feed of balanced organic fertilizer such as blood, fish and bone (follow the manufacturer's instructions for the right quantities to apply). Feed roses now with a proprietary rose fertilizer before their leaves unfurl fully.

LOOK AHEAD

Prepare the borders

Acclimatize plants to the outdoors before setting in well-fed beds, then sit and admire them all summer.

Feed and enrich the borders for planting up early next month by incorporating a general fertilizer such as Growmore at 55g per square metre/1½oz per sq yard into the soil.

Start hardening off your chrysanthemums by putting them outside during the day and taking them in at night over a period of two or three weeks. Keep inside if the weather is severely cold.

WHAT TO SEE

It is always a good idea to keep an eye out for something unusual that could make an added point of interest in your own garden – a tree grown to an unusual shape perhaps, or a new type of flowering shrub.

Prunus 'Amanogawa'

A flowering cherry with semi-double, pale pink flowers. The leaves turn red in autumn. Its branches do not spread, but grow upwards; excellent for small gardens.

Harry Smith

Berberis julianae

A dense-growing small shrub with unusual clusters of yellow flowers showing against glossy dark green leaves. It gives added value with its egg-shaped autumn blue-black berries.

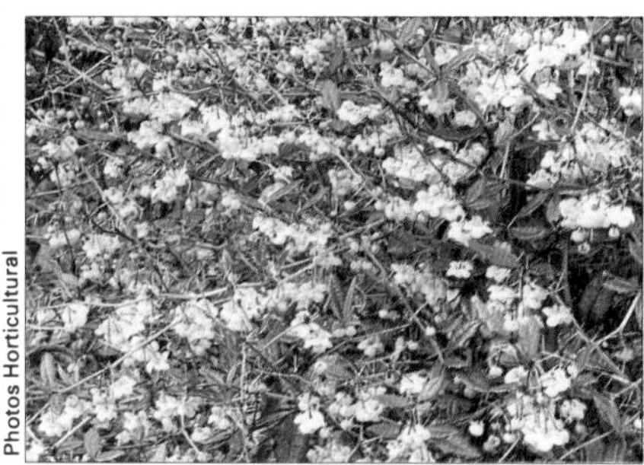

Photos Horticultural

Solomon's seal (Polygonatum)

An elegant shrub with arching stems, from which hang bell-shaped flowers. It prefers shade.

Andrew Lawson

Creeping willow (Salix repens)

A small, bushy shrub that produces silky grey-to-yellow catkins in spring. The leaves, which are silvery green and silky, look pretty as they flutter in the wind. This is a good plant for seaside gardens.

Derek Gould

Euphorbia amygdaloides

A useful semi-evergreen that likes poor soil and grows well in partial shade. In spring it produces a mass of green flowers on its erect stems. These act as a useful background to low-growing, brightly coloured spring-flowering bulbs, such as dwarf tulips and daffodils.

Gillian Beckett

VISITORS

Friends

Birds, ladybirds, bees and the lacewing – which eat aphids.

Foes

Greenfly, blackfly, whitefly, slugs and snails. Catch greenfly and blackfly early on when you can rub them off with soapy water. If badly infested, use an insecticide based on pirimicarb, which will not harm useful insects such as lacewing.

Paul Sterry/Nature Photographers

The lacewing is a welcome sight, as it loves a diet of aphids.

MAKING A SEED BED

Over the next few weeks many seeds can be sown directly into the soil, although it must be properly prepared if you are to get good results. Save a small area of the garden for raising seedlings. They can be planted out into their final positions as soon as they are large enough to handle safely.

Prepare the soil by digging it thoroughly, removing any debris. If necessary, lay a plank across the ground so you do not stand directly on the soil. After a couple of dry days, rake the surface to form a fine tilth – a fine, crumbly texture ideal for seeds to take root.

1 ***Rake the soil level. When you are ready to sow your seeds, use a plank to make a V-shaped drill. The depth of your drill will depend upon the type of seed you are sowing: the larger the seeds, the deeper the drills should be.***

Ray Duns

2 ***Sow the seed thinly and evenly along the drill, according to the instructions on the packet. Gently draw the soil over the seeds and water with a fine rose.***

PRUNING FLOWERING SHRUBS

Many popular garden shrubs produce their blooms on the growth put on this spring. If such shrubs are to give a good display of flowers they will need pruning as soon as possible.

Prune overcrowding in the centre and any dead wood, cutting back to within 15cm/6in of the ground, just above a new shoot.

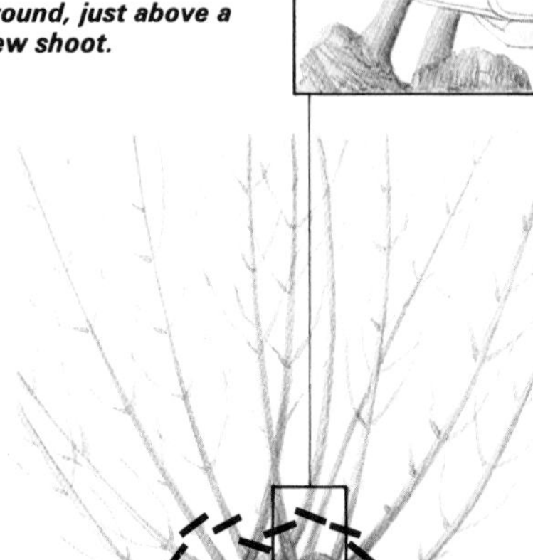

Michael Shoebridge

Cut back Buddleia davidii *to within 5-8cm/2-3in of its base.*

Make cuts in the spring just when the new buds are beginning to break. Prune on outward facing buds with a clean cut sloping outwards.

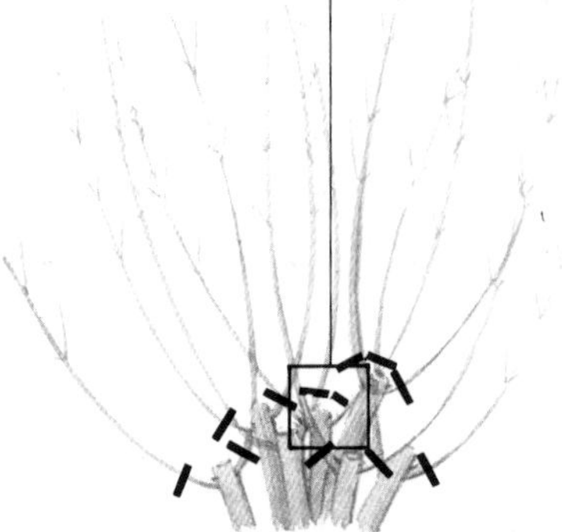

Hardy fuchsias need similar treatment, leaving a crown.

CHOOSING POND PLANTS

If you have a pond in your garden, it is essential to keep its ecological system well balanced. This means the number and varieties of plants and fish should suit the size of the pond.

Oxygenating plants are necessary in any garden pool. Supplied as unrooted cuttings at aquarium shops and some garden centres, you will need about four bunches per square metre/yard of pond surface. If they are supplied with lead weighted ties, remove these and push the cuttings into a pot or bucket of compost and cover the surface of the compost with gravel. This prevents the compost muddying the water when the plants are put in.

Pat Brindley

Elodea will oxygenate your pond.

Recommended oxygenators: Elodea canadensis, *dark green and vigorous;* Callitriche autumnalis, *light green leaves;* Ceratophyllum demersum *(hornwort), free-floating;* Lagarosiphon major, *dark green and vigorous; and* Utricularia vulgaris, *a free-floating carnivorous plant that flowers in early summer.*

If the pond has only recently been filled with water then leave it to stand for a few days before adding plants, so that the chlorine will have dissipated.

PLANTING A NEW LAWN FROM SEED

There is still time to make a new lawn from seed. If you live in an area that is often affected by hosepipe bans during the dry summer months, then it would be better to sow in late summer since a new lawn must be watered regularly until it becomes established.

The most essential groundwork before you sow is thoroughly digging over the area then making sure that it is free of weeds.

1 *Dig over the site really well, scrupulously remove all weeds and their roots by hand and leave for a week or two to allow the soil to settle.*

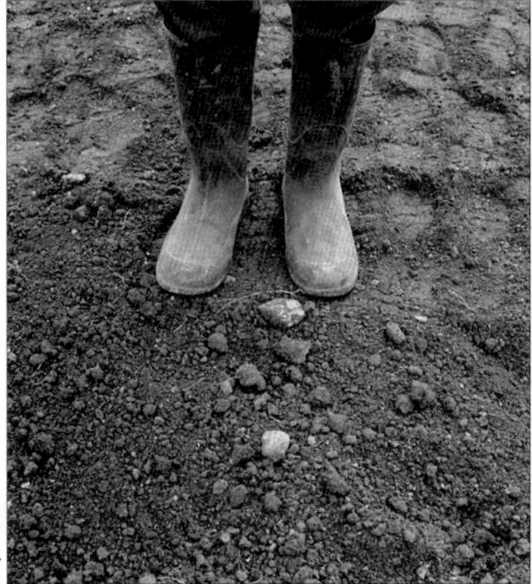

2 *Trample evenly all over the site keeping your feet close together until all the large lumps are broken down. (Do not jump up and down.)*

Ray Duns

3 *Give the soil its first good rake, breaking up the hard lumps and clods of earth. Pick out all the stones and discard them.*

4 *Rake the soil thoroughly to a fine tilth, then level the surface as evenly as possible using the upturned head of the rake.*

5 *Scatter a balanced general fertilizer such as Growmore, at a rate of 60g per square metre/2oz per square yard. Rake into soil evenly.*

6 *Place two strings 1m/3ft apart and then place two canes across them, again about 1m/3ft apart, to make a squared off area.*

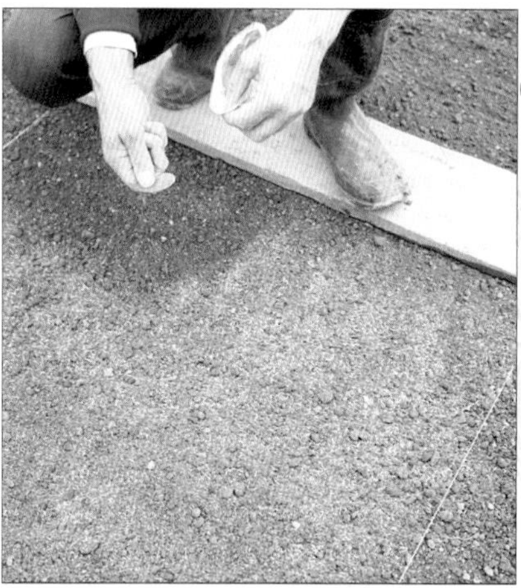

7 *Standing on a plank so as not to compress the soil, scatter the grass seed (35-55g per square metre/1-1½oz per square yard). Lightly rake the surface.*

8 *Turn the plank over, repeatedly, then over again – standing on it between turns – to firm in the seed and even out the soil surface still further.*

CHECKLIST

WHAT TO DO

PREPARE RUNNER BEANS
Decorative and edible

PLANT POND PLANTS
Water lilies

GENERAL TASKS
Protect roses from early blackspot
Clean paths: remove weeds and moss
Buy bedding plants: ageratum, lobelia, geraniums, petunias
Help growth: apply fertilizer; add a mulch

LOOK AHEAD

SOW
Lettuces and radishes

WHAT TO SEE

BORDER PERENNIALS
Aquilegia, aubrieta, bergenia, euphorbia, lungwort, primula

TREES
Magnolia, flowering crab apple and cherry

SHRUBS
Camellia, choisya, kerria, osmanthus, pieris, rhododendron, viburnum

BEDDING PLANTS
Wallflower, forget-me-not, double daisy, polyanthus, primrose, winter-flowering pansy

BULBS
Anemones, daffodils, dwarf iris, hyacinths, grape hyacinths, tulips

VISITORS

FRIENDS
Birds, hedgehogs, ladybirds, bees and lacewings, housemartins and swallows

FOES
Greenfly, blackfly, whitefly, slugs and snails

MID SPRING

WEEK 4

WHAT TO DO

There is a lot to do in the garden at the moment, whether you are preparing for a display later in the summer, tidying up after the winter or carrying on with routine jobs. But all your efforts will pay dividends later in the year when you have plenty of glorious colour for visitors to admire.

Check for pests or diseases

Soft new growth is easy prey to infection and needs particular vigilance to keep trouble away. Small infestations of aphids can be controlled by picking them off by hand or washing off with soapy water. Similarly, local outbreaks of disease can be kept in check by pinching out and disposing of affected shoots (do not put on your compost heap). If attacks persist or are widespread then you may have to resort to using chemical control.

Protect early seedlings and tender new growths from slug attack by sprinkling slug and snail pellets around them.

Continue spraying against rose blackspot and mildew at fortnightly intervals.

Apply fertilizer

Feed beds and borders to be planted up by incorporating a well-balanced, long-lasting fertilizer such as Growmore. Apply about 55g per square metre / 1½ oz per square yard.

Stone chippings

The stone chipping mulch given to alpines and other damp-susceptible plants may well be wearing thin by now. Fill in where necessary with fresh stones after clearing away any winter debris from around the plants and rockery stones.

Replenish stones in rockery gardens.

Act against weeds

Keep on top of new weed growth with regular hoeing. Watch out for the emerging seedlings of quick-growing invaders such as chickweed and shepherd's purse. Established perennial weeds should be removed with as much of the root as possible, so as to avoid regrowth.

Hoe out weeds before they take a hold.

Apply a mulch

Mulch newly planted trees and shrubs with a 5-8cm/2-3in layer of bulky organic manure or garden compost to help conserve moisture around their roots. Make sure the ground is moist before applying the mulch around stem.

Marshall Cavendish

Apply mulch leaving a 5cm/2in gap around stems. This prevents mulch passing on diseases or inducing roots on grafted shrubs.

Try some vegetables

If you would like to try growing some vegetables, start with some quick-maturing ones such as radishes or lettuces. Sow them as thinly as possible in a well-prepared seed bed. Remove weeds and rake soil to a fine tilth.

Hanging baskets

Although it is still too early to set in plants in a hanging basket outside, you can start one off inside the house, garage or greenhouse. It will need a well-lit position out of direct sunlight. The better they are established the better the display will be once transferred outside.

Brigette Thomas/Garden Picture Library

For 'mature' baskets, start them indoors.

Support perennials

Provide good support early for fast developing herbaceous perennial plants such as campanulas and peonies.

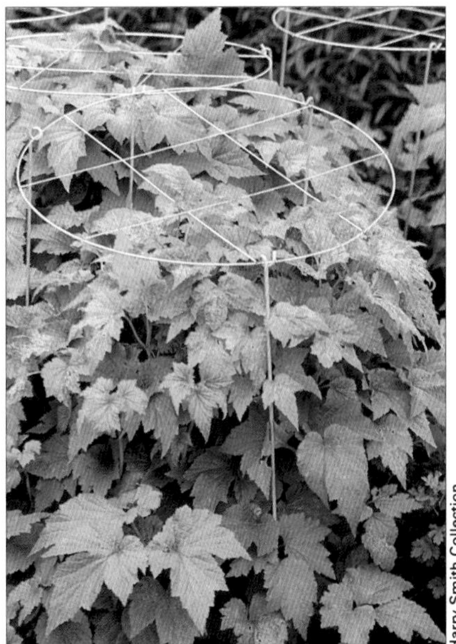

Harry Smith Collection

Give support now to tall perennials.

As the perennials grow up through the wires, the plant foliage splits over and will eventually hide the structure. These clever supports can be reused next year.

LOOK AHEAD

To enjoy a continuous supply of fresh salad during the summer months, make small multiple sowings at fortnightly intervals. Lettuces, radishes, peas and beetroot are good vegetables to start off with.

Sow seed or plant out small plantlets of sweet peas in a sheltered spot to obtain a glorious display of blooms that are perfect for cutting from June onwards.

Start hardening off chrysanthemum plants as they are ready to be planted out about now. They will start to flower in late summer.

WHAT TO SEE

While spring-flowering bulbs are in their full glory, take the opportunity to look around your garden and plan ahead for next spring's colour. You might consider keeping to one or two themes, say blue and white, or add brilliant eye-catching reds and oranges provided by the many varieties of tulips.

Photos Horticultural

The warm colours of tulip 'High Society'.

VISITORS

Friends

Watch out for the arrival of some of our insect-eating friends – housemartins and swallows should be homing in from Africa in the next few weeks, with swifts close behind them. Enjoy summer evenings with their flying feats as they collect their supper.

Hugh Clark/Nature Photographers

Housemartins' nests are reused each year.

GROWING SWEET PEAS AND BEANS

Sweet peas, tall growing peas and beans grow well up a trellis and should be sown within the next week or two. Growing peas and beans not only gives you the pleasure of fresh vegetables for your table but also provides you with colourful flowers and plenty of foliage as well.

The delicate and colourful sweet peas will flower all summer long if cut regularly and runner beans provide red, white or pink flowers. (When planting, tie the stems to their supports loosely to encourage rapid climbing and always twist the stems anti-clockwise.)

There are two advantages of using peat pots. First, they indicate whether your seeds are getting enough water. When the pots are well soaked they turn dark brown, and if kept this way, your seeds will be ensured enough water.

Secondly, you can plant your plantlets out in the pots without disturbing the root systems. The peat pots will break up into the soil.

Marshall Cavendish

1 *Fill 8cm/3½in deep peat pots with a peat-based seed compost to within 2.5cm/1in of the top. Tap pots gently on the table to settle compost.*

2 *Sow seeds by hand, allowing one seed per peat pot; simply place each seed on top of the compost.*

3 *Fill the pots to the rim with more compost and gently firm down. Line the tray with cling film to stop leaks when you water the pots.*

4 *Water the individual pots well (the peat pots turn dark brown when soaked thoroughly). Check the pots regularly – they should not dry out.*

BEDDING PLANTS

By this time of the year most gardening outlets will be selling bedding plants. They are grown in warm, cossetted conditions and will need acclimatizing before planting outside.

Harry Smith Collection

Trays of summer bedding plants.

Ideally, all new purchases should go into a cold frame or a cool greenhouse, with the amount of ventilation being slowly increased. However, if you do not possess either of these in your garden, you can still be successful. Put the trays of young plants outside in a sheltered spot – the porch, for example – for a couple of weeks and bring them in at night time. Do not be tempted to rush plants at this tender stage.

Harry Smith Collection

A cold frame is ideal for 'hardening off'.

Many bedding plants are not frost hardy so it is a little risky putting plants such as lobelia and geraniums outside before the last frost has passed. The time is right when local parks put their plants out.

SPRING CLEANING PATHS AND STEPS

It is essential to clear any algae and moss that has built up on paths and steps during the winter months. If left to get worse these slippery paths can become a real hazard.

The products to use for these cleaning jobs are easily available at most garden centres.

If moss is the problem, then use a proprietary moss killer.

Photos Horticultural

1 *Paths, shaded by a hedge and north-facing wall, produce damp conditions where lichen thrive.*

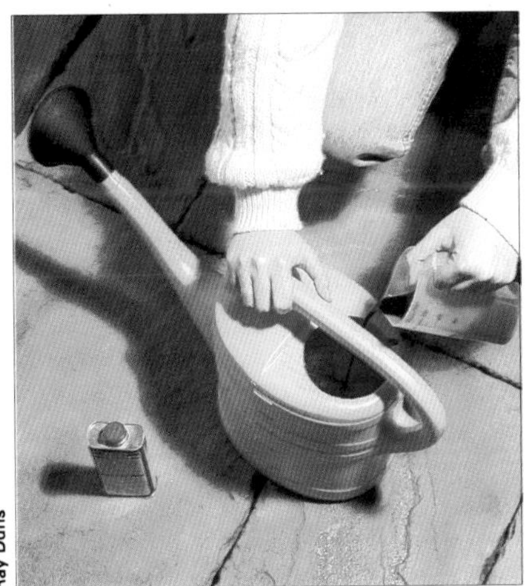

Ray Duns

2 *A garden disinfectant, such as Jeyes Fluid, should be applied with a good stiff brush.*

PLANTING WATER LILIES

Floating plants such as water lilies cover the pond surface and shade it during sunny weather. By reducing light penetration and taking nutrients from the water, water lilies help prevent algae – the bane of every pond keeper's life.

The basket of lilies is raised off the pond bed with bricks. These are removed when growth has started.

1 *Line a special plastic aquatic basket with heavy garden soil not treated with weedkiller or fertilizer.*

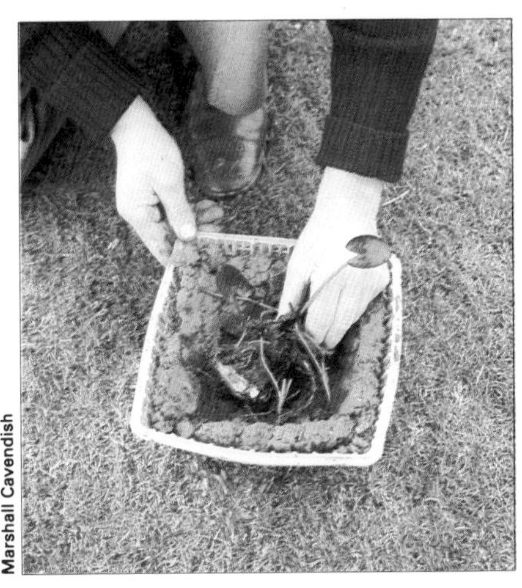

Marshall Cavendish

2 *Spread the roots of the plants out, add a little aquatic plant fertilizer and top up the basket with more soil.*

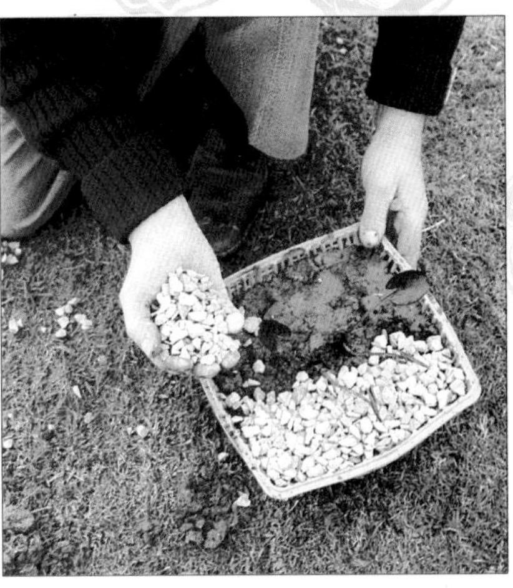

3 *Add a layer of clean gravel on the top to prevent fish disturbing the soil and muddying the water.*

4 *Stand the basket on a few bricks. Lay them easily by using a spade to position them into the pond.*

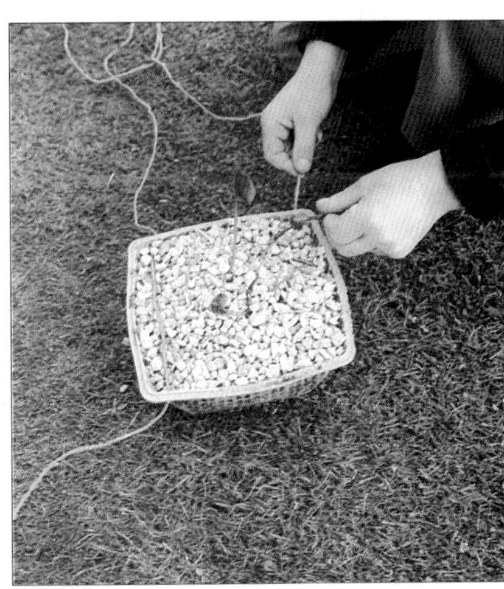

5 *For deep water, thread strong twine through the edges of the basket. Then, with someone's help, lower it in.*

CHECKLIST

WHAT TO DO

TRIM BACK
Tidy up forsythia, privet and heathers

PERENNIALS
Divide Michaelmas daisies, start putting in supports for border perennials

YOUNG PLANTS
Check seedling health and harden off

WAR ON WEEDS
Get on top of annual and perennial weeds

LOOK AHEAD

PLANT
Agapanthus, gladioli corms, nerine bulbs

WHAT TO SEE

BORDER PERENNIALS
Alyssum saxatile, aubrieta, primula

TREES
Amelanchier, magnolia, flowering cherry, flowering crab apple, pyrus

SHRUBS
Berberis, camellia, choisya, fothergilla, kerria, pieris, rosemary, spiraea, viburnum

BEDDING PLANTS
Wallflower, forget-me-not, double daisy, polyanthus, primrose

BULBS
Daffodils, fritillaria, lily-of-the-valley, grape hyacinth, tulips

GARDEN VISITORS

FRIENDS
Housemartins and swallows, ladybirds and bees

FOES
Small white butterflies, sparrows, greenfly, blackfly, whitefly, slugs and snails

LATE SPRING
WEEK 1

WHAT TO DO

In the spring most plants, whether large or small, put out vigorous new growth. This is the best time to trim up straggly growth and get special shrubs, hedges and trees back in shape. Do not worry if they look a little bare afterwards, as branches will soon be covered in lots of fresh new leaves.

Keep in shape

Cut back neglected privet hard to encourage new bushy growth. Trim straggly winter-flowering heathers now that their flowering display is over. Shears are the best tool for this. Weeping trees and shrubs producing any upright shoots should have these pruned out. If left, they will destroy the elegant shape.

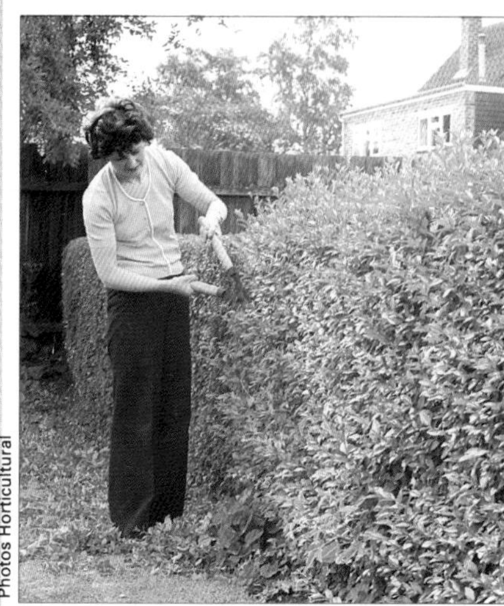

Photos Horticultural

Cut back privet hard to encourage growth.

Dividing daisies

The performance of Michaelmas daisies slowly deteriorates as the crown of roots becomes dense and entangled. Rejuvenate the crown by division every three years or so. First prepare the soil by digging it over thoroughly and incorporating a little compost and bone meal. Dig up the crown now and split it into several sections. Replant a healthy section with plenty of new shoots and a good proportion of the roots. Take care to ensure the roots and buds are not damaged when planting.

Michael Shoebridge

Encourage healthy growth by dividing clumps every three years or so.

Harden off

Continue to harden off new plants bought from garden centres and nurseries. They have usually been raised under protection and if put straight into the garden without a period of acclimatization first, their growth will be stunted and they may even die.

Support perennials

Place stakes or other forms of support among early perennials.

Weed invaders

Don't let up on the war on weeds. Numbers will increase dramatically unless you take some sort of effective control measures now. Temperatures are high enough for most weeds to put in an appearance and soon any bare soil will become a mass of leafy weed seedlings.

Hand weeding is not practical when the weeds are so small. With so many to contend with you are better off with a traditional hoe. The hoe is basically a blade at the end of a pole. The blade is set at an angle so you can push it through the soil, cutting through the stems of annual weeds.

Photos Horticultural

Hoe now to get rid of annual weeds.

Established perennial weeds cannot be culled in this way since, if left in the soil, their root systems soon throw up another burst of growth. Instead, they require careful hand weeding to make sure the whole of the root system is plucked from the soil.

Photos Horticultural

Remove all the roots of perennial weeds.

WHAT TO SEE

The weather is beginning to warm up and suddenly the garden is bursting with colour as the whole of nature is busy preparing for summer. Look out for beautiful flowering shrubs.

Photos Horticultural

Stunning* Kerria japonica *'Pleniflora'.

Harry Smith

***Fluffy balls of* Fothergilla monticola.**

LOOK AHEAD

There is still time to plant summer-flowering corms, bulbs and tubers. They are very rewarding and well worth looking for at your local garden centre.

Gladioli

It is not too late to plant gladioli if you want a dazzling late summer display. You may even find them being sold off cheaply. Plant corms 15cm/6in deep and the same distance apart.

Pink beauties

Nerine bowdenii, *late summer-flowering bulbs, can be planted now in good soil. They like a hot, dry position – the base of a sunny brick wall is ideal. Plant bulbs 10cm/4in deep and 15cm/6in apart. They will produce large, attractive clusters of blooms on tall stems.*

African lily

*Add some colour to a sunny, warm border by planting African lilies (*Agapanthus africanus*) this week. They love a good, fertile, well-drained soil and protection from buffeting winds.*

There are a number of varieties to choose from. The 'Headbourne Hybrids' are moderately hardy. If growing conditions in your garden are not ideal try the more accommodating lavender-blue A. campanulatus *'Isis'.*

Plant with a 5cm/2in covering of soil, leaving 45cm/18in between crowns. Avoid disturbing them after planting.

VISITORS

The great diving beetle,* Dytiscus marginalis, *is a vicious brute which terrorizes the inhabitants of your garden pond. It will attack fish as big as 15cm/6in long. The beetle is about 4cm/1½in long, dark brown in colour and flies from pond to pond.

Nature Photographers

This beetle is a menace in garden ponds.

PLANTING MARGINAL AQUATICS

Plants that grow at the edge of a pond, in shallow water or boggy soil, are called marginal aquatics. These include bulrushes **(Scirpus albescens)** ***and buttercup-like marsh marigolds*** **(Caltha palustris). Saururus cernuus** ***(below), commonly known as swamp lily, will form clumps of heart-shaped leaves with creamy flowers in summer.***

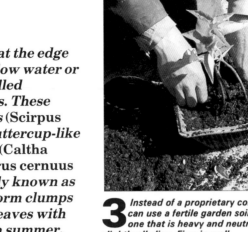

1 *Line the base of a plastic water garden basket, approximately 30cm/12in square and 15cm/6in deep with turf or plastic liner and John Innes No.1 compost.*

Harry Smith

2 *Remove marginal plant from its pot and place in centre of basket. Fill with soil or compost, bringing the level to within 2.5cm/1in of the basket's rim.*

3 *Instead of a proprietary compost, you can use a fertile garden soil, perferably one that is heavy and neutral or slightly alkaline. Firm in well.*

4 *Add a layer of clean gravel to cover the soil's surface. This will give a neat finish and prevent soil from making the water in the pond too muddy.*

Collections/Patrick Johns

5 *Place the finished basket on a shelf at the side of the pond, or on a platform of bricks, to bring the top to 5–7cm/2–3in below the surface of the water.*

LIFTING DAFFODILS

Daffodils actually grow better if left undisturbed for a number of years. In a small garden, though, you may want to move them to make space for summer bedding or, if clumps have become too overcrowded, you may wish to divide and replant them. In either case, lift bulbs and transfer to a spare plot, to be 'heeled in' and left undisturbed until the leaves and stems have shrivelled.

Marshall Cavendish

1 *Lift bulbs carefully with a fork and lay them in a trench in a sunny corner of the garden. Cover bulbs and lower stems with soil and firm with heel of shoe.*

Marshall Cavendish

2 *Don't tidy daffodil leaves and stems by tying them in knots. Leave them fully exposed to the sunlight, which helps the bulbs to 'recharge their batteries'.*

TAKING DELPHINIUM CUTTINGS

Tall delphiniums make an impressive show in your summer border and rather than buy expensive plants you can easily increase your stock by planning ahead and taking cuttings now. Use existing plants from your garden, or buy two or three from your local nursery. Shoots should be 7.5-10cm/3-4in high and the thickness of a pencil.

1 *You will need two or three delphinium plants, rooting powder, earthenware pots, knife, dibber and a mixture of equal parts damp peat and silver sand.*

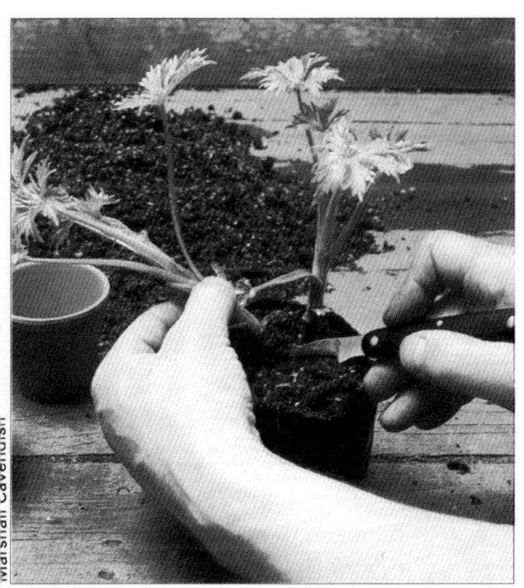

2 *Cut off shoots from below soil level, using a sharp knife. If possible, cuttings should be 7.5cm/3in long and have a heel of old wood attached.*

3 *Trim base of cutting straight across. Discard any hollow stems, as these are not suitable for propagation. Trim off all young leaves at the base.*

4 *Remove excess leaves, including any on lower part of stem. This is best done by pulling them off with a sharp downward movement.*

5 *Overfill pot with the peat and sand mixture, then make a hole in the centre with dibber. Dip cutting into hormone rooting powder before planting.*

6 *Tap pot to settle compost, then use fingertips to firm down. Clay pots are best for propagation as they are porous and so let roots breathe.*

7 *Cover potted cuttings with a polythene bag and stand on a sunny windowsill. Cuttings will take about four or five weeks to root.*

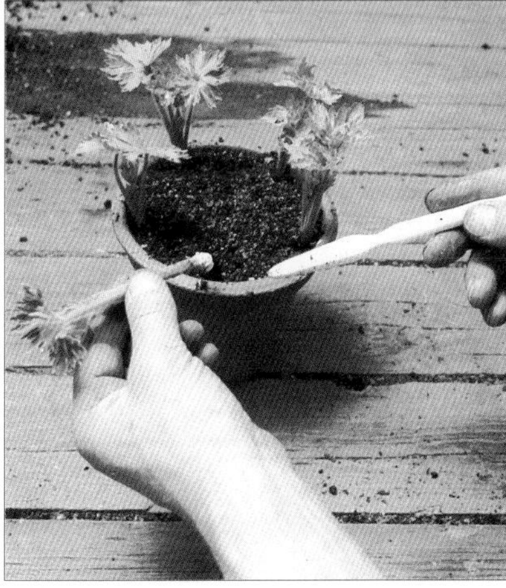

8 *Instead of single small pots, you can use a 12.5cm/5in clay pot which will hold five or six cuttings arranged around the edge.*

CHECKLIST

WHAT TO DO

PLANT
Rhododendrons

PINCH OUT
Sweet peas

GENERAL TASKS
Prune holly and cornelian cherry
Lift and divide red-hot pokers
Trim conifer hedges
Adjust lawnmower blades
Harden off half-hardy annuals

LOOK AHEAD
Sow hardy annuals for a late summer display

WHAT TO SEE

BORDER PERENNIALS
Alyssum, stone cress, bugle, columbine, aubretia, bergenia, hellebore, lungwort, primula

TREES
Chestnut, amelanchier, arbutus, cercis, magnolia, flowering cherry, crab apple

SHRUBS
Ceanothus, choisya, dogwood, flowering currant, broom, beauty bush, kerria, pieris

BEDDING PLANTS
Brompton stocks, campanula, forget-me-not, double daisy, candytuft, honesty, primrose

BULBS
Glory-of-the-snow, cyclamen, fritillaria, hyacinth, lily-of-the-valley, wood lilies

VISITORS

FRIENDS
Small tortoiseshell butterflies, birds, ladybirds, bees and lacewings

FOES
Small white butterflies, sparrows, greenfly, blackfly, whitefly, slugs and snails

LATE SPRING
WEEK 2

WHAT TO DO

It is peak growing season for many shrubs. As they shoot ahead they can look straggly – holly and conifers, in particular, need copious cutting. Lawns demand more frequent mowing and your mower blades should be adjusted accordingly. Even though dry summer weather is a long way off, keep fruit trees happy with regular drinks of water.

Prune conifer hedges
If your conifers are looking untidy now is the time to trim them. A straggly but established conifer hedge should have the growing tips cut back by 15cm/6in. This will encourage the hedge to fill out during the growing season.

Collections/Patrick Johns

Give unruly hedges a spring tidy with a pair of hand shears.

Divide red-hot pokers
It is your last chance to lift and divide clumps of red-hot pokers (Kniphofia species) that have outgrown their allotted space. Although these tall, bright and beautiful plants do not like boggy ground, they will grow in almost all other situations and thrive particularly well in well-drained loam in full sun.

Marshall Cavendish

Red-hot pokers give glorious colour; increase your stock now.

Adjust lawnmower
As mowing the lawn becomes almost a weekly task, your lawnmower blades should be adjusted to give optimum results. Lower the blades from their first-cut setting of about 6mm/¼in to 2.5cm/1in during the summer months. If there is a spell of long, dry weather, then this blade height should be raised again to the less fierce first-cut setting until the grass is growing strongly once more.

Trim holly

If your holly bush is looking straggly and is in need of a trim, cut it back now. Use a sharp pair of secateurs and cut back each stem by making a clean cut just above a healthy bud.

Variegated hollies should be checked over for signs of all-green foliage. This should also be cut out now. The cornelian cherry or Cornus mas *should be pruned after flowering if need be. Once the small golden blooms that appear in clusters along last year's growth have passed their best, the shrub can be cut back quite hard to leave a balanced framework. New growth made this year will flower next spring.*

Collections/Patrick Johns

Give holly a rough shape up with an electric hedge trimmer.

Harden off seedlings

Continue to acclimatize seedling half-hardy annuals such as zinnias, petunias, lobelias and antirrhinums to outdoor conditions before planting out. Tender young plants bought from garden centres should also be hardened-off gradually.

Water thirsty fruit

Make sure that fruit trees growing in pots or at the foot of a wall do not run short of water after flowering. Good care taken with watering now will help to produce a fruitful yield.

LOOK AHEAD

Sow hardy annuals for a late summer display.

Pat Brindley

There is still time to sow candytuft.

WHAT TO SEE

The days are drier and sunnier, but be prepared for the odd thunderstorm and some squally winds. Plants will be bursting with colour in response to the milder climate and there is less danger of night frosts.

There is plenty to enjoy in the garden: perennials, trees, flowering shrubs and bulbs. Take time to revel in the last weeks of the bright and colourful tulips and daffodils.

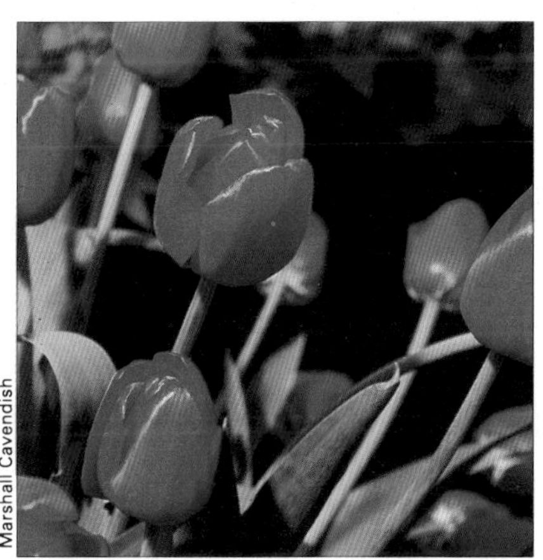

Marshall Cavendish

A blaze of 'Flying Dutchman' tulips.

VISITORS

Butterflies in their pretty, dancing colours are a welcome, enjoyable sight in the garden.

Small tortoiseshell butterflies are useful pollinators, as they search from plant to plant for nectar. Apart from the butterfly bush, honesty, primulas, bugle and aubrieta are attractive to butterflies. Cabbage white butterflies lay their eggs on cabbages, and the emerging caterpillars then eat the leaves.

Greenfly and blackfly are still very much in evidence. If there are plenty of ladybirds around, then nature will take its course, as ladybirds prey on aphids. Hose these pests from leaves and buds.

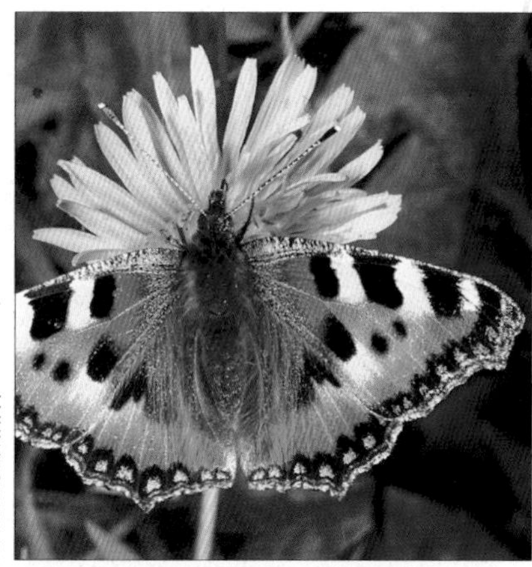

N.A. Callow/NHPA

Tortoiseshell butterflies are pollinators.

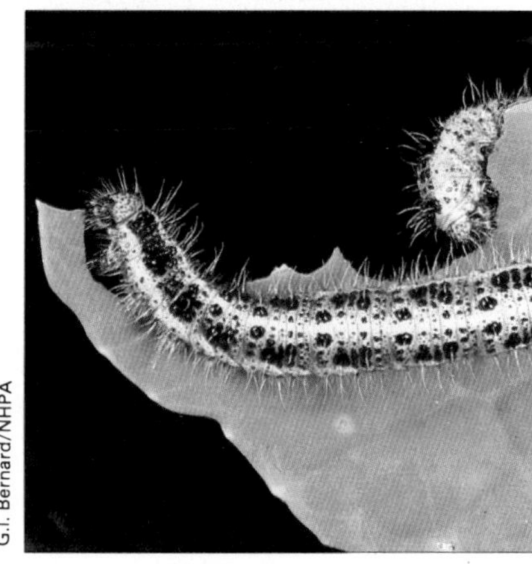

G.I. Bernard/NHPA

Beware, caterpillars destroy cabbages.

THE BEST SWEET PEAS

Delightful and easy to grow, sweet peas are a must for any garden.

The tall garden varieties (Spencer varieties are good) are available in a whole host of vibrant colours from the palest of pastel shades to vibrant reds and purples. Most are highly fragrant and will fill your garden with their heady scent all through the summer months from the early summer right through until the autumn. Grow them over a simple bamboo 'wigwam' or up a trellis, frame or plastic netting. Any sunny location in a well-drained garden soil will do. Just follow these tips to get the very best results from your sweet peas.

Ray Duns

For happy, healthy sweet peas like this one follow these simple tips.

If you look after your sweet peas properly you will be rewarded with armfuls of flowers all through the summer. When the sweet pea plants in your garden are about 10cm/4in high they should be pinched out just above a leaf joint. This encourages each plant to produce several side shoots and gives dense growth.

Some sort of support is essential and you should erect some at this stage if you have not done so already. The tendrils on sweet peas are designed to help them grip the structure onto which they are climbing, but help them along by carefully manipulating them between the netting.

1 Pinch out the tops of 10cm/4in high sweet pea plants, just above a leaf joint. This will encourage the plant to produce vigorous side shoots which produces more attractive bushy plants.

Water well, especially during dry spells. Feed occasionally with a liquid fertilizer which is high in potash – the nutrient that keeps plants flowering. Dead-head regularly as this promotes plentiful blooms.

2 Make sure your sweet peas have good support, not only vertical, but horizontal. As the side shoots grow, help them by twisting tendrils around support.

HARVESTING YOUR RHUBARB CROP

Rhubarb will be ready for harvesting in late spring or early summer but you can go on picking until almost the middle of summer. Tasty new sticks can be picked as required from an established crown (over one year). If you harvest regularly the sticks will be succulent for delicious puddings.

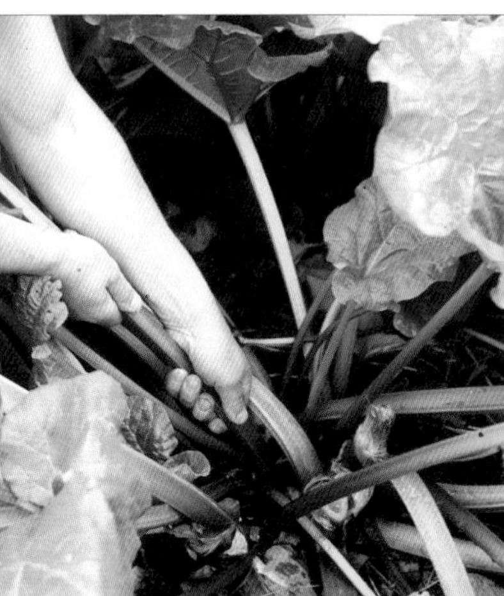

1 Pull each rhubarb stick individually by holding it firmly near its base and giving it a sharp tug. The stick should come away from the crown cleanly.

2 Remove leaves of the harvested stalks and put them on the compost heap before taking the sticks indoors. Remember leaves are poisonous.

PLANTING A RHODODENDRON

Rhododendrons are very popular shrubs, and it is easy to see why. They offer a wide choice of colours and leaf forms, range in size from compact dwarf shrubs to impressive trees, and most kinds are evergreen. The flowering period of rhododendrons is short, so it makes sense to consider the shape and colour of the flowers and foliage when choosing a rhododendron for your garden.

There are many on offer with a wide range of characteristics: R. cambylocarpum *has neat, oval, apple green leaves and yellow flowers while* R. scintillans *has tiny, yellow-scaled leaves and small purple flowers in mid spring.* R. calostrotum *is a compact rhododendron with interesting blue-green foliage and purple or scarlet blooms in late spring; or, for something really stunning, try* R. *'Hawk Crest', a medium-sized hybrid with large leaves, which produces apricot coloured buds and loose bunches of sulphur-yellow flowers in late spring.*

You should also consider the size your plant is likely to reach at maturity. A medium-sized rhododendron will usually grow to a height of 3m/10ft, while a small species might grow to only 1.5m/5ft. If your garden is very small, there are many dwarf varieties available, growing to a maximum of 1m/3ft.

All but a few rhododendrons require an acid soil. If there is any lime present, the plant will not be able to absorb nutrients from the soil. As a result the leaves will yellow and the plant will wither and die. Choose a site for rhododendrons in semi-shade, preferably protected from harsh winds.

If your soil is too alkaline, you need not be deprived of the chance to grow a rhodendron. Buy a dwarf variety and plant it in a large container in a moist, peaty soil. R. yakushimanum *is a pretty, dome-shaped rhododendron particularly well suited to container cultivation. It has a maximum height and spread of 90cm/3ft and subtle pink flowers that gradually fade to white.*

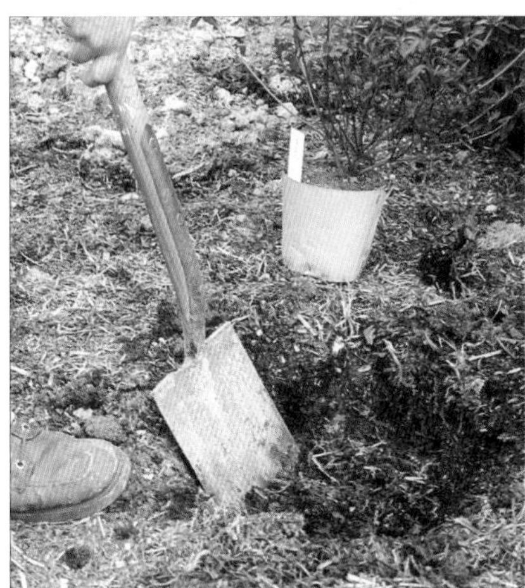

1 ***Carefully select a site in semi-shade and dig a shallow hole. Rhododendrons are shallow rooted and do not like to be planted too deeply.***

2 ***Make sure that the old soil mark on the stem of the container-grown rhododendron is at the same level when it is placed in the planting hole.***

3 ***If the soil in the container is dry, give it a good soaking now. Cut down the side of the plastic plant container and carefully remove the rhododendron.***

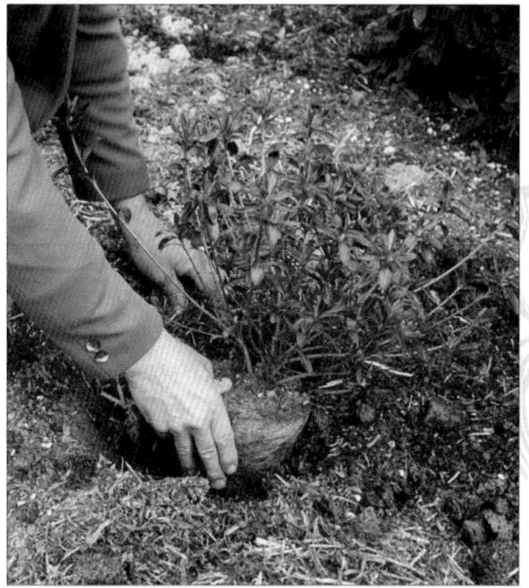

4 ***Add a layer of peat and a handful of bone meal to the bottom of the hole and place the rhododendron in the centre. Fill in the soil around the rootball.***

5 ***Firm in the soil with your hands and give the soil a thorough soaking. It is important to keep the soil moist while the plant is establishing its roots.***

Roses burst into full bloom at the height of the summer – the garden will need careful tending to keep it tidy.

SUMMER

EARLY SUMMER

MID SUMMER

LATE SUMMER

CHECKLIST

WHAT TO DO

GENERAL TASKS
Feed and weed your lawn
Support gladioli
Check roses and gooseberries for signs of pests and diseases
Pick flowers from spring-planted strawberries
Prune hedges of berberis and Leyland cypress
Sow wallflowers, sweet Williams and Canterbury bells

LOOK AHEAD

SUMMER BEDDING
Prepare ground ready for bedding out

LAWNS
Start cutting your lawn at least once a week and tackle rogue lawn weeds as they appear

WHAT TO SEE

BORDER PERENNIALS
Aquilegia, bergenia, dicentra, lungwort

TREES
Crab apple, horse chestnut, Judas tree

SHRUBS
Broom, genista, gorse, kolkwitzia, kerria, pieris, spiraea, viburnum

BEDDING PLANTS
Honesty (*Lunaria annua*), wallflower

BULBS
Fritillaria, grape hyacinths, hyacinths, scilla and trillium

VISITORS

FRIENDS
Butterflies such as peacock, comma, orange-tip, wallbrown, painted lady, red admiral

FOES
Butterflies such as small white, large white. Greenfly, blackfly, whitefly, leaf-hopper, flea-beetle, leaf-miners

WHAT TO DO

Dry spells may occur now and can cause all sorts of problems. Newly planted specimens are particularly vulnerable so take care to keep up with your watering if there is a prolonged period without rain.

Time to feed and weed
There's still time to feed the lawn with a combined fertilizer and weedkiller treatment if you have not already done so. This will give the lawn the food it needs for active spring growth and help to beat the weeds.

Pinch out strawberries
Strawberries planted earlier this spring should not be allowed to fruit during their first summer. This deflowering enables the plant to put all its energies into getting established. Check plants about once a week and pinch out any flowers.

Rose check-up
Check roses for signs of greenfly. Early attacks can be controlled with soapy water and by carefully picking off aphids from around affected buds and shoots. If infestation is well established, tackle it with a garden insecticide recommended for spraying roses.

Also check other shrubs and fruit bushes if you have them, as greenfly are breeding fast and can attack many garden plants.

Sow biennials
There is still time to sow biennials such as wallflowers, sweet Williams and Canterbury bells to flower next year. Prepare the seedbed carefully to produce a weed-free soil that has a well-broken down crumbly texture. Sow in drills (that is narrow channels), and then cover with a light scattering of fine soil. Sow as thinly as possible so that the germinating seedlings have room to develop properly.

Trimming time for hedges . . .
Hedges of evergreen berberis such as Berberis darwinii *and* B. × stenophylla *should be pruned as necessary directly after flowering. Most conifer hedges are trimmed in late summer, but Leyland cypress should also be given its first trim of the year to keep this vigorous hedging plant in control*

Marshall Cavendish

Trim Leyland cypress now to restrain its vigorous growth.

. . . and for lawns

Cut lawns regularly – once a week is best. Collect mowings and mix with other garden waste before placing on the compost heap.

Grass clippings can be used on the compost heap if mixed with other materials.

Mulch agapanthus

Agapanthus planted last month should be mulched with a thick layer of well-rotted manure or compost now. It is also important to keep the soil well watered during dry spells.

Gooseberry mildew

Stay vigilant for signs of mildew and caterpillars on gooseberries. Pick off first offenders, but be prepared to spray later attacks.

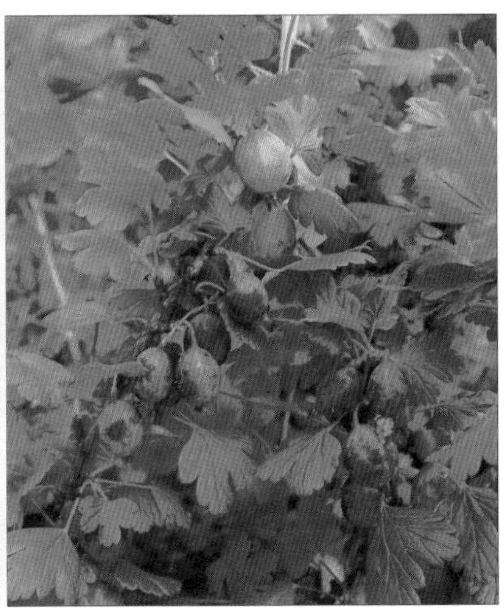

Gooseberry mildew will spoil the crop if not tackled early.

LOOK AHEAD

Now that spring bedding is all but over, it is time to prepare for bedding out their summer replacements.

Prepare for bedding out

First of all clear the bed and then carefully dig it over removing weeds and any debris. Water well. It is important this is done in advance since if planting is carried out in hot, sunny weather the summer bedding plants may suffer from a check in growth if left to dry out.

Before you go and buy your plants it is a good idea to estimate how many you will need. Although individual varieties may need spacing slightly differently, as a rule of thumb edging plants should be spaced about 15cm/6in apart, those in the middle about 25cm/10in and if the border is deep, larger plants at the back may need to be spaced 30cm/1ft apart.

WHAT TO SEE

There are some small trees and shrubs that are versatile enough to be used either as background plants or specimens in the centre of a display. June favourites such as lilac and ceanothus come in this special group.

Lilac *(syringa)*

Lilacs are a common sight in gardens because they are easy to grow and offer a spectacular show of fragrant flowers during late spring and early summer. There are several notable varieties including 'Blue Hyacinth' (pale lilac), 'Mme Antoine Buchner' (deep purple), 'Primrose' (pale yellow), 'Mme Lemoine' (double white).

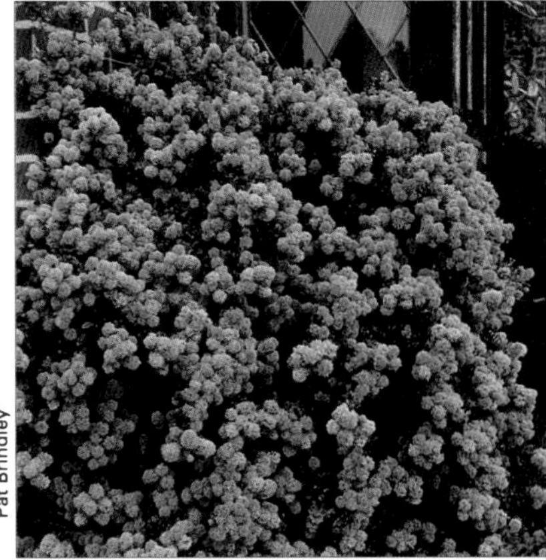

Pat Brindley

Caenothus dentatus *is one of the early-flowering evergreen species.*

Ceanothus

This is a very underrated shrub that needs a warm position sheltered from cold winds. It is commonly called the Californian lilac. During late spring and summer ceanothus varieties such as 'Cascade', 'Delight', and 'Trewithen Blue' are covered in a profusion of densely clustered flowers. Several later varieties are worth looking out for, including the fast growing 'Autumnal Blue' (light mauve), 'Burkwoodii' (bright blue) and 'Perle Rose' (pinkish-red).

VISITORS

Caterpillars can quickly devastate a plant. The magpie moth caterpillar (below) is a common example, but there are many others. Hand pick soon after they have hatched or use derris dust.

Harry Smith

A magpie moth caterpillar.

HOW TO LAYER A RHODODENDRON

Many shrubs, including rhododendrons and azaleas, can be propagated easily by layering – a method that occurs naturally in the wild when stems get covered with soil and rotting plant matter.

Although layering is only suitable for raising a few plants at once, and you will have to wait a year to see the results of your efforts, the resulting plant will be relatively large and should establish itself easily if treated with care.

This kind of layering is traditionally done in late winter or early spring, but it is not too late to try it now, provided you are careful to keep the ground well watered in dry weather.

Fork plenty of peat (and grit if the soil tends to be waterlogged) into the area where the layer is to be made, disturbing the roots of the parent plant as little as possible. Then choose a vigorously growing shoot close to the base, and remove sideshoots for about 15-60cm/6-24in behind the growing tip. Bend the stem down to ground level. To encourage rapid rooting make a slit in the direction of the tip, about an inch or so long. Being very careful to cut only half way through the stem. Do not sever it (if you find this difficult, just tighten a piece of copper wire round the stem, twisting it tight, instead).

Make a slight depression in the ground with a trowel or spade, and peg the shoot down with a piece of bent wire, ensuring it is well buried. Cover with some good soil and, if necessary, weight the branch down with a stone.

Check the layer next spring, by which time it should have rooted. If it has, sever it from the parent plant, but let it grow on undisturbed for another season, when you will have a nice strong plant.

A slit has been made in this rhododendron to encourage rooting.

All photographs Marshall Cavendish

Peg the stem with a piece of wire to hold it in contact with the ground.

It may be necessary to use a stone to hold the layer down.

ROUTINE ROSE CARE

For big blooms on hybrid tea (large-flowered) roses, it is worth disbudding them. If just the main bud is allowed to flower, the resulting bloom will be magnificent so remove any secondary buds.

Do not, however, do this with floribunda (cluster-flowered) roses.

Hybrid tea (large-flowered) roses will produce bigger, more spectacular blooms if just the main bud is allowed to flower. Remove the secondary buds.

Keep climbing roses tied in to their supports, otherwise they can become tangled. Loop the tie around the stem and the support in such a way that the tie will not restrict the shoot as it grows.

Tie the stems of climbers, making sure they have room to expand.

DIVIDING FLAG IRISES

The popular flag irises, one of the jewels of the early June border, can be divided into separate plants straight after flowering. An old, overgrown clump will benefit by being lifted and divided, and you can increase the plants for yourself or your friends at the same time.

Follow these simple step-by-step instructions now and reap the benefits in years to come.

1 *When a clump becomes very large, flowering may be affected so it is time to divide it.*

All photographs Marshall Cavendish

2 *Loosen the soil around the edge of the clump, being careful not to damage any fine roots.*

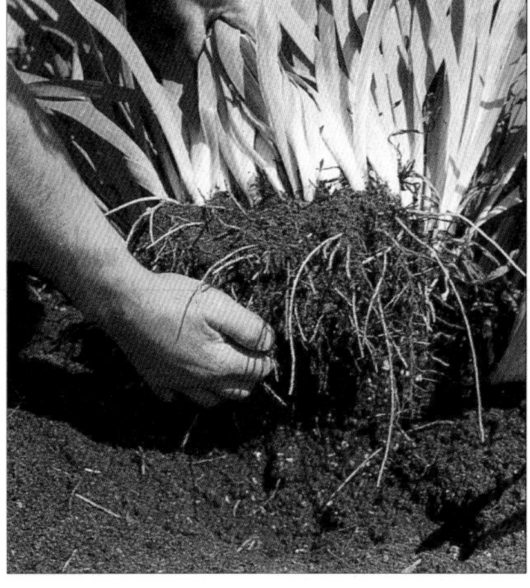

3 *Lift the plant with as little damage to the roots as possible, using a digging fork if necessary.*

4 *Replant a major portion of the clump, but use some of the small rhizomes for propagation.*

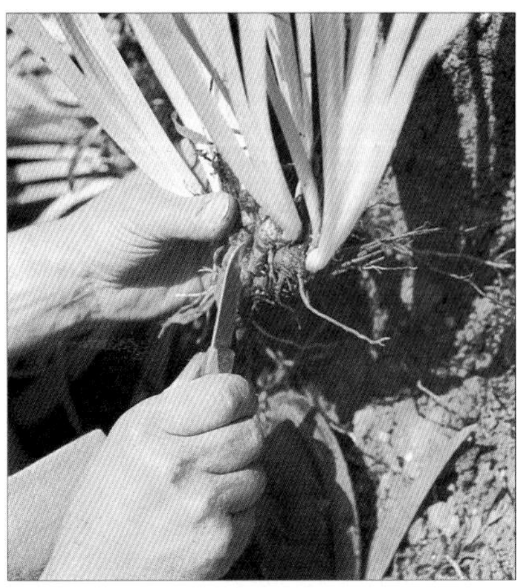

5 *Use a sharp knife to separate individual pieces of rhizome, each with some roots and a fan of leaves.*

6 *To reduce excessive moisture loss and avoid the plant being loosened by wind, trim the leaves as shown.*

7 *Make a hole deep enough to take the fine roots, but be careful not to bury the rhizome too deeply.*

8 *Firm the soil gently around the roots, leaving the top of the rhizome exposed. Water in thoroughly.*

CHECKLIST

WHAT TO DO

GENERAL TASKS
Water lawns in dry weather
Trim foliage from spring-flowering bulbs growing in grass
Check pond fish
Mulch roses
Plant out summer bedding
Plunge in potted Indian azaleas

LOOK AHEAD

CHRYSANTHEMUMS
Pinch out tips to encourage bushy growth

GROUND COVER
Increase by taking cuttings

WHAT TO SEE

BORDER PERENNIALS
Ajuga, masterwort, bergenia, Chinese trumpet flower, saxifrage, poppy, primula

TREES
Hawthorn, laburnum, lilac

SHRUBS
Abelia, smoke tree, broom, kolkwitzia, honeysuckle, senecio, weigela

BEDDING PLANTS
Canterbury bells, eschscholzia, godetia, candytuft, lobelia, stock, viola

BULBS
Allium, cyclamen, gladioli, lily, trillium

VISITORS

FRIENDS
Many butterflies, hedgehogs, moths, birds, ladybirds, bees and lacewings

FOES
Cabbage white caterpillars, butterflies, aphids, leaf-hopper, flea-beetle, leaf-miners, slugs and snails

EARLY SUMMER
WEEK 2

WHAT TO DO

Early summer tends to be dry, a time of light winds and cloudless skies – just the right conditions to enjoy your garden to the full. But don't forget to give thirsty plants an extra drink of water. Danger of frosts should have passed and gardening takes on a new aspect.

Lawn care
Lawns in dry weather can soon lose their lush green appeal. If there is an early spell of drought, water your grass once a fortnight to give it a thorough soaking. Watering little and often can be a big mistake since this encourages the grass to be shallow rooting as it does not need to reach down for extra moisture. The effect will be magnified if drought conditions continue through the summer especially if, because of hose-pipe restrictions, you are unable to continue regular watering.

Eric Crichton

Soak your lawn thoroughly once a fortnight rather than giving small drinks more often.

Mulch roses
Roses reign supreme in the garden now, so keep them blooming well with a mulch of well-rotted manure or compost. This helps reduce water loss from around the roots as well as suppressing weeds. Lawn mowings make excellent mulching material, provided you have not used a weedkiller on your lawn. Whatever you use for mulch, keep it away from the stem of each rose bush.

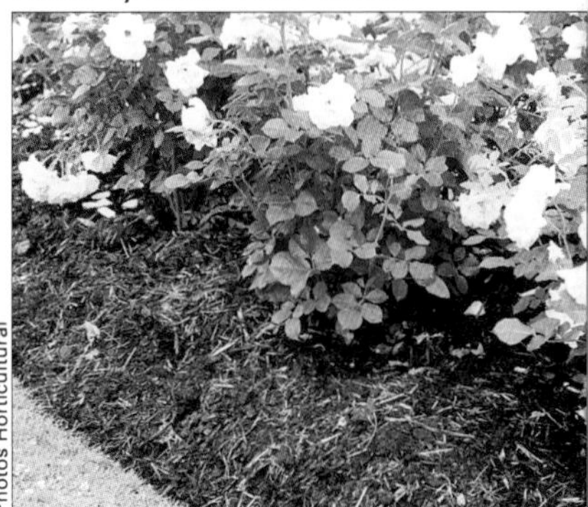

Photos Horticultural

A mulch applied now will smother weeds round your roses while reducing water loss.

Look after pond fish
Feed fish fairly regularly from now on. Start off with small amounts of food. While the fish feed, watch them closely for signs of fungal or parasitic infection. Unusually slow or jerky movements are often a sign that all is not well.

If you suspect something is wrong with a fish, catch it and isolate it in an aquarium. This prevents infection spreading. Then you can check on the problem, treat the fish and cure it before returning it to the pond.

Indian azaleas

Azaleas can now be placed out in the garden to spend the summer outside. Select a shady, fairly well-drained, sheltered spot that isn't too damp. Plunge the pot rim-deep into the soil in a bare corner – but don't forget about it!

Indian azaleas need watering using lime-free water if the weather is hot and dry so if you have hard tap water you need to collect rain water when you can. Make a note in your diary to lift the plant in the autumn to bring it indoors again before the first frosts.

Michael Shoebridge

Your Indian azalea will enjoy a summer outside, but don't forget to bring it in again.

Ready for take-off

As the days – and nights too – are warm, tender plants such as half-hardy annuals should now be fully hardened off and ready to face the outside. Plant into position in the same way as summer bedding. Cloches used to protect plants already in position in the garden can be removed now that there is no longer any danger of frost damage.

Naturalized bulbs

If the foliage of daffodils and other spring-flowering bulbs which were grown in grass has died it can now be cut back and the surrounding grass mown with the rest of the lawn.

LOOK AHEAD

Pinch out chrysanthemums

Any spray varieties of chrysanthemum planted last month should have their growing tips pinched out once the plant is established and growing well – usually at about 20cm/8in tall. This encourages the plant to produce several flowering shoots in the place of each one pinched out to give a really magnificent autumn display. By early summer this process can be repeated with the sideshoots produced from the first pinching out.

WHAT TO SEE

The garden is so full of wonderful colours at this time of year that if you spot something that stands out from all the rest it must be really special. If you are planning a border of one colour now is an ideal time to select the plants.

Red and pink

Thrift; masterwort; begonia; smoke bush; may; cyclamen; bleeding heart; eschscholzia (poppy-like flowers); candytuft; Chinese trumpet flower; calico bush; beauty bush; stock; honeysuckle; London pride; lilac.

Yellow and green

Broom; foxtail lily; avens (border and rock garden perennials); water iris; laburnum; primula; buttercup; nasturtium; canary creeper; marigold; Senecio × *'Sunshine' (shrub).*

Blue and purple

Bugle; ageratum (annuals and biennials); cornflower; purple broom; hebe; heliotrope; campanula; gentian; geranium; lobelia; catmint; navelwort; scilla; veronica.

White and cream

*Arenaria (rock gardens); Shasta daisy (*Leucanthemum × superbum*); hawthorn;* Erinus alpinus *var.* albus *(rock gardens); candytuft; bachelor's buttons; lilac; trillium.*

Multihued

Columbine (Aquilegia vulgaris)*; Canterbury bell; delphinium; rock rose (helianthemum); busy Lizzie; iris; sweet pea; Virginia stock; monkey flower;* Nemesia strumosa *(half-hardy annual); tobacco plant (nicotiana); peony; oriental poppy; petunia; phlox; viola.*

VISITORS

Now that the warmer weather entices evening activity from insects and grubs, their predators are also out and about. The shy hedgehog can be lured to your patio with a plate of canned dog food. Keep competitors away by covering the plate with an inverted plastic flowerpot.

Hedgehogs often make towns and cities their homes, although they prefer a rural environment. Cemeteries, wasteland and parks are favourite sites. They breed in early summer, and usually have four or more young in each litter.

Stephen Dalton/NHPA

Tempt this little chap with canned dog food rather than the traditional bread and milk.

EARWIG TRAPS

Earwigs can devastate many plants, chewing holes in the leaves and flower buds which in turn leads to deformed and disfigured blooms. They trouble mainly herbaceous plants, and are a special problem for dahlias and chrysanthemums, but clematis, delphiniums and pansies are also on their list of desirable eating.

You are much more likely to see their results than the insects themselves, which are dark brown and up to 2.5cm / 1in long. They are not usually seen by day, only coming out at night when they feed.

Instead of an insecticide, trap them by filling a small flower pot with straw or wood shavings, turn it upside down and put it on top of a cane pushed in among the affected plants.

All you need to make your earwig trap is a plastic flowerpot and some straw.

Place the upturned pot on a bamboo cane pushed in among the affected plants. Empty the trap each morning.

WAYS TO WATER HANGING BASKETS

Your hanging baskets require regular and frequent watering – even in wet weather they are often too sheltered by buildings to receive enough moisture – so it makes sense to make the job as easy as possible without too much mess.

Lifting a watering can above head level is tiring, and even using steps can be a chore. A hosepipe will make the job easier, especially if you have a lot of baskets, and you may find it helpful to tie it to a cane if reaching is difficult.

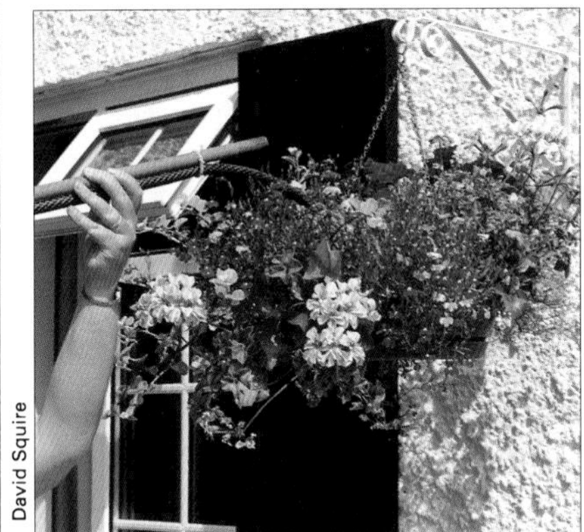

David Squire

Tying your hose to a cane may make watering your hanging baskets easier.

One of the best solutions may be to buy a basket-watering lance to fix to the hose. Alternatively, you might try a special pulley designed to raise and lower the baskets for watering and maintenance. These are not expensive and they also have the added advantage of making it easy to check the basket for pests and diseases.

Inexpensive basket watering bottles (these are like plastic bottles with a long tube and curved spout) work well and they are perfectly satisfactory if you have only a few hanging baskets to water.

THINNING APPLES

A bumper crop of apples at this time of year is not always a good thing. The tree can be overloaded, and if all the fruits mature they will be small and inferior. The branch could even break under the weight of the growing fruit.

Surplus fruit often drops on its own but even if it does further thinning may be advisable.

It is worth doing some initial thinning now, before any natural shedding, to eliminate any malformed or diseased fruits, completing the job at the end of the month. Make sure it is done before mid summer.

As a general guide, thin dessert apples to 10-15cm/4-6in apart, cooking apples to 15-23cm/6-9in apart, but adjust this to suit the tree and the variety.

Thinning apples like this produces larger and better quality fruit later.

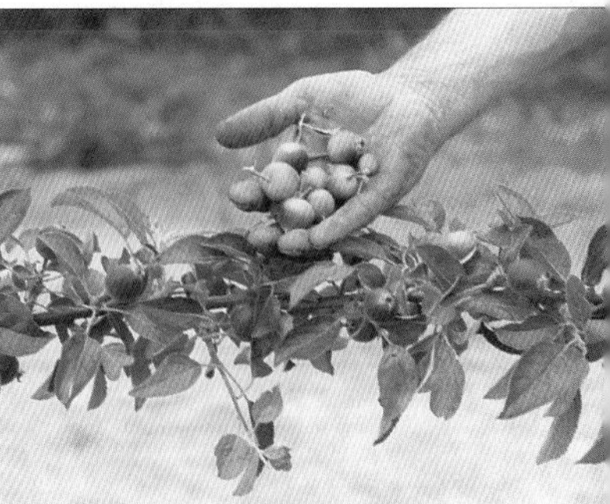

These fruits are now ideally spaced for future healthy growth.

PROPAGATING HYDRANGEAS

Most people love hydrangeas but established shrubs can be quite expensive to buy. In fact, they are really easy to propagate so you can share them with your friends while making more for your own garden too.

If you do not have a hydrangea plant yourself maybe a friend will let you take a few cuttings. You can take them at any time during the next few months.

1 *Choose strong, vigorous and healthy non-flowering shoots for your cuttings. Cut off a piece of shooting stem about 30cm/12in long.*

2 *Using a sharp knife or blade, shorten the cuttings to about 15cm/6in, trimming just below a leaf joint. Remove the bottom pair of leaves.*

3 *As cuttings lose water through their leaves and cannot replace it from their roots, cut the end of each leaf about half-way down to reduce water loss.*

4 *Fill an 8-10cm/3-4in pot with a rooting compost or a mixture of equal parts of sand and peat, or sand and vermiculite or perlite (from garden centres).*

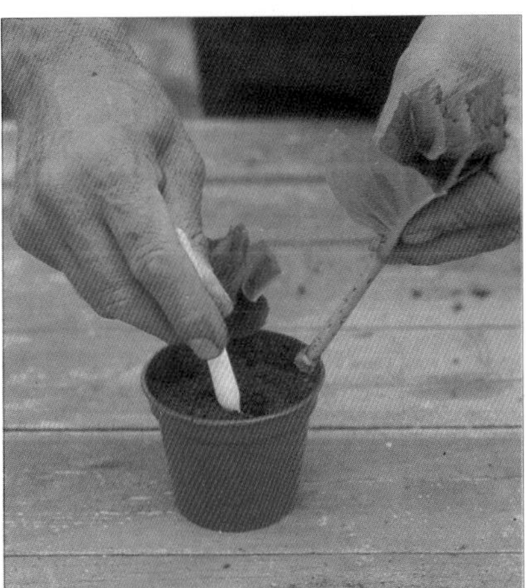

5 *Insert cuttings around the edge of the pot, using a dibber to make holes in compost. Dip the base of each cutting in rooting powder before planting.*

6 *Firm the compost gently around the cuttings with the fingers to ensure that there are no large air pockets that could affect rooting.*

7 *Water the cuttings thoroughly then allow surplus water to drain. Add a fungicide to the water to reduce the risk of the cuttings rotting before they root.*

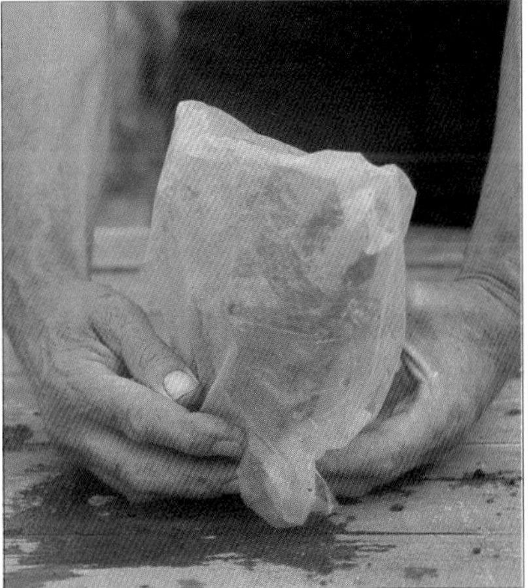

8 *If you do not have a propagator, cover the pot with a polythene bag. Keep cuttings in a light position out of direct sunlight until they have rooted.*

CHECKLIST

WHAT TO DO

GENERAL TASKS
Harvest your last crop of rhubarb
Feed permanent displays of plants in pots, tubs and windowboxes. Lift and divide polyanthus
Check waterlilies to see if they need dividing
Tie in climbing roses
Build a compost heap
Look out for a slug damage

LOOK AHEAD

DEAD-HEAD FLOWERS
Remove dead flower heads to promote further flushes of bloom

FEED TOMATOES
For a bumper harvest later in the season apply a liquid fertilizer to tomatoes in growing bags

WHAT TO SEE

BORDER PERENNIALS
Ajuga, astrantia, bergenia, dicentra, geranium, geum, saxifraga, Oriental poppy

TREES
Foxglove tree, laburnum, red buckeye

SHRUBS
Abelia, *Buddleia alternifolia*, cistus, cotinus, cytisus, deutzia, erica, escallonia, genista, hebe, lilica, lonicera, senecio, weigela

BEDDING PLANTS
African and French marigold, ageratum, begonia, calendula, campanula, candytuft, godetia, lobelia, mimulus, nicotiana, petunia, stock

BULBS
Allium, brodiaea, camassia, cyclamen, iris, ixia, ranunculus, sparaxis, trillium

VISITORS

FRIENDS
Hoverflies, lacewings, ladybirds

FOES
Blackfly, cabbage white butterflies, greenfly

EARLY SUMMER
WEEK 3

WHAT TO DO

Plants which are putting all their energies into growing require constant supplies of food at this time of the year. Supplementing these food supplies can have dramatic results particularly where the plants' rooting area is restricted as when they are confined in containers or growing bags. However, do make sure you apply the right fertilizer, at the recommended dosage, as specified in the manufacturers' instructions printed on the packet.

Apple fruitlet loss
Do not worry if you find a scattering of tiny apples below your apple tree at this time of year. This process is called the 'June drop' and is the perfectly natural way in which the tree sheds excess fruit when too many have set. A tree that carries too many apples will at best bear an abundance of tasteless small fruit.

Andrew Lawson

Trees shed surplus fruit.

Feed tomatoes
Once the first truss of flowers has set and you can see the first pea-sized fruits, give the plants a feed of high-potash fertilizer. Any of the proprietary brands of special liquid tomato fertilizers would be ideal.

Stop picking rhubarb
If you have an established clump of rhubarb in your garden and have been harvesting the tasty leaf stalks regularly throughout the spring, it would be a good idea to take just one more crop before letting the plant have a period to recover during the summer months. If you continue picking, the plant will be weakened and lose its vigour, so producing a smaller crop next season.

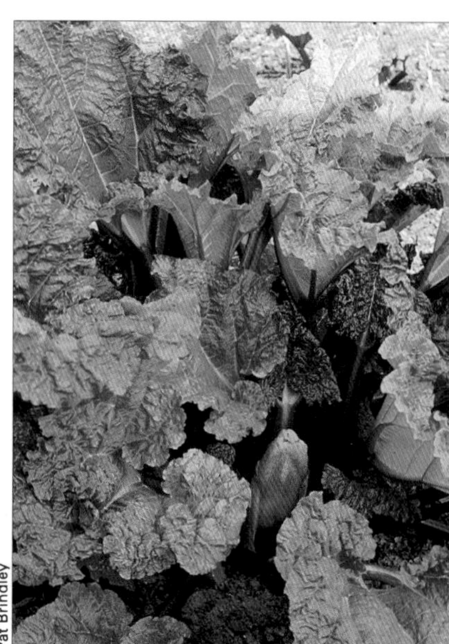
Pat Brindley

Rhubarb 'Early Albert'.

Water lilies

Check established ponds. Water lilies can outgrow the space available which restricts flowering and can swamp other plants. In small ponds this problem can arise quite often, especially when vigorous or semi-vigorous varieties have been planted.

A water lily in need of division.

Where water lilies have become too big they can be lifted from the bottom and divided. The contents of the planting basket should be emptied so that the crown of the plant is easily visible. Divide carefully and replant one section in fresh soil after relining the basket with a new piece of hessian (ordinary potting compost can contain too much fertilizer, which will encourage the growth of algae). Top up the basket with pea-gravel before lowering it once again to the bottom of the pond.

Divide polyanthus

There is still time to lift and divide clumps of polyanthus now they have finished flowering. Using a garden spade, carefully ease out an overgrown clump, then tease it apart, trying to avoid damaging growing points and roots as much as possible. Replant sections in well-prepared border soil. Any 'spares' can be given away to friends and neighbours.

Tie in climbing roses

Climbing roses will be putting on a good deal of growth and some will have started to flower. New growth should be tied into a trellis or other support before it gets too untidy and difficult to manipulate. Use a strong twine or rose ties to secure the stem, but make sure they are not too tight otherwise further growth may be constricted.

Harry Smith

Tie in climbing roses.

LOOK AHEAD

Dead-head displays

Many early flowering plants will produce subsequent flushes of bloom if they are regularly dead-headed. This is a very simple technique of picking off dead flowers. This makes sure the plant puts all its energies into producing further flowers.

Harry Smith

Dead-heading keeps them blooming.

WHAT TO SEE

Many climbers and wall shrubs come into their own now, and perhaps best loved of all are the clematis and honeysuckles.

Clematis

Clematis prefer a sunny position with a shaded root area. This can often be achieved by planting in a sunny site with other shrubs shading the base of the plant.

Photos Horticultural

This clematis is called 'The President'.

VISITORS

Most butterflies are welcome visitors, but the cabbage white is a pest. The eggs are usually laid on cabbages. Remove the eggs if possible or pick off the caterpillars as soon as they hatch.

Stephen Dalton/NHPA

Large or cabbage white butterfly.

SLUG PATROL

Don't let slugs ruin your plants. Go on the offensive before they can do much damage. If you do not want to use slug pellets there are alternatives. You can even drown them in beer.

Slugs can still be a problem, especially among herbaceous borders and in shady corners. They love the new growth on a wide range of plants, but hostas, phlox and delphiniums are among their particular favourites.

Peter McHoy

Slugs and snails love hostas and can ruin them within days at this time of the year.

Slug pellets are most effective but must be placed with care as they can be eaten by birds and pets. It is also important to clear away any dead slugs each morning otherwise the birds will eat them and may be poisoned.

Andrew Lawson

A slug trap that drowns pests.

Alternatively, try making a beer trap. Simply sink a bowl rim-deep into the ground and fill with beer. Cover it from the rain while leaving access for its prey. The slugs will be lured into the trap by the intoxicating smell. There they will drown (but what a way to go!). The trap must be emptied regularly and the liquid 'bait' replaced with fresh.

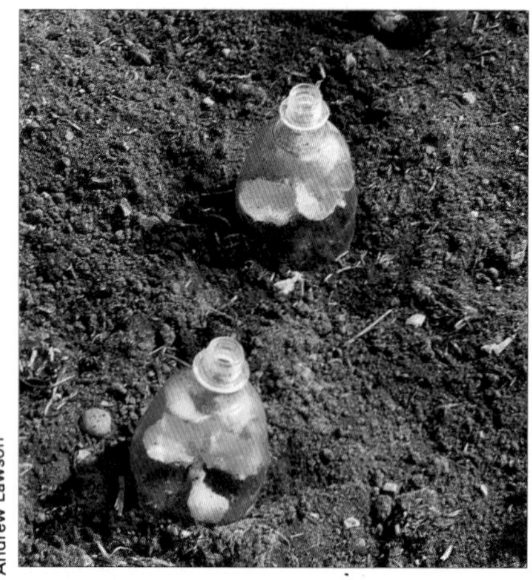

Andrew Lawson

Cut-down bottles protect young plants.

Another way of discouraging slugs and snails from attacking individual plants is to surround them with something rough and scratchy that the slugs don't like to slither across. Sharp sand, ashes or grit are all recommended.

Be warned. In wet weather none of these methods is guaranteed to work.

To keep general populations of slugs down, it is important to clear away any debris or other hiding places the slugs utilize during the heat of the day. Also encourage their natural enemies such as birds who are of course the best slug controllers of all. Birds can be encouraged to guard your garden by offering nesting sites, baths and food supplies – both on a bird table and by growing berry-bearing plants.

GETTING ALPINES INTO SHAPE

Alpines that flowered in the spring, whether growing in the rock garden or in crevices in a path or wall, benefit from a trim at this time of year. This can make the garden look tidier and the plants themselves respond by making more compact growth for next year.

The most important thing is to cut back any seed heads (unless you actually want to save the seeds for propagation purposes). This encourages the plants to put their energy into growing new shoots rather than producing seeds.

Most of the vigorous alpines, like Alyssum saxatile *and aubrieta, can be clipped over with shears, but you can use secateurs if you want to make a neater, cleaner job of it.*

Marshall Cavendish

A rock gypsophila – better for dead-heading and a trim.

Apart from cutting off the seed heads, try to cut back any untidy or sprawling growth to make the plants more compact. New growth during the summer will soon spread to cover the same area without the plant becoming untidy and perhaps dying out in the centre or at the edges.

PLANTING A HARDY FUCHSIA

Although the tender fuchsias that you will find in garden centres already laden with large blooms are tempting and ideal for growing in containers, why not plant a hardy fuchsia, such as F. magellanica, that will give you years of pleasure in the border? These may not look much initially, but eventually will be covered with flowers from summer to autumn.

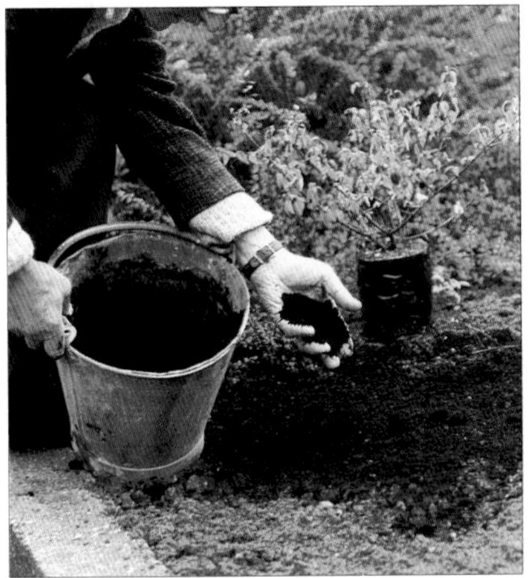

1 *If the soil is poor or sandy, add plenty of peat, garden compost, or other organic material, to improve it. Be generous with the amount you use.*

Marshall Cavendish

2 *Incorporate a balanced general fertilizer, such as Growmore, at about 70g per sq m/2oz per sq yd, or at the rate recommended by the manufacturer.*

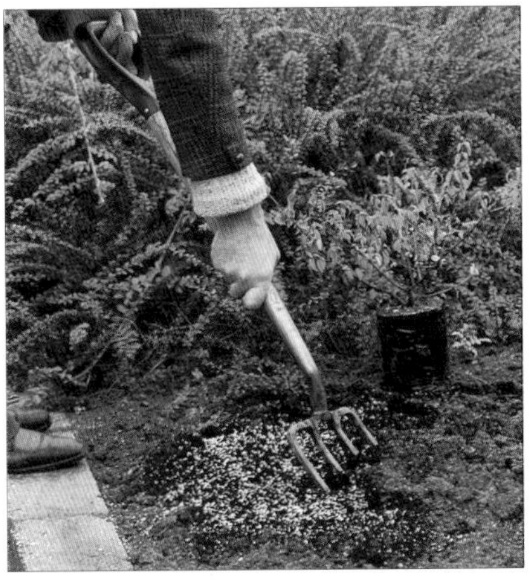

3 *Fork the fertilizer and peat or garden compost into the area where the fuchsia is to be planted, mixing it into the top 15-23cm/6-9in of the soil.*

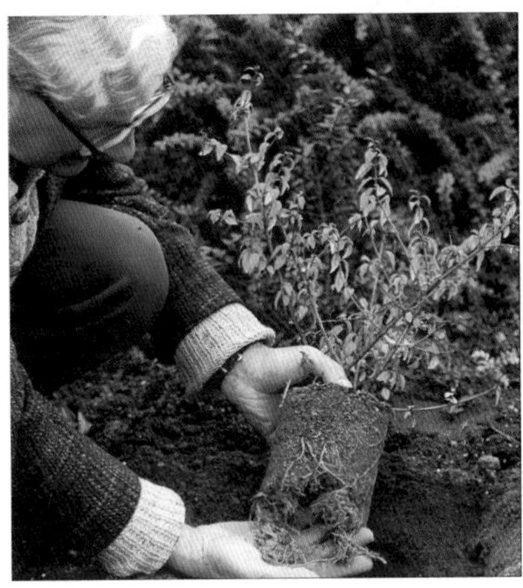

4 *Dig the planting hole slightly deeper than the root-ball of the plant, and mix a little peat or compost at the bottom. Tease out of a few roots before planting.*

5 *Firm the soil but leave the root-ball a little below the surrounding soil to make watering easier. Top it up with soil in the autumn for winter protection.*

PRUNING MOCK ORANGE

Once your mock orange (philadelphus) has finished flowering, which could be any time between now and mid summer, it should be pruned promptly, to encourage the growth of the new shoots that will provide all the flowers next year.

The beauty bush (kolkwitzia), deutzia and weigela can be treated in the same way once these have finished flowering.

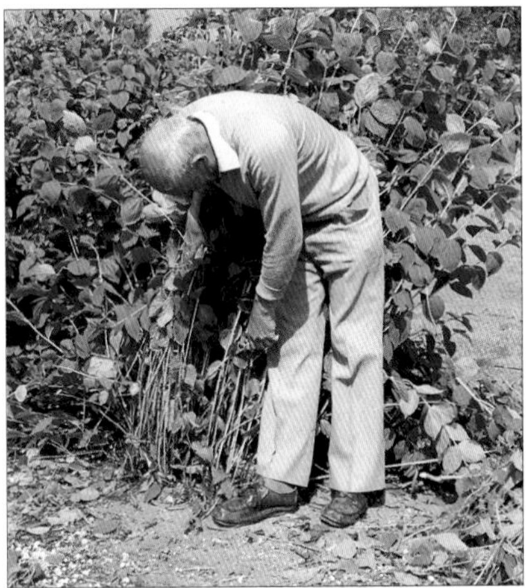

1 *On an established mock orange, cut back some of the stems that have flowered to vigorous young growths, while trying to retain a good shape.*

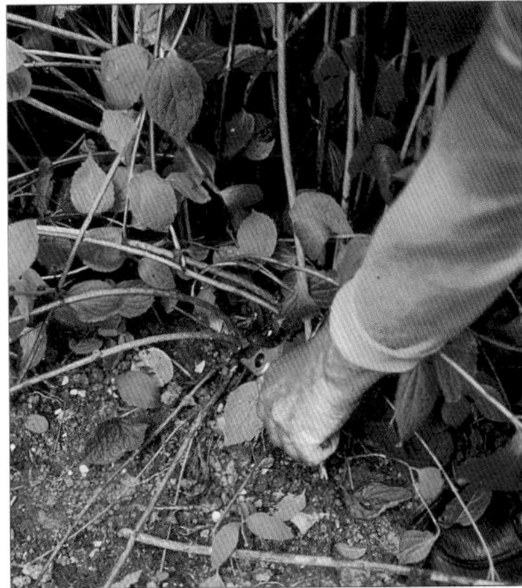

2 *Remove a few old shoots right down to the base, concentrating on the most congested, but do not remove more than a quarter to a fifth of the old stems.*

CHECKLIST

WHAT TO DO

HERBACEOUS BORDER
Dead-head sweet William
Fill gaps with bedding plants
Stake hollyhocks if the site is exposed
Hoe beds and borders to keep down weeds
Mulch dahlias
Propagate strawberries from runners
Protect soft fruit from birds with netting
Trim back vigorous spring-flowering plants

BULBS
Divide and replant big clumps of daffodils

SHRUBS
Remove flowers from cotton lavender

LOOK AHEAD

SOW
Sweet William, Canterbury bell and stocks

PLANT
Amaryllis belladonna bulbs, winter greens

WHAT TO SEE

BORDER PERENNIALS
Carnation, delphinium, cranesbill (geranium), lady's mantle, peony, pink, verbascum

SHRUBS
Mock orange, rock rose (helianthemum), sun rose (cistus), *Viburnum tomentosum,* weigela

BEDDING PLANTS
Begonia, busy Lizzie, floss flower (ageratum), nemesia, sweet alyssum

BULBS
Anemone, ornamental onion (allium)

VISITORS

FRIENDS
Bees, hedgehogs, hoverflies, ladybirds

FOES
Blackfly, greenfly, earwigs

EARLY SUMMER
WEEK 4

WHAT TO DO

As most of the sowing and planting has already been done, you can concentrate your effort on keeping things looking neat and tidy. Aside from weeding, there are lots of nicer pastimes like propagation – and finding time to sit back to enjoy the results of your efforts.

Keep an eye on the biennials
There may still be a few flowers on your forget-me-nots, but ripe seed will be forming all the time and these will germinate and come up like weeds if allowed to drop. Lift up the plants carefully and try to dispose of them without dropping too many seeds unless you want them to spread.

Dead-head sweet Williams. This has a double purpose as it may encourage further flowers to develop and will keep the plants looking tidy, too.

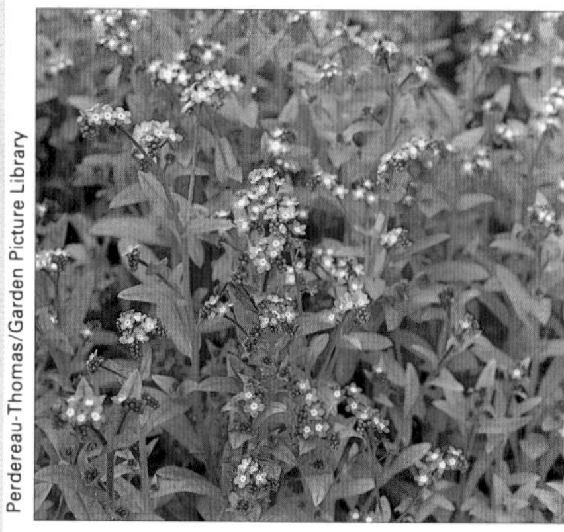
Perdereau-Thomas/Garden Picture Library

Forget-me-nots are rampant self-seeders.

Beat the birds
To stop birds from eating your soft fruit before you get the chance to do so, cover your plants or bushes with small-mesh netting.

Photos Horticultural

Protect your strawberries from birds by using small-mesh netting.

Fill in those gaps
There are often gaps in herbaceous borders at this time, either because plants died during the winter or because early flowering plants have been cut back to make them look tidy. You may find that bedding plants are available very cheaply from garden centres because it is the end of their season. Provided the plants are still in good condition, you can use them to fill any gaps you may have in your herbaceous or mixed border.

Stop weeds now
Weeds will still be germinating rapidly at this time of year, so keep the hoe moving among the plants in beds and borders.

Better foliage than flowers

The grey-leaved cotton lavender Santolina chamaecyparissus *is grown primarily as a pretty foliage plant but it will also start to produce clusters of yellow flowers at about this time. Although the flowers are quite attractive, the plant will have a better foliage effect and will also remain more compact if you trim the plant before it blooms.*

Photos Horticultural

Flowering santolina in an informal setting.

Shaping up alpines

Most spring-flowering alpines require no regular trimming, but vigorous ones like aubrieta and gold dust (Alyssum saxatile) become bare in the centre unless you trim them back to make them more compact.

WHAT TO SEE

Your herbaceous border should still be looking fresh and full of colour at this time. It is worth looking out for some of the border classics like pinks (especially the modern pinks, such as 'Doris', which have a long flowering season) and delphiniums. Among the shrubs, the low-growing rock rose* (Helianthemum nummularium)*, in its many varieties, is well worth making a note of.

LOOK AHEAD

Although you will have done most of your sowing and planting a few months ago, there are always a few things that you can start off. It is not too late to sow biennials such as wallflowers and sweet Williams, and there are a few interesting bulbs still to be planted.

Plant an 'exotic' bulb

Amaryllis belladonna *is not unlike the popular hippeastrum or amaryllis which are grown as pot-plants indoors, though their colour range is rather more limited (white or shades of pink). The showy clusters of big trumpet flowers, often more than 10cm / 4in across, on stiff stems about 60cm / 2ft high are truly imposing when they appear in early autumn.*

Unless you live in an exceptionally mild area, you should be careful to plant them in a sheltered position, perhaps at the foot of a wall that gets plenty of sun. Plant in well-drained ground, with a 15-20cm/6-8in covering of soil.

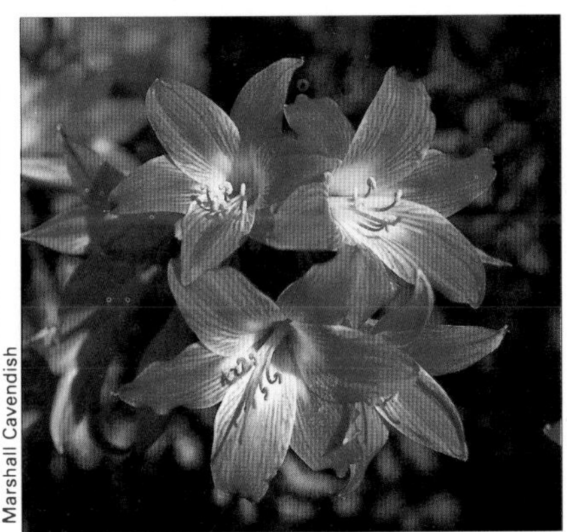
Marshall Cavendish

Amaryllis is stunning in a sunny spot.

Sow now for next year

Biennials (plants that germinate and grow one year and flower then die the next) like Canterbury bells, forget-me-nots, sweet Williams, wallflowers and Brompton stocks can be sown outdoors now. Wallflowers are really perennials, but are best treated as biennials to keep them flowering well as they tend to get rather straggly and thin after a few years.

Brompton stocks are not grown very often but are well worth considering. They look like ordinary stocks, but flower in late spring and early summer, helping to fill the gap between bedding seasons. There are 'selectable' strains available, which enable you to choose those with double flowers before you prick them out. For this method you will need to sow them indoors (or in a greenhouse if you have one).

GARDEN VISITORS

Hoverflies are good mimics – they can easily be mistaken for bees and wasps. Unlike those insects, however, hoverflies can hover and dart backwards and forwards.

The adult flies do not eat pests directly, but they lay their eggs among aphids, and the larvae (grubs) that hatch feed on them voraciously – it is thought that one grub eats about 600 of them.

Marshall Cavendish

Hoverflies resemble bees or wasps.

TAKING CUTTINGS OF ROCK ROSES

Rock roses, also known as sun roses (varieties of* Helianthemum nummularium*), are dwarf shrubs that have a place in every garden, whatever the size. The absolutely stunning bright red, pink or sunny yellow flowers simply smother the plant for months, giving a glorious display.

Helianthemums make a colourful, eye-catching border in this town garden.

Rock roses have one major drawback, however—they begin to deteriorate after a few years and are then best replaced with new plants. With age they tend to become leggy and sparse in the centre, and they lack the compactness and vigour of younger plants. It is so easy to take cuttings from these plants that you should always have a supply of fresh, new specimens coming along to replace your old, tired ones or to give to friends and relations.

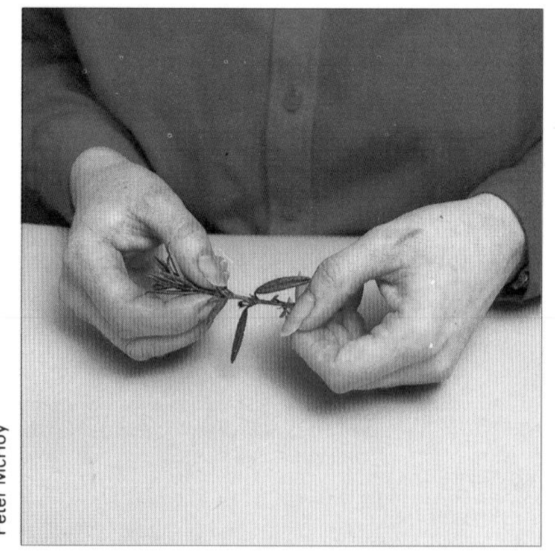

Peter McHoy

1 ***Take small cuttings about 5-7.5cm/2-3in long, using non-flowering shoots. Strip off the lower leaves from each cutting, where it will be inserted into the compost.***

2 ***Dip the end of the cutting into a little water and shake off the excess before dipping it into a hormone rooting powder. Shake off any excess powder.***

3 ***Use a dibber or a pencil to make a hole in the compost. This should be a rooting compost or a mixture of equal parts of peat and sand.***

SOWING BIENNIALS

Biennials such as Brompton stocks, Canterbury bells, double daisies* (Bellis perennis)*, foxgloves (the seeds are poisonous if eaten, so handle with care), sweet William and wallflowers, can still be sown during the next couple of weeks, and you do not even need a greenhouse to bring them on.

Find a small patch of ground that is already weed-free and that you can keep well watered. Do not choose a spot that is out of sight as it may get forgotten and neglected. Hoe and rake the soil so that it is crumbly.

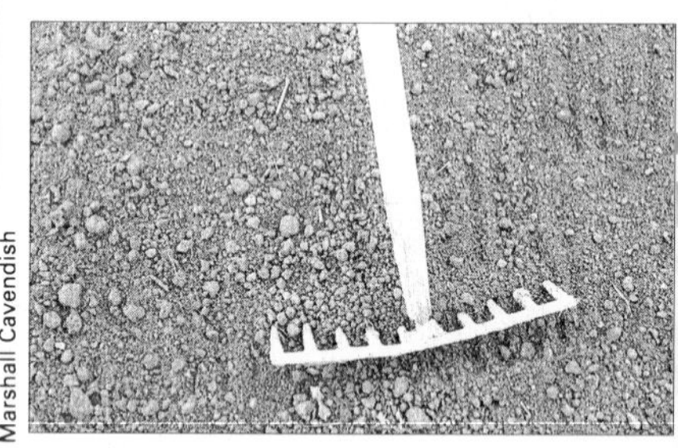

Marshall Cavendish

Before planting seeds, hoe and rake the soil to a fine texture.

Although the seeds can be sown randomly, it is easier to thin and weed your plants if they are sown in regular rows.

Make shallow drills to a depth recommended on the seed packet, 15-23cm/6-9in apart. If the ground is dry, trickle water into the drills and let it soak in before sowing the seeds thinly. Keep watered in dry weather.

After germination, keep the ground weeded and thin the seedlings if they come up too closely. If they are widely spaced enough leave them as they are; otherwise space them out in a spare piece of ground when the seedlings are a couple of inches high. Transfer them to their flowering positions in the autumn.

LAYERING STRAWBERRIES

Strawberries are best replanted every two or three years, as the crops gradually deteriorate if you keep the old plants. They are, however, easy to propagate by layering, so you do not need to keep buying new plants. Now that the runners are beginning to form, this is a good time to start layering. You must, of course, use strong, healthy plants to start with.

1 *Fill 8cm/3in pots with a good compost. Use a piece of bent wire to keep the runners in contact with the compost, to encourage rooting.*

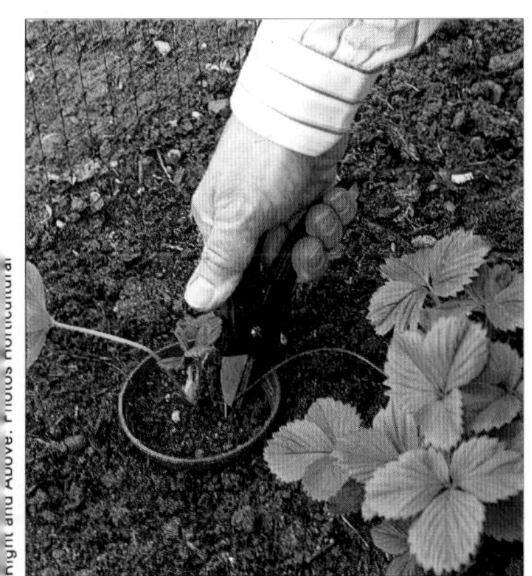

2 *By midsummer the plantlets should have rooted well. Gently remove a pot and tap out the root-ball to check. If so, sever from the parent plant.*

PLANT A MINI-SHRUB BORDER

If you have a small, narrow border that you failed to plant with seasonal bedding, it will probably be looking rather bare now. Try planting an instant mini-shrub border.

By using dwarf evergreens such as hebes, cotton lavender, curry plant and **Pachysandra terminalis**, ***the border will be attractive immediately, and will remain interesting all year round.***

1 *To make sure the spacing is right, position your plants while they are still in their pots. Move them around until you get exactly the effect you want.*

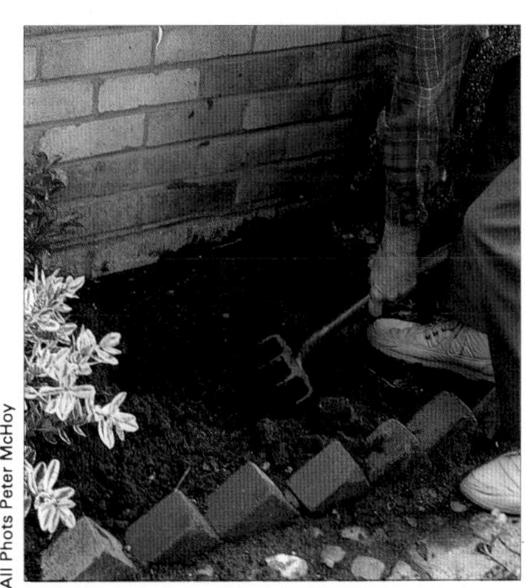

All Photos Peter McHoy

2 *Add plenty of bulky organic material, such as peat or compost. This is especially important on sandy or clay soils. Mix it in with a fork.*

3 *To make sure the plant is set at the right depth, place a piece of wood or a garden cane across the hole and check that you have an even surface.*

4 *Firm the soil well around the plant to make sure there are no large pockets of trapped air that could cause the roots to dry out.*

5 *Water the plant in thoroughly, then mulch the ground around the plant with a thick layer of garden compost or a bark-based mulching material.*

CHECKLIST

WHAT TO DO

LAWNS
Keep watering and mowing

HERBACEOUS BORDER
Cut back early border plants that have finished flowering
Hoe beds and borders to keep down weeds
If dry, water any plants set out this spring
Sow more parsley, dill and chervil
Propagate strawberries from runners
Protect soft fruit from hungry birds

BULBS
Mow grass where bulbs are naturalized

SHRUBS
Prune mock orange, orange ball tree and beauty bush

LOOK AHEAD

SOW
Hardy border perennials such as columbine, delphiniums and geums

PLANT
Container-grown shrubs to fill gaps

WHAT TO SEE

BORDER PERENNIALS
Bear's breeches (acanthus), day lilies, mullein

SHRUBS
Mock orange, potentilla, rose of Sharon, sun rose (cistus) and *Viburnum tomentosum*

BEDDING PLANTS
Antirrhinum, begonia, busy Lizzie, nemesia, ornamental tobacco (nicotiana) and petunias

VISITORS

FRIENDS
Bees, hedgehogs, hoverflies, ladybirds

FOES
Blackfly, greenfly, earwigs, moles

EARLY SUMMER
WEEK 5

WHAT TO DO

At the hottest time of the year many routine tasks are concerned with keeping plants watered and fed. There should still be plenty of time left simply to sit in the sun, relax and enjoy your garden.

Water the lawn

Unless we happen to have a wet spell of weather, the lawn will almost certainly benefit from regular watering now. If there are restrictions on the use of water in your area, however, it is better not to water at all. A surface sprinkling will encourage shallow rooting and simply leave the grass plants more vulnerable in times of drought. The rule, therefore, is: water well or not at all. It is, however, well worth trying to water the area just cut where the bulbs were naturalized, to stimulate the grass into growth in what will now be a yellow or brown area.

Marshall Cavendish

In a drought, shallow-rooted plants – including the lawn – will be the first to suffer.

Keep containers watered

It may seem obvious advice, but not everyone realizes that in very warm weather window boxes and hanging baskets may need watering twice a day for really good results. Because they are often sheltered by a building it may be necessary to water daily even if there have been showers.

Container-grown plants need special care.

Bulbs in lawns

Spring-flowering bulbs that have been planted in the lawn (naturalized) should have been left to allow the foliage to die down naturally. If you chop off the leaves too soon they will not flower well the following year. That means you will have had a patch of long, untidy grass for a few months, where the bulbs are, but now you can cut the grass in that area and reinstate your lawn to its former glory.

Cut back early border plants

Many herbaceous border plants that flower in early summer will be starting to look untidy. Cut back the flowered shoots with shears to tidy the border, but leave some foliage.

Dead-head to prolong life

Removing the dead flower heads from those plants with large blooms (such as pansies and antirrhinums) will make the plants look tidier and may also prolong flowering or encourage a second flush of flowers later. It is not, however, practical for very small flowers such as lobelia.

Marshall Cavendish

Remove all dead flower heads.

Feeding does help

The nutrients in many container composts will already be very depleted by now, so if you did not add a slow-release fertilizer be sure to begin feeding regularly from now on. Plants in containers are planted very densely and become starved very much more quickly than plants in the ground. Follow the manufacturer's advice.

Keep an eye on biennials

With all the colour and interest in the garden it is easy to forget the biennials sown in early summer, yet attention now can be crucial to later success. Those sown recently must be kept watered. Those sown a month ago will probably be ready for thinning: simply remove enough seedlings to leave the others well spaced.

WHAT TO SEE

Summer-flowering heathers should be looking good by now, so if you are planning a year-round heather garden this is a good opportunity to see which kinds you would like to plant. The Irish bell heathers (**Daboecia cantabrica*** ***varieties), bell heathers (*****Erica cinerea*** ***varieties) and cross-leaved heaths (*****Erica tetralix*** ***varieties) should all be giving an attractive display.***

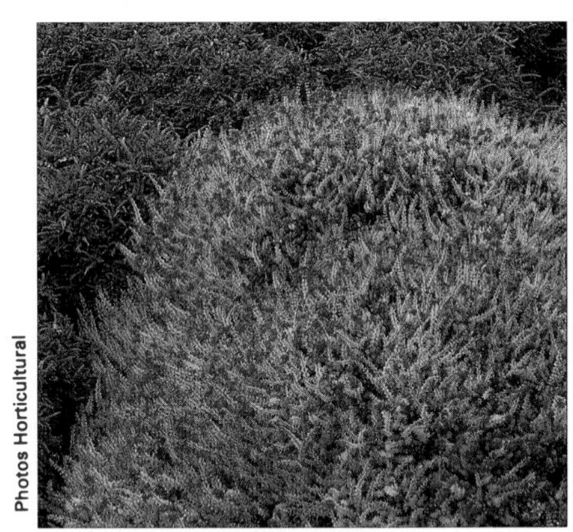

Photos Horticultural

***Erica cinerea* 'Fiddler's Gold'.**

LOOK AHEAD

Container-grown trees and shrubs can still be planted successfully provided you water them well in dry weather. This is also a good time to think about propagating your own plants. You need a little patience but propagation has its own rewards.

Sow border perennials

Those border perennials that can be grown easily from seed, such as columbine (aquilegia), delphiniums and geums, can still be sown. Sow in a cold frame if possible, or in a bed outdoors. Some may flower next year.

Sow annual herbs

Herbs like parsley, chervil and dill still can be sown to provide a succession of pickings.

Marshall Cavendish

Sow seeds at regular intervals to restock your herb patch.

VISITORS

Moles are seldom seen, yet their presence is made abundantly clear when they are in the area: heaps of excavated soil [en] mole hills [en] can ruin the appearance of a lawn and the tunnels that they make below ground can cause the plants above to collapse as their roots are exposed to drying air in the tunnel (this problem is most acute with vegetables and annuals).

You can buy mole traps to insert into the runs, but finding the right position requires experience. Deterrents such as mothballs, garlic and smoke cartridges inserted into the tunnels may be enough to make them move elsewhere.

Peter McHoy

This cute mole is actually a real pest.

CARING FOR ROSES

With the first flush of blooms by now at their peak, it is easy to forget that roses still require plenty of attention if they are to give a long-lasting show.

To keep them growing vigorously, feed with Growmore or a specially formulated rose fertilizer. For top-quality blooms, also use a foliar feed. This means spraying a suitable diluted liquid fertilizer (check the label) on the leaves when the sun is not on the plants.

Roses need watering as well as feeding. If water restrictions mean you cannot water as often as you would like, make sure there is a thick mulch of garden compost or pulverized bark around the plant, to help retain moisture in the soil.

Look out for pests and diseases. Spotted early, you can often pick off affected leaves or shoots and prevent the trouble spreading.

If you do not mind resorting to a chemical approach to keep your roses healthy, apply a systemic insecticide and fungicide. Some products are designed to control both pests and diseases. These should help to control mildew and blackspot as well as greenfly and blackfly, and some contain a foliar feed as well, which means one spraying session instead of three.

Photos Horticultural

Just pull the trigger to eliminate bugs!

TAKING LAVENDER CUTTINGS

Lovely, aromatic lavender is ideal for hedging. It thrives in hot, dry soils and is a particularly good choice for seaside locations.

Mature plants are quite expensive to buy, however, so why not produce your own from cuttings? It is a simple job and, because all the plants come from exactly the same source, will ensure that the hedge is uniform in colour.

***1** Take cuttings 5-7.5cm/2-3in in length, making the cut just below a leaf joint or node. Keep fresh in a plastic bag. Fill pots with a sand and peat mixture.*

All photos Marshall Cavendish

***2** Trim off lower leaves with a sharp knife. If they are not removed those beneath the soil are likely to rot, and this may spread to the cutting.*

***3** Dip the cuttings in hormone rooting powder and push them into the soil. Each pot will hold about 6-9 cuttings depending on its size.*

***4** Water the cuttings. They must remain moist, but not too wet. A mixture of two parts sand to one part peat will be well aerated and moisture retentive.*

***5** Cover the whole pot with a polythene bag. This will ensure a stable environment for the cuttings as well as helping to conserve moisture.*

DIVIDE SAXIFRAGES

Most herbaceous plants are divided in spring, but many spring-flowering rock plants, such as saxifrages, are best divided later – after they have finished flowering. It is not too late to divide large clumps that have become overcrowded, and you will have more plants to spread around the garden or to give to friends. Although you get less plants from division than from cuttings, they are larger.

1 *Lift the plant carefully with a hand fork or trowel, and pull apart sections of the plant from the outside of the clump, ensuring that each has some roots.*

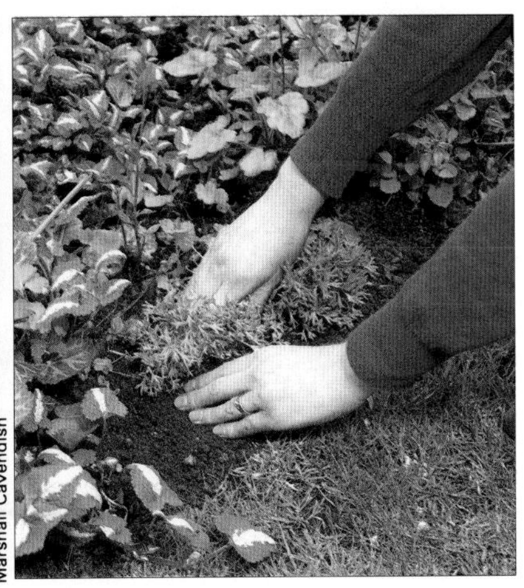

Marshall Cavendish

2 *Replant immediately, before the roots can dry out, working some gritty compost in around the roots. Water regularly until the division is growing again.*

MAKING AN INSTANT BARBECUE

Make the most of these hot summer days with a barbecue. Built-in barbecues can be difficult to construct, and require a suitable patio, while portable ones that you can buy in shops and garden centres are quite expensive. Here is a way to make a barbecue in a couple of hours, using old bricks that you may already have lying around the garden.

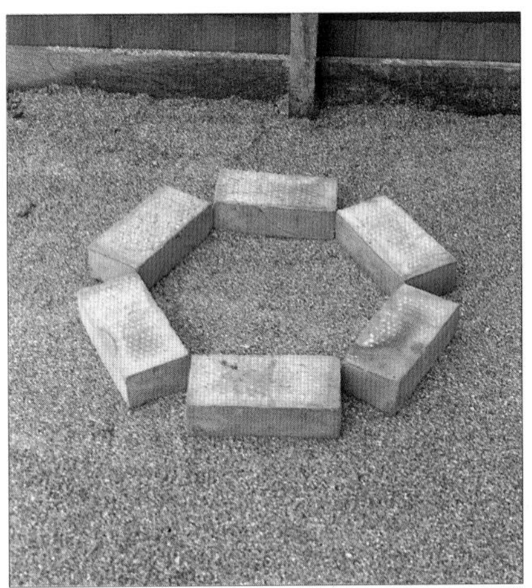

1 *You will need about 60 bricks, but the exact number required depends on the height of the barbecue. Lay the first six bricks as shown.*

Peter McHoy

2 *Place the next six bricks on top of the first layer, but stagger them as shown here. Continue like this until the required height is reached.*

3 *If you do not have a suitable piece of metal, make a cardboard template and ask a metalworker or forge to cut one for you (even a garage may help).*

4 *The last two rows of bricks should be positioned as shown, but for the first course after the metal sheet two half bricks are required.*

5 *A barbecue grill can be bought from a garden centre, or you can improvise with an old one from the kitchen. Place a few bricks behind it and at the sides.*

CHECKLIST

WHAT TO DO

LAWNS
Keep watered and trimmed

BORDERS
Gather lavender and dead-head any border perennials that have finished flowering
Hoe to keep down weeds
Water and feed plants that need a boost
Water vegetables to keep them growing

BULBS
Check lilies for signs of aphids

SHRUBS
Take heather cuttings

ROCK PLANTS
Take softwood cuttings of gold dust and rock phloxes

LOOK AHEAD

PLANT
Container-grown shrubs to fill gaps

WHAT TO SEE

BORDER PERENNIALS
Bee balm, day lilies, hollyhocks, lilies, phlox, pinks, red hot pokers

SHRUBS
Fuchsias, hydrangea, *Hypericum elatum*, lavender, mock orange, potentilla, roses

BEDDING PLANTS
African and French marigolds, ageratum, begonia, busy Lizzie, geranium, nemesia

BULBS
Crocosmia, lilies

VISITORS

FRIENDS
Bees, hedgehogs, hoverflies, ladybirds

FOES
Blackfly, greenfly, earwigs, leaf-miners, moles

WHAT TO DO

With the holiday season coming up, keep on top of routine jobs such as cutting the lawn and tidying beds and borders, so that you do not come back to a neglected-looking garden. If you spend an hour or two each week on these jobs before you go away, the garden will still look good when you return.

Gather lavender

If you are lucky enough to have some lavender plants in your garden, harvest some flowers to dry and use in sachets or pot-pourri. The plants will be coming into flower about now, and the ideal time to cut the stems for preserving is when the flowers on the lower half of the spike are starting to open. Cut them on a dry, sunny morning, tie them into small bunches, and hang the spikes upside down in a cool, airy place. They will retain their colour better if they are hung in a dark place. After a few weeks they will be ready for use.

Alternatively they can be tied into bunches and placed on drying trays in a well ventilated, dark room. Lavender does not dry well in hot, damp places so avoid kitchens and bathrooms. For really quick drying, blast in a microwave for about a minute.

Once flowering has finished, trim the bushes lightly, dead-heading in the process, but do not cut back into old wood.

Give the border a boost

Herbaceous and mixed borders can begin to look a little dull an jaded at this time of year. The main flush of colour is likely to b over and, if the weather has been dry, the plants will probably begin to lack vitality.

If there are no restrictions on watering, spend half an hour or so giving the plants a good soak. This will make the border look green and fresh again, and can b invaluable for later flowering plants. If a young border plant o shrub, perhaps planted last autumn or this spring, does not seem to be growing well or looks as if it could do with a boost, try giving it a foliar feed.

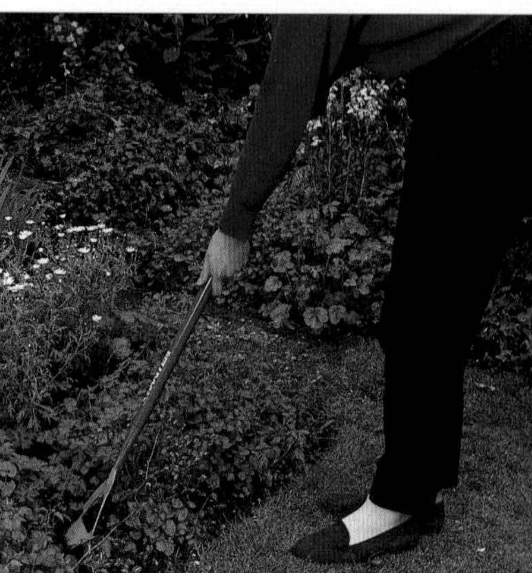
Marshall Cavendish

Clear weeds from the border with a hoe.

Lawn care

If the weather is dry the grass grows slowly at this time of year but in moist conditions it will require frequent trimming. Do no let your grass become too long as this will make it more difficult to cut in the long run.

War on weeds

Before you water beds and borders, give them a thorough once over with a hoe. If you do this when the soil is dry, chopped off weeds will be less likely to reroot. Wait a day or so before watering, to make sure the weeds wither and die first.

Rose care

Dead-heading makes rose bushes look tidier and encourages the plants to continue flowering for longer. This simple chore really is worth the little effort that it takes. If you do not dead-head at this time of year the roses may begin to revert back to their natural state and produce seedheads which are better known as rose hips. On older hybrids and wilder looking roses these can be very attractive. For a pretty cottage garden effect grow a hybrid like Rosa rugosa. *Its large bright red hips make a spectacular display.*

Dead-heading also gives you an opportunity to check for signs of pests and diseases, both of which can spread rapidly at this time. It is especially important to get the plants 'clean' before you go away on holiday, or you may come back to thoroughly infested plants.

Alan Bedding/Garden Picture Library

To prolong flowering, remove dead blooms using a pair of sharp secateurs.

WHAT TO SEE

There are still plenty of border plants and shrubs to see and most bedding plants are coming up to their peak. Those that develop fairly slowly, such as seed-raised geraniums (pelargoniums) and fibrous-rooted begonias, will have made bushy, bold plants and others that flower quite early in the season, such as nemesia and stocks, will also be in their prime.

Harry Smith Collection

Matthiola Brompton stocks flower early.

LOOK AHEAD

During the warm summer months cuttings generally root quickly and seeds germinate satisfyingly fast, provided that you remember to keep both cuttings and seeds moist as well as warm.

Increase your rock plants

Many rock plants are easy to propagate from cuttings at this time of year. Easy ones to try are gold dust (Alyssum saxatile), *rock dianthus, perennial candytuft* (Iberis sempervirens), *rock phloxes (such as* P. douglasii*), and thymes (*Thymus serpyllum *for example). Most of these will root readily from small cuttings taken from the tips of non-flowering shoots. Keep the cuttings in a cold frame or on a window-sill that is well-lit but out of direct sunlight.*

Peter McHoy

Take cuttings from Alyssum saxatile.

VISITORS

You may be lucky enough to see the large tortoiseshell, the pretty common blue, or perhaps the duller but still welcome wall and gatekeeper butterflies.

Think before you chop down clumps of nettles. The caterpillars of the peacock butterfly will probably still be feeding and they love nettles. The butterflies should appear next month. The nettle is also the favourite food plant of the red admiral butterfly.

Peter Wilson/Natural Image

Gatekeeper butterflies lay eggs on nettles.

DAHLIAS

Dahlias come into their own from late summer into autumn, just when most borders are beginning to look bare and straggly. They will flower for months, until an early frost kills the top growth.

The action you take now will determine how good they look later. Dwarf bedding dahlias, which will probably already be coming into flower, require little attention. The larger and taller kinds should have the side buds that form behind the main flower on each stem removed. This, together with feeding, will give you large flowers on long stems which are perfect for cutting and for using in flower arrangements in your home.

Initial staking of tall varieties should have been done at planting time, but the plants will require tying to the stake or support as they grow. You should also start feeding with a liquid fertilizer. Dahlias are prone to pests and diseases. Aphids (both greenfly and blackfly) are attracted to the succulent young growths, and earwigs can also be a problem. Treat them instantly otherwise they may spread viral diseases.

All photos Marshall Cavendish

Remove side buds of tall dahlia varieties.

SWEET PEAS

Sweet peas are one of those wonderful plants that actually respond better if you keep cutting the flowers. Pick plenty of bunches for the house, or deadhead the plants regularly if you want them primarily for garden display. Once you start leaving the flowers to set seed, the plant quickly stops flowering.

Sweet peas will respond well to regular feeding and watering. Apply a soluble fertilizer that is diluted with water to ensure that they are fed as well as watered.

If you want to produce big flowers on long, straight stems, grow your sweet peas up canes. Remove all the tendrils by which they usually climb as they drain the plants' energy away from the important business of flower producing. Once this has been done their natural method of support is lost and you will have to support them artificially instead with small metal rings that go around the stem and cane, or with garden twine. When a plant reaches a cane top undo it, lay it along the ground and take it up a cane further down the row.

For tall sweet peas, grow them up canes.

PROPAGATING PINKS

Carnations and pinks can both be propagated from cuttings or layers. As pinks make compact plants that are less easy to layer it is more usual to take cuttings.

Choose young, non-flowering shoots that are still growing vigorously. Water the plants the day before if the weather is dry.

1 ***Remove the shoot with a sharp knife. Trim the lower leaves off to leave about four pairs of mature leaves at the top. Trim again just below the topmost stripped joint.***

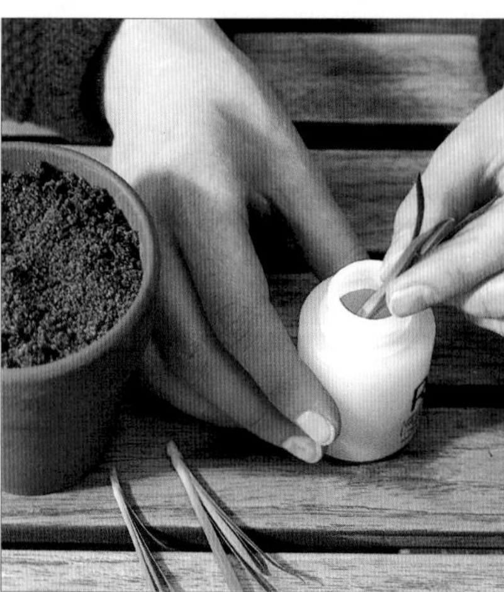

2 ***Insert the cuttings around the edge of a clay pot filled with compost. Water and keep in a cool, lightly shaded position. When rooted, pot up the plants individually and plant out next year.***

TOPPING UP POND WATER

Even if you cleaned your pond in spring, it will greatly benefit from being half emptied and topped up with clean water. Hot, dry weather conditions may have caused some of the water in your pond to evaporate and the level to drop, so topping up may well be necessary anyway.

If you can, use a garden hose fitted with a spray. As you fill the pond, the spray will help to aerate the water.

All photos Marshall Cavendish

Top up your garden pond with fresh water.

At this time of year many water plants are in bloom, such as frogbit (Hydrocharis morsus-ranae) *with its small, three-petalled white flowers, water soldier* (Stratiotes aloides), *also with white flowers, and bladderwort* (Utricularia vulgaris), *an insect-trapping plant with yellow flowers like snapdragons.*

You may wish to trim some of the leaves from your water lilies so that they do not hide the pretty flowers from view. Also, spray against aphids and other pests; and thin oxygenating plants if necessary.

LAYER BORDER CARNATIONS

Anyone who has grown the delightfully fragrant and pretty border carnations so reminiscent of cottage gardens will want to grow more. This is a good time of the year to layer the plants and it is a quick and easy way to increase your stock.

Perennial border carnations tend to deteriorate after a few years, so it is always worth growing a few replacements anyway.

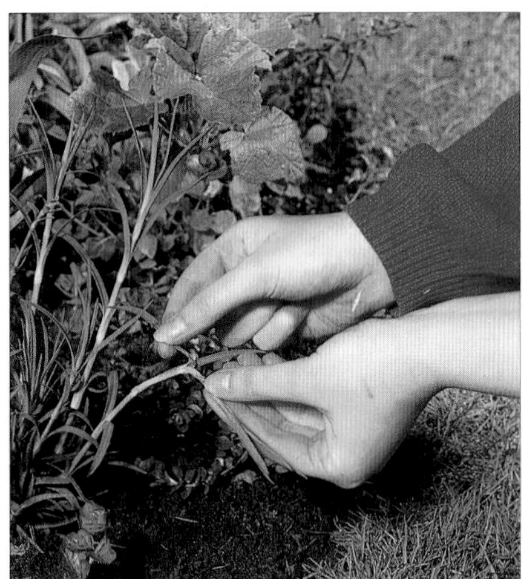

1 ***Choose side shoots from a healthy young plant and strip off the lower leaves, so that just a tuft of fully developed leaves remains at the tip.***

2 ***Use a small, sharp knife to make an upward slit in the stem, just below and into an old leaf joint beneath the cluster of leaves at the tip.***

3 ***Prepare the ground by the side of the parent plant, mixing in sand and/or peat to make it free-draining but moisture-retentive.***

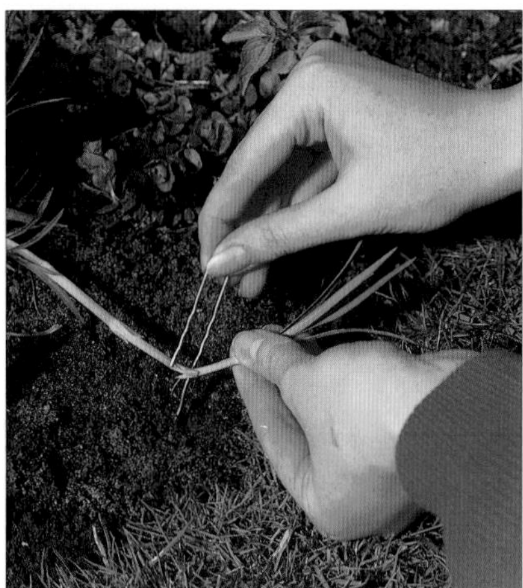

4 ***Make a shallow depression in the prepared soil where the layer is to be pegged down, and bring the shoot down, opening the cut to form a tongue.***

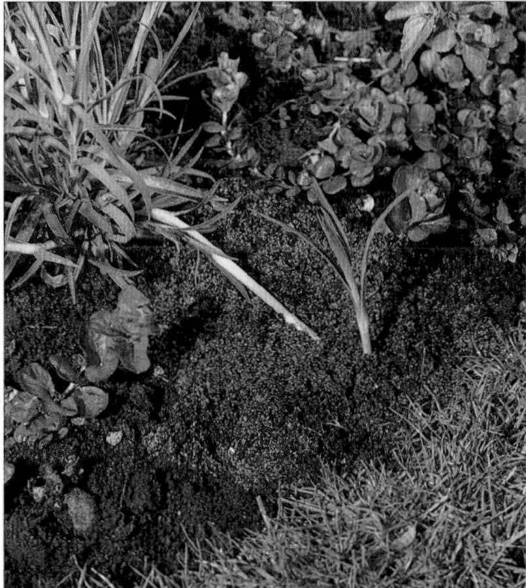

5 ***Peg down the layer using a piece of galvanized wire bent into a U-shape, or improvize with a hair-pin. Cover with soil and keep moist until rooted.***

CHECKLIST

WHAT TO DO

BORDERS
Dead-head plants that have flowered
Start to cut flowers such as globe thistle and Cupid's dart (catananche) for drying
Water and feed plants that need a boost
Water vegetables to keep them growing
Propagate strawberries from runners
Save seeds of rock plants.

SHRUBS
Prune mock orange (philadelphus) after flowering, if not already done

LOOK AHEAD

PROPAGATE
Take cuttings of catmint
Layer summer jasmine

PLANT
Finish planting sprouts and winter cabbages

WHAT TO SEE

BORDER PERENNIALS
African and French marigolds, ageratum, begonia, busy Lizzie, geranium, pansy, petunia *Phlox drummondii*, stocks

SHRUBS
Fuchsia, honeysuckle, lavender, potentilla, roses, sun rose (cistus)

BEDDING PLANTS
African and French marigolds, ageratum, begonia, busy Lizzie, geranium, pansy, petunia *Phlox drummondii*, stocks

BULBS
Crocosmia, lilies

VISITORS

FRIENDS
Bees, dragonflies, hedgehogs, hoverflies

FOES
Blackfly, capsid bugs, greenfly, earwigs, cabbage white butterflies

MID SUMMER
WEEK 2

WHAT TO DO

Most of the jobs at this time of year are concerned with keeping plants growing well for as long as possible – and that means watering, feeding, and dead-heading where appropriate. Do not forget to check those biennial and perennial seeds that you have sown during the last month, as they may need attention at this stage too.

Baskets and boxes

If time or water shortages limit the amount of watering that you can do in the garden, always give priority to the plants you are growing in containers.

Hanging baskets will need abundant watering at this time – twice a day is not too often in very hot weather. More failures are due to water shortage than any other reason. Although some plants, like pelargoniums, will tolerate a degree of neglect if they have to, others (such as lobelia) can be ruined if you let the container dry out for a single day. Window boxes are also vulnerable.

Brigitte Thomas/Garden Picture Library

Window boxes appreciate regular watering.

Feed and water

Dry fertilizers are generally applied earlier in the year and are usually slow acting over a period of weeks or months. At this time of year feed is best given in quick-acting liquid form.

After regular watering, feeding is the other key to success with plants in containers. It really is worth the effort, and those in powder form that you mix with water are very economical.

Do not forget the tomatoes either. They require regular feeding for a good crop. If possible use a feed specially made for tomatoes. Specialized feeds can be obtained at garden centres but also take advice if your tomatoes look deficient in one mineral.

Marshall Cavendish

If time allows, give borders a good soaking.

Pond patrol

At this time of year ponds can start to get overgrown. Marginal plants (those in shallow water around the edge) may be starting to take over, and those that flowered early, like the yellow water iris (I. pseudacorus), *will now be contributing only a mass of leaves. Thin these drastically if necessary.*

Canadian pond weed (elodea) and duckweed (lemna) may also be making a takeover bid. Be drastic with both. Elodeas can choke a pond. Simply use a rake to remove as much as necessary.

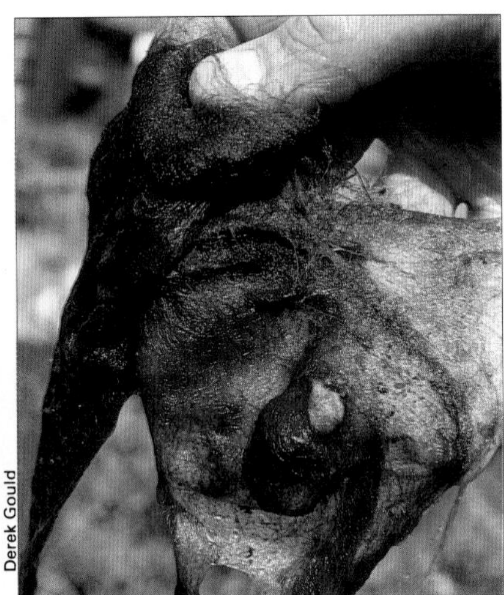

Derek Gould

Clear superfluous blanket weed from ponds.

Duckweed is a floating plant that multiplies so prolifically that it can cover the surface of the water. Use a net to remove as much as possible.

Check biennials

Biennials such as wallflowers, forget-me-nots, and winter-flowering pansies sown in prepared seed beds during the last month or so that have not yet germinated, probably have not been watered enough. If they have germinated, thin to about 10-15cm/4-6in apart. Provided the ground is moist, thinnings can be transplanted to a spare piece of ground.

WHAT TO SEE

Many of the hardy annuals sown earlier in the summer, or in late spring, will now be flowering. Some, like pot marigolds (calendulas), can be in flower from mid spring to late autumn, depending on when you sow them. Others are really plants of mid summer.

This is a good time to see a wide range of hardy annuals in flower at the same time. Good ones to look for (and perhaps sow in your garden next year if you like them) include agrostemma (tall but ideal for cutting), anchusa, baby blue eyes (nemophila), Bartonia aurea *(bright yellow flowers for many weeks) and Californian poppy.*

Candytuft, and the ever-popular blue cornflower are also delightful country garden annuals which are seen at their best now. Cornflowers will flourish in poor soil.

LOOK AHEAD

There are still plenty of plants that you can propagate. Cuttings can be taken from some herbaceous plants, such as catmint and the perennial gypsophila. Many shrub cuttings root well now, too. With a few deft strokes, you can spread resources cheaply.

Catmint cuttings

Take cuttings from new basal shoots about 5cm/2in long, remove the lower leaves and trim the cutting beneath a joint. Insert them in a box or pot of sandy compost and keep them moist in a shady position in the open. They do not need a cold frame.

Layer summer jasmine

The summer jasmine (Jasminum officinale) *is easy to increase from layers. Bend one of the long shoots down so that a portion of it reaches the ground, burying it about 8cm/3in deep in the soil (add some sand to the soil if the ground is heavy), and peg it into position. With luck the layer should root by the autumn and can be transplanted.*

Summer jasmine roots easily.

VISITORS

If you or a neighbour has a pond, look out for dragonflies. These magnificent creatures are very varied in size and colouring, but they can all hover and dart in a characteristic and fascinating way and are very colourful.

Although some are large, they are perfectly harmless and most are very beautiful if you study them closely. Even at rest, their wings stretch out, ready for sudden flight.

Bob Gibbons/Natural Image

Look out for dragonflies, like this spotted chaser emerging from its nymphal case.

SAVE YOUR OWN SEEDS

It is generally not worth saving your own seed of bedding plants and annuals, as the plants they produce are often inferior to the parents (though there are exceptions, such as sweet peas). It is worth saving the seed of many rock plants and some border plants, however, especially if they are species rather than highly-bred hybrids.

Save the seed from choice rock and border plants that are themselves often now long lived, such as primulas and acquilegias, so that you can sow them in a spare piece of ground to produce replacements or extra plants for yourself or to give to friends. The resulting plants may not always be exactly like their parents, but should nevertheless be perfectly satisfactory. Any healthy plant will always brighten an empty piece of ground and may, in time, prosper better than the original.

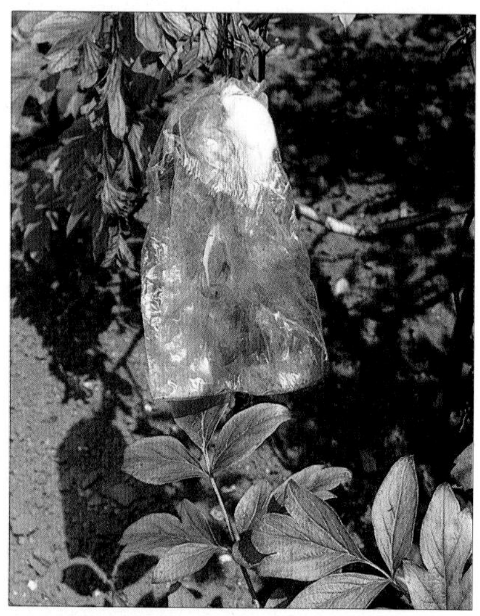

Harry Smith Collection

Never be tempted to collect immature seed heads. When ripe, a plastic bag placed over the plant will help to catch seeds.

Collect the ripe seed heads on a dry day in a small bag or envelope. Collect one type at a time and label them so they do not get mixed up. Do not collect the heads until at least some of them are starting to split open and shed their seeds. This is important because immature seeds will not germinate.

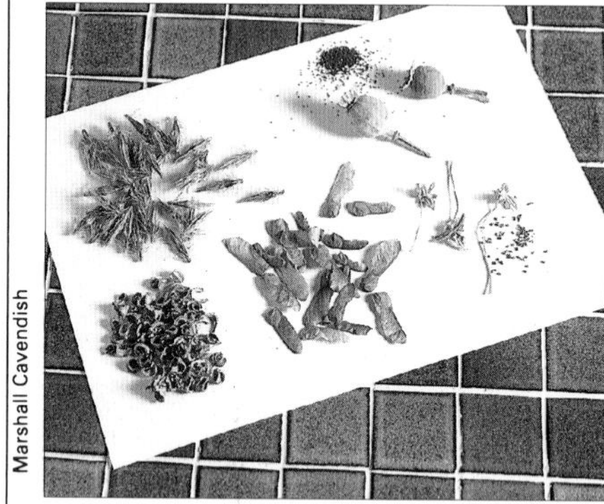

Marshall Cavendish

Spread seeds out to dry, taking care that they do not get mixed up.

Spread out the seed heads on a tray by a sunny window then, when most of the seeds have been shed, blow or sieve them to separate them from the other material.

Marshall Cavendish

Store seeds in paper bags or envelopes (not plastic) to keep them dry. Label to avoid confusion.

It is best to sow seeds that lose their ability to germinate rapidly if stored (such as many primulas) as soon as possible. Others can be stored in a cool, dry place until it is time to sow them.

ROSE PROBLEMS

There are two particular and potentially serious rose problems that begin to appear at about this time: black spot and mildew. Prompt and effective action is a major element of success in controlling these diseases.

Black spot is a disfiguring disease that is adequately described by its name: black spots with yellow fringes start to spread over the foliage, and in a bad attack the leaves will die and fall off. Pick off and burn any affected leaves; then spray the plant carefully with a fungicide. If you can, use one containing benomyl or propiconazole, the most suitable chemicals for this purpose.

Pat Brindley

Check roses carefully for signs of black spot.

Mildew is also a problem associated with summer and early autumn. The buds and leaves become covered with an unpleasant-looking white powdery mould. The fungicides mentioned above will also control powdery mildew.

CHEAP GROUND COVER PLANTS

Buying ground cover plants can be expensive as you need quite a few. Those that spread by underground runners or suckers are usually relatively inexpensive, however, and you can make them go even further by dividing up the plants that you buy. It may take an extra season to cover the ground, but you can get the same results for about a quarter of the cost.

1 *Plants such as rose of Sharon (*Hypericum calycinum*) and this* Pachysandra terminalis *can be made into several plants. Water well first.*

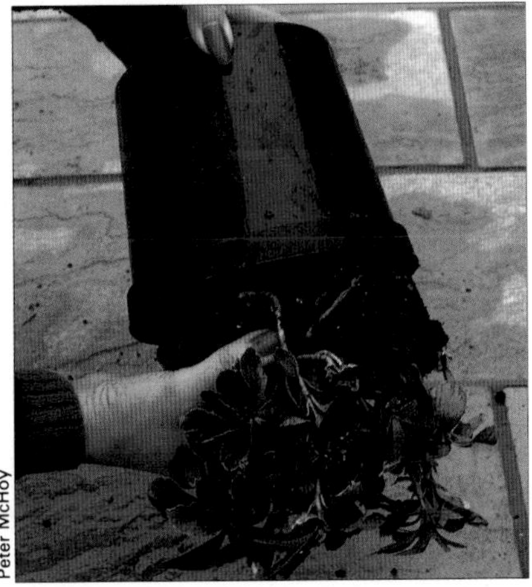

Peter McHoy

2 *Knock the plant out of its pot. It will often come out with a gentle pull once the pot has been inverted. If not, give the rim a sharp tap against a hard surface.*

3 *Pull the root-ball apart gently, as you want to cause as little damage as possible to the roots. Try to pull off pieces with roots and shoots.*

4 *If the crown is tough and the roots are matted, you may find it necessary to use a sharp knife to separate the sections neatly and cleanly.*

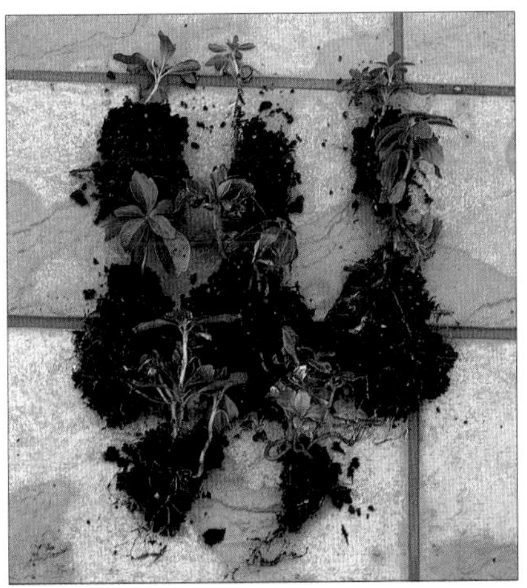

5 *The number of plants that you can obtain from the one pot will depend on its size and the type of plant, but this is typical of a plant in an 18cm/7in pot.*

6 *If you have an empty space ready, plant the pieces immediately where they are to grow. Water well, apply a mulch, and do not let the plants dry out.*

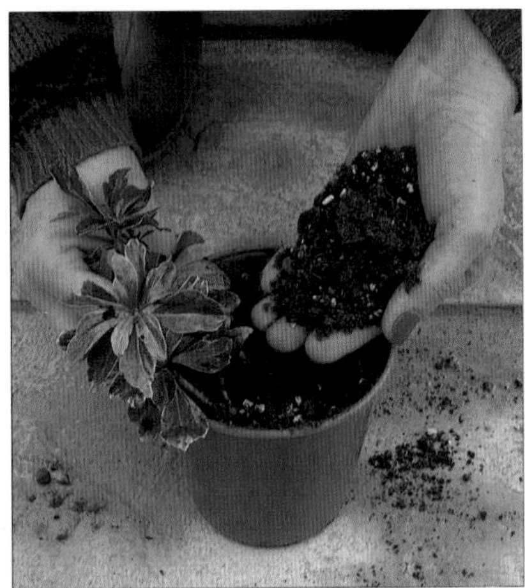

7 *If you want to wait until the plants are larger, and perhaps grow seasonal bedding as a temporary measure, pot them up and grow on for another year.*

8 *Plunge pots to their rims in the ground so that they are less likely to dry out. Choose a light position, and water and feed as necessary.*

CHECKLIST

WHAT TO DO

LAWNS
Take out obstinate weeds by hand

BORDERS
Trim back early border plants that are dying
Support plants that are losing their shape
Water vegetables to keep them growing, especially runner beans
Sow cress, lettuce, radish, sprouting seeds

BULBS
Plant autumn crocuses (colchicums)

LOOK AHEAD

PROPAGATE
Save some self-sown seedlings
Take cuttings of madwort (*Alyssum saxatile*)
Serpentine layer clematis, honeysuckle

WHAT TO SEE

BORDER PERENNIALS
African lily (agapanthus), bergamot (monarda), day lily (hemerocallis) 'Stella D'Oro', gay feathers (liatris), Japanese anemone (*Anemone hupehensis*), phlox

SHRUBS
Daisy bush (*Olearia haastii*), fuchsia, honeysuckle, lavender, roses, sun rose

BEDDING PLANTS
African and French marigolds, ageratum, alyssum, begonia, busy Lizzie, geranium, pansy, petunia, *Phlox drummondii*, salvia

BULBS
Crocosmia, lilies

VISITORS

FRIENDS
Bats, bees, hedgehogs, hoverflies

FOES
Blackfly, capsid bugs, greenfly, earwigs, leaf-rolling sawfly, swift moth

WHAT TO DO

Now you can simply keep things looking tidy, and spend as much time as possible relaxing and enjoying the fruits of earlier labours. Most jobs can be tackled without the sense of urgency there was earlier in the season.

Cut to dry

Flower arrangers generally grow a few border plants for dried flowers to brighten up the winter. Even if you have not specifically planted with this in mind there may be plants already in the garden that you can use. Achilleas, pearl everlasting (anaphalis) and globe thistles (echinops) are among suitable border plants that you are likely to have in flower now.

The flower heads will dry naturally if you leave them on the plant, but wind and rain take their toll, and they never look as good as those cut and dried in the peak of condition.

Cut them before they are past their best – preferably just as they become fully open – on a fine, dry day. Do not collect them when it is damp or when they are still covered with morning dew.

Hang them upside down in small, loose bunches, in a dry, airy place out of direct sunlight. Arrange the bunches with stems of different lengths so that the flower heads are not all bunched at the same point, otherwise they will crush each other.

The leaves will soon dry and shrivel. Keep the bunches in a convenient place until this happens, then remove the leaves and store the flowers somewhere dry where they will not get damaged, such as in a garage or, better still, in a loft.

Eric Crichton

Flowers used for drying are best picked when just fully open.

Sow salads

It is not too late to sow a few salad crops, which you could even plant in growing bags or other containers. Most varieties of radish can be sown as they all mature quickly, but with lettuces it is best to choose a variety like 'All the Year Round'. 'Trocadero Improved' is also suitable for late sowing. It helps if you can provide protection with a cloche later on.

Indoors you can sow mustard and cress, or sprouting seeds like mung beans and alfalfa.

Weed and groom

In dry periods it should not be difficult to keep on top of the weeds as new ones are unlikely to germinate and those that are already growing are easily controlled. The best way to keep the borders weed-free at this time is to hoe carefully, slicing them off at ground level. This will even kill off many established perennial weeds if you do it regularly, and the ground will look much tidier afterwards. Eliminating weeds will also reduce competition for water and nutrients, and your cultivated plants will grow that much better.

Spend a little time making the borders look neat and tidy. Many of the plants that flowered in early summer will now be looking decidedly dejected, with dead flower stems and probably yellowing leaves. Cut off dead flower heads with garden shears, and, if the plant has started to flop onto its neighbours, cut back the stems and foliage to about 15-30cm/6-12in (do not do this with plants that are still growing vigorously, especially if there are more flowers to come).

Some plants, such as oriental poppies and tall achilleas tend to spread and fall, especially after heavy rain or wind, before they have reached their peak. Secure them with some loops of garden twine to hold them upright.

Fill gaps

Gaps in shrub and mixed borders can be very visible at this time, so if you think the border would benefit from another small shrub here or there, why not choose a suitable plant? Provided you water them regularly until they are established, container-grown shrubs can be planted now to provide long-lasting gap fillers.

WHAT TO SEE

Most bedding plants are now at their best, so this is a good time to visit gardens and make a note of what you would like to grow yourself next year.

Make a point of noting varieties of pot marigolds (calendulas) and candytuft (both hardy annuals), which you can sow in a few weeks' time in mild areas to overwinter ready for early flowering next year.

Don Wildridge

The long-flowering day lily 'Pink Damask'.

Day lilies (hemerocallis) and African lilies (agapanthus) have a long flowering season, and are worth noting now. The day lilies especially are easy and tough, and there are many varieties from which to choose. Look out particularly for 'Stella D'Oro', an outstanding dwarf yellow variety that flowers for months.

Garden petunias flower in the summer and autumn and can provide a stunning display of colour (rose, purple, magenta, blue) in sunny borders but they do like light, fairly rich soil and should be grown in a position sheltered from the wind.

LOOK AHEAD

This is a time for enjoying earlier efforts rather than sowing and planting, but if you can obtain the Madonna lily, plant it now.

Collections/Patrick Johns

The Madonna lily with its pretty spikes.

VISITORS

If you grow roses, sawflies, or rather their larvae, may be unwelcome visitors. Many gardeners think the culprits are the larvae of butterflies or moths (in other words caterpillars), but the mature sawflies actually look like flies. You are likely to see them on the wing at this time.

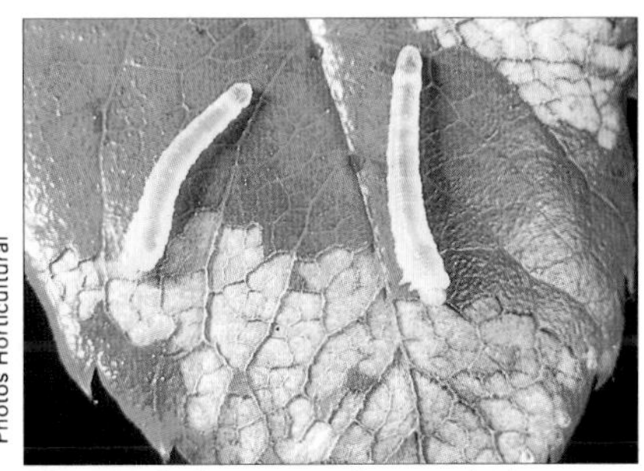

Photos Horticultural

Rose sawfly larvae attack a rose leaf.

Sawflies can bother the gardener at this time of year. Two common ones are the large rose sawfly (young shoots turn black and die after the larvae have eaten into the stems) and the rose slug sawfly, which turns leaves into skeletons. Use a systemic insecticide.

SOW WINTER PANSIES

Pansies can help to make winter seem that much brighter, that little bit shorter. If you choose a suitable variety, such as the Universal range (available in separate colours or as a mixture), they will produce a few flowers whenever there is a mild spell of weather, and by early spring can be in full flower. And you can sow them outdoors now.

***1** Fork or dig over the ground, raking it to produce a smooth, even surface. A fine surface 'tilth' like this encourages the seeds to germinate.*

***2** Work in some garden compost to improve the soil structure and help to retain moisture. Make shallow drills with a cane in which to sow the seeds.*

Simon Hay/Marshall Cavendish

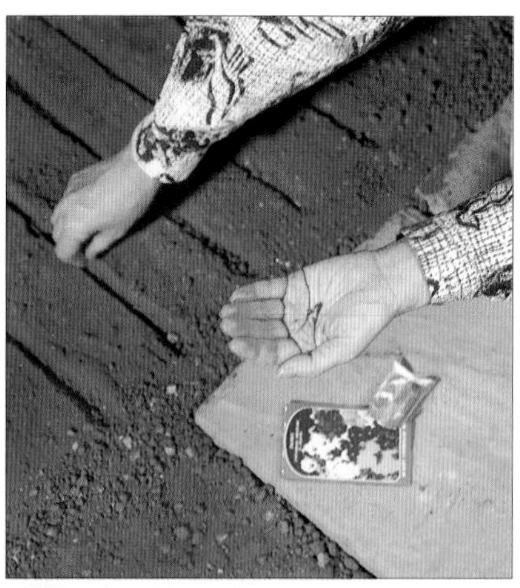

***3** Sow thinly. With large seeds like pansies this is best done by tipping some into the palm of one hand and spacing them individually with the other.*

***4** Cover the seeds carefully, either by drawing a little soil back into each drill with the rake, or sprinkling soil into the drills by hand.*

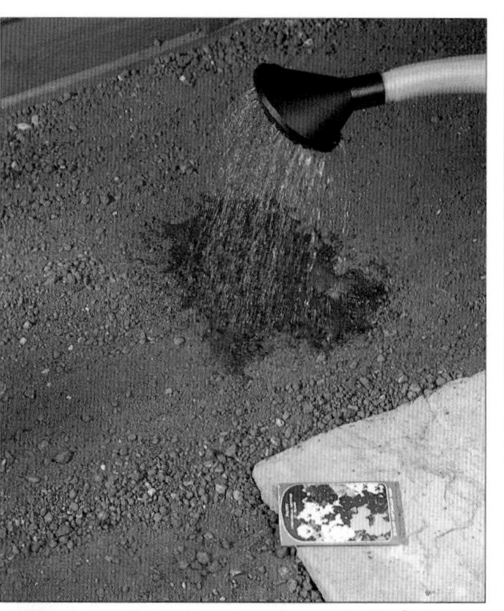

***5** Labelling is always important, but especially so if you are sowing more than one kind. Water well and continue to do so regularly.*

REJUVENATE PANSIES

Pansies often begin to look straggly after the first prolific flush of flowers. Regular dead-heading will help to prolong flowering and encourage fresh young growth, but once they begin to decline it is worth taking more drastic action.

Once a pansy or viola has become too straggly, cut it back to about 2.5cm / 1in above soil level, and cover with about 2.5cm / 1in of potting compost or good soil enriched with bonemeal, worked between the stems.

Keep well watered until new shoots appear, usually after a few weeks. These can be used as cuttings (overwinter them in a cold frame or room if possible), or the plants can simply be left to produce fresh, compact growth. But although reasonably hardy, pansies will not survive excessive winter wet or prolonged periods of frost.

If pansies are infected with pansy stem rot, or 'pansy sickness', it will be necessary to move your plants to fresh ground to save them.

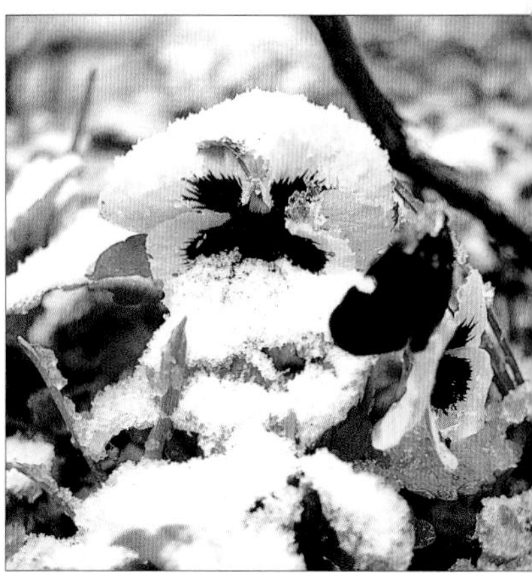

Even winter-flowering pansies will not withstand excessive frost and wet.

SERPENTINE LAYERING

Ordinary layering produces a single plant from each layer, but serpentine layering is a technique that enables you to propagate several plants at once. It is suitable for several climbers with long, trailing stems such as clematis, honeysuckles and summer jasmine. All can be layered now and should be well rooted within a year.

1 *Serpentine layering is a variation on ordinary layering, but it is only possible with long, flexible stems that can be pegged down at various points.*

Peter McHoy

2 *Choose a healthy shoot produced this year. Bend it down to see which leaf joints can be buried; then strip the leaves from these nodes.*

3 *Leave several nodes with leaves attached before stripping another one, so that the stem can be snaked in and out of the soil.*

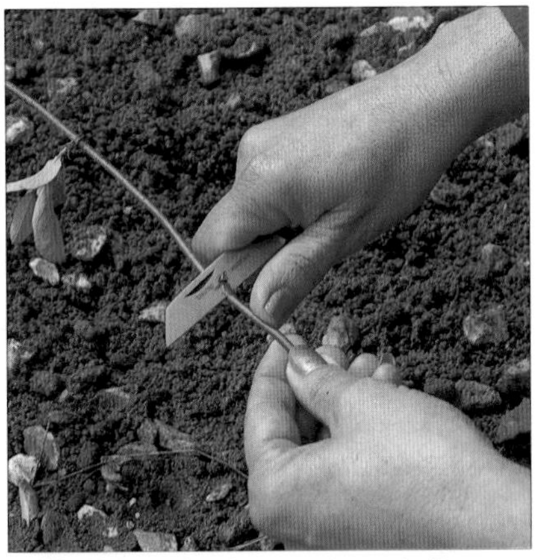

4 *Make a slanting cut almost halfway through the shoot, about 2.5cm/1in long, just behind each node that is going to be buried.*

5 *Pop a small piece of matchstick in the wound to keep the cut behind the node open and to prevent it from closing up and healing.*

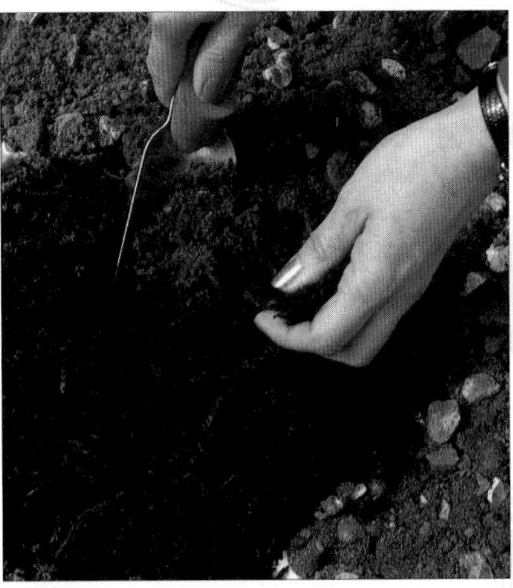

6 *Prepare the ground where the layers are to be pegged down by forking it over shallowly and incorporating plenty of well-rotted compost.*

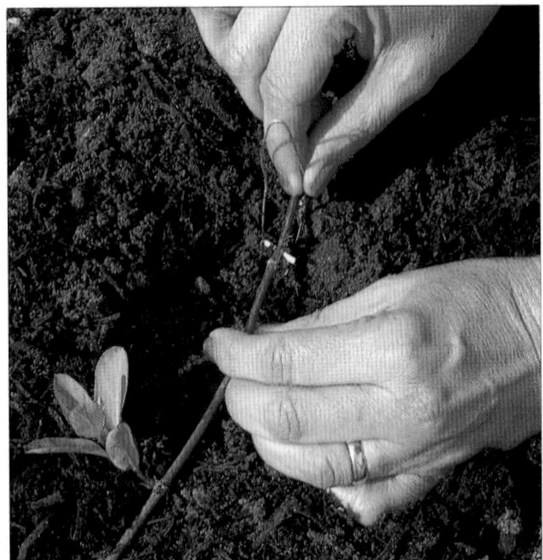

7 *Make small depressions in the soil where the prepared nodes are to be positioned and peg them down with bent wire or small stones.*

8 *Cover the nodes with soil or potting compost. Keep weeded and watered and sever the plants next year when they are well rooted.*

CHECKLIST

WHAT TO DO

BORDERS
Tidy the border by dead-heading and cutting back plants that have passed their best
Stake and disbud large-flowered outdoor chrysanthemums
Harvest vegetables regularly and water often to prevent them deteriorating in the ground
Sow parsley and winter radishes

BULBS
Tie in gladioli and check for thrips

SHRUBS
Fill gaps with container-grown plants
Water hydrangeas in dry weather

LOOK AHEAD

PROPAGATE
Take cuttings of hebes and heathers
Layer border carnations

PLANT
Madonna lily and autumn crocus

WHAT TO SEE

BORDER PERENNIALS
African lily, day lily, golden rod, helenium, mullein, phlox and red hot poker

SHRUBS
Butterfly bush, fuchsia, hypericum, honeysuckle, lavender and roses

BEDDING PLANTS
African and French marigolds, ageratum, alyssum, begonia, busy Lizzie, dahlia, pansy, tobacco plants and verbena

VISITORS

FRIENDS
Bees, hedgehogs, hoverflies and slow-worms

FOES
Blackfly, capsid bugs, garden tiger moth, greenfly, earwigs, rabbits, thrips

MID SUMMER
WEEK 4

WHAT TO DO

The holiday season will no doubt make its own demands on your time, but most of the jobs in the garden can be delayed for a week or two if necessary. Concentrate on keeping your garden looking neat and tidy so that if you do go away on holiday, you will come back to a paradise and not an overgrown jungle.

Smarten up beds and borders
The main flush of colour will already be over in herbaceous borders, although interest will be provided by pockets of summer bedding plants for many weeks to come. Do not let the plants that are now past their best spoil the effect, however. Dead heads and yellowing foliage will detract from the beauty of the flowers of late summer.

Dead-heading makes sense unless you particularly want to save the seeds. The plants look tidier, it encourages them to make vegetative growth rather than putting their energy into producing seed, and will probably prevent self-sown seedlings adding to your weeding chores.

Fill the gaps
Cutting back some of the border plants may leave gaps, especially if they were sparsely planted in the first place, and bare ground is an invitation to weeds.

Use any spaces for growing on seedlings of biennials and perennials sown during the last few months. You may need to move them to a final position next spring, but in the meantime they will benefit from being well spaced out, with plenty of room to grow and develop.

Harry Smith Collection

You may still be lucky enough to find some bedding plants to fill spaces.

Rock garden check
Rock gardens often become untidy at this time of year. Unless the planting has been planned carefully they can lack colour too.

Peter McHoy

Remove weeds from your rockery and trim plants to keep them in shape.

Spend a few minutes trimming back plants that are outgrowing their allocated space. Cut off any dead flower heads to make the plants look neater.

If you let weeds become established and entangled within the rock plants, they can be extremely difficult to get rid of without lifting and replanting, so remove any weeds now.

Water your hydrangeas

Hydrangeas are magnificent shrubs but they are particularly vulnerable to dry soil. Most shrubs fend for themselves in dry weather but hydrangeas need a bit of extra help. Water them regularly in dry weather, and see how they benefit.

Gladioli check

Gladioli will flower over a long period, depending on the variety and when you planted them. Any that are developing flower spikes are worth checking now. Make sure each spike is supported, at least at the base, so that it grows straight. To prevent the plants being damaged by the stake, place the cane on the side from which the wind usually blows.

Stake gladioli for tall, straight stems.

Small, dark insects known as thrips or thunderflies can ruin gladioli but they can be controlled with an insecticide. Check leaves and flowers for the tell-tale signs: a light flecking.

WHAT TO SEE

Many border plants and shrubs will have lost the fresh look they had in early summer. Although there are plenty of mid summer plants still in flower, it is the summer bedding that steals the limelight at this time of year.

*Among the brilliance of all the flowers, however, look for the impact created by seasonal foliage plants. The burning bush (*Kochia trichophylla*) brings height and shape with its cones of feathery green foliage, which will turn brilliant red in the autumn.* Ricinus communis, *the castor oil plant, with its huge hand-like leaves in shades of bronze, purple and red, is exotic looking and quickly grows to 1.4m/4ft or more. Then there are the more common silver-leaved foliage plants like dusty miller (*Cineraria maritima*).*

Don Wildridge

Look out for decorative foliage plants like this Ricinus communis 'Impala'.

LOOK AHEAD

It is too late to plant most seeds (with the exception of parsley and winter radishes) and too early for most bulbs, though it is worth planting autumn crocuses as soon as they are available.

Parsley and winter radishes

With a little planning, parsley, like winter radishes, can be ready to eat in winter. Although you should make your main sowings in spring and early summer, if you have a cold frame for winter protection it is not too late to sow now for winter use. Soak parsley seeds for 24 hours before sowing, to speed germination.

Peter McHoy

Sow winter radishes for a late crop.

VISITORS

Large white butterflies are often a problem at this time, and their caterpillars can devastate cabbages and related crops. They are also partial to nasturtiums.

There are more welcome butterflies, such as the small tortoiseshell, which likes to feed on nettles.

Jim Bain/NHPA

Make friends with slug-eating slow-worms.

Slow-worms may be found basking in the sunshine at this time of year. These snake-like lizards, usually about 30cm/12in in length, are harmless. In fact, they eat lots of slugs, which makes them a gardener's friend.

PLANT AUTUMN CROCUSES

Colchicums are not true crocuses, but the flowers look like giant versions of these flowers, hence their common name of autumn crocus. There are true crocuses that flower in the autumn, but these have much smaller flowers and look like the crocuses that we associate with springtime.

The true crocuses that flower in the autumn (such as Crocus speciosus*) have small corms like spring crocuses and are best planted in a sunny spot in well-drained soil. Naturalize them in short grass if you prefer, planting them randomly and covering them with about twice their own depth of soil.*

Colchicums have much larger corms and require planting 10-15cm/4-6in deep. They will thrive in sun or partial shade and are particularly good in light dappled shade in front of trees or shrubs (but do not choose trees with a dense shadow). They also prefer a well-drained soil.

Pat Brindley

Colchicum byzantinum, ***the autumn crocus, is a larger plant than its cousin the crocus.***

Bear in mind that the leaves that are produced in spring are large (perhaps 20-30cm/8-12in long), so do not place the bulbs where the foliage will hide small spring-flowering bulbs.

TRIM EVERGREEN HEDGES

Many evergreen hedges are trimmed once a year in late summer. Most coniferous hedges, like the Leyland cypress, are best clipped at this time, though to keep it compact it may be necessary to cut your hedge a couple of times a year.

With practice the hedge can be cut by eye, but initially a guide is useful to help keep the lines straight and level.

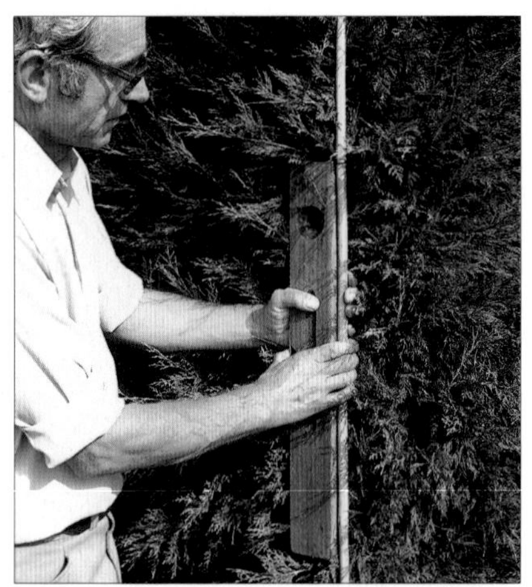

***1** Make a simple cutting guide from a couple of canes and a length of string. Use stout canes. Place one at the end of the hedge and check it is vertical.*

Ray Duns

***2** Place a second cane at the other end and tie a length of string between them at new hedge-top height. (Intermediate canes may be necessary).*

***3** Use a set square to check that the string is horizontal. If necessary, lower or raise the canes or the string slightly to achieve a correct horizontal.*

***4** Keeping the blades of the shears flat along the top of the hedge, trim the top first using the string as a guide to the correct height.*

***5** Once the top has been cut level, trim the sides and the ends. If you wish, a tall hedge can be tapered inwards towards the top to give it a better shape.*

EASY CUTTINGS

Propagation is one of the pleasures of gardening, and there is something especially satisfying about rooting your own shrub cuttings. There are plenty to take now or during the next few weeks, including flowering currant, dogwood and forsythia. Why not get propagating along with your friends, or join a local horticultural society, then exchange rooted cuttings to increase your plants at no expense?

1 *Take cuttings of half-ripe shoots. The size will depend on the plant. Cuttings 5-8cm/2-3in in length are about right for a plant like this hebe.*

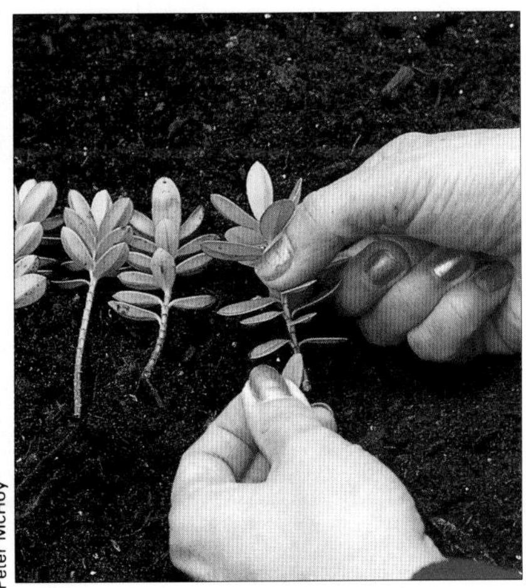

Peter McHoy

2 *Strip all the leaves from the lower end of each shoot, which will be buried in the soil. Trim the shoots to a suitable length if necessary.*

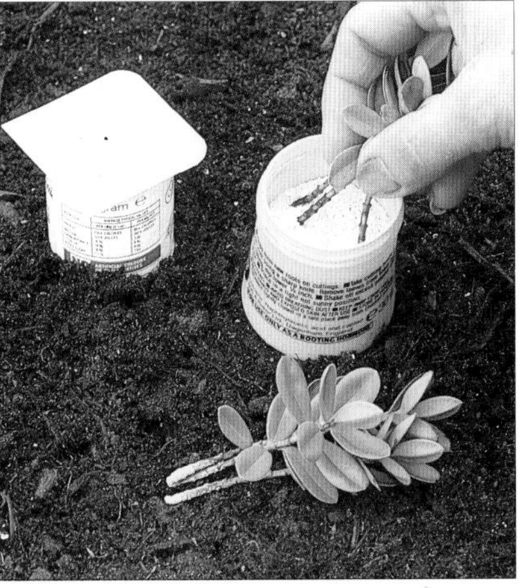

3 *Dip the ends of the cuttings in water, then into a hormone rooting powder. This is not essential but it does usually speed up the rooting process.*

4 *Most shrub cuttings taken now will root in the open ground, but some protection improves their success. Use a frame or cut-off clear plastic bottle.*

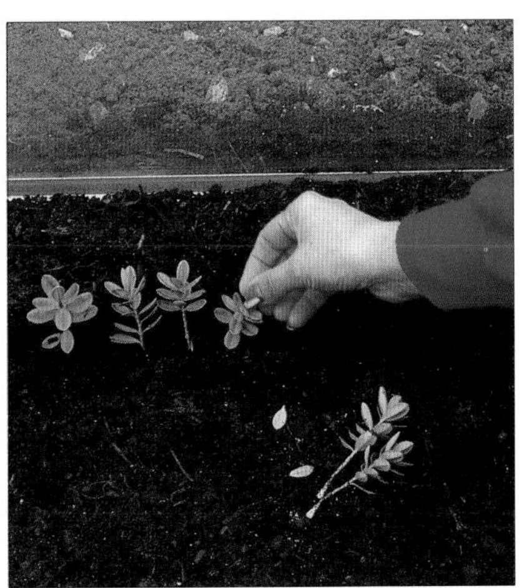

5 *Having made a slit with a trowel, insert the cuttings, spacing them close together to fit in as many as possible (but do not let them touch).*

6 *Push the soil firmly around the cuttings, being careful not to damage them. Make sure there are no large air pockets where the roots will form.*

7 *Water them in. If you add a garden fungicide to the initial watering it may help to reduce the chance of losses through rotting. Keep moist but not wet.*

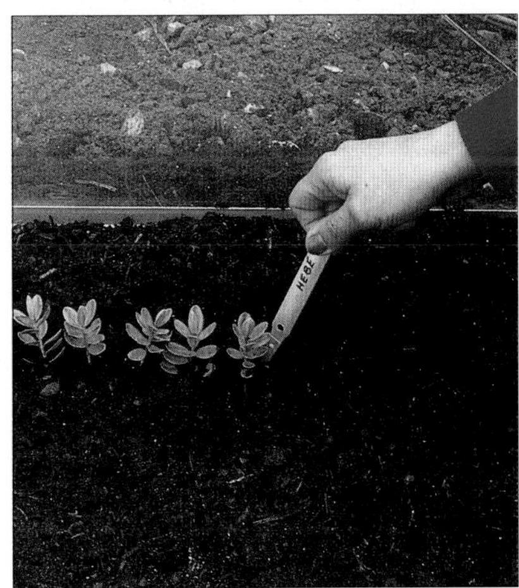

8 *Do not forget to label your cuttings as they may take weeks or months to root. It is surprisingly easy to forget which is which if you take lots of cuttings.*

CHECKLIST

WHAT TO DO

BEDS AND BORDERS
Tidy your borders by dead-heading
Thin Michaelmas daisies and check for mildew
Feed dahlias and fuchsias
Harvest vegetables regularly and water often

ROCK GARDEN
Plant dwarf spring-flowering bulbs

LOOK AHEAD

PROPAGATE
Take cuttings of geraniums (pelargoniums)
Take semi-ripe cuttings of shrubs such as berberis, cotoneaster, deutzia, and escallonia

PLANT
Autumn crocus *(Colchicum autumnale)*, summer snowflake, and belladonna lily

WHAT TO SEE

BORDER PERENNIALS
Dahlia, helenium, mullein (verbascum), perennial sunflower (helianthus), phlox, red hot poker (kniphofia)

SHRUBS
Californian lilac (ceanothus), fuchsia, hydrangea, hypericum, honeysuckle, roses

BEDDING PLANTS
African and French marigolds, alyssum, begonia, bedding dahlia, geranium (pelargonium), petunia, salvia, tobacco plant (nicotiana)

BULBS
Lilies, summer hyacinth

VISITORS

FRIENDS
Hedgehogs, ladybirds, red admiral butterfly

FOES
Blackfly, greenfly, earwigs, large white butterfly, thrips, wasps

MID SUMMER
WEEK 5

WHAT TO DO

Fortunately most of the jobs for this time of year can be delayed for a week or two if necessary, so if you are going on holiday don't worry about your garden – you will not miss out on important tasks.

If you are not going away, it is not too soon to think about next spring so send for bulb catalogues and spend a leisurely afternoon in the deckchair planning for the future.

Bulb time
Next spring may seem a long way off, but it always pays to shop early for spring-flowering bulbs. The longer you leave it, the more likely it is that the bulbs will deteriorate and the varieties you want will be sold out.

If you want 'prepared' bulbs, such as hyacinths and tulips intended for Christmas flowering, it is especially important to buy these early as they have to be planted before the ordinary kinds. (You can plant them later but they probably will not flower in time for Christmas.)

Once bulbs are available in the shops and garden centres it is worth buying them even if you do not plant them yet, as you can pick and choose more readily. Take them out of their bags and store them in a cool, dry place until you are ready to plant them.

Photos Horticultural

***Start thinking about spring-flowering bulbs, like this* Chionodoxa luciliae.**

Do not plant bulbs yet if it means digging up summer bedding displays. In the rock garden, however, there are often spaces where small bulbs can be planted now. Do not forget to leave space to plant autumn crocuses and other autumn-flowering bulbs such as the belladonna lily, which must be planted straight away.

Dahlias and fuchsias
Dahlias and fuchsias, which will probably have been flowering well for some weeks, will continue to bloom until the first frosts. Such long and prolific flowering makes considerable demands on the plants, and they will respond well to feeding.

Use a liquid feed for fast results. Watering well will also help to give these plants a boost.

If you want to produce large dahlia flowers for exhibiting, remove all but the central bud.

Michaelmas daisies

These pretty pink and purple border perennials are a feature of autumn borders, but they can be disappointing if neglected.

For better quality flowers, and big heads, thin the shoots to leave three to five heads of bloom on each plant.

Look out for powdery mildew, which is a particular problem for Michaelmas daisies. The foliage becomes covered with a white powdery-looking growth. To avoid this keep plants well watered and spray fortnightly with a fungicide based on benomyl or carbendazim.

The leaves of a Michaelmas daisy, with the characteristic white growth of mildew.

Ponds

It is worth feeding fish regularly at this time of year, so that they are in good condition to face the winter. Give them sufficient pellets that can be eaten within ten or twenty minutes; do not overfeed fish.

Duckweed covering a pond surface.

Rake out floating pond plants such as fairy moss (azolla) and duckweed (lemna) to clear the pond surface. At this time of year, these may soon cover the whole surface if not removed regularly.

WHAT TO SEE

Choosing the right variety of a particular plant is part of the art of successful gardening. At this time of year, two groups worth studying are the border phlox and golden rods.

Some of the most dependable border phlox are 'Prince of Orange' (orange-salmon in colour, with sturdy growth), Starfire' (deep red and vigorous), and 'White Admiral' (white). The pale purple flowers of 'Norah Leigh' are nothing special to look at, but the ivory and green variegated leaves make this a desirable plant.

Golden rods (solidago hybrids) show their breeding. Years ago golden rods were regarded as weed-like plants with little garden merit. Modern varieties are highly desirable. There are dwarfs like 'Golden Thumb', only 30cm/12in high, compact ones such as 'Cloth of Gold', 45cm/18in, and taller ones of 90cm/3ft or so. All have foaming sprays of yellow flowers.

Photos Horticultural

Phlox paniculata *'Prince of Orange'*.

LOOK AHEAD

This is a good time to take cuttings of semi-ripe wood from a number of desirable shrubs, including berberis, cotoneaster and deutzia.

Semi-ripe cuttings are prepared from wood that has newly grown this year. You can usually find this type of cutting growing on side shoots or at the top of the main growth.

Semi-ripe cuttings are often taken with a 'heel' (pulled off with a sliver of the main shoot attached). Most will root well in a garden frame or in a pot indoors.

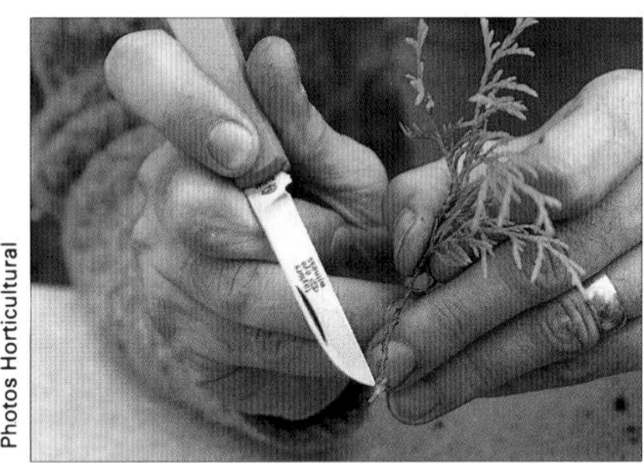

Photos Horticultural

Taking a heel cutting from a thuja.

VISITORS

Wasps can cause a lot of damage to ripening fruit at this time. The cavities caused are often later infected by rots and other diseases. A wasp trap (a jam-jar partly filled with water and a little detergent and baited with jam) can help.

Natural History Photographic Agency

Wasps are a particular nuisance now.

THIN MARGINAL POND PLANTS

The warm days of summer always bring a surge of growth to water plants, and a small pond can quickly become overgrown. Apart from removing most of the carpets of floating plants like duckweed and fairy moss, it is worth thinning or trimming back the more vigorous marginal aquatics such as the yellow flag iris and sedges and rushes, which can become weed-like and dominate a small pond.

Although many marginal plants die down in the autumn and can be divided then or when new growth starts in spring, the yellow iris and rushes like the one illustrated are evergreen and might as well be controlled now to make the pond look better for the rest of the season. Uncontrolled, they spoil the effect by reducing the area of exposed water so making a small pond look smaller. By producing a lot of shade they will also affect the flowering of plants like water lilies and water hawthorn.

All pictures Peter McHoy

1 *If your pond has become overgrown like this one, it is time to thin out some of the more vigorous plants, like yellow flag irises and rampant sedges.*

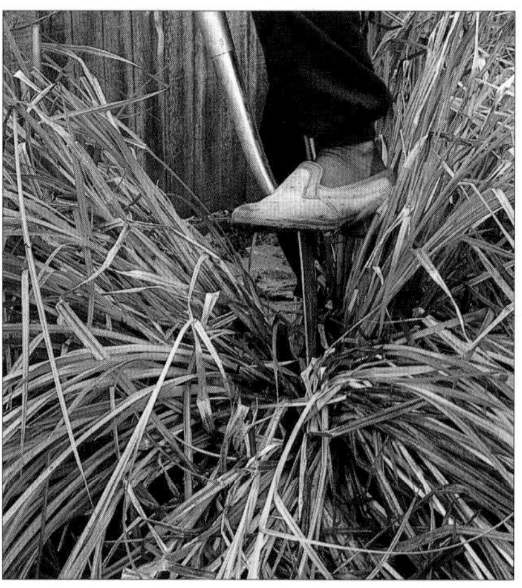

2 *Lift the plant out of the water (a large clump that has not been divided for some years can be heavy, so you may need help), and use a spade to divide it.*

3 *The wet crown of an old clump may be too tough to slice easily with a spade, and it may be more practical to slice through it with a sharp knife instead.*

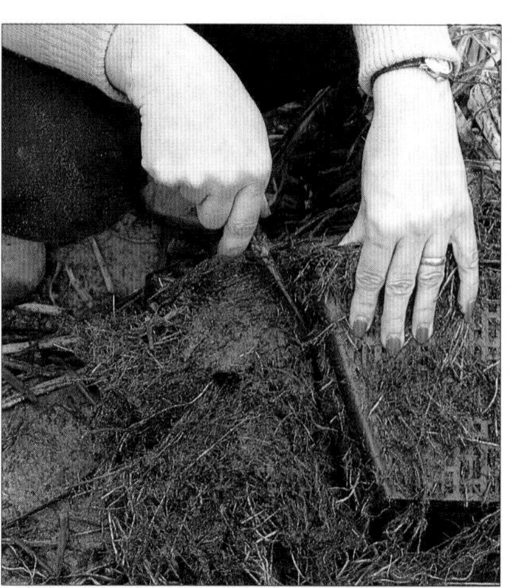

4 *If the plant was originally put in a planting basket but has since outgrown it, reduce the plant to size by cutting the roots back to the basket.*

PLANT BULBS IN A ROCK GARDEN

Although it is too early to plant spring-flowering bulbs in beds still occupied by summer bedding, you may have some space in your rock garden. There are plenty of dwarf bulbs to choose from at this time. Once planted, leave the bulbs undisturbed and they will multiply each year.

Easy and dependable bulbs for the rock garden include varieties of Crocus chrysanthus, *glory-of-the-snow (chionodoxa), grape hyacinth (muscari), snowdrop (galanthus), spring star flower (triteleia), striped squill* (Puschkinia libanotica), *angel's tears* (Narcissus triandrus albus)*, with its icy white bell-like blossoms,* Scilla tubergeniana, *with pale blue flowers, and* Tulipa tarda, *a yellow and white dwarf tulip. All these are inexpensive and should multiply freely, making a better show in your rock garden year after year.*

Cover them with about twice their own depth of soil. All prefer a sunny spot.

Harry Smith Collection

Tulipa tarda ***is an early spring-flowering bulb which reaches a height of 15cm/6in.***

PROPAGATE PELARGONIUMS

Geranium (pelargonium) cuttings will root easily at this time of year and this is a good way to increase your stock. By taking cuttings now, you will have young plants to overwinter indoors (or in a greenhouse, if you have one). Summer cuttings will make bigger plants and flower earlier than cuttings taken in spring and the old plants can be discarded at the end of the flowering season.

1 *Choose non-flowering shoots if possible. This may be difficult, as the plants flower so prolifically; flowering shoots can be used if necessary.*

2 *Make each cutting about 10cm/4in long. Cut shoots off the plant with a sharp knife just below a node (leaf joint). Remove flower or bud stem.*

3 *Trim off the bottom leaves, leaving just two or three at the top. Always use a sharp knife or blade to ensure that a clean cut is made.*

4 *Remove the stipules (the small scale-like growths at the base of each leaf stalk). If left on they may start to rot in the compost and affect the cuttings.*

5 *Fill pots with a cuttings compost. Put several cuttings in a medium-sized pot. Make holes for the cuttings close to the edge of the pot, using a pencil.*

6 *Dust the end of each cutting with a hormone rooting powder. Use one that also contains a fungicide to reduce the risk of rotting. Place a cutting in each hole.*

7 *Firm compost gently and then water carefully to avoid disturbing the cuttings. You can use a small pot for individual cuttings.*

8 *Place the pots in a cold frame or greenhouse, or on a window-sill, out of direct sun. Pot up singly when well rooted. Overwinter in a frost-free place.*

CHECKLIST

WHAT TO DO

BEDS AND BORDERS
Stake and water Michaelmas daisies
Disbud dahlias for large flowers
Dead-head bedding plants with large flowers

KITCHEN GARDEN
Continue to feed tomatoes regularly

SHRUBS
Take cuttings

ROCK GARDEN
Dead-head thymes by trimming with shears

LOOK AHEAD

PROPAGATE
Take cuttings of pelargoniums and fuchsias

PLANT
Autumn crocus (*Colchicum autumnale*), crocus, erythroniums, snowdrops, winter aconites, young border perennials and hardy annuals

WHAT TO SEE

BORDER PERENNIALS
Dahlia, golden rod, helenium, Japanese anemone, mullein (verbascum), perennial black-eyed Susan

SHRUBS
Californian lilac (ceanothus), *Caryopteris* × *clandonensis*, *Clematis tangutica*, fuchsia, hydrangea, honeysuckle, roses

BULBS
Acidanthera bicolor, *Crinum* × *powellii*, lilies, summer hyacinth (*Galtonia candicans*)

VISITORS

FRIENDS
Hedgehogs; lacewings; ladybirds; peacock, red admiral and small tortoiseshell butterflies

FOES
Blackfly, daddy-long-legs (crane fly), greenfly, earwigs, thrips, wasps

WHAT TO DO

Bulbs are in the shops now, but it makes sense to delay the main planting until the summer bedding has run its course – there will be months without much colour so do not cut it short prematurely. Concentrate on keeping the garden looking smart by keeping the lawn trimmed and beds and borders hoed. There are some bulbs, however, that should be planted promptly . . .

Plant for mid winter

Prepared hyacinths (specially treated to flower very early) start to appear in the shops about now. Plant them as soon as possible if you want flowers in mid-winter.

If you are using ordinary pots any peat or loam compost will do but choose a special bulb fibre if you are using a bowl without drainage holes. An odd number of bulbs looks best – three or five.

Harry Smith Collection

An odd number of hyacinths looks best.

Plant the bulbs with their noses just showing above the compost, then put them in a cool, dark place (ideally in a cool, shady spot in the garden). Cover with moist peat, but provide shelter so that containers without holes do not become waterlogged.

Bring them indoors after about six weeks or when the shoots are 3.5-5cm/1½-2in high and keep in a cool position for about a week. Move to a warm, light position for flowering.

You can also bring on tulips such as 'Christmas Marvel' for winter flowering. Prepare in the same way, but cover the bulbs with compost. Plant 14-15 weeks before you want them to flower.

Plant promptly

Autumn-flowering bulbs should be planted promptly, as should those that deteriorate if left unplanted for too long.

Two well worth considering for autumn are the autumn crocuses (colchicums) and lily of the field (Sternbergia lutea), *which looks like a yellow spring crocus. Colchicums look like huge crocuses, but some are double-flowered. Both plants will do well on most well-drained soils, even chalk. They prefer full sun or partial shade.*

Among spring-flowering bulbs that are best planted soon are erythroniums, snowdrops and winter aconites. Snowdrops need no introduction, but both erythroniums and winter aconites deserve to be more widely grown. Both prefer semi-shade and will grow beneath deciduous trees. The most popular erythronium is dog's tooth violet (E. dens-canis), *which has delicate nodding flowers, usually in shades of lilac. The winter aconite* (Eranthis hyemalis) *is an early-flowering ground-hugger with yellow flowers backed by a green ruff of leaf-like bracts. Soak aconite tubers overnight before planting.*

Photos Horticultural
Dog's tooth violet has eye-catching flowers.

Tidy thyme

The carpeting or wild thyme Phymus serpyllum, *also known as* T. drucei *or* T. praecox arcticus) *will probably have finished flowering now. Cut off the flower heads with garden shears to keep the plants dense and compact.*

WHAT TO SEE

This is an excellent time to look at dahlias and make a note of varieties you would like to grow. There are literally hundreds of them, ranging from dwarf edging plants through cactus and decorative types to giant decoratives the size of dinner plates that look more at home on the show bench.

For a patio, look out for the Lilliput dwarfs, which are ideal for container-growing in pots, troughs or window boxes. There are several good named

Marshall Cavendish
A yellow dahlia 'Glorie van Heemstede'.

varieties, such as 'Rapunzel' (clear orange) and 'Red Riding Hood' (bright red).

For general garden display, compact bedding dahlias such as 'Border Princess' (apricot-gold), and 'Park Princess' (pink) have spiky (cactus-type) petals, while 'Margaret Kleene' (apricot-salmon) has flat (decorative-type) petals. The latter is also good in containers. These plants grow 30-75cm / 1-2½ft tall, depending on variety.

This type of bedding dahlia is generally far superior to seed-raised strains. For cutting, the taller small- and medium-flowered decorative and cactus dahlias are generally best.

LOOK AHEAD

Now is the time to plan and plant for spring.

Propagate tender perennials

Most tender perennials used for summer bedding, such as geraniums (pelargoniums) and fuchsias, can be propagated from cuttings now. Overwinter the rooted plants in a frost-free place (such as frost-proof greenhouse or on a light window-sill indoors).

Plant young border perennials

If you sowed border perennials, such as lupins or delphiniums, earlier in the year, move the seedlings into their flowering positions in the border now, before the frosts, to give them a chance to become established while the soil is still warm.

Harry Smith Collection
Delphinium seedlings can be removed from their pots and planted out now.

VISITORS

There are plenty of attractive butterflies on the wing at this time. The peacock, red admiral and small tortoiseshell should all be welcomed – not only are they beautiful but the caterpillars live and feed on nettles rather than on desirable garden plants!

Unfortunately daddy-long-legs (crane flies) also appear at about this time. Although harmless as adults their larvae, leatherjackets, eat plant roots.

Stephen Dalton/NHPA
Daddy-long-legs are now on the wing.

DWARF BULBS TO NATURALIZE

Daffodils are often planted in grass or among other plants and left to 'naturalize' (remain undisturbed to multiply over the years). Some inexpensive dwarf bulbs naturalize just as well in the right setting.

Don Wildridge

Crocuses enliven grassy areas in spring.

Try crocuses and glory-of-the-snow (chionodoxa) in short grass, or plant scillas such as S. siberica *and glory-of-the-snow among heathers.* Anemone blanda *will cover the ground between and among shrubs with a carpet of blue, or you could plant drifts of snowdrops or cultivated bluebells beneath deciduous trees.*

There are two basic points to remember: plant close together for impact in the early years, and be prepared to wait for a couple of years before you see the full effect. But once planted, there's no more to do except enjoy the results . . . year after year.

Eric Crichton

Anemone blanda *can be blue, white or pink.*

PLANT SNAKE'S-HEAD FRITILLARIES . . .

The snake's-head fritillary is a quaint, delicate-looking plant with beautifully chequered nodding bells in subtle shades of pinkish-purple or white at the end of stems about 30cm/1ft high. It seldom fails to attract comment.

Plant as soon as possible, as the bulbs deteriorate quite rapidly if not planted promptly.

Peter McHoy

Fritillaries look good among heathers.

Michael Shoebridge

Bulbs planted close together will produce a wonderful display of flowers in spring.

The snake's-head fritillary (Fritillaria meleagris) *comes in shades of purple, rose and lilac, as well as white. It has relatively few narrow, grey-green leaves. The plant can be grown in a flower border or naturalized in an area of grass that will not be mown regularly.*

In the wild its natural habitat is damp, unploughed meadows that are flooded in winter, cut for hay in summer and grazed by cattle in autumn.

If your soil is heavy, work in some coarse grit or sharp sand to improve the drainage. If the soil is sandy, fork in plenty of garden compost or well-rotted manure. Remove an area of soil about 8cm/3in deep, and work a sprinkling of bonemeal into the bottom of the planting hole. If the soil is very heavy, add more coarse grit.

Space the bulbs carefully – the closer they are the more impressive the result, but do not let the bulbs touch. They will multiply and spread if left undisturbed.

Replace the soil around the bulbs and firm it gently to eliminate any large pockets of air. In grassland mark the area with a few small canes to remind you not to cut the grass until the plants have flowered and seeded.

. . . AND CROWN IMPERIAL

In contrast to the small and dainty snake's-head fritillary, the crown imperial* (Fritillaria imperialis) *is one of the biggest and boldest spring-flowering bulbs. Its cluster of up to five huge orange-red or yellow bell-shaped flowers topped with tufts of green leaf-like bracts is held proudly on stiff stems 60-90cm/2-3ft high. This springtime stunner should be planted now.

Eric Crichton

1 *The crown imperial needs good soil and a sunny, open position to do well. Plant in a mixed border, perhaps with a green shrub or hedge as a background.*

Marshall Cavendish

2 *Plant about 15cm/6in deep. A bulb planter, which takes out a core of soil, is a convenient way to plant these large bulbs, especially in grass.*

SOW HARDY ANNUALS FOR EARLY FLOWERS

In mild areas (area B and parts of area A on the map inside the front cover), some hardy annuals can be sown now to flower much earlier than spring-sown plants next year. Either sow directly in the ground where they are to flower, protecting the plants with a cloche or cold frame, or grow them in pots so you can move them easily when the time comes.

1 *Prepare small pots of a good seed compost, and firm them gently to provide a level surface. Use the base of one pot to firm the compost in another.*

All Photos Peter McHoy

2 *Sow a few seeds in each pot (thin to one later if more germinate). Good plants to use are Californian poppy, candytuft, love-in-a-mist and pot marigold.*

3 *Cover the seeds thinly with more potting compost, or with sand. Sand contrasts better with the compost, making it easy to judge the covering.*

4 *Plunge the pots in the ground in a cold frame or under a cloche to keep the compost moist and protect the seedlings from frost.*

5 *Water thoroughly and remember to label all the plants. It is all too easy to forget which are which by the time spring comes!*

CHECKLIST

WHAT TO DO

LAWNS
Prepare ground for a new lawn

BEDS AND BORDERS
Water Michaelmas daisies; control mildew
Feed dahlias and control pests

BULBS
Buy spring-flowering bulbs

KITCHEN GARDEN
Gather herbs for drying

LOOK AHEAD

PROPAGATE
Cuttings of bay, lavender, rosemary and sage
Cuttings of rock garden shrubs e.g. perennial candytuft and rock roses (helianthemums)

PLANT
Crocus, daffodils to naturalize, erythronium, field lily (sternbergia), hyacinths for winter flowering, snowdrops, winter aconite

WHAT TO SEE

BORDER PERENNIALS
Dahlia, golden rod, helenium, Japanese anemone, perennial black-eyed Susan, perennial sunflower (helianthus), phlox

SHRUBS
Californian lilac (ceanothus), *Caryopteris* × *clandonensis*, *Clematis tangutica*, fuchsia

BEDDING PLANTS
Begonia, buzy Lizzie, bedding dahlia, geranium (pelargonium), lavatera, petunia, salvia

BULBS
Acidanthera bicolor, Crinum powellii

VISITORS

FRIENDS
Peacock, red admiral and small tortoiseshell butterflies

FOES
Blackfly, foxes, greenfly, earwigs, wasps

WHAT TO DO

There are plenty of pleasant jobs to be tackled during the next few weeks, like planting and propagating, but these are tasks that you can be relaxed about as there is not the same sense of urgency as there is in spring. If you want to take a late week away it will not affect your garden, but do find a few minutes to plan for spring.

Border check

Borders can look untidy at this time and detract from the plants that are still blooming. Remove supports that have been used for plants that have now been cut back. Hoe to keep down weeds and improve appearances. Take the opportunity to plant a few bulbs in any reasonably large gaps that are available. These bulbs will provide pockets of interest next spring before most of the border perennials have grown large enough to compete for space.

Feed dahlias and chrysanthemums with a liquid fertilizer to give them a boost.

Photos Horticultural

Blackfly can damage dahlias.

Granular fertilizers applied to the soil in spring will be losing their effect, and these plants may have many more weeks of flowering to come.

Take the opportunity to check dahlias for aphids or earwig damage (the greenfly or blackfly will be easy to see; holes in the leaves or petals are signs that earwigs have been at work).

If your Michaelmas daises have been showing signs of mildew (a white, powdery deposit on the leaves), continue to spray regularly with a fungicide (check the container for suitability and frequency of application).

Plant spring bulbs

John Glover/Garden Picture Library

Plant snowdrops now for spring flowering.

Plant as many bulbs as you can during the next couple of weeks, while they are still in good condition. This applies especially to crocuses, erythroniums, fritillarias, snowdrops and winter aconites. It is worth letting summer bedding flower for as long as possible, but bulbs like daffodils can be planted now in herbaceous and shrub borders, and can be naturalized in grass.

Give hedges a final trim

This is a good time to trim hedges – whether slow-growing evergreens that require just a once-a-year trim, or fast-growing hedges like Leyland cypress and privet. They should produce a little more growth before winter, but most will require no further attention this year.

Hedges will need a final trim.

Shape up evergreen shrubs

The majority of evergreens grown as shrubs require minimal pruning unless they are specially trained in some way. But even the most undemanding shrub will benefit from a little pruning to shape it occasionally. With variegated kinds, prune out any all-green shoots first. Otherwise just prune back any branches that are growing too long or large, to maintain a pleasing size and shape.

Dry herbs for winter use

Even if you manage to keep some parsley and a few other fresh herbs growing during the winter, dried herbs are something that most of us need to fall back upon.

Harvest on a dry day. Tie small-leaved plants like thyme in small bunches and hang upside-down in a shaded, warm and dry but airy place. With large-leaved plants like bay, strip the leaves off, wash in cool water, and spread to dry in shallow containers, out of direct sunlight and in a dry and airy position. Strong light can affect both the colour and flavour of herbs.

Pot up rooted cuttings

Cuttings taken earlier in the summer, such as those of Alyssum saxatile, *pinks, hydrangeas and rock roses, should have rooted. If it has not already been done, pot them up into individual pots. Overwinter in a cold frame.*

WHAT TO SEE

The so-called Japanese anemones deserve to be more widely grown. From now until mid autumn they will be some of the most effective late-flowering border plants.

You may find them sold as varieties of Anemone japonica, A. hybrida, A. × elegans, *or even* A. hupehensis.

Photos Horticultural

The autumn-flowering Anemone hybrida.

Good varieties are 'Bressingham Glow' (rosy-red, semi-double), 'Queen Charlotte' (pink, single), and 'September charm' (pink, single). Heights are typically 45-90cm / 1½-3ft, depending on the variety.

If you want a good late-flowering shrub for your garden, consider a tree hollyhock (Hibiscus syriacus). *This is a marvellous plant with large flowers in a wide variety of colours ranging from white through pink to red and purple, produced in succession from late summer into mid autumn.*

LOOK AHEAD

Garden centres and shops are full of bulbs at this time. Choose yours now, while there is still a good selection, even if you are unable to plant them immediately.

Plan ahead for next year's herb garden by taking cuttings.

Propagate herbs

Many hardy perennial herbs, such as lavender, rosemary, bay and sage, can be propagated from cuttings taken now. In the case of sage and lavender it is always worth raising a few plants from cuttings, as old plants tend to become straggly and are best replaced after a few years.

Take cuttings 8-10cm/3-4in long, and root in a cold frame. Sage cuttings often root better if taken with a heel (a small sliver of old wood attached).

GARDEN VISITORS

Badgers are shy, retiring creatures that few people associate with gardens, but they will venture into rural gardens, and in prolonged dry spells they sometimes eat rootcrops. They can clear a row of carrots in an evening, but you may consider this a small price to pay for such distinguished visitors.

Brian Hawkes/NHPA

At night badgers may forage in rural gardens.

FORCING HYACINTHS

Pot up some hyacinths so you can enjoy the scent and beauty of these easy bulbs in your home next spring. You need specially prepared bulbs for very early flowering. Ordinary hyacinth bulbs, which are cheaper, will also flower long before those in the garden if potted up now.

Plant all one variety together – if you mix varieties they may flower at different times, spoiling the effect.

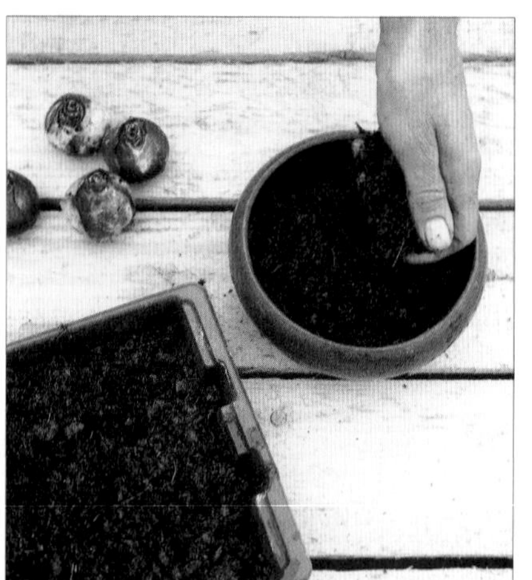

1 *Buy bulb fibre if you are growing in bowls without drainage holes. If planting in ordinary pots, however, you can use an ordinary potting compost.*

2 *Place moist bulb fibre in the base of the bowl, and position the bulbs on top; pack more fibre around the bulbs, leaving the noses exposed.*

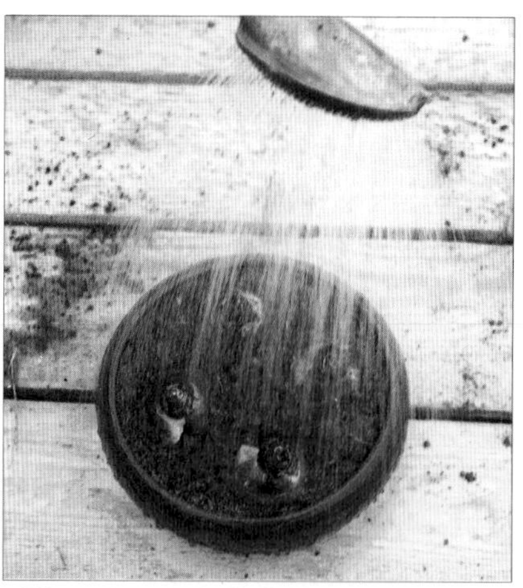

3 *Although the bulb fibre should be moist when you use it, water carefully after planting, being careful not to waterlog. Never let it dry out completely.*

4 *Place the bulbs in a cool position – a shady spot outdoors is likely to be cooler than in the home. Cover with sand or peat to protect the bulbs from light.*

5 *Protect the bowls with straw or even a sheet of polythene. Unless the bowls are sheltered from rain, polythene is necessary to avoid waterlogging.*

A NEW LAWN

Making a lawn need not be a arduous task, and if you use turf the result is almost immediate. Early autumn is a good time to make a new lawn but it is best to prepare the ground now to give it time to settle, and to allow weed seedlings to germinate.

After preparing the ground for a new lawn, check the surface with a spirit level.

Whether planning to start from scratch with seed or to pay a little more and use turf for quicker results, the ground should be prepared a week or two beforehand. It will then be firm and level and will not form depressions and an uneven surface later. If sowing seed you should also allow weed seedlings to germinate first, then kill these off (by hoeing or using a contact non-persistent weedkiller) before sowing the grass seed. This is less important if using turf.

If you want to avoid the hard work, get someone in to dig over the ground for you. Then rake it level, being sure to remove large stones and rubble. To ensure that the finished surface is level, use a spirit-level on a straight-edged piece of timber supported between a series of pegs driven into the ground.

FUCHSIAS FOR NEXT YEAR

Semi-hardwood cuttings root easily at this time of year. This is the best method of propagation to choose if you do not have a heated greenhouse. Take them at any time during the next month, then keep them in a frost-free place during the winter while rooting.

This will provide plenty of good plants to put out in your garden or in your hanging baskets next year.

1 *Choose side shoots 10-15cm/4-6in long, preferably without flowers (though you can remove these). Make sure the plant you choose is healthy.*

2 *Pull the cutting off carefully with a 'heel' (a piece of bark from the main shoot). Although not essential, they tend to root better with a heel attached.*

3 *Remove the lower leaves, and trim the end of the 'heel' with a sharp knife or razor blade. You can dip it in a hormone rooting powder, if desired.*

4 *Insert several cuttings round the edge of an 8-10cm/3-4in pot filled with a cuttings compost, or a mixture of equal parts peat and coarse sand.*

5 *Water thoroughly, then leave to let surplus water drain. It is especially important that peat-based composts are kept moist but not waterlogged.*

6 *Remember to label the cuttings. By the time you plant them next year memory may fail you. Write a brief description if you do not know the variety.*

7 *To provide more stable warmth and moisture during the cool weather fill a 'plunge box' to just above pot rim level with moist peat or sand.*

8 *Place in a frost-free frame or greenhouse, or on a light window-sill in a cool but frost-free room. Keep moist; pot up individually when well rooted.*

CHECKLIST

WHAT TO DO

LAWNS
Sow a new lawn

BEDS AND BORDERS
Water Michaelmas daisies and control mildew
Disbud large-flowered chrysanthemums
Save and store seeds

SHRUBS
Plan for winter interest

LOOK AHEAD

PROPAGATE
Divide aubrieta and rock campanulas
Sow annuals for spring and early summer

PLANT
Spring bedding plants such as wallflowers

WHAT TO SEE

BORDER PERENNIALS
Chrysanthemum, dahlia, golden rod, helenium, Japanese anemone, penstemon, perennial black-eyed Susan, red hot poker

SHRUBS
Caryopteris × clandonensis, Clematis tangutica, fuchsia, heathers, *Hebe* 'Autumn Glory', hydrangea, honeysuckle

BEDDING PLANTS
Begonia, busy Lizzie, bedding dahlia, gazania, geranium (pelargonium), nasturtium, petunia, salvia, tobacco plant, zinnia

BULBS
Acidanthera bicolor, Crinum powellii, golden-rayed lily *(Lilium auratum)*

VISITORS

FRIENDS
Hedgehogs; ladybirds; peacock, red admiral and small tortoiseshell butterflies

FOES
Blackfly, greenfly, leaf-miners, wasps

LATE SUMMER
WEEK 3

WHAT TO DO

Late summer and early autumn is a good time for gardening, for although the bright flowers of summer have passed their peak, the weather is still pleasant enough to enjoy work outdoors, and with holidays probably behind you you can turn your attention to the garden with new enthusiasm . . . and plan for spring.

Naturalize bulbs

Bulbs are good buys, especially if you choose suitable kinds and plant them appropriately. Most of those suitable for naturalizing multiply freely and flower dependably each year. Many bulbs do much better if you can leave them undisturbed rather than lifting them and replanting each year, but you must not cut off their leaves prematurely,

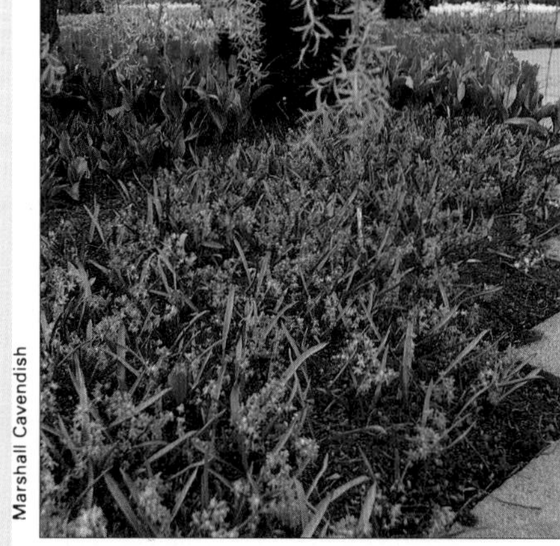

Marshall Cavendish

Glory-of-the-snow and tulips in spring.

simply to make the garden or grass look tidier. It is the fact that they can die back naturally that helps naturalized bulbs grow and multiply so well.

Many bulbs are naturalized in grass, but rather than spread them all over the lawn keep them in one area which you can leave untrimmed while they die down, without making the whole lawn look untidy. Good bulbs for lawns are crocuses, daffodils, glory-of-the-snow (chionodoxa) and winter aconites. In more informal grass, perhaps in an orchard, include Camassia esculenta, *erythroniums and snake's-head fritillary.*

To make the planting look as natural as possible, just scatter the bulbs over the ground, rather than spacing them, and plant where they fall. A bulb planter is useful for planting in a grassed area – you simply press it into the ground (some have a depth gauge on them) and pull out a core of soil, which is replaced once the bulb has been inserted into the hole.

Bulbs can be planted and left to grow undisturbed in herbaceous and shrub borders, where they will perform just as well – and you can include many different kinds, such as anemones, grape hyacinths and ornamental onions. But in this case some element of planned spacing and positioning is necessary because they generally have to fill gaps between other plants.

Order plants from nurseries

The vast majority of the trees and shrubs that you will require for your garden will be available as container-grown plants from garden centres. Sometimes, however, perhaps if you want to buy a particular plant that is not widely available, it will be necessary to send away to a mail order nursery. Many plants are sent out in the autumn. Place your orders quickly so that you are in the despatch queue and they are more likely to have the plants that you want.

Decide what plants you need.

Check stakes and supports

Supports can be removed from border plants that flowered earlier in the summer, and the foliage clipped back a bit if necessary, but for those tall plants that are still flowering it is important to check that the stakes or supports are firm and the plants tied to them. From now on strong winds are common and plants with a lot of leafy growth, like dahlias, can be badly damaged if staking is neglected. Some chrysanthemums may also need careful staking.

Dry herbs

Most herbs will be deteriorating now, so if you have not already done so, dry or freeze some leaves, such as parsley, mint and tarragon, to provide herbs for winter use. There is not much point in drying leaves of bay, rosemary and sage, however, as you should be able to pick a few fresh leaves from the plant during the winter.

Chrysanthemums

These are at their best in autumn. Most border kinds can be left to form mounds of bloom with no special attention, but if you are growing the large-flowered kinds, where the size and perfection of the individual blooms is important, staking and disbudding are necessary. With this type of chrysanthemum the number of shoots should have been reduced earlier. Now the number of flower buds should be reduced by removing the small ones, to leave just one big flower at the top of each shoot.

WHAT TO SEE

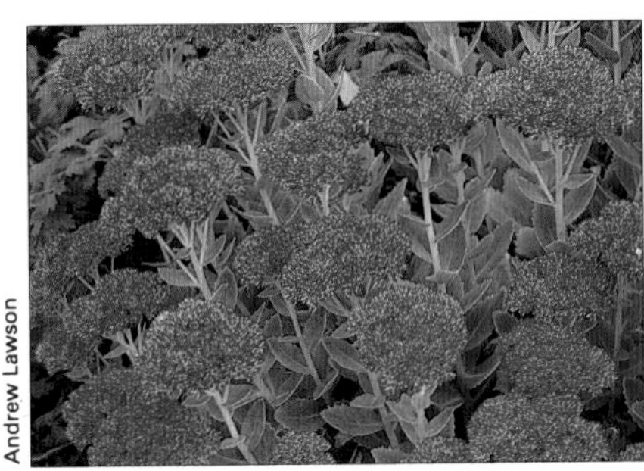

Andrew Lawson

Sedum spectabile *adds late summer colour.*

The sedums are a huge family, but one member,* Sedum spectabile *and its varieties and hybrids, excels at this time of year. The large heads of pink or red flowers, which cap large, succulent-like leaves, are truly magnificent. But there is also the bonus of the wildlife they attract . . . they are often covered with visiting butterflies and wasps.

Two good pinks are 'Autumn Joy' and 'Brilliant'. 'Carmen' is bright carmine, 'Meteor' deep carmine.

LOOK AHEAD

The sooner spring bedding plants like double daisies, pansies, polyanthus and wallflowers are put in, the better the spring display.

If you are planting where there is still summer bedding it will be a compromise between letting the summer bedding continue to flower as long as possible and getting the new plants in. As soon as the existing plants look tatty, tidy up the beds, fork out the ground and rake it level, then plant your bulbs and spring bedding plants. If mixing bulbs with plants, insert the plants first, and put the bulbs in between.

VISITORS

Leaf-miners, the larvae of which bore tunnels within the leaves or stems, are mainly a problem of early summer, but on holly the grubs will be in the 'mines' waiting to pupate in the spring. Pick off affected leaves. The carnation leaf-miner (carnation fly) starts to tunnel into the stems and leaves of carnations, pinks and sweet Williams about now. Spray with dimethoate if symptoms appear.

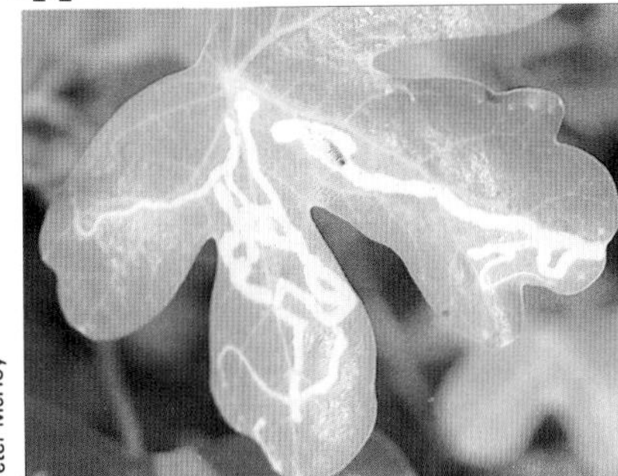

Peter McHoy

The signs of leaf-miner on canary creeper.

SAVE YOUR OWN SEEDS

It can be rewarding to save your own seeds, but bear in mind that it is not always worth doing so. Do not save the seed from F1 hybrids – the seedlings will not be like the parent. Even ordinary varieties may produce variable plants, but it may be worth saving seed from true species, or varieties of plants like sweet peas, alyssum, and lobelia, most of which will produce good seedlings.

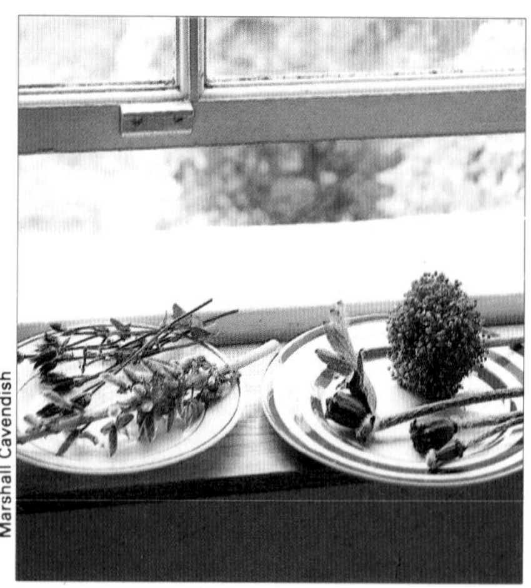
Marshall Cavendish

Collect your seed pods and place them indoors on a window-sill until they open. This can be a project in which children will be keen to participate.

Collect the seed pods once they have ripened and the seeds are just about to shed (if you collect them too early, while the seeds are still immature, they will not germinate).

Harvest on a dry day, and spread the pods out on a tray on a window-sill until the seeds have been shed.

Blow or shake off the dust and pieces of pod, then put the seeds in envelopes in a sealed tin, or directly into small airtight jars. Do not forget to label them. Store in a cool dry place until it is time to sow.

MULTIPLY AUBRIETAS

Most plants are divided in spring, but some rock plants that have crowns that develop naturally into several individual plants, such as aubrietas and many rock campanulas and gentians, can be divided now. (The autumn-flowering **Gentiana sino-ornata** ***should be divided in the spring, not now.)***

This quick and easy method produces good-sized plants very quickly.

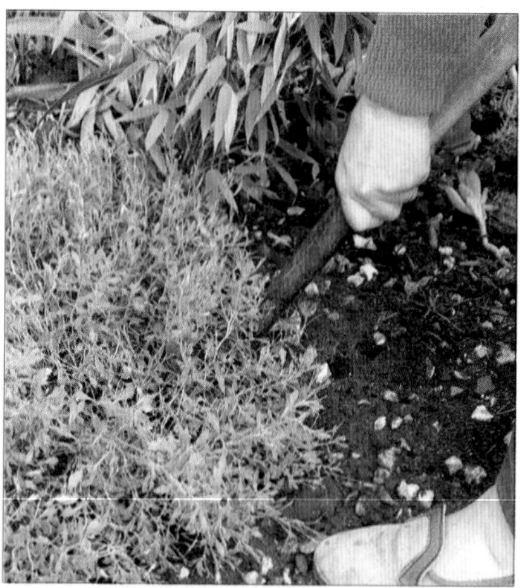

1 Lift the plant carefully with hand or garden fork, trying not to damage the shoots. Small vigorous clumps often produce more plants than neglected ones.

All photos Peter McHoy

2 Gently shake off surplus soil so that the clump is easier to handle and you can easily see what you are doing. Do not remove more than necessary.

3 Tease the pieces apart with the fingers or a hand fork. You can use a knife if necessary, but usually the distinct parts of the crown can be pulled apart.

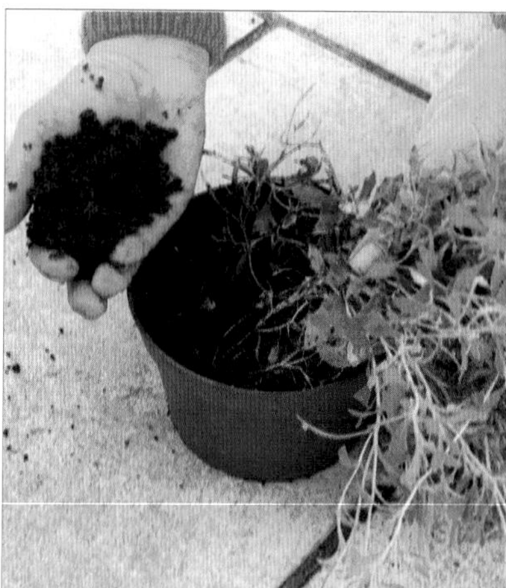

4 Replant immediately, preferably where the plants are to grow. If you want to give some plants to a friend, pot up some pieces too.

5 Remember to label the plants (with the colour if you do not know the variety), and water in thoroughly. Be prepared to water regularly for some weeks if it is dry.

CHEERFUL CHIVES

Chives are great to grow in the flower garden, or even on the kitchen window-sill. The grass-like foliage is attractive in its own right, and the flowers are as pretty as those of thrift, which they resemble. Grow it as an edging in the flower garden, and just harvest a few leaves when you need them.

You can divide established clumps now . . . and while doing so pot up some to grow indoors for winter use.

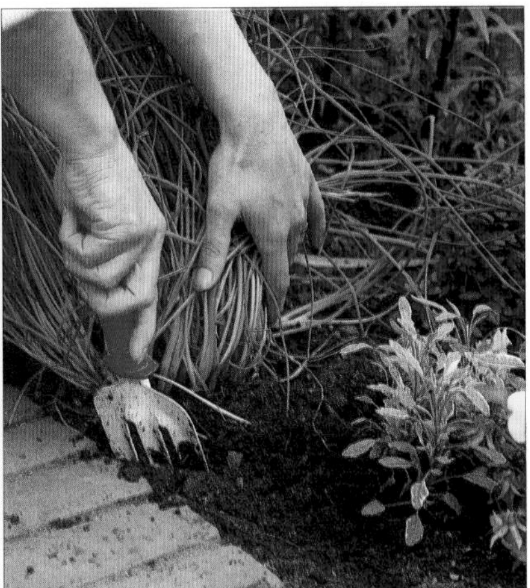

1 *Lift the clump with a small hand trowel – they are not deep-rooted and will come up easily. Separate the clump into small pieces by pulling it apart.*

2 *Replant about 15cm/6in apart to form a pretty edging to a flower bed or vegetable plot. Pot up a large piece to grow on the kitchen window-sill.*

MAKING THE MOST OF MINT

Mint is such an easy herb to grow that it is often taken for granted, but fresh leaves are always at a premium early and late in the season. It is easy to extend the harvesting period by lifting some roots now and potting them up to provide fresh mint in winter and early spring. You can do this any time within the next month, whether you have a greenhouse, a cold frame or just a window-sill.

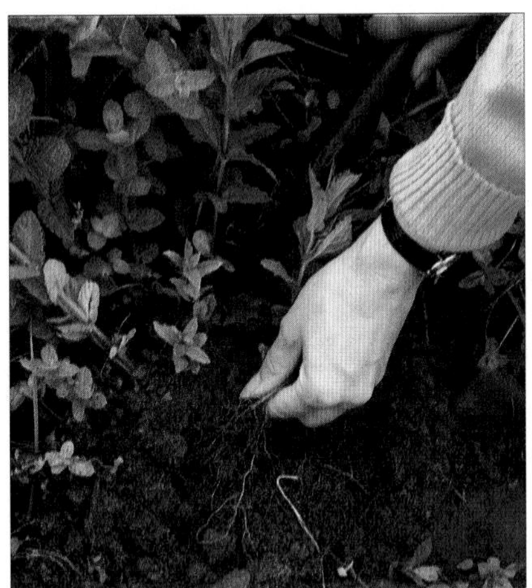

1 *Lift a large, established clump, using a fork or spade. Any pieces of root left behind will grow again, so remove all roots if not replanting in the same place.*

All photos Peter McHoy

2 *Pieces can usually be pulled off by hand, but if necessary use a garden knife to separate sections of root. Do not use any shoots with diseased leaves.*

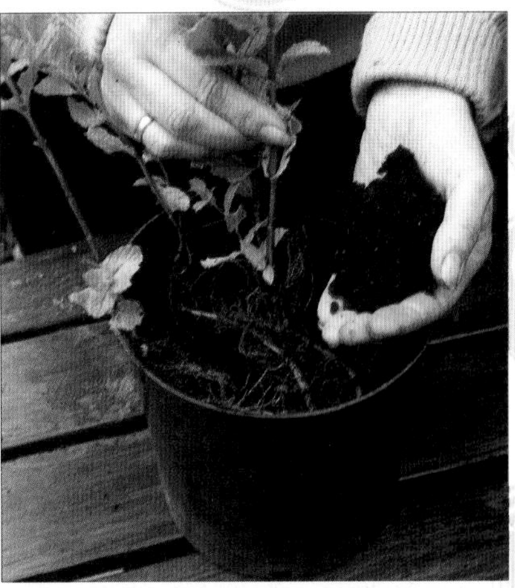

3 *Three-quarters fill a 20-25cm/8-10in pot with compost for use indoors. Spread the roots out and cover them with compost. Keep on a light window-sill.*

4 *For a greenhouse, spread the roots in a seed tray half filled with compost, then cover and keep in the light. New growth will start early next year.*

5 *If you have a cold frame, plant in an old growing bag used for a previous crop. A pot of mint indoors, however, saves you going out in bad weather.*

CHECKLIST

WHAT TO DO

BEDS AND BORDERS
Cut back foliage that is dying back
Order plants for autumn delivery

SHRUBS
Continue to dead-head and spray roses
Give hedges a final trim if necessary

ROCK GARDEN
Move plants in unsuitable positions

LOOK AHEAD

PROPAGATE
Evergreen shrubs

PLANT
Bulbs for spring bedding and naturalizing
Spring bedding plants such as wallflowers

WHAT TO SEE

BORDER PERENNIALS
Californian fuchsia *(Zauschneria californica)*, chrysanthemum, dahlia, Japanese anemone

SHRUBS
Californian lilac (ceanothus), *Caryopteris × clandonensis, Clematis orientalis, Clematis tangutica,* fuchsia, heathers, hydrangea

BEDDING PLANTS
Gazania, geranium (pelargonium), nasturtium, salvia, tobacco plant (nicotiana)

BULBS
Acidanthera bicolor, Crinum powellii, summer hyacinth *(Galtonia candicans)*

VISITORS

FRIENDS
Hedgehogs; ladybirds; peacock, red admiral and small tortoiseshell butterflies

FOES
Blackfly, daddy-long-legs (crane flies), greenfly, earwigs, sawflies, caterpillars, wasps

LATE SUMMER

WEEK 4

WHAT TO DO

This is a period of transition between summer and autumn – in the colder parts of the country the garden may already be assuming an end-of-season appearance. Make the most of the late summer colour by tidying up the more dejected summer bedding plants.

Tidy beds and borders

Towards the end of the season some summer bedding plants will have finished while others will still be blooming, and may continue until the first frost. Some plants, such as the burning bush (kochia), are at their best in the autumn, when the feathery green foliage becomes flushed in shades of red and purple. Make the most of this late colour . . . do not let dead plants spoil the effect.

Pull up any bedding plants that have finished flowering, even if it involves leaving some gaps around those plants that are still blooming well. Then hoe the soil to keep it weed-free and smart.

It may be possible to plant appropriate spring bedding plants, such as forget-me-nots, to fill in the spaces.

Herbaceous and shrub or mixed borders also benefit from a general tidy at this time. Dead-heading benefits the plants and improves the appearance. If the foliage is turning yellow and

Marshall Cavendish

Pull up bedding plants that have died.

beginning to die away it is best t cut herbaceous plants down to ground level.

Prepare for autumn planting

Container-grown plants can be planted at any time of the year if the ground is in good condition, but early autumn is an ideal tim to plant shrubs of all kinds as th soil is still warm enough to encourage root growth before the cold weather sets in.

Bare-root trees and shrubs, which are usually sent out from nurseries, are ideally planted in autumn – immediately in the cas of evergreens, after the leaves have fallen in the case of deciduous trees and shrubs. If possible prepare the ground in advance of planting.

Dig the area thoroughly, incorporating as much garden compost, well-rotted manure, or other organic material as you ca spare, and rake in a generous sprinkling of bone meal (avoid strong, quick-acting fertilizers at this time of year).

Preparing the soil in advance allows it to settle and lets weed

Dig in compost before planting shrubs.

seedlings germinate so that they can be hoed off.

If buying by mail order, make sure you post the order as soon as possible, otherwise the nursery may sell out of the plants that you require, and as most are dispatched in rotation, a delay now may mean your plants arrive late or at an inconvenient time.

Autumn lawn care

If your lawn is in good condition it will probably not require feeding, but if it looks jaded or yellow after the effects of a summer's use, an autumn feed may bring it back to health.

Choose a special autumn lawn fertilizer – a normal summer or general feed will contain too much nitrogen, which will cause soft, lush growth that is likely to be damaged by cold winter weather.

Special autumn lawn feeds contain nutrients that encourage strong root growth rather than sappy shoots. Follow the manufacturer's instructions for application rates.

Your lawn will almost certainly benefit from aeration.

The ideal aerating tool is a hollow-tined aerator, which takes out a core of soil. You can use a garden fork instead if the lawn is small, but as this is tiring you will only want to treat a small area at once. Push the prongs of the fork into the grass to a depth of about 10-15cm/4-6in. Repeat in rows about 10cm/4in apart.

Slitters that you can fix to the front of your conventional mower do a similar job.

If you find aerating a chore to do each year, try to do about a third of the lawn each autumn, or divide the job between autumn and spring.

If possible brush sand or a mixture of sand and peat into the aeration holes or slits, although simple slitting or spiking alone will benefit the grass.

Harry Smith Collection

A lawn spiker will aerate your turf.

WHAT TO SEE

Marshall Cavendish

Clematis orientalis *flowering in autumn.*

Clematis are justifiably popular plants, and you can have different species and varieties in flower from mid spring through the summer until early autumn or even later. Two excellent species that are a real feature in September are **C. orientalis *and*** **C. tangutica.** ***Both have masses of nodding yellow flowers set against feathery foliage, which will be followed later by pretty fluffy seedheads that will last for a couple of months.***

LOOKING AHEAD

Semi-ripe cuttings (those from shoots produced earlier this year and now hardening at the base) can be taken from most evergreens during the next month or two.

Evergreen cuttings

Most hardy evergreens can be propagated from cuttings of semi-ripe shoots taken now. Examples are griselinia, heather (calluna), Mexican orange blossom (choisya), skimmia and spotted laurel (aucuba). If you have a heated propagator, preferably with a mist unit, choice shrubs such as camellias and rhododendrons can also be rooted at this time.

VISITORS

The large white and small white butterflies are usually regarded as a problem of cabbages and related vegetables, but the caterpillars can also devour ornamentals such as mignonette, nasturtiums and canary creeper. Autumn often sees another brood of these pests, so check vulnerable plants regularly.

The small white caterpillar is green with blackish hairs. The large white caterpillar is greenish with yellow stripes and whitish hairs.

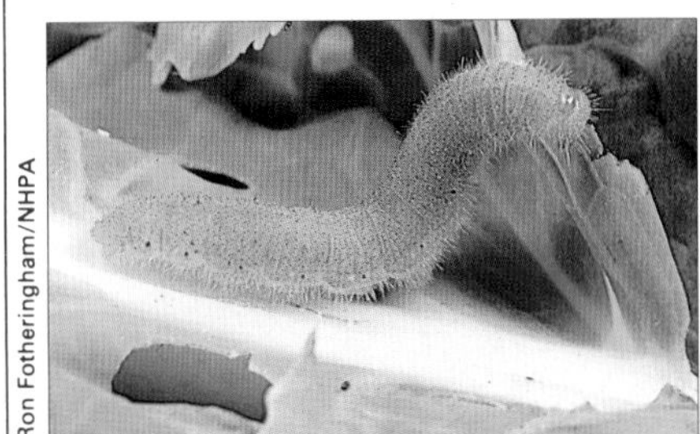

Ron Fotheringham/NHPA

A small white butterfly caterpillar.

MAKE THE MOST OF YOUR DAHLIAS

Dahlias are the crown in many borders at this time of year, combining the virtues of an abundance of flowers that will continue until the first frosts with bushy and leafy growth that helps to fill out gaps left by earlier border plants that have now finished.

Marshall Cavendish

Dahlia *'Gerrie Hoek' flowers into autumn.*

And of course they provide a wonderful supply of cut flowers for the home.

As the season progresses, however, the flowers will become smaller and fewer, and the leafy top growth is prone to wind damage, so spend a few minutes checking your dahlias and giving them a boost. They will continue to provide a super display.

Dahlias require a lot of water and a lot of feeding to do really well. If the weather is dry, find time to water them, and if growth seems to be lacking vigour give them a boost with a foliar feed or liquid feed to the roots (granular fertilizers applied to the roots may not act quickly enough at this time). Dead-head the plants, and make sure the shoots are tied in to canes or stakes (except for dwarf and bedding types).

LILIES FROM SCALES

Raising new plants from scales is a fascinating way to increase your lilies. You may already have lilies in your garden that you can use (you do not even have to dig up the bulb), otherwise buy a few bulbs as soon as they are available. The fresher the bulb, the greater the chance of success.

You do not need any special equipment, and this is a way to have beautiful lilies at minimal cost.

1 *Remove a few outer scales from the lily bulb, snapping them off. If you have a bulb in the garden draw some soil away and do this without lifting it.*

All photos Peter McHoy

2 *Dust the scales with a fungicide powder, such as sulphur, to reduce the risk of the scales rotting. Put them in a bag and shake them in the fungicide.*

3 *Mix equal parts damp peat and grit, or use perlite or vermiculite for rooting. Partly fill a polythene bag with the rooting medium and add the scales.*

4 *Inflate the bag slightly and secure the top with a tie. Shake the rooting compost and scales to mix them, then place the bag in an airing cupboard.*

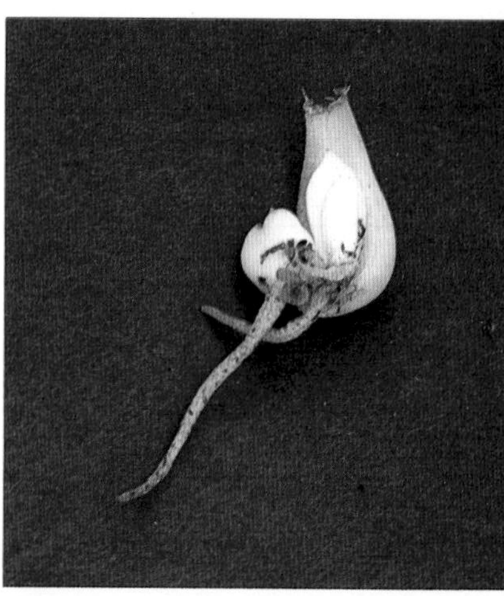

5 *When bulblets appear at the base of the scales (usually after a month or two), pot them up in John Innes No. 1 compost, burying the bulblets.*

BULBS IN WINDOW BOXES

Tulips and other bulbs can be planted in window boxes to brighten up those spring days, but choose dwarf or compact varieties, and try to use them with spring bedding plants or other kinds of bulbs to extend what can otherwise be a relatively brief period of interest. By 'stacking' the bulbs you can cram in more colour and extend the period of flowering too.

1 *Place a layer of drainage material and an inch or so of compost in the window box, then plant those bulbs that need deep planting, such as tulips.*

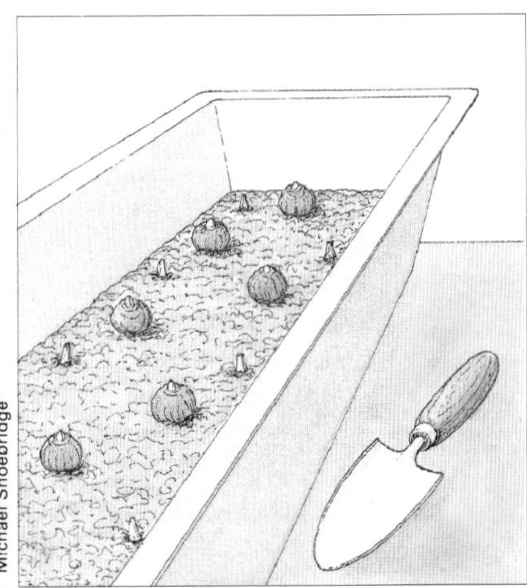

Michael Shoebridge

2 *Add enough compost to cover the first layer of bulbs, leaving the noses just exposed, then add more bulbs between them, such as scillas.*

PLANT DAFFODILS

Most spring-flowering bulbs can be planted during the next two months, but it makes sense to plant them once space is available.

Except for a few species, tulips do not naturalize well, and they deteriorate if left in the ground (they succumb to diseases, and the bulbs split up into smaller ones that take years to reach flowering size) so plant fresh ones each year. Daffodils should flower each year.

1 *Fork over the ground, working in some coarse grit if the soil is prone to water-logging. Rake in a sprinkling of bone meal (do not use a general fertilizer).*

All photos Peter McHoy

2 *If the area will be used for summer bedding, a bulb planting tray makes lifting easier. After flowering you can lift it and replant elsewhere.*

3 *If planting with a trowel, lay the bulbs on the soil where you want them to grow, to adjust spacing, then plant each one using a trowel or a hand fork.*

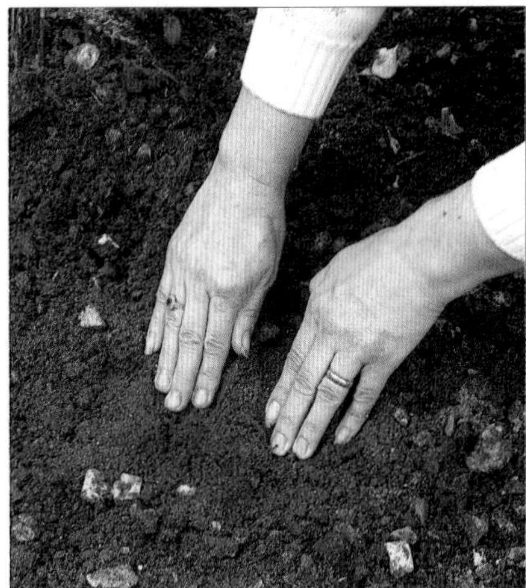

4 *Pull the soil back over the bulbs, or rake the soil level if planting a large area. Firm the soil round the bulbs with the hands to eliminate pockets of air.*

5 *Do not forget to label. If spring bedding plants are to be planted too, mark each cluster of bulbs with small split canes to avoid them when planting.*

CHECKLIST

WHAT TO DO

LAWNS
Repair damaged lawn edges

BEDS AND BORDERS
Dead-head and tidy border plants
Hoe to control weeds
Move plants from unsuitable positions

SHRUBS
Feed and water young trees and shrubs
Pot up rooted cuttings taken in the summer

LOOK AHEAD

PROPAGATE
Peonies if they are large enough to divide

PLANT
Spring-flowering bulbs and lilies
Spring bedding plants such as double daisy

WHAT TO SEE

BORDER PERENNIALS
Californian fuchsia, chrysanthemum, dahlia, Japanese anemone, red hot poker, rudbeckia

SHRUBS
Californian lilac (ceanothus) *Caryopteris* × *clandonensis*, fuchsia, heathers, *Hebe* 'Autumn Glory', hydrangea, rowan

BEDDING PLANTS
Aster, begonia, busy Lizzie, bedding dahlia, nasturtium, pansy, salvia, tobacco plant

BULBS
Acidanthera bicolor, Crinum powellii

VISITORS

FRIENDS
Peacock, red admiral and small tortoiseshell butterflies, swallows and swifts

FOES
Blackfly, greenfly, sawflies, small and large white butterfly caterpillars, wasps

LATE SUMMER

WEEK 5

WHAT TO DO

There is a definite hint of autumn in the air. Although there are many more weeks of colour to be enjoyed, with berries and autumn tints, it is a reminder that there are lots of jobs to do before autumn brings growth to an end.

Prepare for planting

Hardy shrubs and border plants can be planted in the autumn, but it makes sense to leave those of borderline hardiness, like hebes and New Zealand flax (phormiums) until spring. The advantage of planting in the autumn, however, is that it takes pressure off you next spring when there are so many other jobs. And with evergreens you can have the benefit of the plant during the winter.

Plants that flower in the spring or early summer, such as Lenten roses and pyrethrums, along with spring-flowering rock plants, are best planted in the autumn.

There is plenty of time to plant during the next month or two, but if using container-grown plants it is worth planting while the soil remains warm and gardening outdoors is still pleasant.

Check your borders to see whether there are gaps to be filled or plants to be moved, and make a note of what is required. This is better than buying plants on impulse then trying to find space.

Photos Horticultural

Use a fork to dig up deep-rooted weeds.

Tidy up the surrounding plants and dig over the ground. Remove the roots of any deep-rooted perennial weeds like couch grass and bindweed.

Moving established plants

Sooner or later you will put plants in the wrong place – either they will be too large or too close to neighbouring plants, or they will need more sun or more shade to do well. This is an ideal time to move them. Even quite large shrubs that have been planted for a couple of years can be moved with a good chance of success.

Water the ground a few hours before you move the plant, and dig a large enough hole in the new position before you start to lift it.

Dig a trench all around the plant, about 30-45cm/12-18in from the stem or crown, depending on size, then gradually undercut it with a spade, severing the roots if necessary. Try to lift a shrub with a large ball of soil attached to the fibrous roots. Unless the plant is still small you will need help — an established shrub plus soil can be very heavy.

Move it straight to its new planting hole without delay, pack new soil around the root-ball without disturbing it too much, and water thoroughly until it is re-established.

Continue dead-heading

Do not ease up on the dead-heading just because the end of the season is in sight. Dead-heading may not do much to promote further flowering now, but it will make the garden look tidier. And in the case of border perennials and shrubs like roses it will encourage the plants to put all their energies into producing better plants for next year rather than into forming seeds.

Hoe and water

Keep the hoe moving to prevent weeds becoming established or setting seed. And do not forget to water late-flowering plants like dahlias and Michaelmas daisies if the weather is dry.

If you have to hoe and water, do the hoeing first while the soil is dry, and wait until the weeds have withered before watering.

Marshall Cavendish

Do not let Michaelmas daisies dry out.

LOOK AHEAD

Once summer bedding is over or looking decidedly dejected, it is often best to clear the ground. Lightly fork it over and rake it level, then plant bulbs and spring bedding.

Propagating peonies

Do not disturb peonies unnecessarily (they may sulk and refuse to flower for a season or two), but large clumps can be divided.

Lift the roots carefully with a garden fork, then cut through the tough crowns with a sharp knife, ensuring that each piece has a dormant bud as well as some roots. Replant immediately.

Eric Crichton

Now is a good time to divide peonies.

WHAT TO SEE

Californian fuchsias or humming-bird's trumpets, which have the much less attractive Latin name of Zauschneria californica, deserve to be better known as they can contribute so much to a garden in late summer and early autumn. The compact plants grow to about 30cm/12in and are ideal for growing in a rockery or at the base of a sunny wall, where the profusion of tubular scarlet flowers on short spikes will make a cushion of colour.

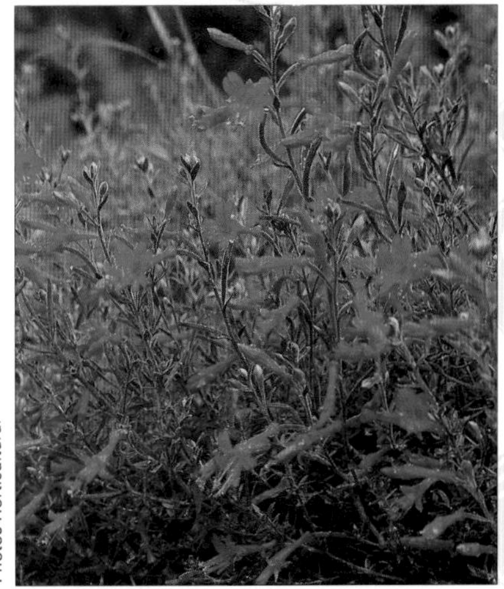
Photos Horticultural

The scarlet flowers of Californian fuchsia.

They have just one drawback – they may succumb in a bad winter. But you can overwinter cuttings in a greenhouse or frame as an insurance against winter losses.

VISITORS

Swallows, swifts and house martins are among the summer visitors that will be paying a final visit to our gardens before migrating.

Although it is sad to see the summer visitors depart, within weeks the winter guests, such as fieldfares and redwings, will be arriving.

W.S. Paton/Nature Photographers

Swallows will soon be flying to Africa.

MAKING A WINTER WINDOW BOX

Do not confine your window boxes to the garden shed once the summer bedding has been removed. Plant them up with evergreens and spring-flowering plants to provide subtle but welcome colour throughout the winter.

If you want to replant the boxes with more colourful summer bedding next year, the dwarf shrubs can be planted in the garden next spring.

1 *Place a layer of fresh compost in the box – do not attempt to use the old compost, unless just plunging the plants in pots (see step 4).*

Marshall Cavendish

2 *Plant small evergreen shrubs such as spotted laurel,* Fatsia japonica, *hebes, and grey-leaved shrubs like the curry plant and cotton lavender.*

3 *Soften the front of the window box with some small-leaved ivies. Remove from their pots and plant them at a slight angle so that they trail.*

4 *If the window box is to be replanted with summer bedding next year, keep the plants in their pots, plunged to their rims, so they can be planted out later.*

5 *No matter how attractive foliage plants are, a splash of colour is welcome. Plant polyanthus, winter-flowering pansies or crocus bulbs.*

BRIGHTER WINDOW BOXES

If you plant short-season bedding plants in your window boxes they may be looking rather sad by now. Even boxes containing plants that normally flower well into autumn may have suffered while you were on holiday.

You can plant bulbs immediately but you will have a bare box for a few months, so why not use pot plants for a final fling of brilliant colour for a few weeks?

1 *It is still warm enough to use pot plants for instant colour, and year-round pot chrysanthemums are ideal. Plunge the pots into the compost or peat.*

Peter McHoy

2 *Heathers will also bring instant colour. These are* Erica gracilis, *a tender kind, but you could use hardy ones that you can plant in the garden afterwards.*

REPAIRING A DAMAGED LAWN EDGE

A lawn takes a lot of wear, especially if you have children who use it as a play area or even as a football pitch! Edges are particularly vulnerable and often become trodden down.

Repairs are easy, however, and the result is almost instant. Make good those damaged lawn edges now and the grass will be as good as new by next summer.

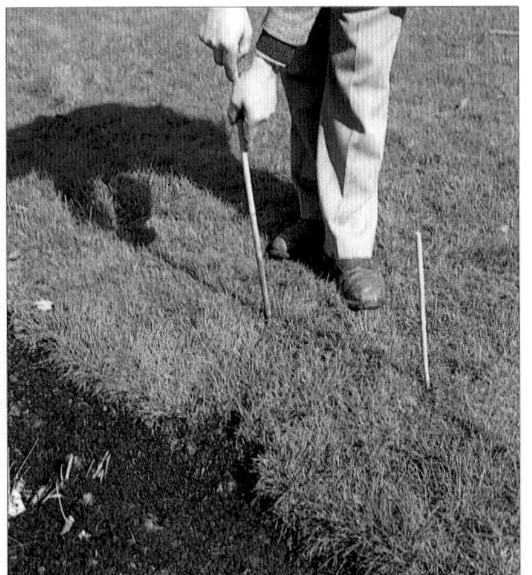

1 *This kind of damage to the edge of a lawn is easily repaired by cutting out the affected area and reversing the turf, leaving it looking as good as new.*

2 *Use canes to mark out a square or rectangle of turf that includes the damaged area. It must be right angled with parallel edges.*

3 *Using a spade (or better still a half-moon edging tool) with a straight-edged piece of timber as a guide, cut a neat rectangle or square.*

4 *Use a spade to slice beneath the area of turf to be repaired. Try to keep the spade blade horizontal to produce a slice of turf of even thickness.*

5 *Once you have cut carefully all the way underneath the piece of turf, lift it up slowly, making sure it stays in one piece.*

6 *Reverse the piece of turf so that the damaged area is on the inside. Press it down to ensure good contact. If need be, add or remove soil to make it level.*

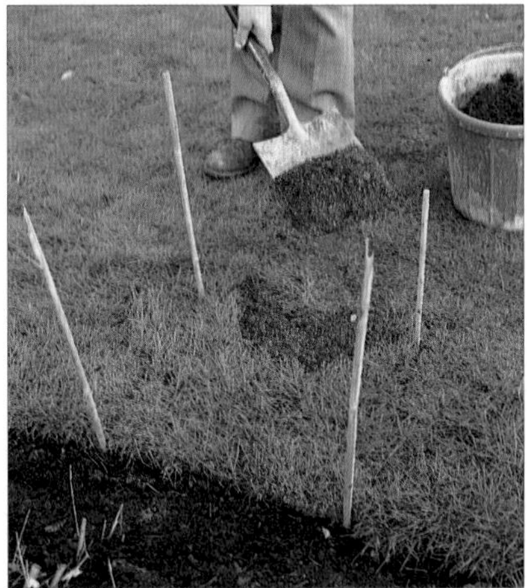

7 *Fill the hole left on the inside with fine soil, and sprinkle some grass seed over the area. Cover with fine netting or a sheet of polythene until it has germinated.*

8 *To prevent future damage you could try edging your lawn with stiff plastic. Wooden planking or bricks are alternative edging materials.*

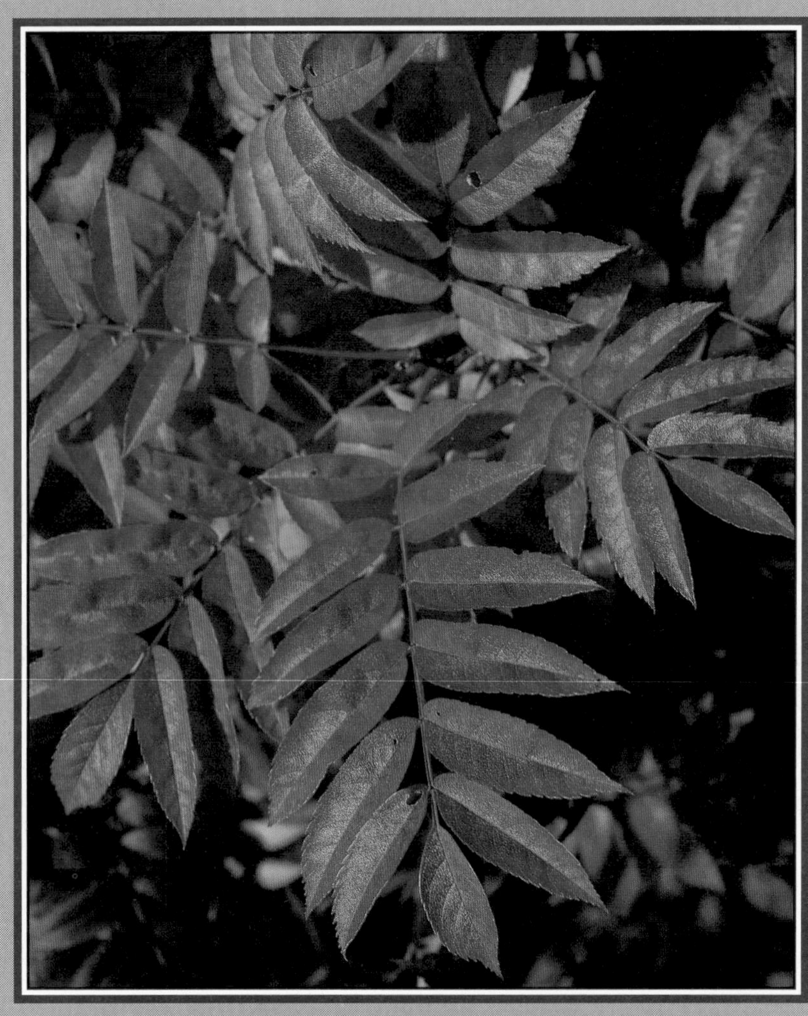

The rich red leaves of the Mountain Ash reflect the autumn sun – enjoy the fruits of your labours before preparing the garden for next year.

AUTUMN

EARLY AUTUMN

MID AUTUMN

LATE AUTUMN

CHECKLIST

WHAT TO DO

BEDS AND BORDERS
Prepare soil for biennials

SHRUBS
Move rooted cuttings of shrubs of doubtful hardiness to a cold frame
Shorten shoots on wisteria

LOOK AHEAD

PROPAGATE
Take semi-ripe cuttings of shrubs such as flowering currant, forsythia and mock orange

PLANT
Spring-flowering bulbs and biennials

SOW
Hardy annuals to overwinter in mild areas
Chives as a decorative border edging

WHAT TO SEE

BORDER PERENNIALS
Californian fuchsia *(Zauschneria californica)*, chrysanthemum, dahlia, Japanese anemone

SHRUBS
Clematis tangutica, fuchsia, heathers, *Hebe* × *andersonii*, *Hebe* 'Autumn Glory', viburnum

BEDDING PLANTS
Aster, begonia, busy Lizzie, bedding dahlia, gazania, geranium (pelargonium), pansy, salvia

BULBS
Acidanthera bicolor, autumn crocuses (colchicums), *Sternbergia lutea*

VISITORS

FRIENDS
Hedgehogs; common blue, peacock, red admiral and small tortoiseshell butterflies

FOES
Blackfly, greenfly, small and large white butterfly caterpillars, squirrels, wasps, weevils

EARLY AUTUMN
WEEK 1

WHAT TO DO

Early autumn is an ideal time to plant biennials and perennials as the ground is still warm enough to encourage root growth. The soil is not usually as dry as in the summer and this means plants become established quickly. And at this time of year the weather is still pleasant enough to make gardening outdoors pleasurable.

Planting priorities

Give priority to spring bedding plants, which will give the best display next year if they are moved early. If you move them later the ground may be too cold and they will take longer to recover from transplanting.

Most bulbs should be planted within the next few weeks if possible, but they will generally flower just as well even if you delay planting for another month, provided they are suitably stored and do not begin to rot. Only early-flowering bulbs require prompt planting. Tulips are perfectly satisfactory if planted in mid autumn, though there is no point in delaying if you have time to plant them now.

Bare root deciduous trees and shrubs are not moved until the leaves have fallen, but evergreens should be planted as soon as possible to allow them to settle before the cold winter winds.

Container-grown trees and shrubs can be planted at any time of the year, but this is a good time to plant them if you can.

Autumn lawn care

If you simply want a play area for the children, moss and coarse grasses in the lawn probably do not matter, but if you want a good sward there are jobs to do.

Lawns gradually build up a 'thatch' of dead grass around the roots, especially if the clippings are not collected. Over a long period this begins to affect the growth of the grass. Scratching out the thatch will often give a lawn the boost that it needs.

Spread a moss killer now on the lawn.

If you have a moderately large lawn, a powered lawn rake is a worthwhile investment. It takes all the hard work out of the job, and will do it both thoroughly and quickly. For a small lawn, however, raking with a lawn rake is perfectly adequate, if a little slower. You must use a lawn rake, however, as an ordinary garden rake will damage the lawn.

Raking will pull out a lot of moss, too, but it will not actually eliminate it. If you have a very mossy lawn the underlying problem may be too much shade – try pruning overhanging trees and shrubs. If the moss is due to poor drainage this is difficult to improve once the lawn has been laid, but it can be done by digging slit drains.

For persistent moss, apply a proprietary moss killer based on dichlorophen or chloroxuron. Do not use lawn sand as a moss killer because it usually contains sulphate of ammonia, which will stimulate the grass too much at this time of year.

Garden hygiene

Keeping beds and borders tidy not only improves the appearance of your garden, it also helps garden hygiene. Weeds allowed to grow and overwinter will not only create a problem for next year but may act as hosts to pests and diseases. Many live on weeds as well as ornamental plants.

Flowerheads left to rot on a plant invite the spores of diseases to germinate. Dead leaves and litter provide ideal hiding places for slugs and other pests.

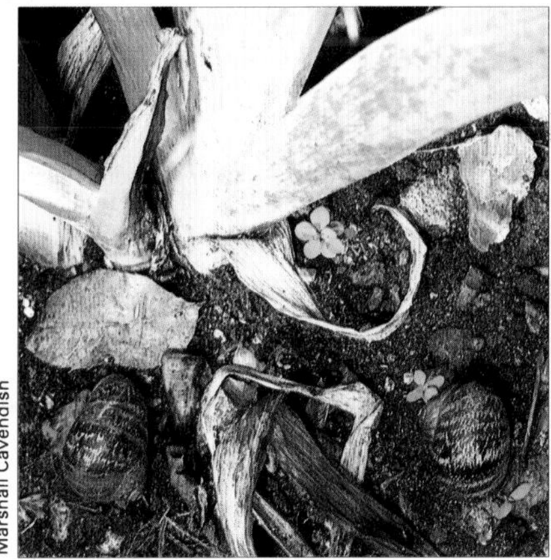

Marshall Cavendish

Remove snails' hiding places by tidying up.

WHAT TO SEE

Autumn-flowering bulbs are now coming into bloom, and you may mistake some for crocuses. There are true crocuses that flower in the autumn, but the plants most often seen are, in fact, imposters. The yellow* Sternbergia lutea *is one of these. It is easy to grow in a warm, sunny and sheltered position and deserves to be better known.

Peter McHoy

Sternbergia lutea *is related to amaryllis.*

The colchicums, popularly known as autumn crocuses, have flowers the shape of true crocuses, but they are much larger and there are double forms. The commonest species is C. autumnale, *the meadow saffron, which has pale pinkish-lilac flowers. There are also pink and white forms with single or double flowers.* C. speciosum *is another good one to try. It stands up to the weather.*

LOOK AHEAD

Propagation is one of the great pleasures of gardening, and there are still plenty of shrubs that can be raised from cuttings taken now. And it is not too late to sow selected seeds. In favourable areas try suitable hardy annuals, or sow a decorative edging of chives along a flower border.

Shrub cuttings

Semi-ripe cuttings of many shrubs will generally root readily if taken now. Semi-ripe cuttings have hardened wood at the base but are still soft at the tip. Root them in pots or in a cold frame. Those to try include berberis, cotoneaster, flowering currant, forsythia, mock orange (philadelphus) and weigela.

VISITORS

There are many kinds of weevil, but those that can cause particular problems for ornamental plants include the leaf weevil, clay coloured weevil and the vine weevil (which does not confine its attentions to vines). Among the plants likely to be attacked by weevils are euonymus, roses and rhododendrons. Adult weevils nibble the edges of leaves, but it is the larvae of the vine weevil that do the most damage, causing pot plants to collapse because the roots have been eaten. If a problem, dust with HCH dust.

Nature Photographers

Vine weevil nibbling at the edge of a leaf.

SOWING HARDY ANNUALS

***If you live in a mild area, you may be able to have some of your annuals in flower much earlier next year by sowing outdoors now. Not all kinds are suitable, but it is worth trying Californian poppies, cornflowers, godetia, love-in-a-mist, pot marigolds (calendulas) and the annual poppy* Papaver rhoeas.**

For the cost of a packet of seeds it is worth having a go – you might be surprised.

1 *Make sure the ground is free of weeds by digging or hoeing, being sure to pull out the roots of any perennial weeds like couch grass. Rake level.*

2 *Take out drills to the recommended depth with the corner of a rake or a hoe. Unless it has been raining, run water into the drills to wet the soil.*

All photos: Marshall Cavendish

3 *If sowing in straight rows, space the drills at the recommended distance. Space the seeds as evenly as you can, so that thinning is easier later.*

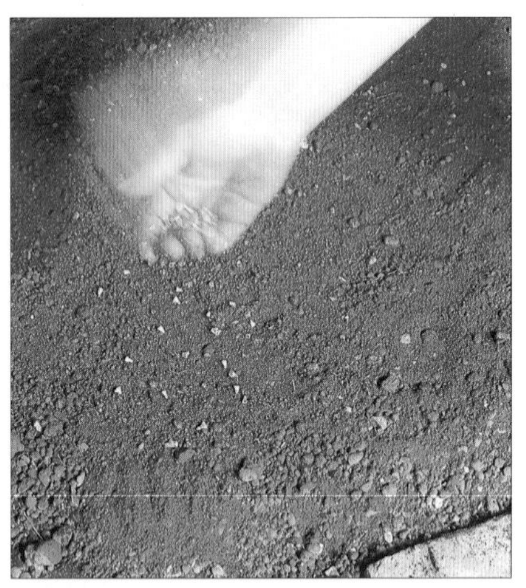

4 *For filling gaps in borders or for an informal cottage-garden effect, you can sow 'broadcast'. Do not bother with drills but simply scatter the seeds.*

5 *Use a rake to draw soil over the seeds. It is especially important to rake in those scattered broadcast on the surface. Do not forget to label them.*

PLANTING BIENNIALS

Biennials for spring flowering, such as forget-me-nots and wallflowers should be planted as soon as possible Follow the advice on the seed packet or plant label with regard to spacing. The more compact varieties are usually planted closer together than standard kinds. You should allow a little extra space if you want to interplant with bulbs such as tulips or hyacinths.

1 *If you have grown your own plants, water the ground thoroughly about an hour before lifting them. Always lift with a good-sized ball of soil if possible.*

2 *If buying the plants, try to buy in pots or strips (wallflowers are sometimes sold in bundles with bare roots). Press the soil firmly around the root-ball.*

PLANTING EVERGREENS

Early autumn is a good time to plant evergreens, especially those sold as 'root-balled' plants (these are lifted from the field instead of being grown in a container, and have a ball of soil held in place with hessian or a plastic fabric). Rhododendrons are often sold this way, and they are likely to be less expensive than equivalent container-grown plants. Plant now while the soil is still warm.

1 *Whether planting a balled or container-grown plant, water it about half an hour before planting. Dig the site, and work in compost or manure.*

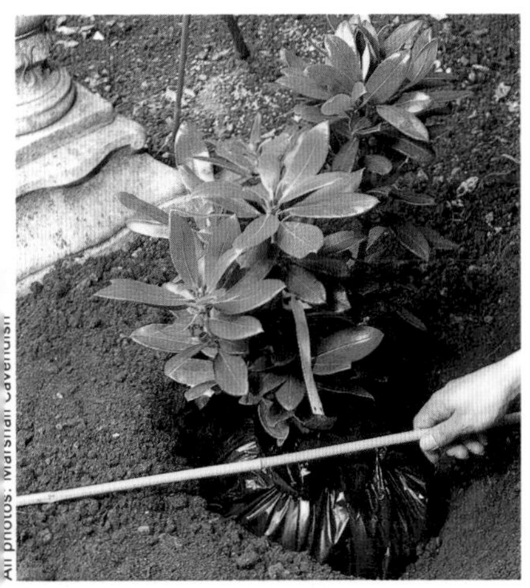

2 *Excavate a hole large enough to take the root-ball, and place the plant in the hole, still root-wrapped or in its pot, to check the depth. Use a cane as a guide.*

All photos: Marshall Cavendish

3 *If planting a container-grown plant, carefully knock it out of its container and tease out a few roots if they have been tightly wound around inside the pot.*

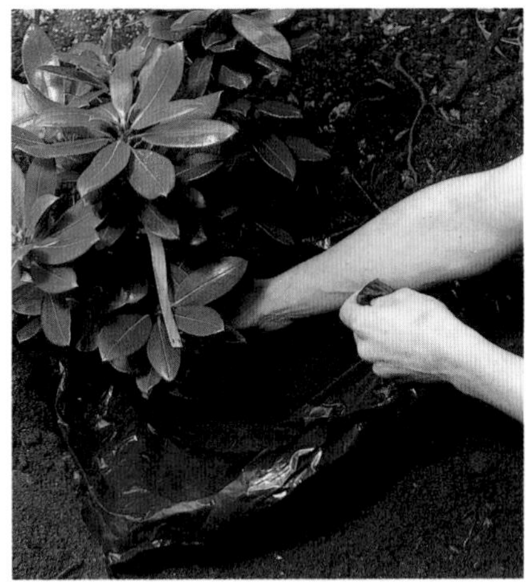

4 *If planting a balled plant, place it in the hole, untie the wrapper and slide it out. Lift the plant slightly as you do so. Never leave the wrapper on.*

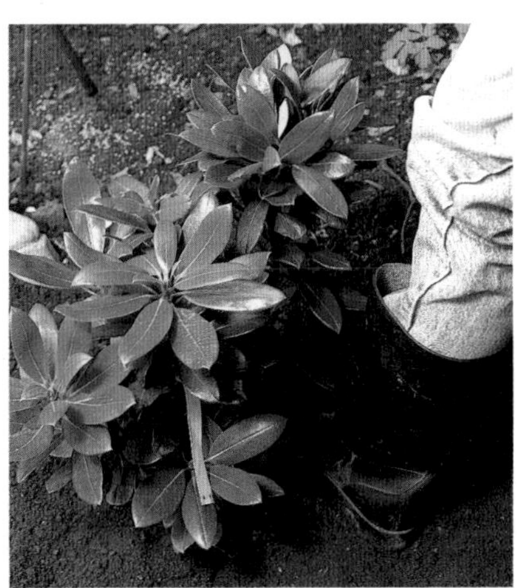

5 *Replace the soil around the roots, being careful not to knock the clump of soil off the roots of a balled plant as you do so. Firm well with your feet.*

6 *Water thoroughly, then apply a mulch of pulverized bark, peat or a peat alternative, or garden compost, but keep it out of direct contact with the stem.*

7 *Evergreens lose moisture through their leaves and may be damaged by cold winter winds. It is worth protecting choice plants for the first winter.*

8 *Make a protective wind shield by fixing several layers of fine mesh netting or a sheet of polythene round four canes, but leave the top open.*

CHECKLIST

WHAT TO DO

LAWNS
Rake and aerate

BEDS AND BORDERS
Plant border biennials

SHRUBS
Move young shrubs not in the right position
Plant evergreens

LOOK AHEAD

TAKE CUTTINGS
Rhododendrons, cypress (*Cupressus* spp.), griselinia and roses

SOW
Sweet peas to overwinter in a frame

WHAT TO SEE

BORDER PERENNIALS
Chrysanthemum, dahlia, golden rod, Japanese anemone, rudbeckia, *Sedum spectabile*

SHRUBS
Strawberry tree (*Arbutus unedo*), *Ceratostigma willmottianum*, *Clematis orientalis*, *Clematis tangutica*, *Fuchsia magellanica*, heathers, *Hebe* × *andersonii*, *Hebe* 'Autumn Glory', hydrangea

BEDDING PLANTS
Aster, begonia, busy Lizzie, bedding dahlia, burning bush (*Kochia scoparia*), French marigolds, geranium (pelargonium)

BULBS
Acidanthera bicolor, autumn crocuses (colchicums), *Sternbergia lutea*

VISITORS

FRIENDS
Peacock, red admiral and small tortoiseshell butterflies

FOES
Blackfly, greenfly, earwigs, rose leaf-hoppers, caterpillars, wasps, weevils

EARLY AUTUMN
WEEK 2

WHAT TO DO

This is the time of year when regional variations begin to become very apparent, with colder areas experiencing chilly days and nights, often with frost, while the milder parts still have the feel of summer. But no matter where you live, it is worth checking the weather forecast regularly so that tender plants can be protected from harmful conditions.

Frost watch

It makes sense to leave tender plants to flower for as long as possible. You can leave those that are dispensed with at the end of the season until they are killed by frost. But there are many tender perennials, such as geraniums (pelargoniums), dahlias and most fuchsias, that you will want to lift and protect so that you can plant them again next year.

Those plants with protected tubers or corms, such as dahlias and gladioli, can be left until the first frosts have arrived. The tops of dahlias will turn black and collapse, but these first frosts are unlikely to be so severe that they penetrate deep enough into the soil to harm the tubers.

Some fuchsias are hardy enough to be left in the garden in many areas, but many of those used in hanging baskets and other containers will be killed if left outside. If you are not overwintering the plants as cuttings, move them to a frost-fre place before severe frosts arrive. is especially important to move a standard fuchsia, which will ha taken years to train, to a frost-fre place now. It may be happy in a conservatory or a warm porch if you do not have a greenhouse.

If you have to save plants threatened by an unexpected ear frost, give priority to tender plants, such as spider plants tha you may have used for bedding, c tradescantias in an outdoor hanging basket.

Most of the seed-raised tender bedding plants are discarded at the end of the season. It is easier to raise fresh ones each year and they are often more compact too.

Marshall Cavendish

Lift bedding begonias to grow on indoors.

Harry Smith Collection

Dahlias soon wilt when caught by the frost.

But some gardeners like to lift a few fibrous-rooted begonias or busy Lizzies to grow on as pot plants indoors for a few more weeks. These must be taken indoors before the first frost.

Border maintenance

Once the majority of plants begin to look decidedly dejected, it is time to tidy the borders. Even though there will be areas that look quite bare after you have done it, the border will look much neater and smarter, and those plants that are still blooming well will stand out that much more effectively.

Herbaceous border plants that flowered during the summer and now have straggly and yellowing foliage are best clipped back with shears to just above ground level. The leaves of some plants, such as bear's breeches (Acanthus mollis and A. spinosus), will probably still look good, so just clip off dead flower spikes and damaged leaves to leave a mound of decorative foliage.

Most plant labels fade in time, or become brittle and snap. If you do not replace them while the old ones are still legible or your memory fresh, the chances are you will have more unidentified plants in your garden. Write new ones now, as you will have too many other tasks next spring.

Plant border biennials

Although most biennials, such as wallflowers and forget-me-nots, are planted in beds or containers, some biennials are more appropriate for the herbaceous or mixed border. Canterbury bells and sweet Williams are among those that look good in a border. Some short-lived perennials, such as hollyhocks, are often treated as biennials. This reduces the risk of hollyhock rust becoming a

Harry Smith Collection

Canterbury bells bloom from spring to summer.

problem with this species.

You can buy most of these plants now, so use them to fill gaps in the border.

Bulbs for the border

Use spring-flowering bulbs such as daffodils and crown imperial (Fritillaria imperialis) to fill gaps in the border. Plant some lilies, too, for a stunning effect next summer.

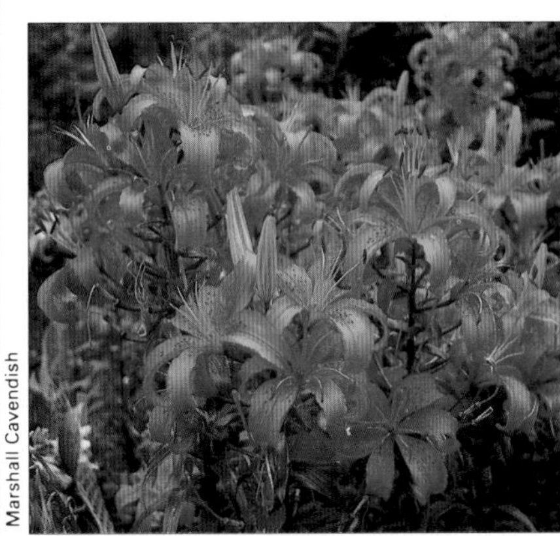

Marshall Cavendish

Lilies always look spectacular.

WHAT TO SEE

The Abyssinian gladiolus (Acidanthera murielae) deserves to be better known and more widely grown. It lacks the impact of a proper gladiolus, but flowers in autumn and contributes a special beauty late in the season. The sweetly scented

Photos Horticultural

Acidanthera (or Gladiolus callianthus).

flowers are white with a purple blotch in the centre.

Acidantheras are best planted in a border or in front of a warm, sunny wall. Except in very mild districts, the corms will have to be lifted and stored in a frost-free place over the winter.

VISITORS

Rose leaf-hoppers produce a second generation of adults about now and they can be a problem in some gardens. The insects look like little green bugs, and can be seen jumping and flying from one leaf to another. Affected leaves, which often drop prematurely, show tell-tale fine white mottling on the upper surface.

Control is relatively easy if you use a contact insecticide, such as malathion, or a systemic one, like dimethoate. Any spray that you use against greenfly will have some effect.

Photos Horticultural

Leaf-hopper damage to rose leaves.

TAKING ROSE CUTTINGS

Most roses that you buy are grafted or budded. These are difficult techniques for an amateur, so it is worth trying cuttings for those roses that may do well on their own roots. Ramblers and most climbers should do well, and vigorous floribunda (cluster-flowered) roses are also worth trying, as well as miniatures. Large-flowered (hybrid tea) roses can be difficult.

1 *Choose a mature side shoot of a rambler or climber, and take a cutting about 30cm/12in long. The shoot should have been produced this year.*

2 *Trim off the weak top of the shoot, to leave the cutting about 23cm/9in long, and trim the bottom off straight just below a leaf joint and bud.*

All photos Peter McHoy

3 *Remove the thorns by pressing them sideways with a thumb so that they snap off, then trim off the lower leaves, leaving just one pair at the top.*

4 *In a shady but not dry part of the garden, excavate a shallow slit about 15cm/6in deep, with one edge straight. Put coarse sand in the bottom.*

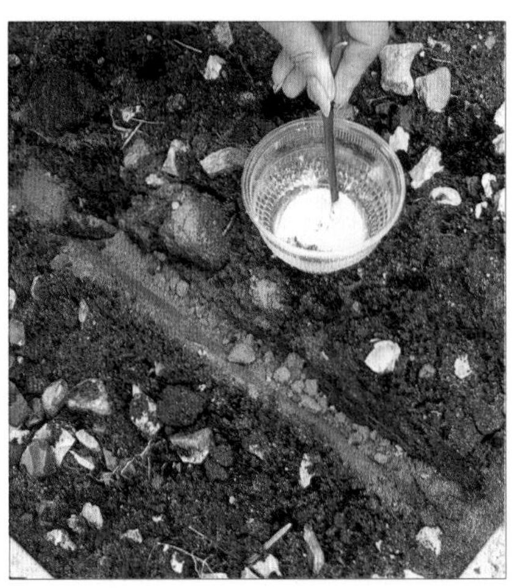

5 *It will increase the chances of rooting if the bottom of each cutting is dipped in a rooting hormone. Space the cuttings about 15cm/6in apart.*

6 *Firm the soil around the cuttings to eliminate air pockets, and water well. Keep watered in dry spells. Plants should be ready to move in 12-15 months.*

7 *Cuttings of vigorous floribunda (cluster-flowered) roses can be taken in the same way. Choose a mature side shoot from growth produced this year.*

8 *Miniature roses are easily raised from cuttings, and they will remain dwarf. Make the cuttings about 8cm/3in long and insert around a pot.*

AUTUMN LAWN CARE

Lawns take a lot of punishment and they welcome a little kindness at this time of year. The grass is still growing strongly enough to respond to a manicure and overhaul so that it starts the winter in good condition. If you do not feel able to tackle the whole treatment, do some of the jobs this autumn, and the rest next spring or autumn. If moss is a problem you will want to make the moss treatment a priority.

1 *Raking the grass with a lawn rake will help to prevent a 'thatch' of dead grass building up, which in time causes the lawn to deteriorate.*

2 *Besides removing dead grass and debris from around the base of the grass plants, raking will also remove much of the moss if this is a problem.*

All photos Peter McHoy

3 *After raking, aerate the lawn. You can buy tools that remove a core of soil, but you can improvize by pushing the prongs of a fork 15cm/6in into the ground.*

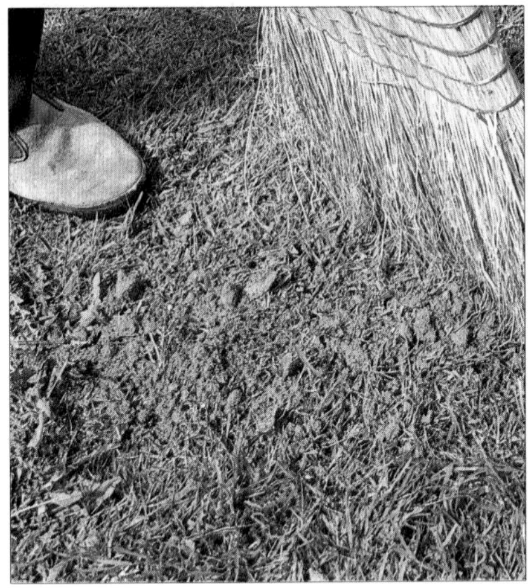

4 *If you garden on heavy clay, brush sand into the holes; if you garden on sandy soil, brush in peat to improve the structure and encourage root growth.*

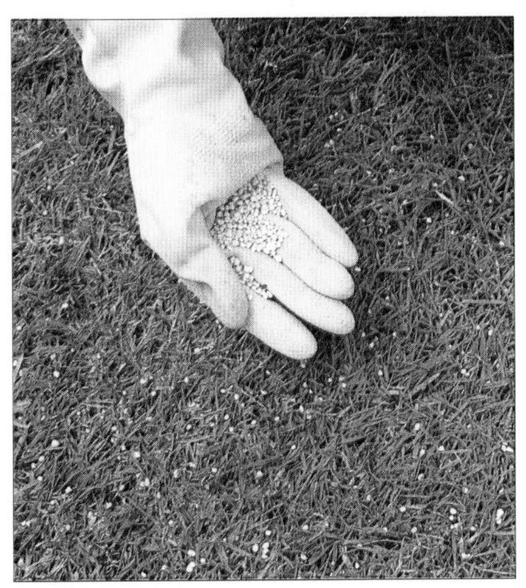

5 *If the grass has been looking yellow or the growth poor, apply a lawn feed. Use one intended for autumn; summer feeds have too much nitrogen.*

6 *If moss is a problem, use a moss killer intended for autumn use (the type known as lawn sand may contain too much nitrogen for use at this time).*

7 *Smarten up the edges by using edging shears or a nylon-line trimmer to cut long grass. If the edge is uneven, use a half-moon edger against a straight-edge.*

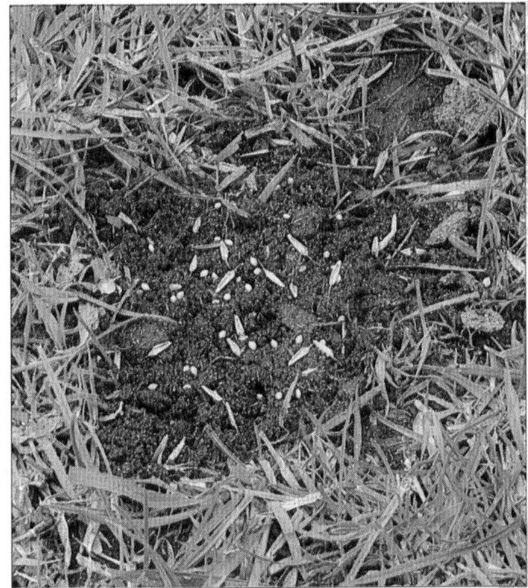

8 *Bare patches can be reseeded very successfully now. Small amounts of seed are available for this job. Loosen the surface first, and keep moist.*

WHAT TO DO

LAWNS
Rake and aerate

BEDS AND BORDERS
Plant spring bedding

SHRUBS
Plant evergreens

LOOK AHEAD

TAKE CUTTINGS
Box, conifers, rhododendrons, roses

SOW
Sweet peas to overwinter in a frame

PLANT
Spring-flowering bulbs
Lilies for summer borders

WHAT TO SEE

BORDER PERENNIALS
Chrysanthemum, dahlia, Japanese anemone, rudbeckia, *Sedum spectabile*

SHRUBS
Strawberry tree, *Ceratostigma willmottianum, Fuchsia magellanica*

BEDDING PLANTS
Burning bush (*Kochia scoparia*), French marigolds, geranium (pelargonium)

BULBS
Acidanthera bicolor, autumn crocuses (colchicums), kaffir lily (schizostylis), *Sternbergia lutea*

VISITORS

FRIENDS
Swallows and house martins; red admiral, painted lady and peacock butterflies

FOES
Rose leaf-hoppers, small and large white butterfly caterpillars, wasps, weevils

EARLY AUTUMN

WEEK 3

WHAT TO DO

This is a time for note-taking, recording the successes and failures of the summer to take into account next year, and deciding what to grow for late colour this time next year. It is worth making a special effort to grow plenty of plants that bridge the gap between the flowers of summer and the colourful foliage and berries later in the autumn.

Weather wise

Keep an eye on the weather forecasts so that you can bring in any vulnerable plants if frost threatens.

It is possible to prolong flowering of bedding plants like buzy Lizzies by covering them with newspaper when a light frost is forecast. This is not practical for a large number of plants but for a small bed or a window box or trough it can be worthwhile. Use plenty of sheets, and peg them down with canes to prevent them blowing about. Remove them in the morning.

If a prolonged cold snap is forecast it is not worth attempting to protect tender plants like this.

If house and greenhouse plants that have been standing outside for the summer have not yet been brought in, do so without delay. This applies to plants like Christmas and Easter cacti, indoor azaleas, and other pot plants that are not particularly decorative during the summer and benefit from a spell outdoors.

Pat Brindley

Easter cactus needs protection from frost.

Pest patrol

It is tempting to ease up on pest and disease control towards the end of the season, but infestations left untreated now may quickly build up to problem proportions next year.

It is worth taking a walk round the garden looking for potential problems. Often by nipping them in the bud you save work later. Few of us actually look for trouble, but this is one occasion when it is worthwhile.

Simple garden hygiene, like picking up dead and rotting leaves and debris, will eliminate many of the hiding places for slugs, snails and woodlice.

Plant border perennials

This is a good time to fill gaps in the herbaceous border. Garden centres usually have a good selection of basic border plants, but to save money you can divide and replant existing ones. They will fill out well next year.

WHAT TO SEE

Chrysanthemums are among the most magnificent autumn flowers, yet they are not widely grown as border plants. Because some have huge show-bench blooms people sometimes assume that they are difficult to grow. If you choose the right types, however, they are no more difficult than, say, Michaelmas daisies or dahlias.

If you want plants that you can leave in the ground like ordinary border plants, choose varieties of Dendranthemum zawadskii *– like the florist's spray chrysanthemums but hardy. This species makes a dome-shaped plant about 75cm/2½ft tall, covered with pink daisy-type flowers, but there are*

The early flowering pompon 'Mei-kyo'.

varieties in a range of colours. 'Clara Curtis' is a clear pink, 'Duchess of Edinburgh' is copper red and 'Mary Stoker' is an attractive peachy yellow.

Korean dendranthemums are also hardy, and these form low mounds of blooms in a whole range of colours at this time of year. They resemble small spray chrysanthemums.

The traditional outdoor spray chrysanthemums that are popular with enthusiasts can be used in the herbaceous border. The roots are usually lifted for the winter, except in the mildest areas, and fresh plants are raised from cuttings in the spring.

LOOK AHEAD

Hedges require a lot of plants, but you can keep the cost down by raising your own from cuttings. Most conifers and evergreens, such as box and yew can be rooted from cuttings taken now.

Gillian Beckett

Pot up semi-ripe conifer cuttings now.

If you do not already have a suitable mature plant from which you can take the cuttings, buy a few large young plants from a garden centre to provide suitable cuttings material.

Whenever possible, take all the cuttings from the same plant, as this will ensure even growth – that is especially important for dwarf box hedges.

For fast rooting, use a heated propagator if you have one, otherwise put them in a garden frame, or even in pots on a light windowsill, covered with a polythene bag to retain humidity.

Conifers such as cypress (cupressus), false cypress (chamaecyparis) and arbor-vitae (thuja) can all be propagated from semi-ripe cuttings taken now. Make sure there is at least 12mm/½in of brown, well-ripened wood at the base of the cuttings. Yew is best grown in a propagator.

VISITORS

Swallows and house martins are among the many migrants that are likely to be gathering for their long migration back to Africa. Swallows traditionally herald the summer (though they actually arrive in mid spring) and it is always sad when they depart on their return journey. Make the best of their company when they come swooping down into the garden to catch insects on the wing.

House martins will also be departing about now, and these are especially companionable. As their name implies, they nest on houses. They can be distinguished from the swallow by the shallower fork in the tail and the noticeable white rump which is visible in flight. If you live in a rural or suburban area they may have left the remains of their homes under the eaves of the roof. These cup-shaped mud nests are constructed from pellets of mud bound with grass and hair and mixed with saliva. This hard-wearing cement is surprisingly robust.

Among the arrivals to look out for are fieldfares and redwings. They generally only venture into town gardens when the going gets tough in the winter, feeding on the berries on our trees and shrubs when wild supplies are over.

E.A. Janes/Nature Photographers

House martins gathering before migration.

LIFTING GLADIOLI

The early flowering varieties of gladioli will be ready for lifting soon. In very mild areas they can be left in the ground if you do not mind taking a risk, otherwise lift them and store the corms in a frost-free place.

If you have a little patience it is worth taking the opportunity to use the cormels (tiny corms that form around the base of the old corm) to increase your stock of plants. They should flower in about two years.

Gladiolus byzantinus *is a fully hardy species and is one of the few gladiolis that can be left undisturbed in the ground over the winter.*

1 *Use a garden fork around the base of the plant to loosen the soil. The corm should come from the loosened ground easily if you pull gently on the stem.*

All photos Marshall Cavendish

2 *Trim off most of the foliage and let the plants dry for a few days. When dry, remove any soil and cut off the old stems with a sharp knife.*

3 *Remove the cormels from around the base of the old corm. If you want to use them for propagation, store and plant out in a nursery bed next year.*

4 *Dust the corms with a fungicide, such as sulphur, and store in open boxes or paper bags in an airy, frost-free place. Check periodically for pests or diseases.*

TYING IN CLIMBERS

Climbers and wall shrubs will have made a lot of growth during the summer, and need to be tied to support wires or secured with wall fixings before the autumn gales damage them.

If horizontal wires are already fixed to the wall, tie the shoots to these. If there are only a few shoots, vine eyes or other fixings can be used to secure them. Some come with a kind of super-glue that makes fixing easy.

1 *Raffia or a soft string that will eventually disintegrate is better than synthetic string that may cut into the stem as it expands. Tie loosely but securely*

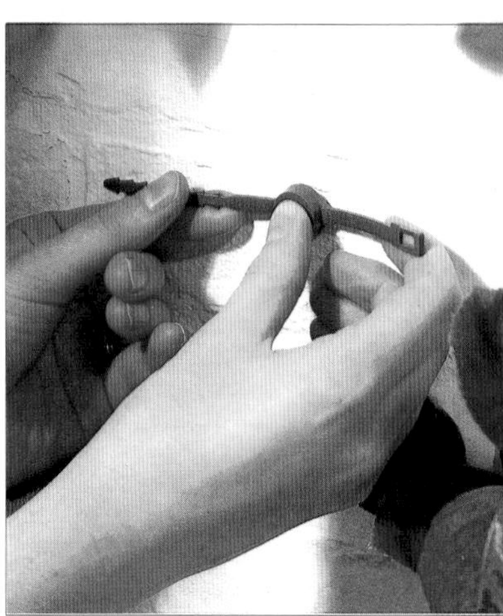

2 *This tie uses an epoxy bond which w[ill] stick to any wall, even a pebble-dash finish. Use it where just a few ties are needed, perhaps for a rose around the door*

LANTING SPRING BEDDING

Spring bedding should be planted as soon as possible now so that it has a chance to become well established before the cold weather arrives. Although beds of a single kind of plant can be very effective, do not be afraid to try mixing different kinds, such as wallflowers and forget-me-nots, to add variety and extend the season of interest. Try interplanting with bulbs for more colour.

1 *Clear the bed of any remaining summer bedding, then fork over the ground. Deep digging is unnecessary and you do not need to add compost.*

2 *Make sure all weeds are removed, then rake the ground level. Add a sprinkling of bone meal, but do not use any fertilizer containing a lot of nitrogen.*

3 *Space out the plants on the ground before planting, so that you know you have enough for the area. Allow extra spacing if planting more than one kind.*

4 *Lay the next kind of plant in position on the soil such as forget-me-nots between wallflowers. It may be necessary to respace them slightly.*

5 *Plant them with a trowel and firm them in well with the hands. Remove any foot marks as you proceed, unless bulbs still have to be planted.*

6 *If planting bulbs, lay them out between the plants first, so that you know you have enough to complete the bed. You may need to adjust spacing.*

7 *Plant the bulbs with a trowel – a bulb planter is not so convenient in this situation. After burying the bulbs, loosen any soil compacted by your feet.*

John Glover/Garden Picture Library

8 *Bulbs such as grape hyacinths can be used to edge the bed, but winter-flowering pansies are particularly popular. Primulas will also look good.*

CHECKLIST

WHAT TO DO

LAWNS
Rake and aerate

BEDS AND BORDERS
Finish planting spring bedding
Bring in tender pot plants
Protect tender plants if frost threatens
Lift dahlias and tuberous begonias

SHRUBS
Check ties on wall shrubs and standard roses
Plant hedges

LOOK AHEAD

TAKE CUTTINGS
Box, cotton lavender, rhododendrons, roses

PLANT
Spring-flowering bulbs
Lilies for summer borders

WHAT TO SEE

BORDER PERENNIALS
Chrysanthemum, dahlia, Michaelmas daisies

SHRUBS
Strawberry tree, heathers (varieties of *Calluna vulgaris*), *Hebe* 'Autumn Glory', mountain ash (berries), viburnum (berries)

BEDDING PLANTS
Aster, burning bush (*Kochia scoparia*), French marigolds, geranium (pelargonium)

BULBS
Autumn crocuses (colchicums), kaffir lily (schizostylis), *Sternbergia lutea*

VISITORS

FRIENDS
Painted lady, peacock and red admiral butterflies

FOES
Blackfly, cats, greenfly, small white and large white butterfly caterpillars, weevils

EARLY AUTUMN
WEEK 4

WHAT TO DO

The weather at this time of year can be unpredictable. Some years have an Indian summer at this time, with warm days and still plenty of colour in the garden. In other years even the mild areas experience quite severe frosts. Gales are to be expected. It is a time for enjoying the good days and being vigilant in the garden on the bad ones.

Check ties
Windy weather can be a particular problem at this time when many shrubs are still fully clothed with summer leaves and offer much more wind resistance than in winter.

Spend half an hour tying in shoots on wall-trained shrubs, pruning out any growing in the wrong direction or extending beyond their allotted space. Check tree stakes and ties (it is not a good idea to stake trees for too long – it can produce a weaker tree than one allowed to flex in the wind). It is worth checking existing tree ties as they may require loosening so that they do not restrict the expanding stem and damage the plant.

Harry Smith Collection

Make sure your ties are secure, but give trees and plants room to move.

Overwinter geraniums
The best way to save your old geranium (pelargonium) plants for another year is to keep them in a frost-free place indoors or in the greenhouse. But if your window-sills are full and you do not have a greenhouse you might have to resort to some of the less reliable methods.

Marshall Cavendish

Geranium trays can be kept on windowsills.

Try packing a number of plants close together in large pots or deep trays – you will have to shake most of the soil off the roots and remove some of the leaves – so that you can pack more on your window-sills. Or keep them on a window-sill in the garage with a mini-heater turned on just to keep the frost away.

If you do not have space even for this, lift the plants, trim off the leaves but keep a ball of soil around the roots, then pack them in dry peat or vermiculite in deep boxes. Place the boxes in a cold frame or garage and cover with another thick layer of peat or vermiculite to insulate them. If you cannot even do this, dig a trench about 30cm/1ft deep in the ground, and lay the plants in this, covering them with a layer of peat or vermiculite then returning the soil. You may lose them, but often they can be retrieved in spring and potted up to make a gradual recovery.

WHAT TO SEE

Eric Crichton

S. coccinea *'Major' brightens any border.*

The kaffir lily (*Schizostylis*) deserves to be more widely grown. It makes a bold show in the border just when a boost of late colour is needed, and it will produce its rather fragile looking spikes of red or pink flowers right to the end of autumn.

Kaffir lilies are actually members of the iris family and not lilies at all. They look best in well-established clumps that have been left undisturbed to multiply. In mild parts of the country you will have no problem growing them, but in cold parts they are not dependably hardy. They can often be overwintered successfully outdoors in borderline areas by covering the roots with a layer of bracken or leaves before the severe weather arrives.

The plant commonly grown is S. coccinea *'Major', with deep red flowers, but others that you may find include 'Mrs Hegarty' (clear pink), 'Sunrise' (salmon) and 'Viscountess Bying' (pale pink). There are less common varieties, including a white one (*S.c. alba*).*

The time to plant kaffir lilies is early spring, but make a note of which you like best now, and order them for spring delivery from specialist border plant nurseries or from bulb merchants. You may also find them in some garden centres.

LOOK AHEAD

There is still time to plant spring-flowering bulbs if you have not already done so. Tulips in particular are often best planted during the next couple of weeks, but the choice of varieties in the shops is often very limited towards the end of the season, so buy your bulbs now if you have not already done so.

Bulbs such as daffodils are often reduced in price towards the end of the planting season, and although it is not wise to delay, because bulbs can deteriorate, this is often a good way to fill a large area that you want to plant with naturalized bulbs.

New plants from suckers

*Some suckering shrubs provide 'instant' stock to plant elsewhere, or to give to friends. Snowberry (*Symphoricarpos*) and the stag's horn sumach (*Rhus typhina*) sometimes produce suckers – shoots arising from the roots around the plant. By severing these and replanting them you can increase your plants with the minimum of effort.*

This is not a good idea if the plants are budded or grafted onto a rootstock, however, like most lilacs and some rhododendrons. Shoots arising from the base of these plants will be those of the rootstock, which will almost certainly have inferior flowers to those produced by the main plant.

Andrew Lawson

Stag's horn sumach often produces suckers which can be replanted.

VISITORS

At this time of year, when the ground has probably been cultivated and bulbs and spring bedding planted, cats can be a nuisance. Being clean animals, they always dig themselves a hole and tend to choose soft, freshly cultivated soil. And as many cat owners know they often prefer to use a neighbour's garden. Even cat lovers can find it frustrating to have their bulbs and plants dug up.

A few simple tricks will reduce the problem. Keeping the recently cultivated areas well watered may help deter the cats, and the plants will benefit too. Pepper dust and other proprietary repellents have some effect.

Peter McHoy

Cats can curl up in annoying places.

LIFT DAHLIAS

As soon as the tops of your dahlias have been blackened by frost you can lift the tubers to store them for the winter. There is no need to lift them before the first frost, but do so before penetrating frosts reach the tubers.

Seed-raised bedding dahlias are generally discarded and fresh plants raised or bought each year, but you can save the tubers if you think it is worth doing so. Be sure to store them in a frost-free place.

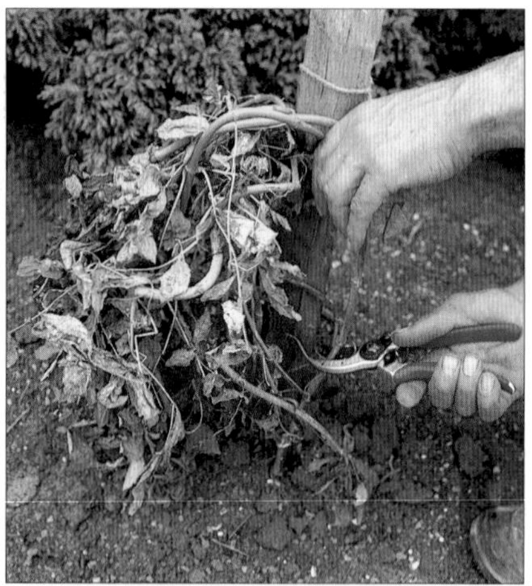

1 *Once your dahlias have been blackened by frost, cut off the dead tops an inch or two above ground level. Put them on the compost heap.*

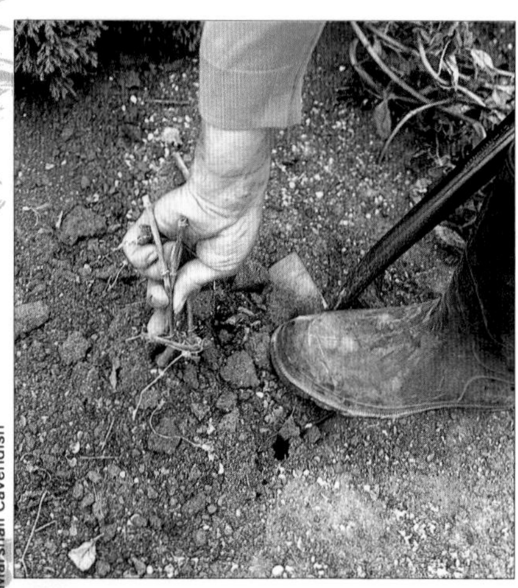

Marshall Cavendish

2 *Lift the tubers with a garden fork, or a spade if this is more convenient, being careful not to spike or slice the tubers as you do so.*

3 *Rub off any surplus soil. If the soil is reasonably dry it will come off easily, but if it is wet you may have to dry off the tubers first.*

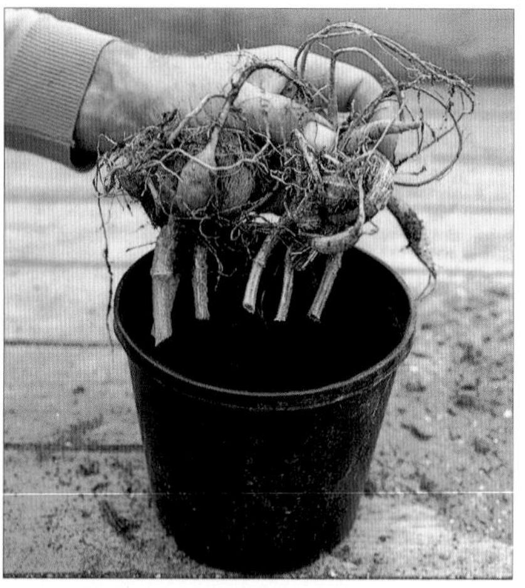

4 *Make sure the tubers have dried off before storing. Stand them upside down, in trays or in empty pots, in a frost-free place indoors or in the greenhouse.*

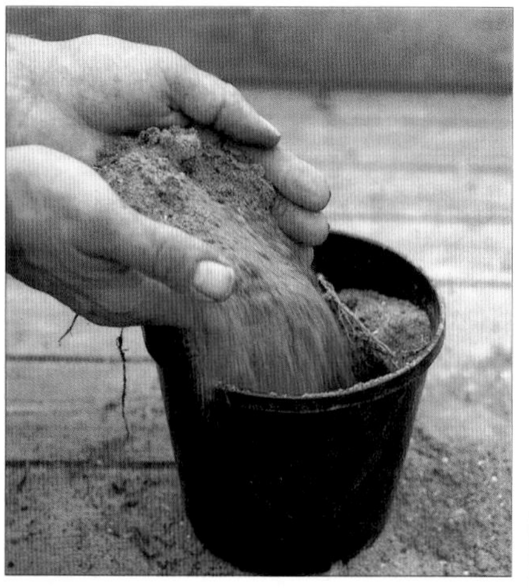

5 *When dry, trim off surplus stem, but keep the clump intact – if you pull off individual tubers they may not grow. Cover with sand, peat or vermiculite.*

LIFT TUBEROUS BEGONIAS

The small-flowered fibrous-rooted begonias (Begonia semperflorens varieties) used for summer bedding are discarded once they are killed by frost. Lift one or two before the first frost to grow in pots.

The larger-flowered tuberous bedding begonias can be saved for another year. Like dahlias they must be stored in a frost-free place until next spring.

1 *Lift your begonia tubers before the first frost (they sit near the surface and are not buried deeply like dahlias). Plant in trays of moist peat until the leaves drop.*

Vana Hagerty

2 *Once the leaves have fallen, break off the stem and allow the tubers to dry off. Store in dry peat, vermiculite or sand, or in paper bags, in a frost-free place.*

SOW SWEET PEAS

It comes as a surprise to many people that autumn is the time when most sweet pea experts sow their seeds, but sweet peas are tough plants and by sowing now you will have plants in flower weeks or months ahead of those sown in the spring.

You can sow them where the plants are to flower, but it is much better to grow them in pots and keep them in a cold frame – they do not require heat.

1 *To speed germination soak the seeds in water overnight before sowing. Do not leave them for longer, otherwise they may rot before they germinate.*

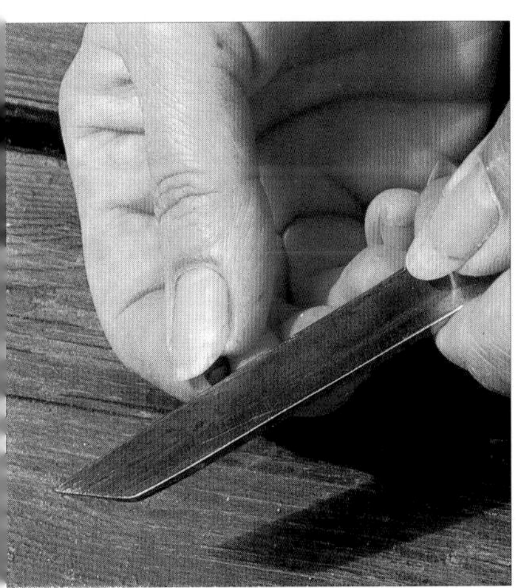

2 *Some sweet peas have a very hard seed coat. If there are any black seeds that have not absorbed water, nick them opposite the 'eye'.*

3 *If sowing directly in the open ground, dust the seeds with a fungicidal seed dressing. Do this even if sowing in pots if the seeds are very pale or mottled.*

4 *Fill small 8-10cm/3-4in pots with a good seed compost, such as John Innes seed compost. A loam-based compost is preferable at this time of year.*

5 *Using a dibber or a pencil, make holes about 15mm/¾in deep, and insert the seeds. Sow four to seven seeds in a 10cm/4in pot. Cover with compost.*

6 *Label the seeds carefully, so that you do not forget the varieties by next spring, and keep them in a cold frame or a cool or unheated greenhouse.*

7 *Cover the pots with a piece of glass or fine-mesh netting to protect the seed from mice. Remove when the seeds have germinated. Keep watered but not wet.*

8 *Although germination will be less satisfactory, you can sow in the ground where the plants are to flower. Sweet peas are very hardy.*

CHECKLIST

WHAT TO DO

BEDS AND BORDERS
Lift and store tender bulbs, corms, tubers
Cut back herbaceous plants and tidy borders

SHRUBS
Trim back long shoots that are casting shade
Check ties on wall shrubs and standard roses

LOOK AHEAD

TAKE CUTTINGS
Box, cotton lavender

DIVIDE
Bergenias

SOW
Sweet peas to overwinter in a frame

PLANT
Spring-flowering bulbs
Lilies for summer borders

WHAT TO SEE

BORDER PERENNIALS
Chrysanthemum, dahlia, Michaelmas daisies

SHRUBS
Strawberry tree (*Arbutus unedo*), cotoneaster (berries), sorbus (berries)

BEDDING PLANTS
(*until cut back by frost*)
Burning bush (*Kochia scoparia*), French marigolds, geranium (pelargonium)

BULBS
Autumn crocuses (colchicums), Guernsey lily (*Nerine bowdenii*), kaffir lily (schizostylis)

VISITORS

FRIENDS
Hedgehogs, squirrels

FOES
Blackfly, greenfly, weevils

EARLY AUTUMN

WEEK 5

WHAT TO DO

The transition from summer to winter is often very pronounced at this time. The garden can look rather dejected, with summer-flowering plants dying and some perhaps blackened by frost. The beauties of the season, with its autumn tints, berries and the odd late-flowering plant, can be lost if surrounded by the remnants of summer. If you clear these up, however, the gems of autumn can be seen in all their glory.

Autumn clean

Tidy beds and borders as a priority. Go round with a pair of shears, secateurs, hoe and a barrow, and work your way round the garden methodically. It is better to tidy up one part thoroughly first, rather than simply cutting back a few plants here and there. By concentrating on one bed or part of a border, you will see immediate improvements.

Cut back all herbaceous border plants except those that flower late and, of course, those few evergreen types, such as elephant's ears (bergenias). It is worth leaving the foliage on bear's breeches (acanthus), as this is big and bold and will remain satisfyingly showy until the really bad weather arrives.

Harry Smith Collection

Trim borders to improve autumn looks.

Clip back any shrubs that have outgrown their space. Proper pruning may be necessary, too, but even shrubs that do not require regular pruning, such as many evergreens, benefit from being trimmed back to size.

Finally, remove any large weeds by hand, then hoe to kill any weed seedlings and to make the earth look more presentable.

Buy and plant

Bare-root trees and shrubs are not planted until the leaves have fallen and they are dormant. Most of us, however, buy container-grown plants. The sooner these are put in, the better chance they will have of making some new root growth before winter sets in.

Lift and store

Tender plants, like dahlias, geraniums (pelargoniums) and most fuchsias (not hardy types), should be taken into a frost-free place as soon as possible.

Lift tubers and corms of plants like dahlias and gladioli before penetrating frosts can reach them

Marshall Cavendish

Ensure bulbs are healthy.

Plant bulbs

Bulbs should be planted without delay. Make sure they are still firm and healthy; do not plant any that are going soft or mouldy, or already have long shoots.

WHAT TO SEE

The Guernsey lily* (Nerine bowdenii) *will flower from early to late autumn. In most places it is at its best in mid autumn, when it will provide an excellent focal point for this time of year. The big heads of pink flowers, on stems about 45-60cm/1½-2ft tall, appear before the leaves and are all the more striking for that.

If planted in front of a wall, perhaps in a narrow bed in front of the house, or with dark shrubs as a background, it will add the kind of vibrant colour that takes the eye across the garden.

Guernsey lilies are outstanding, not only because they flower so late but also for so long . . . they last for weeks and also make great long-lasting cut flowers.

They are more expensive than most common daffodils and hyacinths, but with a little care they will be an investment that will reap dividends for years. In the right site, they can be left to grow and multiply for many seasons to come.

For such a rewarding plant you need to make a special effort to choose a suitable spot. It is not fully hardy everywhere, so plant it in a sunny, south-facing position.

Buy and plant in spring. 'Fenwick's Variety' is a good, deep pink form to look for.

Pat Brindley

The Guernsey lily thrives in autumn.

LOOK AHEAD

Fresh herbs in winter are always welcome. So, if you have herbs in pots or other containers that can be moved, why not take them into a cold greenhouse or conservatory, or even into a very light room? Chervil, parsley, sage and thyme should retain leaves through the winter.

Harry Smith Collection

Bay, mint and parsley do well indoors.

Bay is fairly hardy and in most winters it will survive outdoors, but the leaves are then often windburned and unappetizing. If you can, take your container-grown bay tree into the shelter of a conservatory.

Always trim back any straggly growth and remove any dying or diseased leaves before moving herbs into the greenhouse or conservatory.

Chives and mint are best cut back so that new shoots are produced as soon as there is sufficient warmth and light to stimulate growth.

Do not feed the plants, and give them only enough water to prevent the compost drying out.

VISITORS

Hedgehogs are welcome visitors, not only because they are great fun to watch as they explore the garden on a summer's evening but also because they help to control many garden pests. Their diet includes beetles, caterpillars, slugs and earwigs.

Unfortunately many die because they find the centre of an unlit bonfire or a pile of rubbish a particularly desirable residence. Before you light that autumn bonfire have a quick check to make sure that it is only rubbish that you are burning.

If you know that hedgehogs visit your garden, encourage them by providing a winter shelter. A simple lean-to of wood, against a shed or the garden fence, may be enough to tempt them to take up residence and stay with you next year. Fill it with straw.

Don Wildridge

Make your local hedgehog welcome.

PROPAGATE ELEPHANT'S EARS

Elephant's ears (bergenias) make excellent evergreen ground cover plants, but it can be expensive to buy enough plants to cover a large area. If you propagate your own you will have enough plants to use them freely as ground cover or to plant them at the edge of a pond or in the front of a border. If you do not already have a plant, buy a few good-sized specimens from a garden centre.

1 Bergenias make excellent ground cover by suppressing weeds with their evergreen leaves. You will need enough plants to set them about 30cm/12in apart.

All photos Peter McHoy

2 Lift a well established plant with a garden fork. The rhizomes lie close to the surface, so the plants will come up very easily.

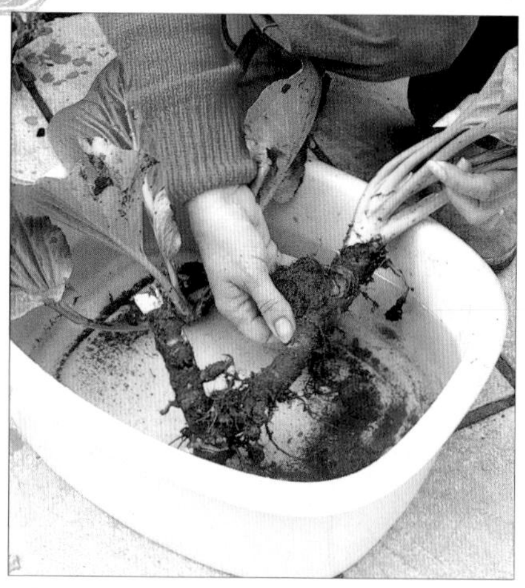

3 Although not essential, you may find it easier to work with the plants if you wash the soil off the rhizomes, but be careful not to damage the roots.

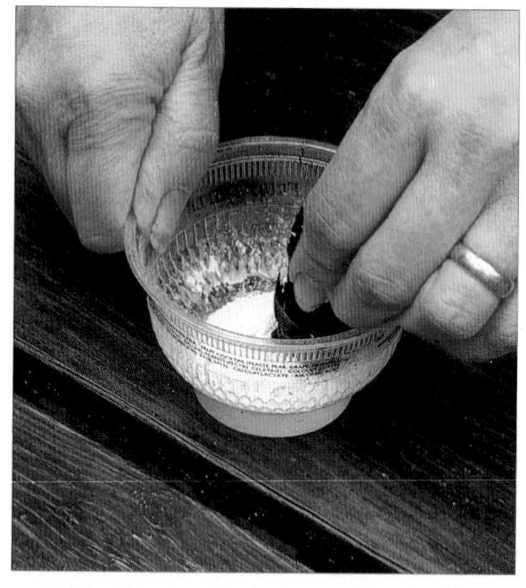

4 Using a sharp knife, cut the rhizome into sections about 8cm/3in long. Dust them with a fungicide to reduce the risk of them rotting where wounded.

5 Replant the pieces as soon as possible, where they are to grow, in well-prepared soil. Replant so that the top of the rhizome is just level with the soil.

6 If you want even more plants, and do not mind waiting to plant them, cut the rhizome into 18mm/¾in sections, each with a bud and some roots.

7 Place these smaller sections of rhizome in trays of cuttings compost, burying them horizontally to half their depth. Keep in a cold frame or greenhouse.

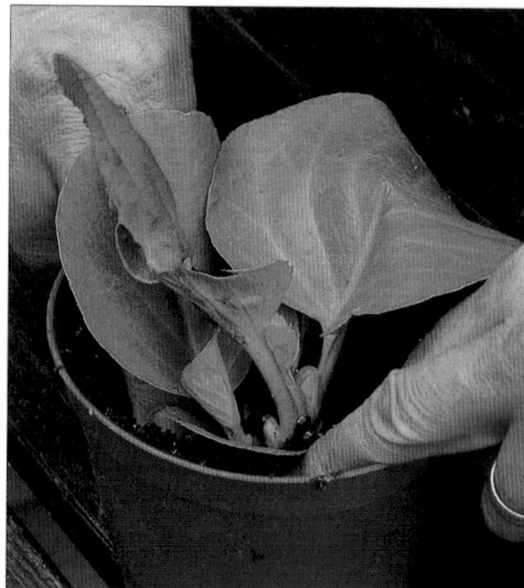

8 Next summer pot up the plants and grow them on for a year before planting out, or plant them in a nursery bed to grow on for a season.

A COTTON LAVENDER HEDGE

Cotton lavender **(Santolina chamaecyparissus), *with its feathery silvery foliage and compact habit, is an ideal shrub to use at the front of a shrub border or in the herbaceous border, where it can contrast with green-foliaged plants. It looks good with summer bedding and acts as a contrast to bright flowers like begonias. You can even use it to edge your flower beds.***

1 *An established plant will provide plenty of cuttings. Choose semi-ripe shoots (those still soft at the tip but mature at the base), about 5-8cm/2-3in long.*

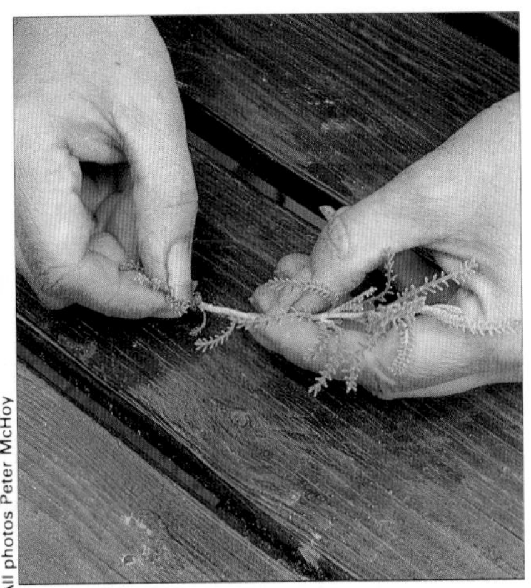

All photos Peter McHoy

2 *Trim the leaves off the bottom 2.5cm/1in of the cutting, pulling off or using a sharp knife. Trim off the growing tip if the growth is still very soft.*

3 *Fill some small pots with a cuttings compost. Use equal parts peat and sand or perlite, or buy a proprietary cuttings compost from a garden centre.*

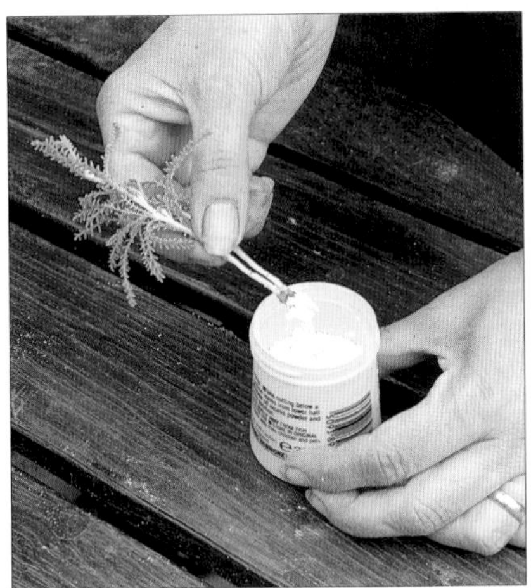

4 *Dip the tip of each cutting in water, then in a hormone rooting powder. The powder should contain a fungicide as well as a rooting hormone.*

5 *Insert the cuttings around the edge of a pot or half pot, using a small dibber like the one shown, or a pencil if you do not have a dibber.*

6 *Remember to label the cuttings. Water the pots thoroughly and place them in a cold frame or an unheated greenhouse. Plunge the pots in the soil.*

7 *If the compost is kept moist but not waterlogged, the cuttings should be ready for individual 9cm/3½in pots in mid spring. Use a potting compost.*

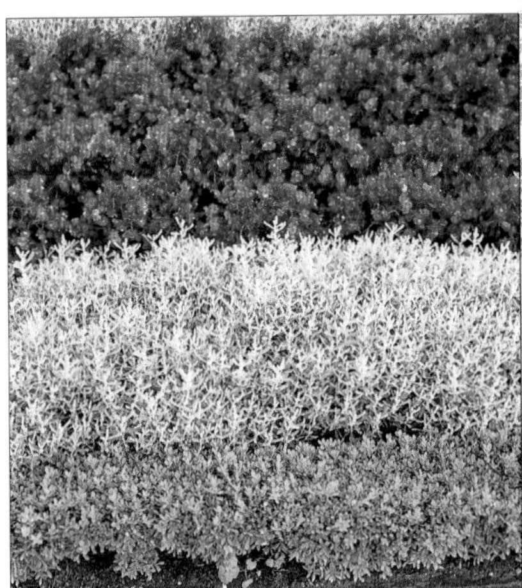

8 *The young plants can be set out in the ground in the autumn. If planting a dwarf hedge, space them about 30cm/12in apart. Trim to make shapely.*

MID AUTUMN

WEEK 1

CHECKLIST

WHAT TO DO

LAWNS
Lay a lawn with turf

BEDS AND BORDERS
Renovate neglected borders
Cut back herbaceous plants and tidy borders

SHRUBS
Plant a container with foliage shrubs for year-round interest

ROCK GARDEN
Protect woolly-leaved alpines from winter wet with a sheet of glass

LOOK AHEAD

DIVIDE
Border plants such as bergenias and rudbeckias

SOW
Sweet peas to overwinter in a frame

PLANT
Spring-flowering bulbs and summer lilies
Biennials such as wallflowers, sweet Williams and Canterbury bells
Heathers

WHAT TO SEE

BULBS AND BORDER PLANTS
Guernsey lily (*nerine*) and kaffir lily (*schizostylis*)

SHRUBS AND TREES
Cotoneaster (berries and foliage), crab apple (fruit), pyracantha (berries), *Rosa rugosa* (hips)

VISITORS

FRIENDS
Squirrels

FOES
Mottled umber moths, winter moths

WHAT TO DO

Although the garden now lacks much of the vibrant colour of summer, there are still the more muted and subtle shades of autumn to be enjoyed, with none of the pressures associated with spring and summer gardening. It is a time for pottering and tidying and for enjoying the garden in all its autumn glory.

Renovate old borders

Herbaceous and mixed borders become overgrown in time, with the more vigorous plants swamping many of the choice but less robust kinds. The balance of the border can be lost, and it can soon look neglected.

Some plants die and need replacing. Some would be better moved to another position in the border, perhaps where their height or habit is more appropriate, or simply to achieve a more pleasing juxtaposition.

Often it is sufficient to lift the offending plants, taking the opportunity to divide them before replanting. Sometimes, though, it is best to lift a whole section of border and to start afresh.

Plant them in a spare piece of ground while you dig over the border and clear any weeds. Then divide and replant them.

Delphiniums and autumn-flowering border chrysanthemums are best propagated from cuttings taken from new growth. Pot up a few clumps in boxes or deep seed trays to keep in the cold frame or a cool greenhouse to provide early shoots next year for cuttings.

Plant biennials

All biennials for spring and summer flowering, such as wallflowers, Canterbury bells and sweet Williams, should be planted as soon as possible. Many of these, such as wallflowers and double daisies, are often used along with bulbs for spring bedding. If you have a few plants over put them in the perennial border to add welcome clumps of colour there next year.

Alpine protection

Derek Gould

Glass or polythene sheets keep off the wet.

Alpines are used to cold conditions and few will object to low temperatures. But some, especially those with hairy, silver or felted leaves, may succumb to too much wet. Vulnerable types are best protected with a sheet of glass or perspex.

Sow sweet peas

If you love the sight and scent of sweet peas, extend the flowering season next year by sowing some now to flower in early summer. Sow another batch in the spring, where they are to flower, and these will carry on blooming well into autumn.

Photos Horticultural

Sow sweet peas now in pots.

Sow some now in pots and germinate them in a warm place, perhaps on a light windowsill or in a cold frame, as it is too cold to sow them outdoors. Once they have germinated, however, be sure to keep them in a cool light place, such as a cold frame or unheated greenhouse.

If you pinch the growing tips out when they are a few inches high, and keep them in a cool but light and sheltered place, you will have sturdy, bushy plants to set out in the garden in spring.

Finish planting bulbs

Most bulbs can still be planted, and you may find some bargains as it is now late in the season, but make sure they are firm and in good condition. Tulips are especially satisfactory if planted in mid or late autumn.

Plant a heather garden

Autumn is a good time to plant a heather garden, so why not find a suitable part of the garden and prepare the ground for planting during the next few weeks?

WHAT TO SEE

The big and beautiful florist's cyclamen, which is an indoor plant, has some charming, dainty yet hardy relatives that you will find flowering in the garden even at this unlikely time of year.

C. hederifolium *(also known as* C. neapolitanum) *can start to flower in early autumn and still be putting on a worthwhile display in late autumn. The small mauve to pale pink or white flowers are perfect miniatures of the florist's cyclamen on plants only 10cm/4in high. The foliage, which can persist through to late spring, is usually attractively marbled silver.*

Harry Smith Collection

Hardy cyclamen; the variety* album *is white.

Look out for them in gardens now, and next year plant a group of them in your rock garden, or a drift of them in front of shrubs with bold autumn foliage.

You will often find the tubers on sale in garden centres in the autumn, just before they start to grow, but specialist nurseries may sell them as growing plants in pots. If possible buy pot-grown plants, as once the tubers have dried out they can be difficult to start into growth.

You can grow these hardy cyclamens on most free-draining soils, but enriching the ground with leaf mould will definitely encourage them, as will a thin mulch of leaf mould over the tubers in summer.

VISITORS

The adult moths of some of the major fruit tree pests emerge about now. The caterpillars of the winter moths are a pest on apples, pears, plums and cherries, as well as on many ornamental trees, such as flowering cherries and flowering crab apples. The moths will be starting to lay their eggs now.

There are three different species of moth that are commonly grouped loosely as 'winter moths', and two of them will be on the move now: the mottled umber and the winter moth. These make their way up the trunk of the tree to lay their eggs, having pupated in the soil. The eggs will hatch in spring and it is the caterpillars from them, which all move with a looping motion, that do the damage to the tree.

You can wait until spring and try to control them with an insecticide, but a good, 'green' control is to trap the female moths on their way up the trunk by 'grease banding'.

You can buy ready-greased strips, which you must fix tightly around the trunk so the moths cannot crawl under the band.

Paul Sterry/Nature Photographers

A mottled umber; females are flightless.

DIVIDE RUDBECKIAS

Perennial rudbeckias or cone flowers (sometimes known as black-eyed Susan) are excellent border plants for late summer and autumn, with their big, bright yellow, daisy flowers and contrasting dark centres. They will be coming to an end now if they have not already done so, and this is an ideal time to divide an old clump to keep it flowering vigorously and to provide new plants for yourself or for friends.

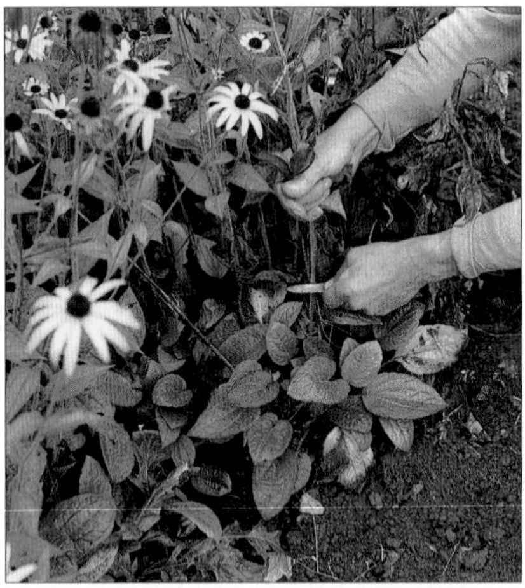

1 Choose a large clump to divide. Cut off any remaining flower stalks to leave a manageable clump of foliage before lifting the plant.

All photos Marshall Cavendish

2 Use a garden fork or a spade to lever up the crown and ball of roots. If it is too large to lift in one piece, chop through it with a spade and lift with a fork.

3 Before breaking the crown into smaller pieces by hand, use two forks back to back to prize apart the clump into more manageable pieces to handle.

4 The clump can be pulled apart into smaller pieces by hand. Use pieces from the outside and discard the old centre. Trim off dead foliage.

5 Fork over the ground and rake in bone meal. Replant the pieces in groups of three or five, spacing them well to provide a good display next year.

PLANT A FOLIAGE CONTAINER

Most gardeners plant their containers with bright summer flowers, but it is worth planting one or two with colourful evergreen shrubs that will have year-round appeal. Try growing a New Zealand flax (phormium),* Hebe × *franciscana 'Variegata' and the grey-leaved curry plant (*Helichrysum angustifolium*). The hebe and phormium are unsuitable in very cold areas.

1 Choose plants with contrasting shapes and colours, and move them around while still in their pots to create an attractive arrangement before planting.

Vana Haggerty

2 Plant in a good loam-based compost, and water in thoroughly. Cover the compost with a decorative mulch of gravel or expanded clay granules.

LAY A LAWN FROM TURF

Autumn is an ideal time to make yourself an instant lawn with turf. The grass will be well established and ready to use by next spring.

Although turf is more expensive than seed, it will not cost much for a small lawn and you should be able to complete it in less than a day if the ground has already been dug over and weeded. Although the ground should be level and weed-free, it does not need such thorough preparation as for sowing grass seed.

Turf can often be bought from garden centres, but if you require enough for a large lawn it may be best to order it from a turf specialist (look for advertisements in local papers, or in the telephone directory under the listing Turf Supplies).

A good supplier will be able to offer various grades raised from different seed mixtures. Explain what type of lawn you want. You will probably want one that is hard-wearing, or a high quality one that is mainly decorative. The better the quality of grass, the more expensive the turf will be. But if you want a good looking lawn that is easy to lay and will soon be ready, it is worth the additional expense.

Try to have the ground dug and levelled before delivery. Lay the turf as soon as possible, but if the ground is frozen wait until it has thawed out before starting.

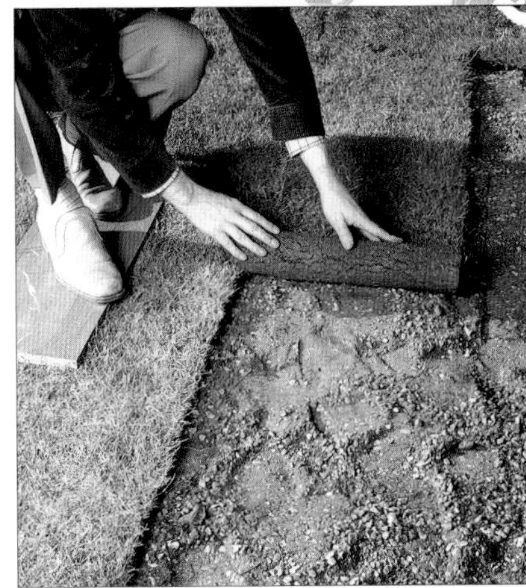

2 *Lay subsequent rows, making sure the joints are staggered; cut the first turf in the row shorter if necessary. Work from a board to spread your weight.*

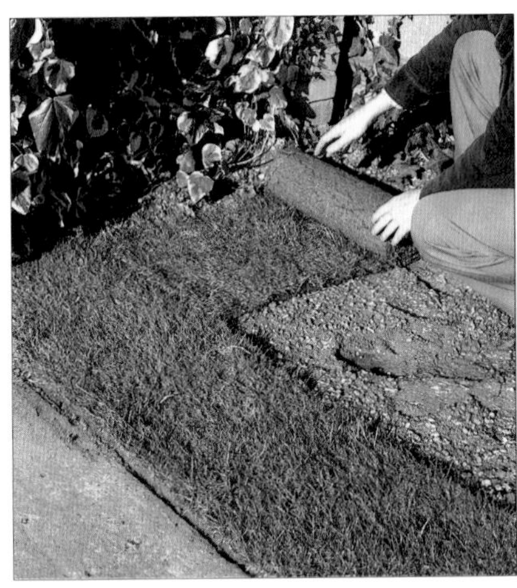

1 *Make sure the ground is firm and level, then unroll the turf along one side and one end to start with. These must be straight as later rows are laid to them.*

3 *Once an area has been laid, bang it flat to ensure good contact with the soil. The back of a spade can be used, but a 'beater' made from wood is better.*

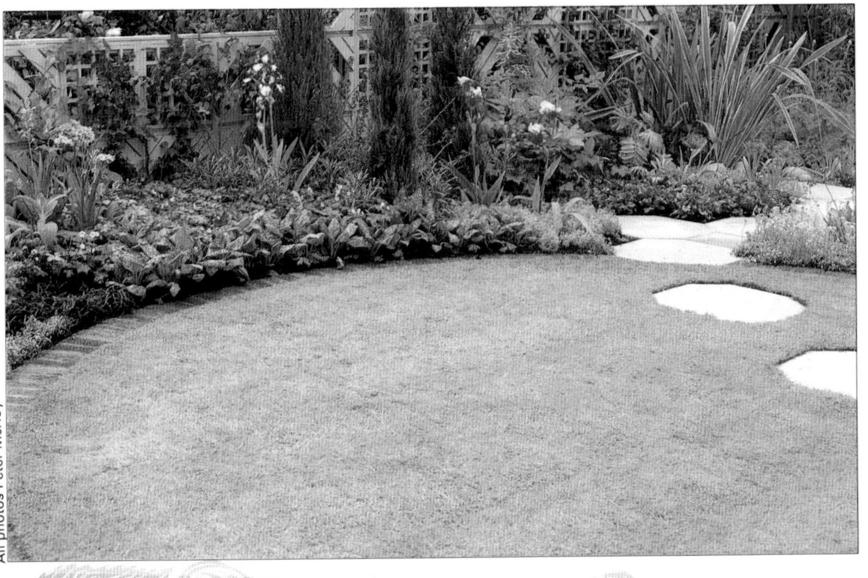

A lawn newly laid with turf looks good almost immediately. The joints, just visible here, soon disappear. The turves have been neatly trimmed to fit around stepping stones and within the brick surround.

All photos Peter McHoy

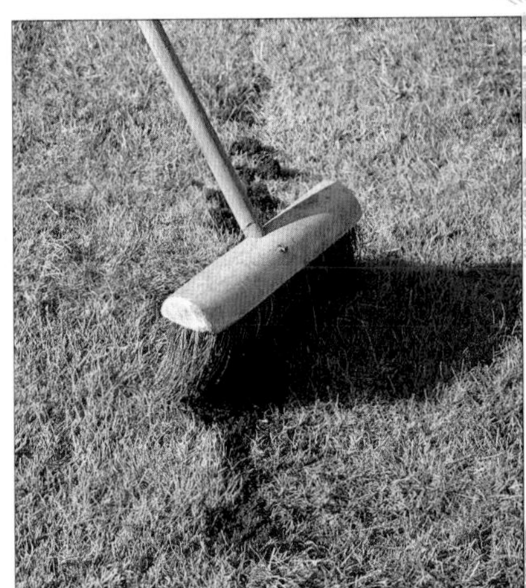

4 *Brush peat, fine compost or a mixture of peat and sand into the joints to help the turf knit together. Water well and keep watered in dry weather.*

CHECKLIST

WHAT TO DO

PONDS
Clear leaves, cut back large plants

BEDS AND BORDERS
Cut back herbaceous plants and tidy borders
Pot up lemon balm

SHRUBS
Trim back plants around shrubs with berries
Shorten shoots of the butterfly bush
Dead-head and tidy up roses. Spray with a fungicide. Remove suckers
Plant container-grown and bare-root deciduous trees and shrubs

ROCK GARDEN
Protect woolly-leaved alpines from excess winter moisture with a sheet of glass

LOOK AHEAD

DIVIDE
Herbaceous border plants

SOW
Lettuces in a frame or greenhouse

PLANT
Tulips for spring and lilies for summer
Biennials such as double daisies (*Bellis perennis*) and wallflowers

WHAT TO SEE

BULBS AND BORDER PLANTS
Pampas grass (*Cortaderia selloana*)

SHRUBS AND TREES
Cotoneaster (berries and foliage), pyracantha (berries), *Viburnum opulus* (berries)

VISITORS

FRIENDS
Blackbirds, thrushes

FOES
Greenfly, winter moths

MID AUTUMN
WEEK 2

WHAT TO DO

The bounty of berries and fruits as well as the abundance of autumn foliage colour make this a time to be enjoyed to the full before the colder weather makes gardening outdoors a less attractive proposition. It is also a time when regional variations are very pronounced – in cold areas it can seem as though winter has arrived, while in favourable regions there are often warm days when it still seems like summer.

Make the most of berries

Berries provide invaluable pockets of colour at this time, so make the best of them.

Cut down and tidy up any herbaceous plants in front of berrying shrubs so that these do not detract from their beauty. This often exposes low branches covered with berries. Trim back any surrounding shrubs that are hiding berry-laden branches.

Harry Smith Collection

Berries on Viburnum opulus *'Compactum'.*

Shorten shoots

Full pruning of late-flowering deciduous shrubs, such as Buddleia davidii, *is usually done in the spring. However, it is worth cutting the shoots back by half now to reduce wind damage and to make the plants look neater.*

Plant trees and shrubs

Autumn is an ideal planting time, whether you buy container-grown plants or bare-root ones. Bare-root deciduous trees and shrubs can be planted at any time while they are dormant, but it makes sense to do it while the soil is still reasonably warm and workable.

It is best to wait until spring before planting any that are on the borderline of hardiness, in case we have a severe winter. Hebes, for instance, are much better planted in spring so that they have time to become established before they have to cope with very cold weather.

Roses

Remove any lingering dead flowers, and cut back any very soft shoots. Most people leave the main pruning until spring, but cutting out soft shoots now reduces the risk of die-back.

Pick up any fallen leaves that show signs of black-spot or other disease, and give the plants a final spray with a fungicide.

LOOK AHEAD

Plant tulips

If you have not yet planted your bulbs for a spring display, do so before it is too late. Concentrate on tulips, which usually do well if planted late. Choose compact ones like early double tulips and hybrids of species like Tulipa kaufmanniana *and* T. greigii *for window boxes and other containers in exposed positions. Try the yellow and white dwarf* T. tarda *in the front of an herbaceous or mixed border – although ground-hugging, this bright and bold tulip will usually thrive for years if left undisturbed.*

Sow some lettuces

If you have a greenhouse or cold frame you may be able to grow some lettuces for late winter and spring – there is a real sense of triumph in harvesting your own lettuces while they are still expensive in the shops.

Lettuces growing in a cold frame.

You must choose a suitable variety. If you have a heated greenhouse (7°C/45°F is adequate), sow 'Dandie' or 'Diamant' (the latter is worth trying in an unheated greenhouse or cold frame). 'May Queen' is also a tough variety that you can grow over the winter in a cold frame to harvest in spring.

WHAT TO SEE

Pampas grass is one of those plants that you simply cannot fail to notice at this time of year. A grass of simply huge proportions, some species have white or silvery plume-like flower spikes well over 1.8m/6ft tall. These long-lasting flowers often appear in early autumn and the spikes can still look respectable in early winter. They are ideal for cutting and taking indoors for winter decoration in the home.

Eric Crichton

Cortaderia selloana *'Sunningdale Silver'*.

It is worth looking at the different types of pampas grass to see which might be suitable for your own garden, and noting where they look best. These are not an easy plant to place successfully, and the tall ones are often best as specimen plants grown in isolation in a lawn – they make an excellent focal point at this time of year. The more compact kinds, and especially the variegated ones, are easier to integrate into a large herbaceous or mixed border.

For a very large and tall plant, Cortaderia selloana *is the pampas grass to choose, and 'Sunningdale Silver' is a particularly good form of it with larger, loose white plumes. For small gardens, however, it is best to choose 'Pumila' which is more compact (about 1.2-1.5m/4-5ft).*

A variegated variety like 'Gold Band', which is compact and has green and yellow leaves, has year-round appeal.

VISITORS

Berries and birds are both attractive in the garden, and one will tend to attract the other. At this time of year both can be enjoyed as there is still plenty of alternative food around. Although birds will be attracted by the berries they should not be so hungry that they strip the bushes (in harsh winter weather a flock of birds like redwings can strip a whole tree within a couple of days).

It is their resident relatives, the blackbird, song thrush and mistle thrush, that are most likely to be tempted by berries now. Cotoneaster, berberis, firethorn (pyracantha) and holly are likely to be on their menu. Starlings will also take berries, but at this time of year they usually still have a plentiful supply of other natural food, so they are not usually much of a problem.

Netting is the most effective way of protecting the plants, but this is far from attractive and it may be better to risk losing a few berries and enjoying both the plants and the birds, even if the display will not be so long-lasting.

E.A. Janes/NHPA

A redwing eating hawthorn berries.

PROTECT THE POND

Autumn is a crucial time for ponds. They can easily become polluted with leaves, especially if there are trees or deciduous shrubs nearby. The leaves will pollute the pond as they decay, particularly in winter if the pond becomes frozen and toxic gases cannot easily escape. It makes sense to prevent at least some of the leaves falling in. Trimming back dying pond plants will help keep the water clean.

1 *Rake out as many leaves as you can, from the surface and the bottom of the pond. You can use a garden rake but a spring-tined lawn or leaf rake is ideal.*

2 *Thin out submerged oxygenating plants like elodea if they are beginning to dominate the pond. Pieces can be removed easily with a garden rake.*

Peter McHoy

3 *Trim off any dying leaves from marginal plants or those beyond the edge of the pond, before the leaves start to decay in the water.*

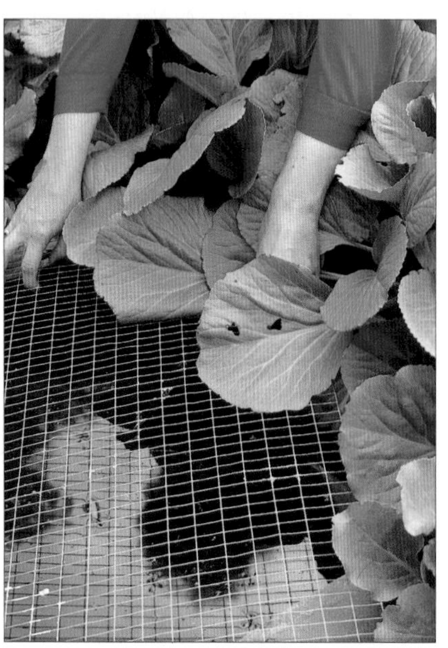

4 *To prevent further leaves falling in, cover the pond with netting, pegged into position around the edge. This fine wire mesh will catch most leaves.*

POT UP LEMON BALM

Lemon balm is hardy in most areas, but it is sometimes killed in a cold winter in areas where the climate is harsh. It is worth potting up few small pieces to overwinter in a cold frame or a cool greenhouse, as an insurance against losing your plant if the winter is severe. your outdoor plant survives you can still use your potted pieces, forcing them for some early lemon-scented foliage.

1 *Lemon balm soon makes a big plant so just pot up one or two small pieces from around the edge of the plant, lifting them with a trowel or hand fork.*

Vana Haggerty

2 *Firm the compost or soil, then trim back long shoots to make the plant more compact. Water well and stand in a cold frame or a cool greenhouse.*

REMOVE ROSE SUCKERS

Suckers are shoots that arise from the rootstock, usually from some form of wild rose, rather than the variety you bought. Not all roses are grafted or budded onto different roots, but most hybrid teas (large-flowered) and floribunda (cluster-flowered) roses are. This is because they do not grow so well on their own roots. If you let suckers grow they will gradually dominate the plant.

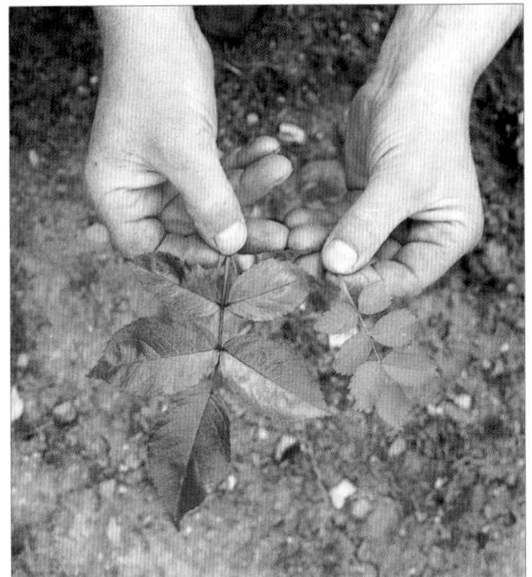

1 *Suckers arise from below soil level, and the leaves usually have a different appearance. Most hybrid roses have five leaflets, suckers usually have seven.*

Marshall Cavendish

2 *Dig away the soil and pull the suckers off with a firm tug. If you find this difficult, cut them off with a sharp knife. Return the soil and firm it well.*

PLANT LILY-OF-THE-VALLEY

Lily-of-the-valley* (Convallaria majalis) *is such an appealing plant that it is surprising it is not grown in almost every garden. The small, dainty sprays of nodding white bells are pretty for cutting and are charming in the garden. They also provide that wonderful lily-of-the-valley scent.

They make fine ground cover plants once established, and if they already grow in your garden you can multiply your stock by dividing established plants now.

Eric Crichton

1 *Lily-of-the-valley can be forced to flower early indoors. It also makes an excellent ground cover plant for the garden, flowering in mid and late spring.*

Marshall Cavendish

2 *If you buy plants they will probably have crowns like these. Plant them about 8-10cm/3-4in apart, with the tips just below the surface of the soil.*

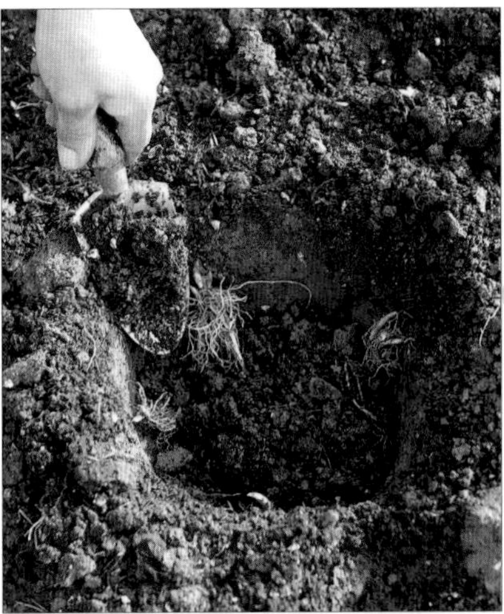

3 *Return the soil and firm it gently around the crowns. If possible, add garden compost or peat, or a peat substitute, to the soil. Water thoroughly.*

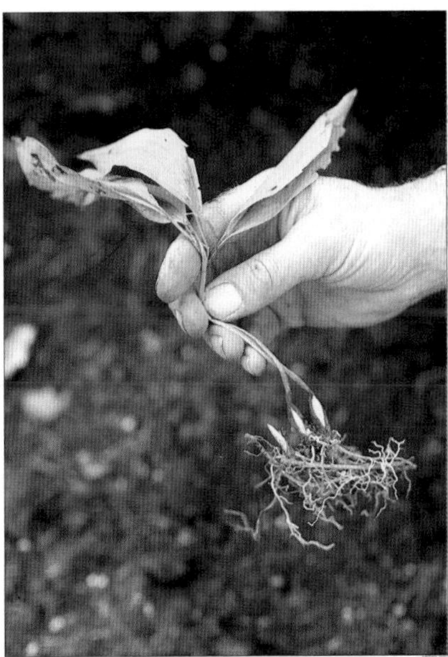

4 *If you already have some plants and want to multiply them, lift a few roots and separate them into sections about the size shown. Replant them without delay.*

CHECKLIST

WHAT TO DO

LAWNS
Continue to cut the grass
Repair damaged areas

BEDS AND BORDERS
Cut back herbaceous plants and tidy borders
Prepare the ground for sweet peas

SHRUBS
Check stakes and ties
Dead-head and tidy up roses. Spray with a fungicide. Remove suckers
Plant container-grown and bare-root deciduous trees and shrubs

ROCK GARDEN
Remove fallen leaves covering plants

LOOK AHEAD

POT UP
Freesia corms

HEDGES
Prepare ground for a new hedge

PLANT
Tulips for spring and lilies for summer
Heathers

WHAT TO SEE

BULBS AND BORDER PLANTS
Pampas grass (*Cortaderia selloana*)

SHRUBS AND TREES
Acers (foliage), cotoneaster (berries and foliage), Japanese cherries (foliage), pyracantha (berries), snowy mespilus (foliage)

VISITORS

FRIENDS
Blackbirds, thrushes

FOES
Greenfly, short-tailed voles

MID AUTUMN

WEEK 3

WHAT TO DO

Strong winds are common at this time of year, and cold nights occur even in favourable areas. So there is still plenty to do in the garden, staking plants and making sure they are adequately protected.

The colder weather brings its compensations. Although sharp frosts can cause leaves to fall suddenly, a cold spell often heightens the autumn tints of trees and shrubs.

Check stakes and ties

Do not wait until strong winds cause damage to plants and stakes – check supports and ties now and renew them if necessary.

Pay special attention to supports for plants like standard roses, as the stakes are usually thin and the plant will be ruined if its main stem snaps in a gale.

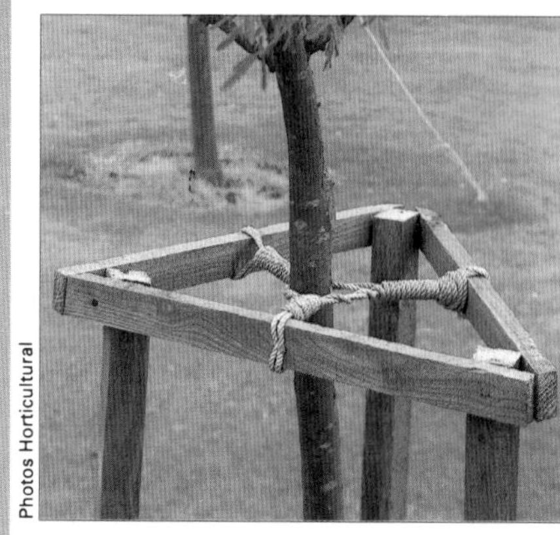
Photos Horticultural

Ties supporting trees should be firm and not too tight or too loose.

Pull a little soil away from the base of the stake to make sure the timber is still sound (replace the stake now if it shows signs of rot)

Take the opportunity to adjust old ties that are becoming too tight; add new ones if needed.

Plants on trellises and pergolas are particularly vulnerable. Check that these structures are sound and if necessary remove surplus growth to reduce wind resistance.

Super sweet peas

You can grow perfectly satisfactory sweet peas for a garden display by sowing the seeds in spring where they are to flower, without a lot of special preparation. But enthusiasts who want really super flowers with long stems on vigorous plants like to prepare the ground in autumn. They often overwinter seedlings to get a head start next year.

If you know where your sweet peas are to be planted, dig the ground deeply now (to a depth of about 50cm/20in), adding in a lot of compost or manure.

If you have sown your sweet pea seeds recently, do not forget to keep them well watered. If several seeds were sown in each pot, thin them to one seedling. You may be able to transplant the surplus seedlings into new pots.

Lawn care

Lawns require only infrequent cuttings at this time of year, but do not let the grass become too long otherwise it will be difficult to cut in the spring. Provided the grass is still growing, keep it mown occasionally, but set the blades higher than you would for summer mowing.

LOOK AHEAD

Plant tulips

It is not too late to plant tulips, and you may find the bulbs reduced in price at the end of the season. Provided they are sound (press gently around the base to make sure they are firm, and check that there are no signs of mould on them), they are worth planting.

If you do not have space in the ground you will probably have a container left over from summer that can be put to good use.

*Keep to dwarf kinds, such as the species tulips and their hybrids (*T. kaufmanniana *hybrids for instance) or early double tulips. In tubs and large pots, however, you can grow any of the taller kinds, especially if you provide a sheltered position.*

Brian Carter/Garden Picture Library

A tub of tulips looks lovely in spring.

If you need a new hedge . . .

Late autumn is a good time to plant a new hedge, but try to prepare the ground a couple of weeks before planting if possible. Although not essential, if you prepare the ground in advance you will probably make a more thorough job of eliminating difficult perennial weeds like couch grass. If the weather is mild and some weed seedlings germinate, you can hoe them off.

WHAT TO SEE

If there has been a cold snap in some areas, followed by strong winds, the leaves may have fallen from certain trees, but elsewhere the autumn tints may be at their best. It is tempting to buy trees and shrubs for your garden that take your eye at this time. However, if your garden is small you should look for those that also have other periods of interest as well as good autumn colour.

Don Wildridge

***Bright autumn leaves of* Malus tschonoskii.**

The maples (acers) are justifiably popular for autumn colour, but if space is limited choose one with good colour and an interesting bark for the whole year – like Acer griseum, *the attractive paperbark maple. Some of the crab apples have good autumn tints and one of the best –* Malus tschonoskii *– has spring blossom and small 'apples'. It also grows in a narrow, upright fashion, which makes it a good candidate where space is limited.*

The snowy mespilus, which can be grown as a small tree or a large shrub, is so showered with white flowers in spring that it makes a real focal point. The flowers may be followed by berries in early summer, and the season is rounded off with foliage that turns rich orange and red.

Many of the Japanese cherries, among the most beautiful of all flowering trees, also have colourful autumn foliage.

VISITORS

Short-tailed voles (also known as field voles) are among the most common small rodents in Britain. They are rarely active during the day so we may not be aware of them.

They can do much damage by eating the bark off young trees, and consuming seeds and bulbs. To be fair to the short-tailed vole, it does eat many insect pests too.

In rural areas voles are controlled by owls, weasels and other predators. In the garden, cats will help to control their numbers. Trapping and baiting are rarely practical forms of control as more tend to move in.

It is better to accept that they are part of the natural wildlife of our gardens. Take precautions, therefore, to protect seeds in vulnerable places and to protect newly-planted trees if necessary.

Stephen Dalton/NHPA

A short-tailed vole eating a nut.

PLANT LILIES FOR SUMMER

Except in chilly areas where the ground is already very cold, this is a good time to plant lily bulbs. You can plant in spring, but planting now gives you more chance. Many lilies fail because the bulbs have dried out too much by the time they are planted.

Most lilies prefer a soil on the acid side (pH6-6.5), but some, including* Lilium candidum*, will do well on alkaline soils.

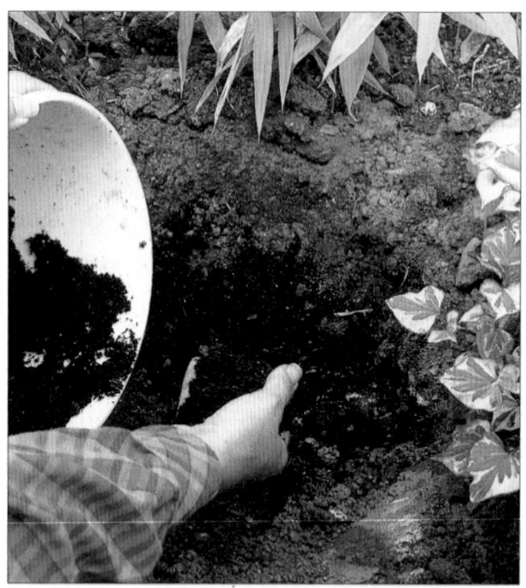

1 *Lilies require well-prepared soil. Dig deeply and work in as much garden compost as you can. If the soil is poorly drained, add plenty of coarse grit.*

All photos Peter McHoy

2 *Lilies are best planted in groups, so remove an area of soil to a depth of about 20cm/8in. Add a layer of coarse grit or sand, and a sprinkling of bone meal.*

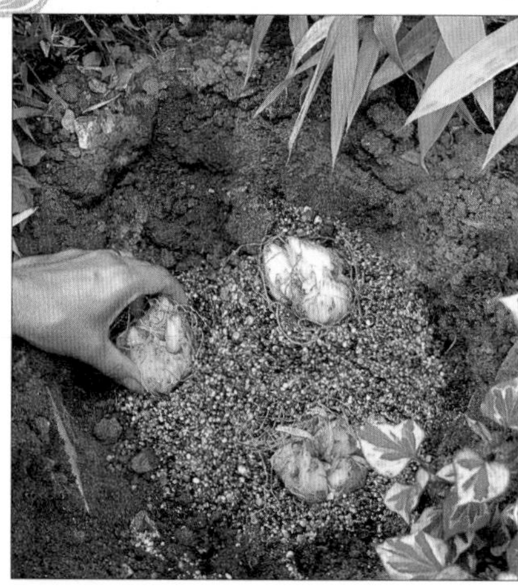

3 *Space the bulbs about 15cm/6in apart, and make sure the hole is deep enough for the bulbs to be covered with about twice their own depth of soil.*

4 *To encourage good drainage and to deter slugs, bed the bulbs on coarse sand and sprinkle more sand over them before returning the soil.*

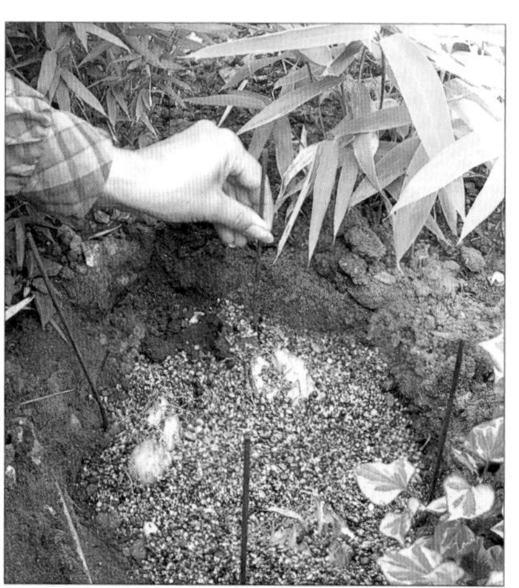

5 *Place small sticks or canes around the area before returning the soil, so that you do not damage them while hoeing. Remember to label them.*

POT UP SOME FREESIAS

Fragrant freesias are not as difficult to grow as you might think, and you can plant them now to bloom in late winter.

You can grow freesias from seed, but it is much quicker, easier and more certain to buy corms. For early flowering indoors you can grow them on a very light window-sill, but they will be sturdier if you can grow them in a cool greenhouse until flowering starts.

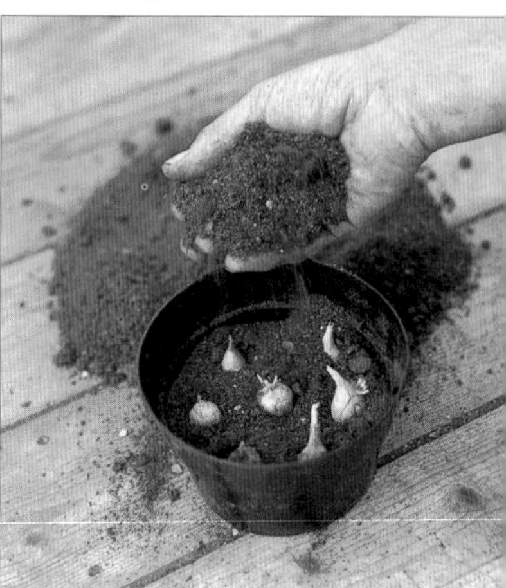

1 *Grow your freesias in pots about 20-23cm/8-9in in diameter, and use a good potting compost, or good garden soil with some sharp sand added.*

Marshall Cavendish

2 *Space corms 2.5cm/1in apart and cover them with 2.5cm/1in of compost. Tap the pot on a table to settle the soil, then water thoroughly.*

PATCH UP THE LAWN

Lawns receive a lot of hard wear, especially if they have to act as a play area for a young family.

You do not have to let bare or worn patches spoil your lawn. Now is a good time to patch up those less than perfect areas.

You may be able to lift some turf from a spare piece of grass elsewhere in the garden, otherwise buy it from a garden centre.

1 *Mark out a rectangle that includes the worn area, using canes or string, then use a half-moon edger (or a spade) to cut round the area to be removed.*

2 *Use a spade to lift the worn patch, keeping the blade as horizontal as possible so that you remove an even slice of turf.*

3 *Level the area as much as possible by slicing off more soil if necessary, then prick over the surface with a fork to loosen the compacted ground.*

4 *Rake the soil level, tread it lightly to remove any large pockets of air, then rake it smooth. If need be, add a little more fine soil to make it the right depth.*

5 *Lay the prepared new piece of turf in position. Make it slightly larger than the area so that you can trim it to size once it is in position.*

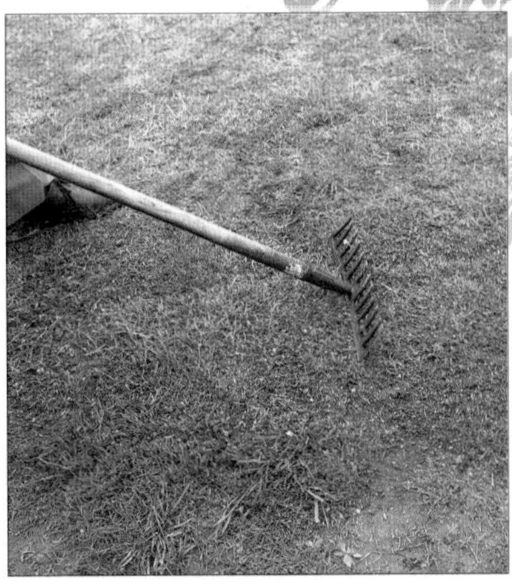

6 *Firm the new turf into position by tapping it with the back of a spade or rake. If it does not appear level, remove the turf and add or remove soil.*

7 *Small bare patches can be reseeded, but if this is not done by mid autumn it is best to wait until spring. Loosen the ground then tamp it level.*

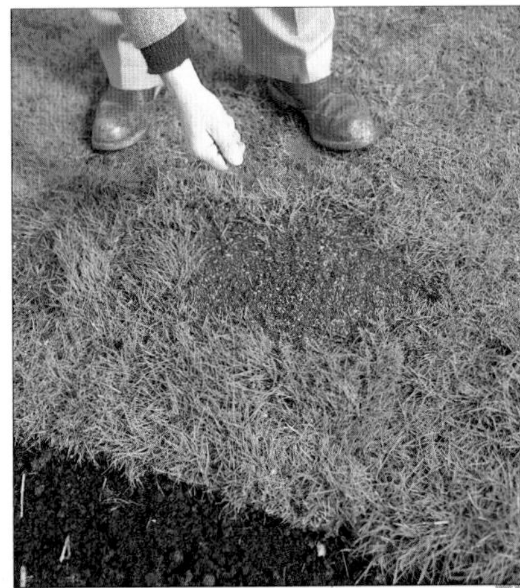

8 *Sow an appropriate grass seed (choose one containing ryegrass for a hard-wearing lawn). Water in and cover with clear polythene until germinated.*

MID AUTUMN

WEEK 4

CHECKLIST

WHAT TO DO

LAWNS
Rake up and collect autumn leaves

BEDS AND BORDERS
Tidy borders and store stakes and supports
Lift tender bulbs, corms and tubers

SHRUBS
Plant roses and other deciduous shrubs
Dig and prepare soil for new borders

ROCK GARDEN
Remove fallen leaves that are covering the plants
Protect vulnerable alpines from winter wet with a sheet of glass

LOOK AHEAD

TAKE CUTTINGS
Propagate shrubs such as dogwoods from hardwood cuttings

HEDGES
Prepare ground for a new hedge

PLANT
Tulips for spring and biennial bedding plants

WHAT TO SEE

BULBS AND BORDER PLANTS
Pampas grass (*Cortaderia selloana*)

SHRUBS AND TREES
Cotoneaster (berries and foliage), guelder rose (*Viburnum opulus*, berries), pyracantha (berries), strawberry tree (*Arbutus unedo*, *A. × andrachnoides*)

VISITORS

FRIENDS
Blackbirds, thrushes

FOES
Voles, woodlice

WHAT TO DO

In cold areas frosts will already have begun to penetrate the ground, but elsewhere they are unlikely to have damaged tender bulbs, corms and tubers yet. The tops may have been killed, however, so unless you go round the garden and lift them you may find it difficult to remember where they are, or simply forget to protect them so that they live to flower another year.

Lift tender bulbs, corms and tubers

Dahlia tubers should be lifted as soon as possible if not already done (seed-raised bedding dahlias are generally discarded and sown afresh each year). Gladioli will sometimes come through the winter unscathed in mild districts, but it is not worth risking it. Acidantheras, though they flower late, should be treated like gladioli and lifted.

Any other vulnerable plants, such as cannas and tuberous begonias, should be salvaged whenever possible.

Clean glass

Plants in cold frames and greenhouses need all the light they can get from now on. Make sure any summer shading wash is cleaned off, and wash all the glass thoroughly, inside and out.

Peter McHoy

Clean off greenhouse shading to let in light

Dirt accumulates where panes of glass overlap. Clean them out with a jet of water from a hose or sprayer, and push a plastic plant label between the panes to dislodge stubborn dirt.

Improve the soil

Your plants will only be as good as your soil allows them to be. Improving the soil is the best route to more successful gardening, and during the next few months you have an ideal opportunity to make a start.

If you are making a new bed or border, or have an area set aside for vegetables, dig it over before winter makes the ground too hard to work. Add plenty of organic matter. Whether your soil is acid or alkaline, heavy clay or light sand, humus-forming material such as compost or well-rotted manure will work wonders.

Few of us have enough material so concentrate on those areas that you most want to improve, rather than spreading your humus thinly all around the garden.

LOOK AHEAD

Last call for spring bedding

Plant spring bedding plants such as pansies, polyanthus and wallflowers and bulbs such as tulips as soon as possible, otherwise they will not become established before the really cold weather arrives.

You can still plant biennials such as Canterbury bells and sweet Williams in the border to flower next year. Avoid these in spring bedding schemes, as they flower too late for the bed to be cleared for summer bedding.

Roger Hyam/Garden Picture Library

Plant up wallflowers and tulips for spring.

Plant shrubs

Late autumn is a good time to plant shrubs. It reduces the number of tasks to be tackled in spring, and if you plant now you can use bare-root deciduous shrubs, which may be cheaper than container-grown plants.

If you have ordered the less common kinds from specialist nurseries most of these will probably be dispatched in late autumn.

Bare-root roses are sometimes available in shops at this time (the roots may have damp peat packed around them to reduce the risk of them drying out), but these should be bought and planted while the stock is still fresh and before they begin to dry out and deteriorate.

WHAT TO SEE

Strawberries at this time of year, and growing on trees, too,may sound an unlikely prospect. This, however, is the time of year when the strawberry tree (Arbutus unedo) ***is at its best.***

Eric Crichton

Arbutus unedo ***has dramatic fruits.***

Its white or pink-tinged flowers, which resemble lily-of-the-valley in appearance, are produced in abundance in late autumn and early winter. On established trees these are followed by globular edible fruits that look like strawberries from a distance. These fruits are often still present when the next season's flowers are produced. The combination of white flower and red fruit set against evergreen foliage would make this a desirable large shrub or small tree at any time, but especially so at this time of year.

It has a challenger, however, in A. × andrachnoides, *the Killarney strawberry tree. This has attractive cinnamon-coloured bark as a bonus.*

There has to be a drawback to plants as good as these. They are slow-growing for the first 15 years or so, and dislike alkaline soils. A. × andrachnoides, *however, tolerates lime.*

VISITORS

Turn over almost any rock, lift any piece of rotting wood, or move a heap of autumn leaves, and you are almost sure to find woodlice – those armour-plated grey creatures that either scurry away to some dark spot if disturbed or curl themselves up into a ball. There are about half a dozen species that you are likely to encounter in the garden, but the three most common ones outdoors are the common woodlouse, granulated woodlouse and pill woodlouse – the latter often rolls itself into a ball if disturbed.

Woodlice are usually grey, but the colour varies from pale yellow through brown to dark grey.

Trying to eliminate them from the garden is an almost impossible task, so it is best to live with them and to control them only where they are likely to damage vulnerable plants.

They can live on dead and decaying material but they also eat the leaves and stems of a wide range of living plants. Seedlings are most vulnerable, however, so concentrate on trying to eliminate them from areas where there are young plants.

Clear away rubbish and debris and eliminate as many hiding places as possible. Additional protection can be given by using gamma-HCH dust.

Stephan Dalton/NHPA

Woodlice live in dark, damp places.

PROPAGATE DOGWOODS

Dogwoods grown primarily for their colourful stems, like the red-stemmed* Cornus alba *and its varieties, and the green-stemmed* C. stolonifera *'Flaviramea', are easy to increase from hardwood cuttings. Because the plants are dormant when the cuttings are taken you can put them in and almost forget about them until spring. Use the same method for willows and purple-leaved plums.

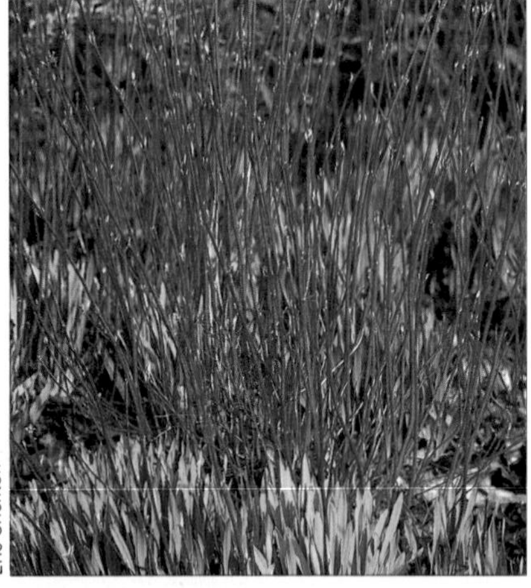

Eric Crichton

1 *Cornus alba 'Sibirica' is grown for its coral-red stems in winter. Take hardwood cuttings from mid summer to early autumn.*

Marshall Cavendish

2 *Select stems that have grown this year, cutting them off cleanly with secateurs. One shoot should produce several usable cuttings.*

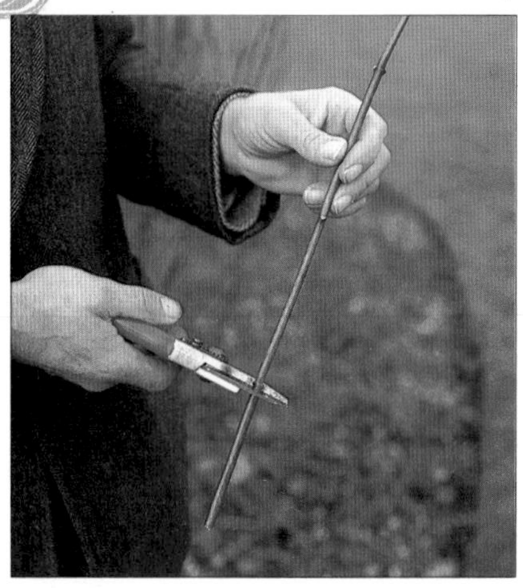

3 *Make each cutting about 15cm/6in long, cutting straight across just below a node (point where leaves were) with the secateurs or garden knife.*

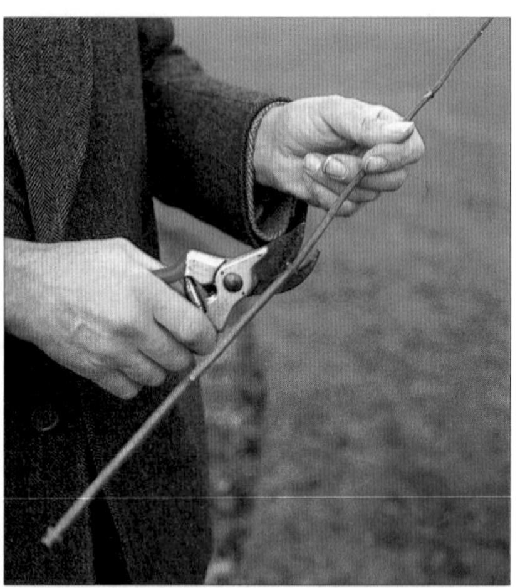

4 *Make the second cut, about 15cm/6in above the first, at an angle, just above a node or bud. Make sure later you plant with the sloping cut at the top.*

5 *Choose a sheltered position in the garden, or in a cold frame, and make a slit with a spade. Insert the cuttings 10cm/4in deep and the same distance apart.*

HOW TO GERMINATE DIFFICULT SEEDS

The seeds of some perennials, such as trees and shrubs and especially alpines, need a cold period to break their dormancy. If you simply sow them in spring most of them will not germinate for a year until they have experienced winter conditions.

To break their dormancy, the seeds require 'stratification' so that they will germinate more readily when spring arrives.

1 *Space out large seeds like these rose hips. Small seeds can simply be sprinkled on. Very small seeds are best chilled in the refrigerator.*

Marshall Cavendish

2 *Cover with a 2cm/¾in layer of sand and keep moist for a few days. Place the pot in a cold part of the garden. Be prepared to protect them from mice.*

PLANT A ROSE

Container-grown roses are available all the year round and can be planted at any time, provided the ground is not waterlogged or frozen. At this time, however, rose nurseries often send out their roses 'bare-root'. You will also find bare-root plants in shops and garden centres and they are often cheaper than container-grown ones. They will quickly become established if you plant them with care now.

1 You can enjoy roses like this next summer if you plant now. Bare-root plants, available now from shops and garden centres, are often quite inexpensive.

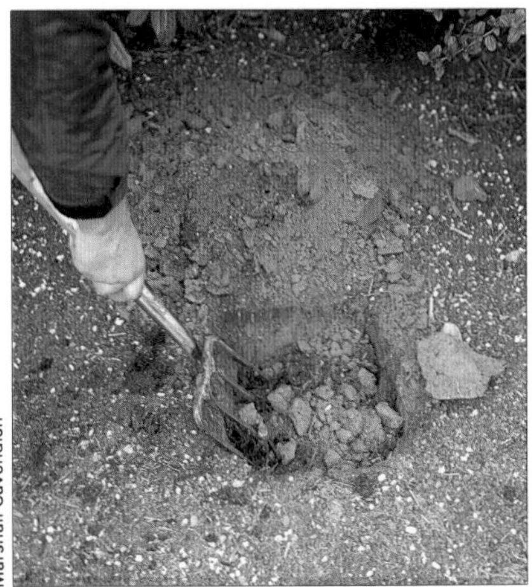

Marshall Cavendish

2 Dig a hole large enough to take all the roots when spread out, and fork in as much garden compost, or proprietary planting mixture as you can spare.

3 Remove the rose from its packing, or from the ground if it has arrived at an inappropriate time and been 'heeled in'. Trim off any damaged roots.

4 Plant at its original depth (you will be able to see the old soil mark), and be sure to spread the roots out well before returning soil to the hole.

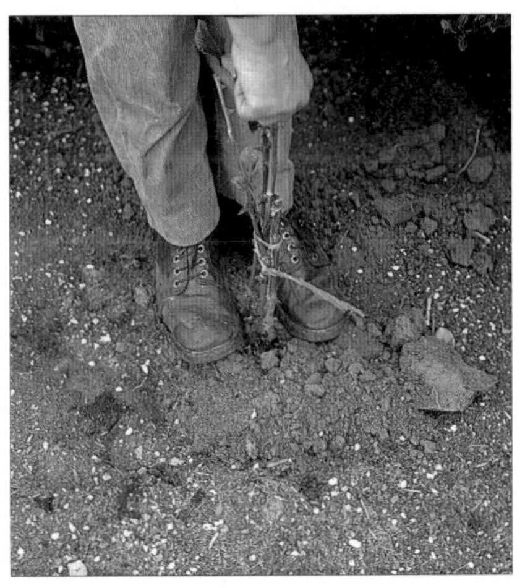

5 Firm the soil well, using your feet to tread the ground. Give the plant a gentle tug to make sure it has been planted firmly. Hoe or loosen the surface.

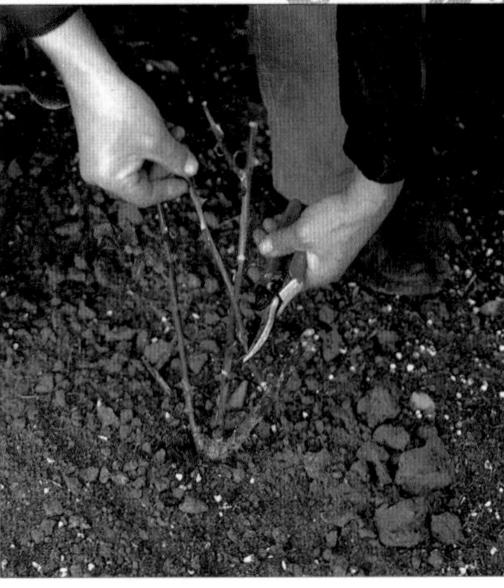

6 Cut the shoots back to about 15-20cm/6-8in above the ground, to reduce the chance of winter winds rocking the plant and loosening the roots.

7 If the rose is in a container, planting is even more simple. Prepare the soil and remove the plant from its container, keeping the root-ball intact.

Right and above: Peter McHoy

8 Tease out a few of the larger roots that have become wound around the root-ball and spread these out in the hole. Use a cane to check the hole depth.

CHECKLIST

WHAT TO DO

LAWNS
Rake up and collect autumn leaves

BEDS AND BORDERS
Tidy borders and store stakes and supports
Compost plant debris and leaves

SHRUBS
Plant roses and other deciduous shrubs
Plant hedges

ROCK GARDEN
Pick off fallen autumn leaves
Top up stone chippings

LOOK AHEAD

TAKE CUTTINGS
Propagate shrubs such as dogwoods from hardwood cuttings

DIVIDE
Iris sibirica

PLANT
English irises, lilies, ornamental onions, prepared lily-of-the-valley

WHAT TO SEE

BULBS AND BORDER PLANTS
Algerian iris (*Iris unguicularis*), pampas grass (*Cortaderia selloana*)

SHRUBS AND TREES
Heathers (*Erica* × *darleyensis*), cotoneaster (berries/foliage), guelder rose (*Viburnum opulus*, berries), pyracantha (berries), strawberry tree (*Arbutus unedo*)

VISITORS

FRIENDS
Blackbirds, grey squirrels, thrushes

FOES
Rabbits, voles, woodlice

MID AUTUMN
WEEK 5

WHAT TO DO

Do not let the season's ever-lengthening evenings and increasingly cold and dull days give you a negative attitude to gardening. Pick a few blooms from the garden to cheer up the home, and look on outdoor tasks like clearing up the beds and raking up autumn leaves with a positive attitude. You can smarten your garden even if it lacks the colour of previous months – and some useful recycling can be done.

Recycle for the future

Collections/Patrick Johns

Rake up leaves so they don't kill the grass.

For gardeners there is nothing new about recycling – they have been doing it for generations. The compost heap is a perfect recycling machine, enabling you to put all that goodness back into the soil next year. Tidying up borders and consigning the remains of the summer bedding to the compost heap is a valuable contribution to next year's plants.

Compost as much material as you can. If you do not have a compost heap, this is an ideal time to start one as there is so much material available – but do not use diseased plants.

Compost fallen leaves, too, but use any that rot down slowly, like beech and oak, in a separate heap to produce leaf-mould.

Pick some flowers for the home

At a time when flowers are few and far between in the garden it may take courage to cut some for indoors, but even a small garden produces a few spare blooms for table decoration. Choose a simple display using just two or three flowers, or a couple of sprays of blossom enhanced with foliage.

*The winter-flowering Algerian iris (*I. unguicularis*, sometimes sold as* I. stylosa*) is starting to flower about now, but the blooms are often damaged by birds, so pick a few just before the buds open to enjoy indoors.*

*A few shoots of winter-flowering plants that produce a mass of bloom all winter, if the weather is not too severe, such as winter jasmine and laurustinus (*Viburnum tinus*), will do much to brighten up the home.*

Tidy the rock garden

Many choice alpines die each year because fallen leaves deprive them of light and act as a haven for slugs, snails and woodlice. Pick them off and pull up any weeds. To improve appearances, top up any depleted stone chippings from the rock garden.

LOOK AHEAD

Summer bulbs to plant now

Lilies can still be planted, except in very cold areas, as they are less likely to deteriorate in the ground than if allowed to dry out until spring. But get them in the ground without delay.

Border bulbs such as English irises and many alliums that flower in early or mid summer will do better if planted in the autumn. Towards the end of the season these bulbs are often reduced in price at garden centres. It is getting late for planting in some areas but they can be a good buy provided you plant them without delay.

English irises are great for cutting, so if you do not have a suitable spot for them in the border, try growing them in a spare piece of ground for use as cut flowers. They prefer a rich, moist soil, and some shelter or winter protection (such as a cloche or a thick mulch of peat or pulverized bark) in cold areas. If conditions suit they can be left undisturbed to flower each year.

Allium karataviense *flowers in late spring.*

WHAT TO SEE

Eric Crichton

Erica × darleyensis *'Silberschmelze'.*

Heathers are year-round plants and, by choosing appropriate species and varieties, you can have them in bloom at any season. The winter-flowering kinds are especially useful, however, and help to fill that awkward gap when the autumn flowers have finished but the winter ones are not yet at their best. **Erica × darleyensis** ***varieties are valuable, as many of them start to flower in late autumn and provide pockets of colour right through until spring. This heather is lime tolerant and is an excellent plant for ground cover.***

If possible, try to see them growing before choosing varieties for your own garden, as this gives you a better idea of their habit and final size. Otherwise, small plants in garden centres will give you a good idea of flower and foliage colour . . . and you can plant them now.

One of the finest varieties is 'Silberschmelze' (also known as 'Molten Silver'), a silvery white heather that flowers for a long period. 'Arthur Johnson' is one of the most reliable and long flowering pink varieties; 'Darley Dale' is another dependable pink.

VISITORS

Children and most nature-lovers adore the cheeky and friendly grey squirrel, especially in parks and gardens where it is tame enough to feed from the hand. But there are people who resent its numbers and blame it for ousting the red squirrel. It is more likely that the red squirrel declined through disease, however, and the grey squirrel simply moved in to fill the gap.

The grey squirrel came from America and was originally released from captivity at places like London Zoo. It found things so to its liking there that it soon bred and spread to most parts of the country.

It is active all year round but, at this time, is often busy in gardens laying up a winter store of beech-mast and fruit and nuts of many kinds. They may visit the bird table if bird food with nuts and other tasty morsels is on the menu.

If there are squirrels in the area you may think it is worth feeding them so that they become regular visitors.

Stephan Dalton/NHPA

Although attractive, the grey squirrel may eat garden plants and damage saplings.

DIVIDE *IRIS SIBIRICA*

Iris sibirica ***is a popular plant for the margin of a pool, but it also makes an attractive border plant if the soil is not too dry. Large clumps tend to die out in the centre after a few years, however, so it makes sense to divide and replant established clumps every four to five years. This also provides an opportunity to give pieces to your friends or to expand the plant's territory to other fairly damp parts of the garden.***

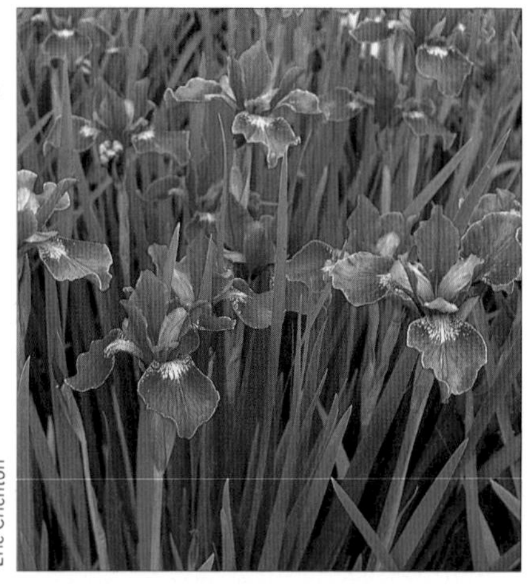

Eric Crichton

1 *Iris sibirica has many attractive varieties in shades of pale and dark blue, pink, violet and white – this is 'Orville Fay'. All flower in early summer.*

Marshall Cavendish

2 *Lift the clump after loosening it all round with a fork or spade. An ideal time to do this is when the soil is neither too dry nor very wet.*

3 *Pull the pieces apart by hand. If the rhizomatous roots are difficult to separate into suitable sizes, cut through them with a sharp knife.*

4 *A clump of moderate size like the one above will produce about half a dozen pieces of generous size with plenty of roots and a tuft of foliage.*

5 *Replant as soon as possible. You can make a convenient slit with the spade or use a trowel. Plant about 30cm/1ft apart to make a bold new clump.*

LILY-OF-THE-VALLEY

Lily-of-the-valley **(Convallari[a] majalis)** ***is not difficult to force, but you must buy specially prepared crowns if you want them to flower in the next 4-6 weeks. You may find these in garden centres; otherwise order them by pos[t].***

They will be more expensiv[e] than ordinary crowns. But yo[u] can plant ordinary crowns or even lift some from the garde[n] to grow in pots – they will flowe[r] later. Their wonderful smell seems more intense indoors.

1 *Pot crowns into 13-15cm/5-6in pots, using a peat-based or peat substitute compost. The crowns should be just below the surface.*

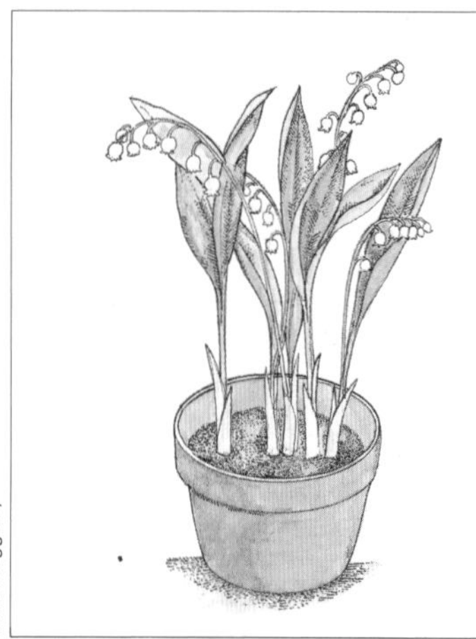

Vana Haggerty

2 *Keep moist, in a dark, vermin-proof place at 10-13°C/50-55° until the leaves are about 10cm/4in high, then bring into a light position to flower.*

PLANT A HEDGE

Hedges can be planted at any time of the year if you use large container-grown plants, but that is an expensive method, requiring many plants. Bare-root plants or small specimens grown as bundled plants in a container are best planted in the autumn, or any time during the dormant season if the plants are deciduous or semi-evergreen. Look for plants in the hedging section at the garden centre.

1 *Prepare the ground well. If the area is covered with grass, skim this off with a spade. Use a garden line to provide a straight edge for the trench.*

2 *Remove the soil to a depth of about 25cm/10in, placing it to one side of the trench. Bend your knees so that they, rather than your back, take the strain.*

All photos Peter McHoy

3 *Work in as much humus-forming garden compost, rotted manure or shrub planting mixture as you can spare. Fork it into the bottom of the trench.*

4 *Return the soil to the trench, mixing more organic material in with it if you have enough to spare. Apply a good sprinkling of bone meal and rake it in.*

5 *At this time of year you will find some hedging plants simply bundled as bare-root plants. You will find them in containers like this at any time of year.*

6 *A container like the one shown will usually hold about 12 plants, but the number will vary. Keep them in the container until you are ready to plant.*

7 *Spacing will depend on the type of plant, but 38-45in/15-18in is fine for most kinds. Make sure the holes are large enough to spread the roots.*

8 *Bare-root plants must be planted firmly. Tread the soil around the plants to eliminate large air pockets. Keep well watered in dry weather.*

CHECKLIST

WHAT TO DO

BULBS IN BOWLS
Keep watered and check growth

BEDS AND BORDERS
Tidy borders
Clean and store canes
Test the soil

SHRUBS
Plant deciduous trees and shrubs
Plant hedges

ROCK GARDEN
Remove fallen autumn leaves
Protect plants with hairy leaves under glass

LOOK AHEAD

TAKE CUTTINGS
Propagate shrubs such as dogwoods and flowering currants from hardwood cuttings

SOW
Prepare perennial seeds that need prechilling

PLANT
Lilies, ornamental onions and lily-of-the-valley for forcing

WHAT TO SEE

BORDER PLANTS
Algerian iris (*Iris unguicularis*), Pampas grass (*Cortaderia selloana*)

SHRUBS AND TREES
Autumn cherry (*Prunus subhirtella* 'Autumnalis'), heathers (*Erica* × *darleyensis*), laurustinus (*Viburnum tinus*), pyracantha (berries), strawberry tree (*Arbutus unedo*)

VISITORS

FRIENDS
Blackbirds, robins, squirrels, thrushes

FOES
Cutworms, rabbits, voles

LATE AUTUMN

WEEK 1

WHAT TO DO

As gardening becomes increasingly difficult outdoors, make the most of those fine days that do occur to tidy beds and borders, and protect any vulnerable plants against the colder weather that will come.

There are cheerful and promising signs of growth to offset the gloom of deteriorating weather. Bulbs that were planted in bowls to flower in early winter may be starting to shoot.

Check bulbs in pots

Those bulbs planted in pots or bowls in early autumn should be checked every week to ensure that the compost is neither dry nor waterlogged. Check too whether the plants are ready for moving into a light position.

Once the shoots are about 4–5cm/1½–2in tall, bring the bulbs indoors and place them in a sunny but cool position. Try to keep them below 10°C/50°F, otherwise the stems may become too drawn and weak.

You can make the pots and bowls look smarter and more interesting by covering the surface with moss (gathered from the garden) or grass. Sow the grass seed now so that it will germinate before the bulbs flower.

Peter McHoy

Plunged bulbs may be ready to bring in.

Check the rock garden

The majority of rock plants are very tough and hardy. They will succumb, though, to a covering of leaves that keeps out the light and creates conditions that encourage fungus diseases and pests. Slugs and snails, which love to hide beneath leaf litter and other debris, will soon munch their way through a small rock plant.

To keep losses to a minimum, take a few minutes to remove fallen autumn leaves from the plants and from surrounding areas. If necessary, top up the stone chippings around vulnerable plants to deter slugs and ensure that water drains freely away.

Leaves are best removed by hand, as rakes are not effective among rocks and you may actually uproot the plants.

Plant trees and shrubs

This is a good time to buy and plant deciduous trees and shrubs. If you layered your own shrubs last year, they may be ready for

Eric Crichton

Layers may be ready to sever and plant.

severing and replanting. Check that they have rooted well before cutting and moving them.

Prechill difficult seeds

Some seeds require a cold period to help them germinate, especially those that in nature would lie dormant through a cold winter before germinating in the spring. This includes most alpines, many trees and shrubs, and even a lot of perennial border plants.

You could sow the seeds in seed trays or pots and keep them outdoors for the winter, but vermin can be a problem, especially if the seeds are large. It is often more convenient to create an artificial winter in your fridge.

If you can buy such seeds early, or if you have collected them from plants in your own garden, sow them on moist kitchen paper in a margarine tub or similar small container with a lid, then place them in a cold part of the fridge (you do not need to place them in the freezing compartment). The container must have a lid otherwise the paper and seeds will quickly dry out. Check periodically to make sure the seeds are still moist, but they should not be waterlogged.

When you sow them properly in the spring they should germinate much more quickly than those not treated to a cold period.

WHAT TO SEE

Border plants that flower from mid autumn to early spring are scarce, so the Algerian iris deserves a special place in the garden.

You are likely to find the Algerian iris sold as Iris stylosa *or* I. unguicularis, *an ugly name for a beautiful plant. The flowers are typically iris shaped, about 6-8cm / 2½-3in across, usually in shades of soft lavender or lilac with a yellow blaze on the lower petals. They are great for bringing a little winter cheer into the home on a dull day. Pick them in bud.*

Named varieties include 'Mary Barnard' (dark mauve) and 'Walter Butt' (pale blue).

Eric Crichton

Iris unguicularis *'Mary Barnard'*.

There is also a rare white form: I. u. alba.

The strap-shaped leaves are evergreen, but this is not the attraction it may at first appear, for they tend to hide the flowers that nestle low down in the plant. Try cutting the leaves back to about 30cm / 12in to make the flowers more visible.

Early autumn is certainly the best time to plant, but put them in a warm, sunny spot with well-drained soil. Then be patient – they can take a year or two to settle down before they flower well.

VISITORS

Cutworms are not worms at all but the caterpillars of various moths. They live in the top few centimetres of the soil for most of the time, attacking stems of young plants, though they will also damage roots, tubers, bulbs and corms. They are most active during the summer, but caterpillars from the second generation overwinter in the soil and pupate in spring.

If you see dull-coloured caterpillars curled up in the soil when you are digging at this time of year, they are likely to be cutworms so take the opportunity to destroy them. Just leaving them exposed on the surface may be enough if birds such as robins are around.

Fat, soft brown, yellow or green caterpillars with a line of dark markings on the side are likely to be from the large yellow underwing moth. Grey-brown ones with fine dark spots on the body are probably from the turnip moth or heart and dart moth.

If they are apt to become a real nuisance in the spring (they often cause most damage to young plants by chewing the stems at ground level), dust with a soil insecticide such as bromophos.

Ron Fotherington/NPHA

Caterpillar of cloud-bordered brindle moth.

TEST YOUR SOIL

There is only a limited amount that you can tell about a soil simply by looking at it. Its appearance may not tell you how acid or alkaline it is (important if you want to grow acid-loving or chalk-loving plants), or whether it is deficient in major nutrients. To know how best to treat and manage your soil, you need to test for pH and nutrient levels . . . and it is very easy with a kit from your local garden centre.

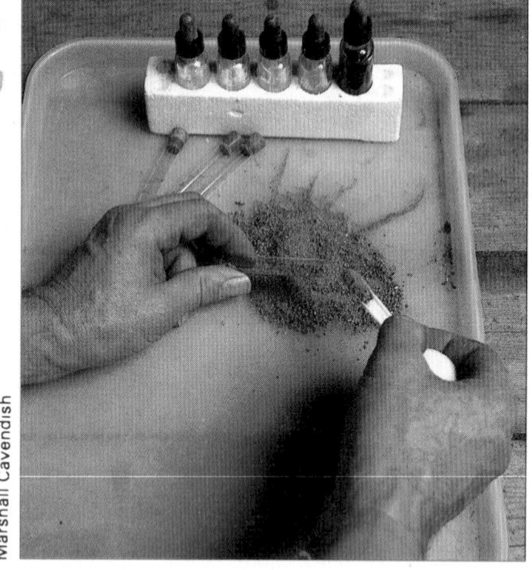

Marshall Cavendish

1 Kits vary in detail, but most are similar to this one. Take soil samples as advised by the manufacturer, from various parts of the garden.

2 Place a measured amount of soil in a test-tube and add the indicator fluid. It is convenient to start with the pH test, but be guided by the manufacturer.

3 Shake the stoppered test-tube well, then allow it to stand to let the particles settle and the fluid clear, or it will be difficult to judge the colour.

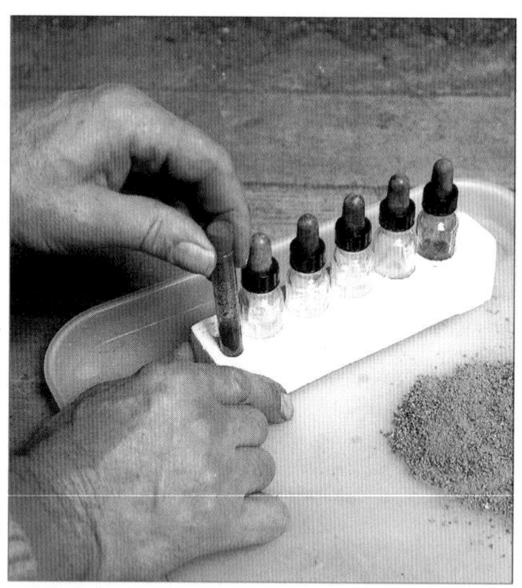

4 The approximate pH can be read off against the special colour chart provided. Hold it the right distance away from the chart, in good light.

5 Read off the levels against the colour chart. Follow a similar routine to test for the major nutrients, nitrogen (N), potassium (K) and phosphorus (P).

PRESERVE THOSE CANES

Bamboo canes are less expensive than most other types of plant support, and they look more natural than the majority of alternatives, but they will soon rot if you neglect them. It makes sense to preserve your investment – a quick and easy job.

Rots thrive in the damp, so do not leave your canes in the garden for the winter. Clean them, dry them off and store them in a dry shed.

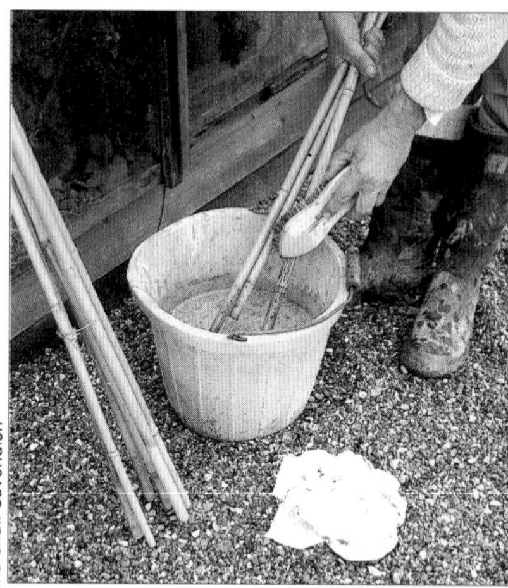

Marshall Cavendish

1 Before storing garden canes for the winter, scrub them clean with a stiff brush, using a garden disinfectant. Concentrate especially on the ends.

Peter McHoy

2 Wipe them with a dry cloth, and allow the canes to dry off. Then stand the bottoms (the broad ends) in a wood preservative overnight before storing.

BUILD A RETAINING WALL

Do not be deterred from building a low retaining wall like this one because you lack bricklaying experience – it is an ideal first project, and the heavy mixing and lifting involved is minimal. If you do not rush the project you will not strain yourself.

Choose a frost-free spell to make the footing and lay the bricks. Protect the wall from frost until the concrete and mortar have set.

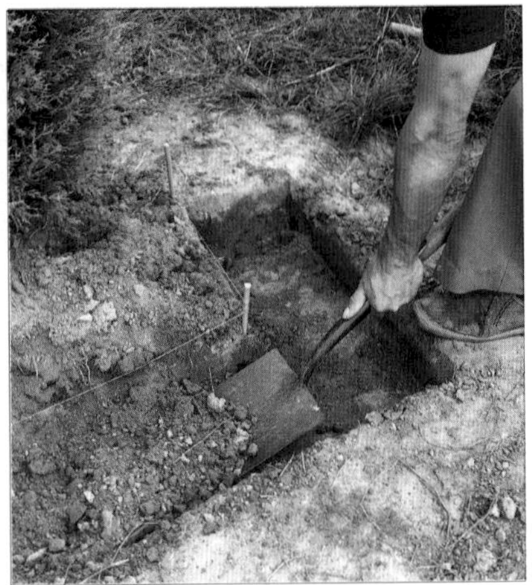

1 *Excavate a trench about 30cm/12in wide and 10cm/4in deep where you want the wall to be. Use strings between wooden pegs to outline the area.*

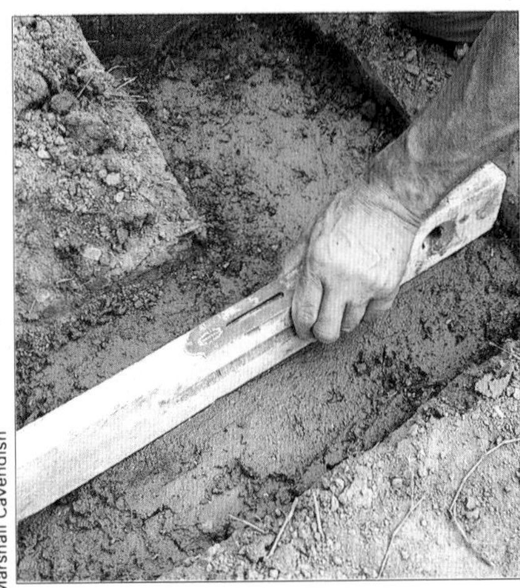

2 *Use a concrete mix suitable for footings, to form a level bed about 7.5cm/3in thick. For an area like this premixed concrete is not too expensive.*

3 *Once the base has set firm you can lay the bricks. It is important to use string guides to ensure that they are laid absolutely straight.*

4 *Bed the first course of bricks on mortar, using a spirit-level to check levels. Premixed bagged mortar will make life easier, though more expensive.*

5 *Build the wall to the required level, working from the corners. Use a string stretched between the ends to provide a guide as you lay.*

6 *Use the spirit-level to check both horizontals and verticals, and across the corners as shown. Tap the bricks level and add more mortar if necessary.*

7 *Point the bricks to produce a neat finish, using the same mortar mix. Push mortar into the joints, then strike it clean with a bricklaying trowel.*

8 *Do not make the wall too high – this needs stronger foundations and a more complicated laying pattern. Fill with good soil to make a planting area.*

LATE AUTUMN
WEEK 2

CHECKLIST

WHAT TO DO

BULBS
Keep bulbs in bowls watered and bring indoors those for early flowering
Check tender summer-flowering bulbs, corms and tubers in store

BEDS AND BORDERS
Tidy borders

SHRUBS
Plant deciduous trees, shrubs and hedges

GREENHOUSE
Clean pots and seed trays

LOOK AHEAD

TAKE CUTTINGS
Take hardwood cuttings of shrubs such as dogwoods, flowering currants, viburnums and willows
Take root cuttings of drumstick primulas, oriental poppies, perennial border phlox and verbascum

ORDER SEED CATALOGUES
Order catalogues if not already on mailing list

WHAT TO SEE

BULBS AND BORDER PLANTS
Algerian iris (*Iris unguicularis*)

SHRUBS AND TREES
Autumn cherry (*Prunus subhirtella* 'Autumnalis'), cotoneaster (berries), heathers (*Erica* × *darleyensis*), laurustinus (*Viburnum tinus*), pernettya (berries), pyracantha (berries), winter jasmine

VISITORS

FRIENDS
Blackbirds, robins, squirrels, thrushes

FOES
Cutworms, rabbits, voles

WHAT TO DO

When the weather is particularly dull as well as cold, there is always the temptation to turn your back on the garden and to content yourself with the delights of planning and dreaming that come from reading about it in books, magazines and catalogues. Make the most of fine days, however, to finish those few jobs that you can still do outdoors.

Order seed catalogues

Seed catalogues are advertised in newspapers and gardening magazines at this time. Browsing through catalogues is not only a pleasant way to spend a few hours, it is also a practical contribution to next year's gardening.

It makes sense to order your seeds as soon as possible so that you receive those that require a long growing season, such as pelargoniums (geraniums), in time to sow early. If you wait until spring to order, your seeds may arrive late, as orders are almost always despatched in rotation.

Marshall Cavendish

Catalogues will give you plenty of ideas.

Check stored bulbs and tubers

Check tender summer-flowering bulbs, corms and tubers, such as gladioli and dahlias, every couple of weeks to make sure none have started to rot. It is especially important to check them over at this time as any that were not properly dry when stored may be decaying, and the rot can quickly spread to others.

Remove and destroy those that are affected. Dust others in close proximity with a fungicide such as sulphur dust. Make sure stored bulbs, corms and tubers are kept well ventilated.

Protect young evergreens

Unlike deciduous trees and shrubs, which lose little water during the winter because they have no leaves through which to transpire, evergreens continue to lose moisture right through the winter. Drying winter winds can increase the rate at which water is lost from the leaves.

This does not matter much with well established plants, but newly planted evergreens will not have produced enough roots through which to replace moisture. A simple windbreak of polythene, netting or sacking may be enough to save a newly-planted evergreen.

LOOK AHEAD

Clean pots and trays

Clay pots will last for many years if looked after, and even plastic pots and seed trays should last for several seasons. Keep them out of strong sunlight as much as possible (this makes many plastics brittle). You are almost sure to have amassed a collection of old pots and trays and within the next month or two you will need them again for seed sowing and pricking out.

It is lovely to start with clean containers.

Make the most of this slack time in the garden to clean containers thoroughly, so that they are ready for use. This will help to reduce the chance of diseases attacking vulnerable young seedlings.

Wash off any soil first, then scrub containers thoroughly in a bowl of water containing a disinfectant, before rinsing and drying off. This is a job you can do indoors if the weather is unfavourable.

Store the cleaned pots and trays in a dry, protected place, such as a garden shed or garage.

Take the opportunity to clean old labels ready for re-use. Wooden ones can be repainted, plastic ones can often be cleaned with a kitchen cleanser.

WHAT TO SEE

Berries and birds are not compatible for long, though some berries seem less attractive to birds and these will remain decorative for many more weeks. Make a note of these if you are planning to introduce berried shrubs into your borders to provide a few splashes of colour in early winter.

Some firethorns (pyracanthas) are quickly stripped once the hard weather arrives. Those that normally retain their berries well into winter include P. angustifolia *(with orange-yellow berries, often until spring) and 'Orange Glow' (bright orange-red berries).*

Cotoneasters are invaluable berrying shrubs and the popular herringbone cotoneaster, C. horizontalis, *usually retains its berries in early winter. For a dwarf, almost prostrate, cotoneaster for the front of a border,* C. salicifolius *'Autumn Fire' can be depended upon for a profusion of long-lasting red berries. For something different, the tall* C. *'Rothschildianus' has yellow berries that ripen late and also last well.*

Eric Crichton

Cotoneaster horizontalis *covered in berries.*

Hollies can generally be relied upon to carry a good crop of berries until mid winter.

If you choose a variety that is brightly variegated, such as the gold and green Ilex x altaclarensis *'Gold King' or the weeping white and green* I. aquifolium *'Argentea Pendula', you will have really striking winter-interest plants.*

Pernettyas require an acid soil. They retain their large pink, red or white berries well into the new year. 'Bell's Seedling' can still have attractive-looking berries when next year's flowers arrive.

Berries on the common mountain ash (Sorbus aucuparia) *often disappear by early autumn, but the gleaming white ones of* S. cashmiriana *and* S. hupehensis *hang until mid winter.*

VISITORS

The cheery and cheeky robin is a year-round resident, but it visits gardens more frequently during the winter. Robins seem to appear from nowhere once you start digging, and will often keep you company, pecking at grubs exposed as you turn over the soil.

Although they will sometimes eat fruit and berries, they prefer grubs and insects so they should be encouraged. They will also accept crumbs and scraps, so you should be able to keep them as regular visitors.

Stephen Dalton/NHPA

Robins can become remarkably tame.

TAKE ROOT CUTTINGS

Root cuttings are an interesting alternative to stem cuttings for some plants. If you have never tried this method of propagation you will find it rewarding. Most root cuttings are only successful if taken during the plant's dormant season.

Among the plants that you can propagate now are anchusa, drumstick primula **(Primula denticulata)*****, oriental poppies, phlox and verbascum.***

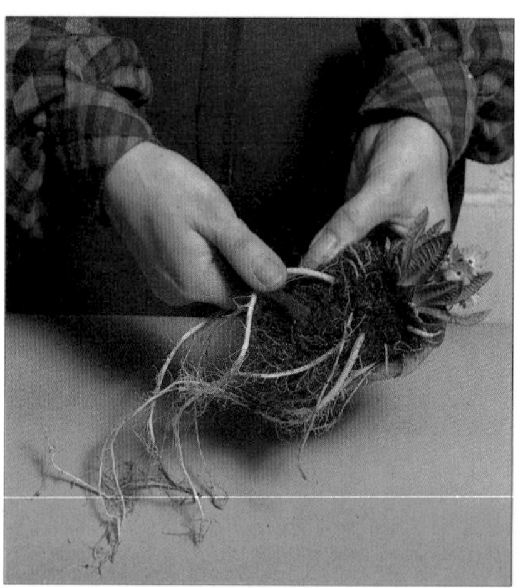

1 Lift a young but established plant with plenty of vigour, and shake off the soil to expose the roots. Cut off the roots you wish to use, then replant the crown.

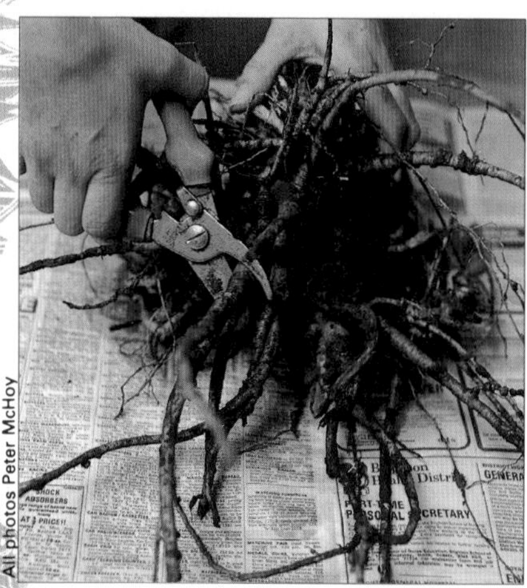

All photos Peter McHoy

2 Small plants like the drumstick primula, shown in the first step, are easily prepared with a knife, but secateurs may be needed for thick roots.

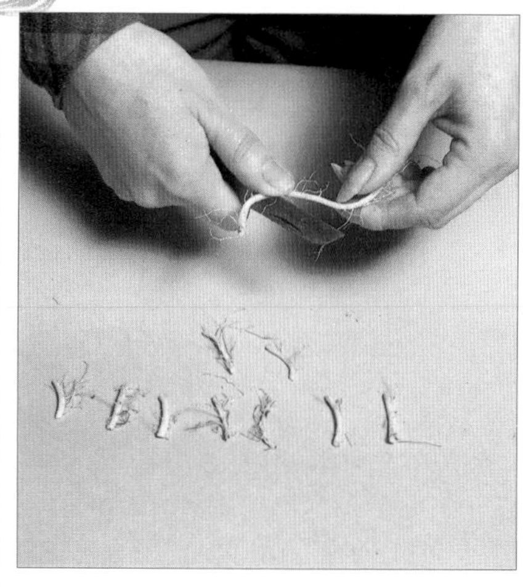

3 Cut the roots into lengths about 2.5-5cm/1-2in long. To remind you which way up to plant, cut the top straight across and the bottom at a slant.

4 Cuttings with fine roots can be laid horizontally in a seed tray and covered with compost; insert thicker ones vertically in pots, just covering the top.

5 By early summer the cuttings should have formed new roots and shoots, like these drumstick primula cuttings, ready to be separated and planted.

KEEP THE COLD FRAME COSY

A cold frame will provide enough protection to overwinter many cuttings a plants that need a little protection from the worst o the winter cold, such as young hebes.

Old-fashioned frames had brick or wooden sides, whicl offered good protection, but modern all-glass frames do n retain warmth so well, and ca be draughty. They can easily b insulated, however, for little co

1 If there are gaps between the glass and the aluminium frames, seal them with draught-proofing strips sold for windows and doors.

2 Insulate the sides and ends of the frame with sheets of expanded polystyrene (sold by DIY stores). Just cut the pieces to size with a knife or saw.

HARDWOOD CUTTINGS

Many popular shrubs, such as dogwoods, flowering currants, viburnums and willows, can be propagated from hardwood cuttings taken now. Ideally, the shrubs should have been pruned hard a year ago to stimulate plenty of vigorous new shoots, but you should be able to find suitable shoots even if this was not done. Most of the cuttings will root by next autumn, and can be planted the following spring.

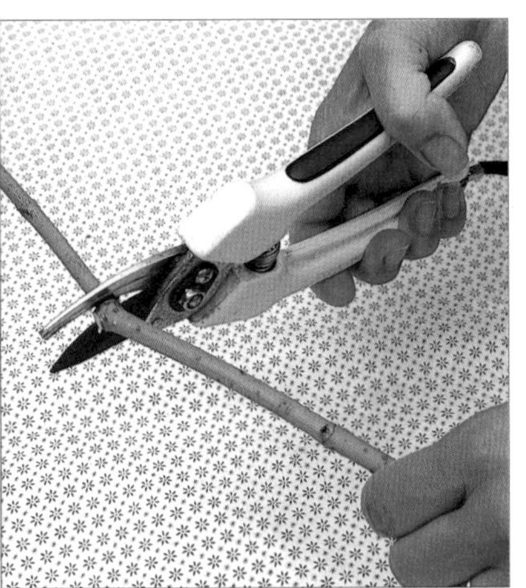

1 *Use hardened shoots, not those that are still soft, and make a slanting cut above a bud at the top. You can make several cuttings out of a long shoot.*

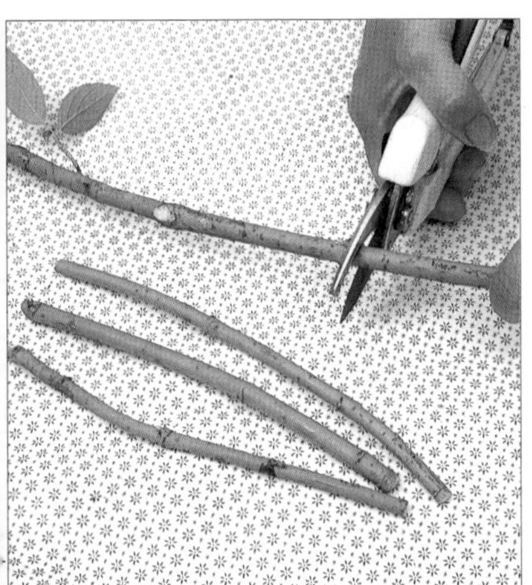

2 *Cut the bottom of each one at right angles to the stem. An ideal length for hardwood cuttings is 15-20cm/6-8in, though longer ones are sometimes used.*

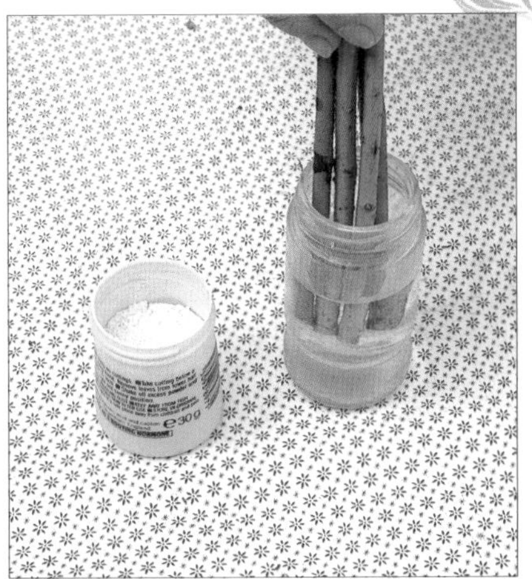

3 *A hormone rooting powder should increase the success rate with plants that are difficult to root, but most root easily without hormone treatment.*

4 *If using a hormone powder (liquids are also available), dip the end in water before inserting into the powder. Treat only the end of each cutting.*

5 *Make a slit trench about 10-20cm/4-8in deep in ground where the cuttings can be left undisturbed for a year. A spade is ideal for making the trench.*

6 *If the ground is poorly drained, trickle a layer of coarse sand or fine grit into the bottom of the trench. This will prevent the cuttings becoming waterlogged.*

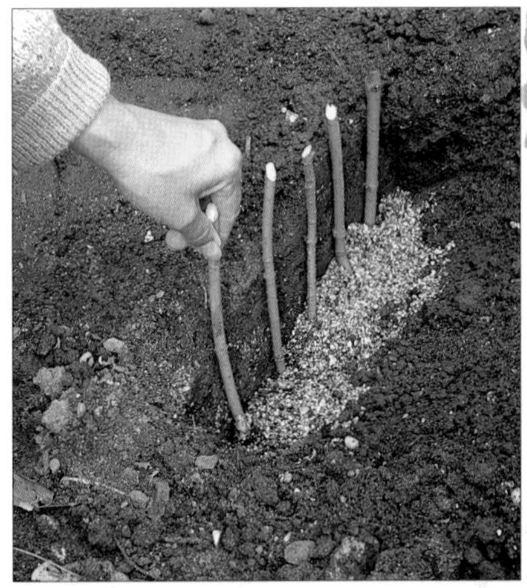

7 *Insert the cuttings vertically against the back of the trench, spacing them an inch or two apart. Leave about 2.5-5cm/1-2in standing above the ground.*

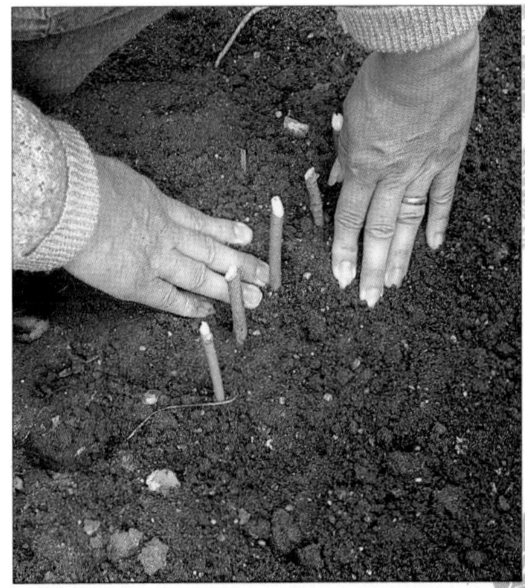

8 *Firm the soil well to ensure that there are no air pockets trapped around the cuttings. After frosty weather the ground may need to be firmed again.*

CHECKLIST

WHAT TO DO

BULBS
Check bowls of bulbs to see whether they should be brought into the light

BEDS AND BORDERS
Hoe or lightly fork over the soil
Plan design changes for next year

SHRUBS
Plant deciduous trees, shrubs and hedges
Plant trees in containers
Protect vulnerable shrubs in pots and tubs

ROSES
Pick up leaves and tidy rose beds

LOOK AHEAD

TAKE CUTTINGS
Take hardwood cuttings of shrubs such as dogwoods, flowering currants and willows
Take root cuttings of drumstick primulas, oriental poppies and perennial border phlox

ORDER CATALOGUES
Order seed catalogues if you are not already on a mailing list

STORE TOOLS
Clean tools before putting them away

WHAT TO SEE

BORDER PLANTS
Algerian iris (*Iris unguicularis*)

SHRUBS AND TREES
Autumn cherry (*Prunus subhirtella* 'Autumnalis'), cotoneaster (berries), heathers (*Erica* × *darleyensis*), laurustinus (*Viburnum tinus*), pernettya (berries), winter jasmine, winter sweet (*Chimonanthus fragrans*)

VISITORS

FRIENDS
Robins, squirrels

FOES
Cutworms, rabbits, woodpigeons

LATE AUTUMN
WEEK 3

WHAT TO DO

Dark evenings and dull weather will not encourage you to go out and garden. It is worth making the effort, however, because even ten minutes a day can help to keep the garden looking smart and tidy. Jobs done now will ease the pressure during the busy spring months next year.

You might be surprised at what colour you can still find in your beds and borders

Loosen border soil

Borders tidied up in the autumn will benefit from another going over with the hoe. Some of the weeds that can become a real nuisance, such as chickweed, groundsel and bittercress, can germinate and make quite a lot of growth during the sometimes warm days of late autumn. They may even start to flower and spread their seeds around the garden whenever there is a long spell of good weather.

Chop off any lingering weeds with the hoe. Loosening the soil will also improve the appearance of what is often a large expanse of bare soil at this time.

Alternatively, fork over the ground to a depth of about 5-8cm 2-3in to bury the weeds.

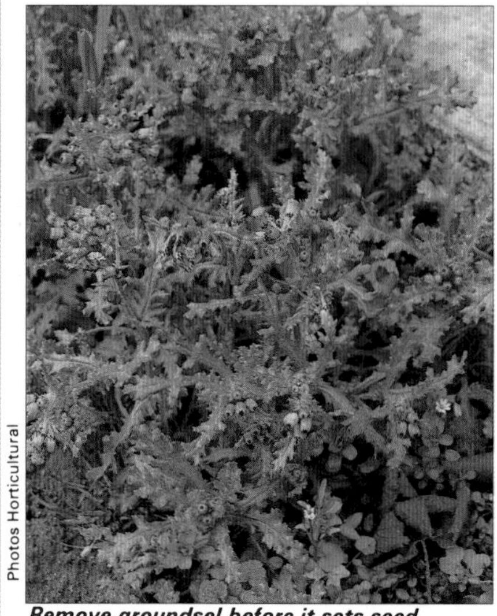

Photos Horticultural

Remove groundsel before it sets seed.

Send for seed catalogues

Send off for your catalogues now so that you can sit and plan your summer garden for next year when the weather is too cold to work outside.

Plant trees and shrubs

If you have ordered trees and shrubs by post, deciduous kinds may arrive bare-root at any time during the dormant season. Hedging plants are often bought bare-root because they are much cheaper in this form than container-grown ones.

If they arrive at an inconvenient time, heel the plant in, using a spare piece of ground.

Tidy rose beds

Pick up and burn any fallen leaves from around your roses then loosen the soil to keep down weeds. This is more than just a cosmetic job – many rose diseases, such as black spot, can overwint

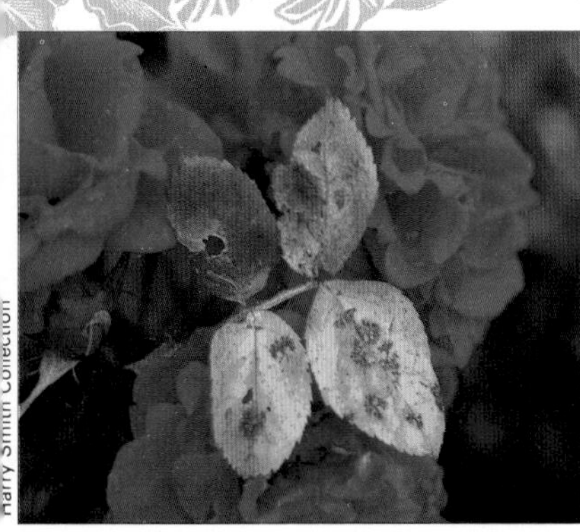
Harry Smith Collection

Destroy rose leaves that have black spot.

on fallen leaves and debris. Destroy them now to reduce the extent of any attack next year.

Check the ties on standard roses, as these plants are vulnerable in winter gales. Make sure climbing roses are tied in, and that existing ties are not too tight (if necessary remove the old tie and use a new one).

LOOK AHEAD

Plan improvements

Great gardens often begin on a sheet of paper. Time spent with paper and pencil now can save time and expensive mistakes in the garden next year.

If is tempting to start by planning which plants to buy and where to put them, but the biggest improvements often come from small changes in design.

If you have a lot of small beds in the lawn, would the effect be better if they were made into fewer large ones? Would the garden be more interesting if you set the lawn at a 45 degree angle to the house, or trimmed it to a circular shape? Could the lawn's appearance be improved and the grass cutting made simpler by easing out some of those tight curves? Would a focal point, such as a sundial, a birdbath or some other garden ornament, improve the appearance of a large expanse of grass? Would the garden be more interesting if you divided it up with a few plant-covered trellises into different areas?

Look at some of the gardens you like in My Garden, *and see whether you could introduce some of the features into your own. Try to draw your garden to scale on a piece of graph paper, then take several photocopies of the plan and spend an hour or so trying out ideas to see how many improvements you can make.*

WHAT TO SEE

If the weather is relatively mild, the garden will have many pockets of colour and interest. The bare branches of cotoneasters will still be studded with berries. Pyracanthas and pernettyas, too, should be bright with berries.

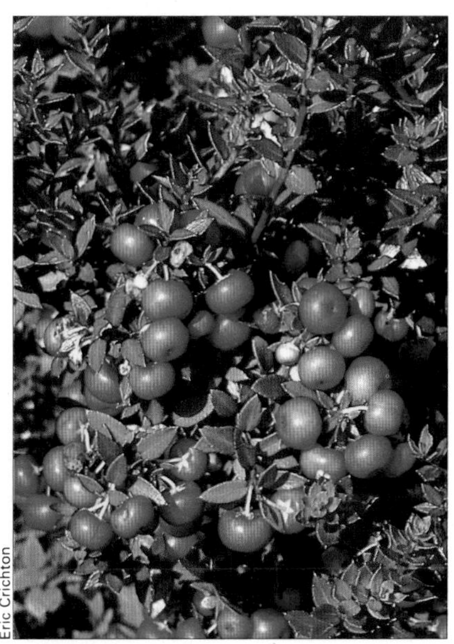
Eric Crichton

Pernettya mucronata *has vivid berries.*

*Winter-flowering shrubs, such as winter jasmine and laurustinus (*Viburnum tinus*), will be in full flower and, unless it is very frosty, the autumn cherry (*Prunus subhirtella *'Autumnalis') will be producing its small but attractive semi-double white flowers.*

In a mild autumn and early winter the greatest thrill can come from those tough summer plants that just seem to keep on flowering. There are even pond plants that do this.

*The water hawthorn (*Aponogeton distachyos*), for instance, starts flowering in early summer and in a mild season will still be producing fragrant white flowers well into early winter.*

VISITORS

Woodpigeons are regular winter visitors to the garden in some areas, and they can cause devastation among vegetables such as cabbages and Brussels sprouts once the weather becomes harsh. They will also damage many other garden plants if they become very hungry.

If they have been a problem in previous years, net vulnerable plants now. This is not always possible in a border, but it is a relatively simple job in a vegetable garden.

You can try bird scarers in other parts of the garden. For these to be effective you will need to move them around frequently, and use several different types in rotation.

Janey Sauvanet/NHPA

Woodpigeons can be a problem.

CHECK BULBS IN BOWLS

Keep a regular eye on bulbs that are in the dark – either in cupboards or plunged in sand or peat outside. They will be ruined if you let the compost or bulb fibre dry out, or if the shoots become too elongated before you bring them into the light.

Those planted early, especially 'prepared' hyacinths for early flowering, will be well advanced by now; others may not yet be ready.

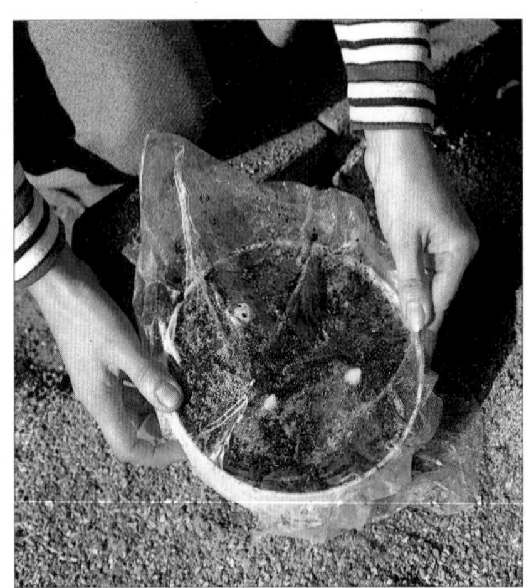

1 *Expose the bowls by removing the sand or peat used to keep the bulbs in the dark. Make sure the compost or bulb fibre is still moist.*

Peter McHoy

2 *Check bowls in cupboards, too, and bring them into the light once the shoots are 2.5-5cm/1-2in high. Keep in a cool position until the buds emerge.*

LOOK AFTER YOUR TOOLS

It makes sense to look after your tools. They are often expensive to buy, and looking after them will extend their life considerably. Clean, shiny tools are also easier and more pleasant to work with than dirty and rusty ones.

It takes only a few moments to clean your tools at the end of a gardening session, and it will not take long to give them extra treatment before storing them for the winter.

1 *Scrape off the soil at the end of a session. An old label or a small piece of wood is perfectly adequate, and it only takes a moment or two.*

Marshall Cavendish

2 *A cloth, ideally lightly oiled, is ideal for removing any remaining soil to leave the tool clean and bright. Do not forget the backs of tools such as spades.*

3 *To help prevent rusting if the tool is wet, or is to be stored for some time, brush it lightly with oil. This will give a protective coat.*

4 *Wood also needs protecting. Use a scrubbing brush to clean it. As diseases can be spread by tools, it makes sense to add a disinfectant.*

5 *At least once a year paint the wood when it is dry with a wood preservative. It will help to prevent th wood rotting and improves appearances to*

PROTECT TENDER POTTED SHRUBS

Do not let those choice shrubs in containers, such as bay (Laurus nobilis) and the cabbage or Torbay palm (Cordyline australis), succumb to the ravages of winter. Plants in containers are much more vulnerable than those in the ground. Even if you cannot put them in a porch, greenhouse or a conservatory for the winter, there are things you can do to protect them.

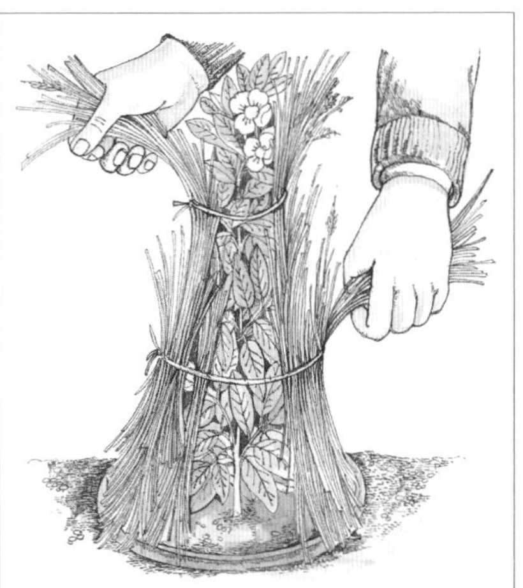

1 *Protect shrubs of borderline hardiness by plunging the pot into the ground and tying straw or bracken around the top growth during the coldest months.*

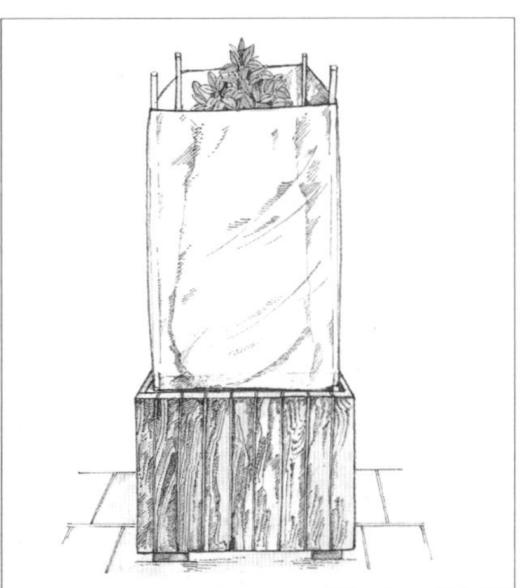

2 *Plants like bay trees are generally tough but they can be damaged by cold winter winds. Fix clear polythene around the plant, supported on canes.*

GROW A TREE IN A TUB

No matter how colourful your patio containers, or how pretty they are when planted with a succession of seasonal bedding, you will almost certainly appreciate the sense of permanency and extra height provided by a small tree. You can always add a dash of colour around the base with a few flowers.

Wait until spring before planting an evergreen. You can plant deciduous trees now.

All photos Peter McHoy

1 *Dwarf trees like this Japanese maple are usually used for containers, but taller kinds can be grown as the pot or tub will keep them compact.*

2 *Place a 5cm/2in layer of broken pots or coarse gravel in the bottom of the tub to provide good drainage, then part fill with a good loam-based compost.*

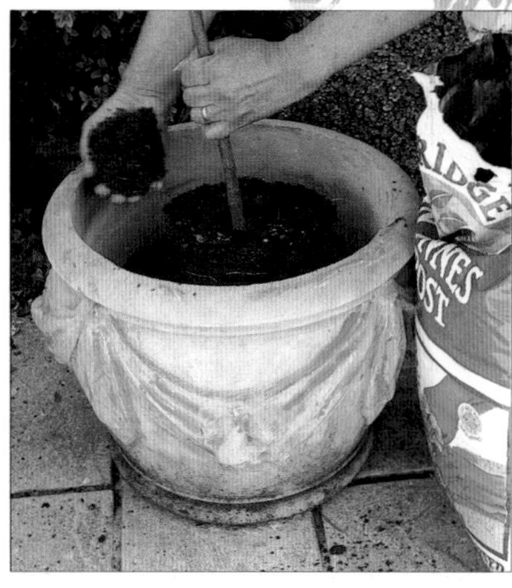

3 *Remove the tree from its pot and stand the root-ball in the container. Make sure there is a 5cm/2in gap between the root-ball and the top of the container.*

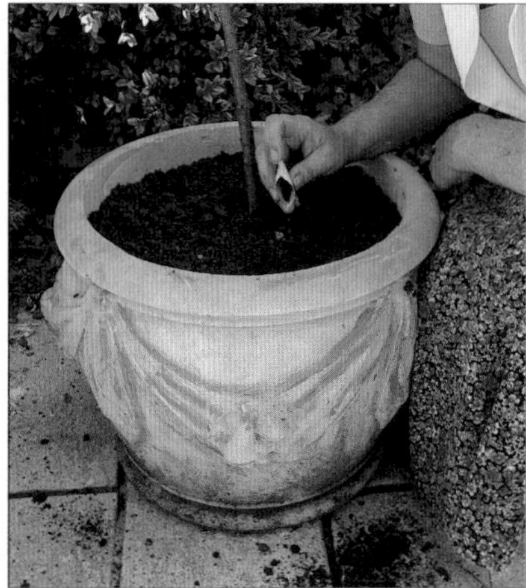

4 *Pack compost around the root-ball, firming it well. Plant some dwarf bulbs around the edge; in spring you can sow hardy annuals.*

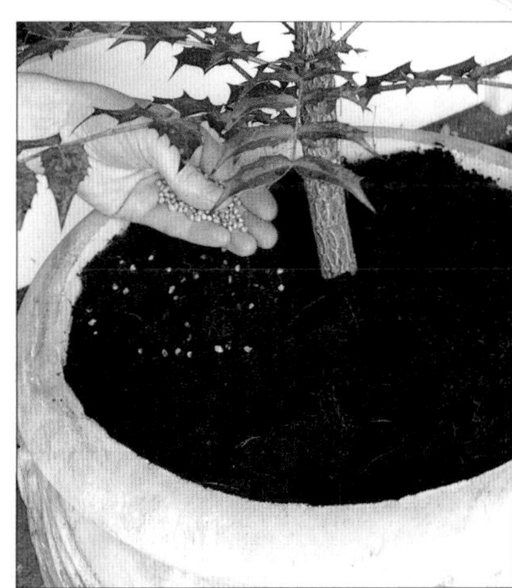

5 *Trees require feeding, so each spring sprinkle a slow-release fertilizer onto the surface, then carefully fork it in, trying not to damage the roots.*

Snowdrops push their delicate heads up into the thin, cold winter air – it is a busy time for the gardener as spring approaches.

WINTER

E A R L Y   W I N T E R

M I D   W I N T E R

L A T E   W I N T E R

CHECKLIST

WHAT TO DO

BULBS
Check bowls of bulbs to see whether they should be brought into the light

BEDS AND BORDERS
Continue winter digging

SHRUBS
Plant deciduous trees and hedges
Protect tender wall shrubs and figs

TROUGHS
Plant winter-interest alpines

FENCES
Apply a wood preservative

LOOK AHEAD

MAKE A HANGING BASKET
How to make one from wood

GARDEN MACHINERY
Have mowers etc. overhauled

CLEAN TOOLS
Clean tools before putting away for winter

WHAT TO SEE

BORDER PLANTS
Algerian iris (*Iris unguicularis*)

SHRUBS AND TREES
Autumn cherry (*Prunus subhirtella* 'Autumnalis'), cotoneaster (berries), heathers (*Erica* × *darleyensis*), laurustinus (*Viburnum tinus*), pernettya (berries), *Mahonia* 'Charity', *Malus* 'Red Sentinel' (a crab apple; berries), winter jasmine, winter sweet (*Chimonanthus fragrans*)

VISITORS

FRIENDS
Robins, squirrels

FOES
Rabbits, wood mice, woodpigeons

EARLY WINTER
WEEK 1

WHAT TO DO

Make the most of those days when the soil is still workable and the weather kind to dig over beds and borders. Tackle maintenance jobs, like painting walls and preserving fences, which are so much easier once branches of trees and shrubs are bare.

Evergreens in the garden can be cut for winter arrangements. Use berry-laden shoots to compensate for the lack of winter flowers.

Paint walls

Small courtyard gardens and backyard or basement gardens often have dark walls that can make the area seem small and gloomy. Paint them with a light-coloured masonry paint to reflect the light and to show off the plants. Most plants look better against a pale white or even a pink background, as it shows off their shape and profile and acts as a suitable backdrop for flowers.

Don Wildridge

Paint masonry walls white or a pale colour.

Continue winter digging

If you have a kitchen garden, continue with winter digging. On clay soil it is best to complete this as soon as possible so that winter frosts can break down the clods. On light, sandy soil it does not make much difference if you complete it in the spring, but doing it as soon as possible will leave you more time for sowing and planting in spring.

Preserve fences

Fences invariably turn an unappealing silvery-grey colour after a few years. A timber preservative will bring back some colour as well as arrest rots.

Creosote is a good preservative, but is not kind to plants and can be unpleasant to work with. If nearby plants are dormant, however, they should come to no harm as any damaging fumes will have gone by the time the plants come into leaf again (but try to avoid splashing any on the plants). If you do not want to use creosote, buy one of the 'plant safe' alternatives. These are less powerful preservatives than creosote, but they will keep the wood sound if used regularly and will improve its appearance.

Untie plants growing against the fence and lay them on the ground. Retie them again later. Take the opportunity to thin some of the growth if the plant has become too large or bushy.

If the plant is on a trellis, it may be possible to release the whole panel and to lay it on the ground while you paint the trellis and thin out the plant.

LOOK AHEAD

Overhaul garden machinery

Most garden machinery is expensive to buy, so do not let your investment fall into a poor state of repair. Overhaul machines now so that they are ready for the new season.

Mowers, especially, benefit from annual servicing. If you wait until spring, when you need to use the mower, a professional service is likely to take much longer because of increased demand. At this time of year the job should be done quickly, and some specialists offer special rates to generate work at a slack time.

Photos Horticultural

Clean mowers and other machinery.

Much routine maintenance, such as oiling and cleaning, is simple to do yourself. If you have a petrol mower, make sure the tank is drained and the machine suitably prepared for the winter.

WHAT TO SEE

Mahonias are hardy evergreen shrubs, grown for their large, spiny foliage and clusters of yellow bell-shaped flowers. Most of them are spring-flowering, but some are among the boldest of all winter-flowering shrubs.

The winter-flowerers are mainly tall plants with an upright habit, and they make imposing shrubs. They grow 1.8-3m/6-10ft tall, yet, because of their modest spread they can suit small gardens.

Mahonia lomariifolia *will not flower until mid winder, but the hybrid 'Charity' can bloom in late autumn.*

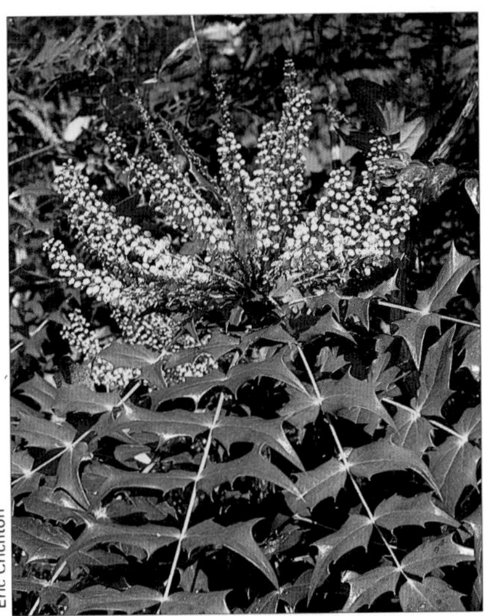

Eric Crichton

The yellow blooms of* Mahonia *'Charity'.

'Charity', with its cascading sprays of yellow flowers, is one of the most striking winter-flowering shrubs. The blackish berries in spring and early summer are a bonus.

'Charity' is widely available at most garden centres (you may even be able to buy it in flower now), and there are two similar but rare 'sisters', 'Hope' and 'Faith'.

VISITORS

Wood mice (also known as long-tailed field mice) do not hibernate, but often move into outbuildings, garden sheds and greenhouses during the winter. During mild spells they will make forays into the garden. Despite their name, they are creatures of hedgerows and gardens more than of woodland. If they can gain convenient entry to your home in the autumn, they will certainly do so.

The adult wood mouse is greyish-white beneath, brown above, and the tail is relatively long. The large prominent eyes are a clue to its nocturnal habits.

Although relatively harmless in the summer, when there is plenty of food about, they can cause considerable damage in winter and spring by eating bulbs and seeds. And if they can gain access to your apple store they will completely ruin the fruit.

Mouse poisons can be used, but these can be risky if you or your neighbours have pets. Mouse traps are a practical solution if you place them where domestic animals will not be harmed. Try baiting them with carrot or apple.

Stephen Dalton/NHPA

Wood mice can cause damage to plants.

MAKE A WOODEN BASKET

A wooden basket like this will add a bit of character to your hanging displays next year. It has a sturdy, rustic appearance and is best planted for a bold rather than subtle summer display with, for example, begonias, pelargoniums and lobelias.

You could even use it indoors for a display of suitable houseplants in the meantime. The basket is very heavy, however, so make sure the hook is strong and secure.

You may be able to use wood that you already have, otherwise buy approximately 7.3m/24ft of 20mm × 20mm (¾in x ¾in) softwood. You can buy suitable small-link chain from good hardware shops.

Cut the wood into 25 strips about 29cm/11½in long and smooth the sawn ends with sandpaper.

Cut and drill all the pieces before you start to assemble them. You will need to drill holes the width of the chain or slightly wider in all pieces except seven for the base.

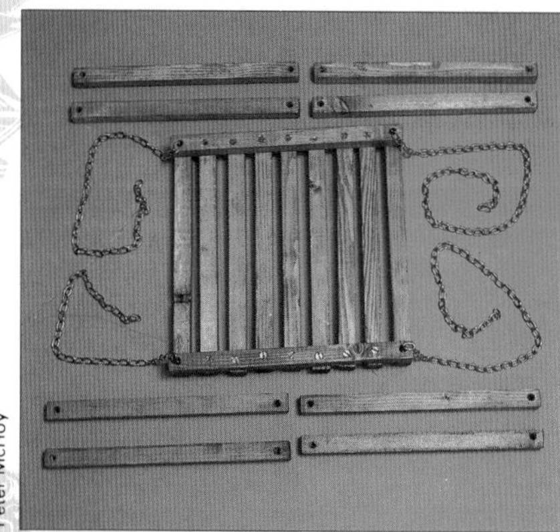

Peter McHoy

1 *Cut the wood to the lengths above. Keep seven pieces for the base, and drill holes for the chain in the rest. Paint with preservative. Assemble base.*

2 *Space and screw the seven base pieces as shown. Cut the chain into suitable lengths. Thread them first through ends of the base and side pieces.*

3 *If you just want to plant in the top of the basket, insert a plastic planting basket (sold for ponds) and line it with moss or plastic to hold the compost.*

4 *If you want to plant in the sides, it is better to line the basket with black polythene, so that plants can easily be inserted through slits in the side.*

5 *Insert plants with large leaves through the small spaces in the sides by rolling the leaves up in a piece of fairly stiff cardboard – easy with practice.*

6 *Add compost to the level of the slit, then push the rolled tube through from the inside. Let the card unfurl on the outside to release the undamaged leaves.*

7 *This kind of basket can be used indoors or out, but the wood makes it very heavy, so use a light compost and a strong hook fixed securely.*

PLANT A WINTER-INTEREST ALPINE TROUGH

Instead of letting window boxes and troughs stand empty, plant them up with evergreens. Dwarf shrubs are a popular choice, but if you have a terracotta trough or window box, alpines can be just as interesting.

You can plant them in the rock garden in spring if you want to use the container for summer bedding.

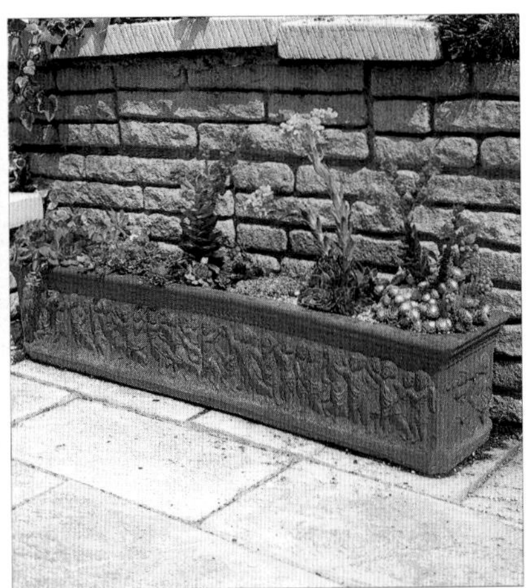

1 *This trough contains houseleeks (sempervivums), sedums and* Raoulia australis. *They will not flower like this until summer, but all are evergreen.*

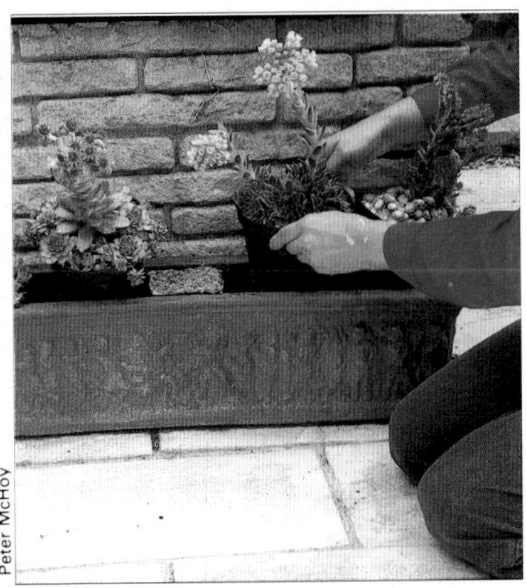

Peter McHoy

2 *Experiment a little before planting, to make sure the effect is right. Position the plants still in their pots to see how they look best.*

3 *Add a layer of broken clay pots or gravel and then some gritty loam-based compost. If necessary, remove some compost from the root-ball.*

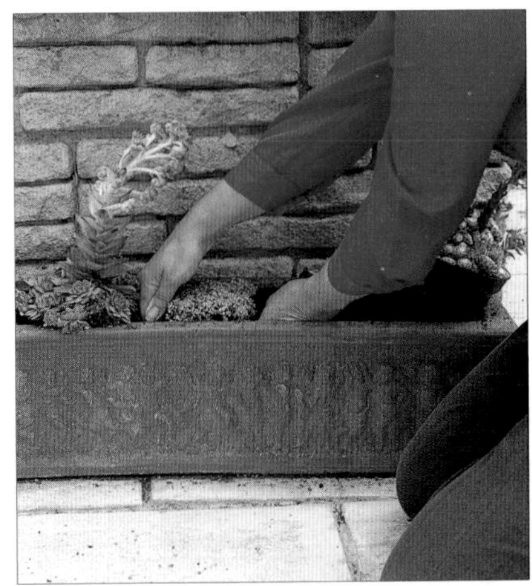

4 *Make sure the plants are set to the same depth below the rim, then pack more gritty compost between them. Firm to remove any large air pockets.*

5 *Water well to settle the compost around the roots, then finish off with a layer of coarse grit or stone chippings to improve the appearance.*

PROTECT TENDER WALL SHRUBS AND FRUIT

In some areas shrubs on the borderline of hardiness and wall-trained figs benefit from winter protection. In the case of slightly tender deciduous shrubs, this can be as simple as pushing a few cut branches of an evergreen around the base to provide some protection against biting winds and heavy falls of snow. It is wise to do this now.

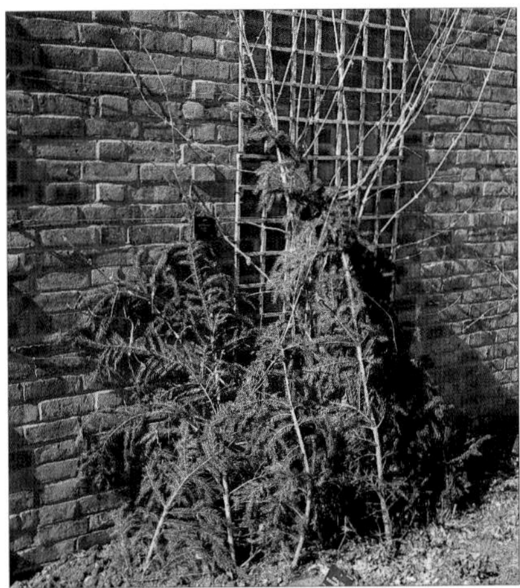

1 *Protect slightly tender compact or deciduous wall shrubs with a few branches of an evergreen. Angle these into the ground, against the wall.*

2 *Figs are fairly hardy, but bracken fronds or straw will protect the embryo figs at the tips of the shoots, which can be damaged by very cold weather.*

CHECKLIST

WHAT TO DO

BULBS
Continue to bring in bowls and pots of bulbs for early flowering indoors
Check stored bulbs, corms and tubers

BEDS AND BORDERS
Dig over vacant beds, borders and plots

SHRUBS
Plant deciduous trees, shrubs and hedges provided the ground is not frozen
Check trees and shrubs planted earlier

LOOK AHEAD

MAKE A BIRD TABLE
Home-made tables are often best

ORDER SEEDS
Get your seed order in early

PREVENT FREEZE-UP
Be prepared to protect your pond and fish

FEATURE GRAVEL
A gravel garden can be simple to make

WHAT TO SEE

BULBS AND BORDER PLANTS
Algerian iris (*Iris unguicularis*)

SHRUBS AND TREES
Autumn cherry (*Prunus subhirtella* 'Autumnalis'), heathers (*Erica* × *darleyensis*), laurustinus (*Viburnum tinus*), *Mahonia* 'Charity', *Malus* 'Red Sentinel' (a crab apple; berries), *Viburnum* × *bodnantense*, *V. farreri* (*V. fragrans*), winter jasmine, winter sweet (*Chimonanthus fragrans*), witch hazel

VISITORS

FRIENDS
Blue tits, great tits, robins, squirrels

FOES
Fieldfares, redwings, wood mice

EARLY WINTER

WEEK 2

WHAT TO DO

Make the most of those cold bright days that can be so invigorating. A little winter digging will soon get the circulation moving and you will probably be able to enjoy the company of birds like robins and blackbirds.

If the ground is too hard to work outdoors, make yourself a bird table instead. Or sit down indoors and write out your seed order.

Check recently planted shrubs

Check shrubs and roses planted in the autumn and early winter to make sure that hard frosts have not loosened them in the ground. If necessary, refirm them by treading firmly around the base.

If supports have also been loosened or blown over, refix them securely. New stakes in soft ground are particularly vulnerable in strong winds.

Order early

Advance planning pays dividends. Work out what you want to grow during the coming year, then get your seed order in as soon as possible. Seeds of hardy annuals will not be needed for several months, and many tender bedding plants are often best sown in early or mid spring. But a few (pelargoniums and fibrous-rooted begonias, for instance) are best sown in mid or late winter to make large enough plants to flower soon after planting out in early summer.

If you order later, you may have to wait longer for your seeds and this could hold you up when you want to sow. Another reason for ordering early is to avoid the disappointment of some varieties being sold out.

Check corms and tubers

Check over stored corms such as gladioli and acidantheras, and especially fleshy tubers such as dahlias. Unless dried off thoroughly before storing, some may have started to rot, and these can quickly affect the others. Check regularly and remove immediately any that are not completely healthy.

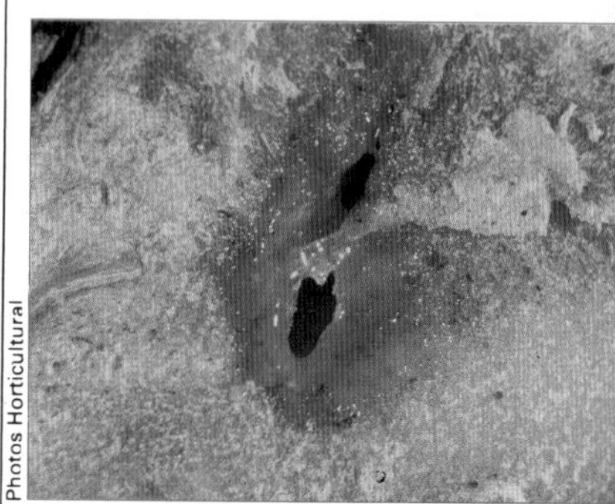

Photos Horticultural

Rot on a corm can quickly spread.

Sweet peas

On very cold nights protect sweet peas which were sown in the autumn and are being overwintered in a cold frame. Cover the frame with a piece of old carpet or some other form of insulation. Remove it the next morning so that the plants get enough light. If not already done, pinch out the tips after the second or third pair of leaves.

LOOK AHEAD

Prepare the greenhouse

If you have a greenhouse, even a small lean-to or a mini-greenhouse put it to good use for seed raising this spring. You need not spend a lot of money on heating: start your seedlings off indoors where heat is available for no additional cost, then transfer them to the greenhouse, which can be cooler, to grow on in the better light.

It is too soon to sow the majority of seeds, but prepare the greenhouse now so that it is ready when you need it.

Wash greenhouse glass inside and out.

Scrub all the frames and staging with a garden or household disinfectant to reduce the risk of overwintering pests and diseases. If woodlice are lurking in crevices, dust in nooks and crannies with BHC; use a slug bait if there is evidence of slugs and snails (you can close up the greenhouse so that there is no danger to pets or wildlife).

Greenhouse fumigation smokes are also worth using so that you start the season with the minimum of pests and diseases.

Wash the glass inside and out, then use bubble polythene insulation to cut heating costs. Check that the heater works.

WHAT TO SEE

Winter jasmine* (Jasminum nudiflorum) *is such a familiar sight in gardens that it is hard to accept that it was unknown to most gardeners a century ago. It was introduced from China into Britain by the plant hunter Robert Fortune and since then it has become one of the most colourful and dependable of all winter-flowering shrubs.

Photos Horticultural

*Winter-flowering jasmine (*J. nudiflorum*).*

Its masses of small yellow flowers are produced from late autumn to late winter and, although the blooms can be damaged by a severe frost, more are soon produced. In any mild spell it will be covered with bright blooms.

This accommodating plant will grow happily in shade or sun, as a free-standing plant in a border or grown against a wall (it generally does best against a sunny wall). It is not, however, a natural climber and lacks self-supporting stems, so needs to be threaded through a trellis or tied in to a support. If planted at the top of a wall, it will cascade downwards as it grows.

There is an uncommon variegated variety ('Aureum') with yellow-blotched leaves.

VISITORS

Redwings and fieldfares are two common winter visitors that sometimes descend on gardens in large numbers when the weather is severe. They are particularly attracted to berries whenever snow makes foraging for insects and grubs difficult, and a flock of them can strip a tree or bush within a couple of days. They will take large fruit, such as ornamental crab apples, as readily as the small berries on cotoneasters.

Both birds are members of the thrush family. The fieldfare is the size of a blackbird but has a speckled front like a mistle thrush, a chestnut-brown back and a grey rump and head. The redwing is smaller and more like a song thrush. It can be distinguished by its rufous flanks and a white 'eyebrow'.

E.A. Janes/NHPA

Redwings will attack fruit.

PROTECT THE POND

Thin ice that melts in a day or so will not do much harm to your pond or its inhabitants, but a prolonged freeze may produce thick ice that is slow to melt and is a hazard for fish. The surface acts as the pond's lung, allowing oxygen to enter the water and toxic gases to leave. If sealed, the gases that build up can harm or kill the fish. So try to keep a small area of the pond's surface free from ice.

Marshall Cavendish

1 *Anything that will be compressed by ice, such as a piece of wood, will take the strain off the pool (even liners can tear). Remove it to expose open water.*

2 *Balls serve a similar function, but ice often forms beneath them and pushes them out if the freeze is severe. Tap them periodically to break thin ice.*

3 *If you are caught unprepared and the ice remains solid after a few days, stand a pan of hot water on the ice to make a breathing hole. Repeat as necessary.*

4 *Tie a piece of string to the handle of the pan if you have to leave it unattended to melt the ice, so that it is easy to retrieve if it sinks.*

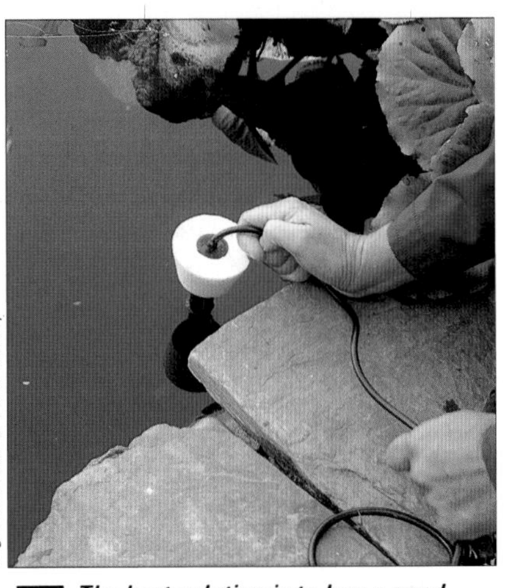
Right and above: Peter McHoy

5 *The best solution is to buy a pond heater. They are safe if you use a low voltage type and are cheap to run. They keep a small area ice-free.*

MAKE A PRETTY BIRD TABLE

You can buy a bird table from a garden centre, but it will almost certainly lack the character of the home-made one illustrated here.

Bird tables should be practical and functional, but they can also be attractive. The one shown here has been made into a focal point, with bright colours adding a touch of cheer to a winter scene and fun features like a house name, cut-out wooden tree and a crooked chimney stack.

You may be able to make one for minimal cost from pieces of wood that you have lying around the garden shed, and you can use our picture as a guide for an entertaining design. Let your imagination contribute, too, and modify or adapt it to suit your own taste and the materials available.

Remember, however, that the base must be stable, and the platform as high as possible above the ground.

Peter McHoy

A home-made bird table can be much more interesting than one you purchase. You can be creative, too.

MAKE A GRAVEL GARDEN

A gravel garden is quick and easy to make, and is an ideal project for the winter – you can even lay gravel in cold and frosty weather.

If you have a suitable area with a clearly defined edging to retain the gravel, no further preparation is required other than to level the ground if necessary. Even levelling does not have to be done very accurately as any slight unevenness will be accommodated by the gravel.

Choose a gravel that suits the style of garden that you want to create. Most builders' merchants stock a range of different kinds, from the small rounded pea shingle to larger and more angular types of gravel.

To prevent weeds becoming a problem, lay sheets of heavy-grade polythene over the ground before tipping on the gravel. Rake the gravel level, making sure it is in about a 5-8cm/2-3in thick layer.

A gravelled area is quick and easy to construct. Just rake the gravel level over a sheet of weed-suppressing polythene.

COMPLETE WINTER DIGGING

Dig over vacant ground. This will ease the pressure in spring when there are so many other things to do, and the frosts will break down the clods into more crumbly pieces, making sowing easier.

Single digging is adequate for most beds and borders, but double digging enables you to work plenty of compost into the lower levels and is useful for a vegetable plot.

1 *Double digging cultivates the soil deeply and helps heavy or poorly drained ground. Remove a trench about 40cm/16in wide and 25cm/10in deep.*

2 *Spread a generous amount of garden compost, manure, spent mushroom compost or other organic material in the base of the trench.*

3 *Use a fork to break up the bottom of the trench as you mix in the organic material. Some soils may be difficult to dig, but it will improve their structure.*

4 *Use a garden line as a guide for a straight edge, and excavate another trench the same width and depth, throwing the soil forward into the first one.*

5 *Take small bites of soil, 'cutting'the side first as shown in the previous picture. When the area has been dug, fill the last trench with soil from the first.*

CHECKLIST

WHAT TO DO

BULBS
Check stored bulbs, corms and tubers

BEDS AND BORDERS
Protect Christmas roses needed for cutting

TREES AND SHRUBS
Plant deciduous trees, shrubs and hedges provided the ground is not frozen

DESIGN
Create a fun focal point for winter cheer

LOOK AHEAD

PREPARE LABELS
Replace faded labels and write new ones to save time in spring

ORDER SEEDS
Send off your seed order

SOW A TREE
Pretreat tree seeds for sowing later

MAKE AN ALPINE SINK
Transform an old glazed sink into an attractive 'stone' one for alpine plants

WHAT TO SEE

BULBS AND BORDER PLANTS
Algerian iris (*Iris unguicularis*)

SHRUBS AND TREES
Heathers (*Erica × darleyensis, E. carnea*), laurustinus (*Viburnum tinus*), *Mahonia* 'Charity', *Viburnum × bodnantense, V. farreri (V. fragrans)*, winter jasmine, winter sweet (*Chimonanthus fragrans*), witch hazel

VISITORS

FRIENDS
Blue tits, great tits, robins, squirrels, weasels

FOES
Fieldfares, redwings, pigeons, wood mice

EARLY WINTER

WEEK 3

WHAT TO DO

The garden always looks very pretty cloaked in snow, but plants may need a helping hand at this time.

Snow will provide a degree of insulation for many plants, and most alpines and evergreen border plants will come to no harm, but trees and hedges can be spoilt if the weight of heavy snow damages the branches. Lawns can also suffer.

Snow precautions

The weight of snow can damage evergreens, especially conifers. Those with an attractive dome or cone shape are particularly vulnerable and if a branch gets bent down and broken it will leave a scar where the dark unclothed inner branches are exposed. Spend a few minutes going round with a broom or stick to knock off thick accumulations. Shake any weighed-down branches to release the snow.

Tie the branches of conical conifers that have been damaged in the past. Loop string or wire around the circumference in several places, to help keep the shoots upright. The ties can be removed in the spring.

Hedges with flat tops are also vulnerable. Knock off deep snow with a broom. Hedges with a tapered top are somewhat less liable to snow damage.

Remove heavy snow with a broom.

Snow on the lawn is unlikely to be a major problem unless it lies for a very long time, when the lack of light may cause the grass to turn yellow, and some fungus diseases may be encouraged. Generally, however, recovery is rapid once the better weather returns. Do not pile further snow from cleared paths on the lawn, however, as areas of compacted snow that are slow to melt may damage the grass.

Christmas roses for cutting

Christmas roses (Helleborus niger) *are very hardy, but the delicate-looking blooms can be damaged by frost, and because they are low-growing they often become mud-splashed and sodden in wet weather. Place a supported sheet of glass, a cloche, or even a mini 'tent' of polythene over one o*

Protect the white blooms of Christmas rose.

two plants. Protecting them from the worst weather will ensure some welcome blooms in good condition to bring into the house over the festive season.

LOOK AHEAD

Prepare labels

Good gardeners know the importance of good labels. Clear labelling becomes essential when you have lots of pots and trays of seedlings in spring, many of which will not yet have seedlings to give you a clue. Border perennials that die down in the winter also need labels so that you know where they are when you hoe or tidy the border, and of course they help you remember what the plants are a year later.

Cold winter days are an ideal time to check labels and to write new ones.

Go round the garden to see which have become faded or broken, and replace them while the old ones are still legible enough to read the names.

For permanent plants like shrubs and border perennials, aluminium labels that you write on with a pencil are a good compromise between cost and a long and legible life.

For short-term plants, such as seedlings and annuals, plastic labels are perfectly adequate and very inexpensive. Some come with markers and these are generally more satisfactory than using an ordinary pencil.

Last year's plastic labels can usually be cleaned up and reused. Try rubbing them with a cream kitchen cleanser, then rinse and rub with a clean cloth.

Wooden labels can look good in the kitchen garden or herbaceous border. Make your own from scraps of wood, then paint them white using an emulsion paint.

Save time later by writing labels for seeds that you have ordered and will be sowing during the next few months.

WHAT TO SEE

Heathers provide the mainstay of winter colour in many gardens, and they look especially good as ground cover, particularly around silver-barked birches.

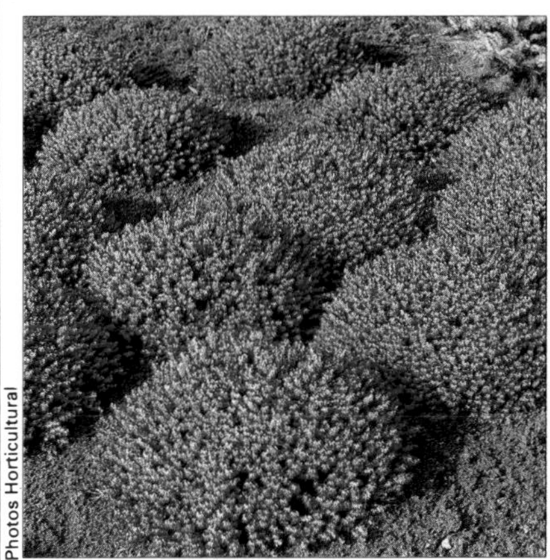

Photos Horticultural

Clumps of* Erica carnea *'King George'.

Varieties of Erica × darleyensis *and* E. carnea *(also known as* E. herbacea*) provide most of the interest, and there are scores of good ones. They flower from early winter to late spring, but the exact flowering span depends on the variety. For mid winter flowering, try varieties of* E. carnea *such as 'King George' (pink, compact), 'Pink Spangles' (pink, very free-flowering), 'Springwood Pink' and 'Springwood White'.*

Both Erica carnea *and* E. × darleyensis *are lime tolerant, so you can enjoy these heathers even if you do not have an acid soil.*

There are hundreds of winter-flowering heathers, so look out during the next few months for those that you like, then when you plant your own heather bed you can plant for a succession of flowers from early to late winter.

VISITORS

Weasels are rare visitors in towns, but are not uncommon in large rural gardens. You are more likely to notice them now when there is less cover and protection, as they will be hunting by day and night for their prey. They are not only beautiful animals but are good for the garden, killing mice, voles and even rats.

The weasel resembles a stoat but is smaller (typically about 23-25cm/9-10in long). The upperparts are a redder brown than in the stoat and the white underparts are a purer white.

Michael Leach/NHPA

Weasels are unusual but welcome visitors.

SOW A TREE . . . OR A SHRUB

Growing trees and shrubs from seed can be a slow business, but the satisfaction of having raised a tree from seed makes the wait well worthwhile.

It is best to keep to species and not varieties if you save your own seed, unless you want to gamble with what the resulting plants will be like. Most seedsmen offer a small selection of trees and shrubs, so why not try a packet?

All photos Peter McHoy

1 *The seeds may need special treatment to stimulate germination. Some benefit from covering with boiling water and being left to soak for 24 hours.*

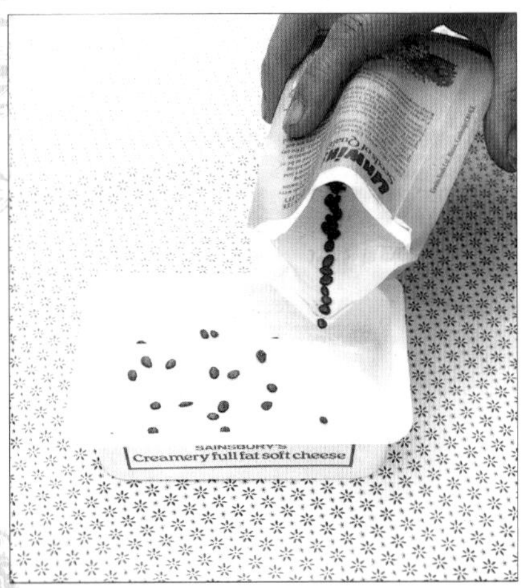

2 *Prechilling is another way to break dormancy. Place the seeds on moist kitchen roll in a small container that you can cover and place in the fridge.*

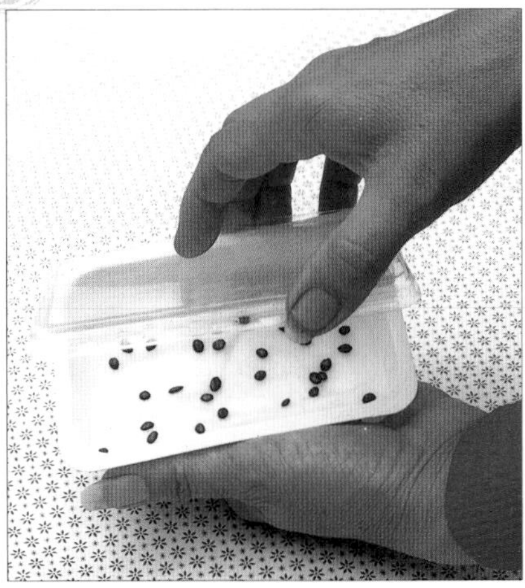

3 *Place the container in the cool or chilling compartment of the refrigerator (about 5°C/40°F) for about seven weeks. Keep paper moist.*

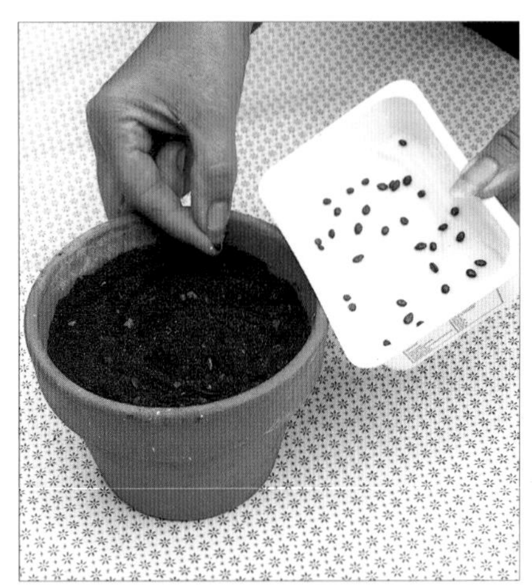

4 *Take seeds from the fridge and space them out on a pot of seed compost. If you have enough, leave some in the fridge for a few weeks longer.*

5 *After watering, be sure to label – they may germinate erratically over a long time – and place in a warm place (about 15°C/60°F) to germinate.*

CREATE A FUN FOCAL POINT

Garden fences can look dull and boring at any time, but especially so in winter when there is little colour elsewhere in the garden to capture the eye. Ornaments can be used as focal points, but these generally look better with a background of foliage, rather than a wooden fence. If you do not mind being a bit outrageous, and have a sense of fun, you can try livening up an unexciting backdrop with some colourful art or a fun feature like the one below.

Here some bright yellow sunflowers have been created from exterior grade plywood and fixed to the fence so that they appear to come out of a vase. When there is little colour in the garden, a fun feature like this can cheer up a dull winter's day, and the choices are limited only by your imagination.

Remove them once the garden bursts into bloom and you have the real thing.

A bit of outrageous fun that could bring a little colour to a dull corner of the winter garden. A real urn acting as a vase adds an extra touch of humour.

CONVERT A GLAZED SINK

Genuine stone sinks make great sink gardens, but they are very expensive and difficult to find. Reconstituted stone substitutes are an alternative, but if you have an old glazed sink why not transform it into a convincing 'stone' sink for your alpines?

A sink can be heavy, so it is best to 'convert' it close to where you want to use it in the garden, as the finished sink will be even heavier.

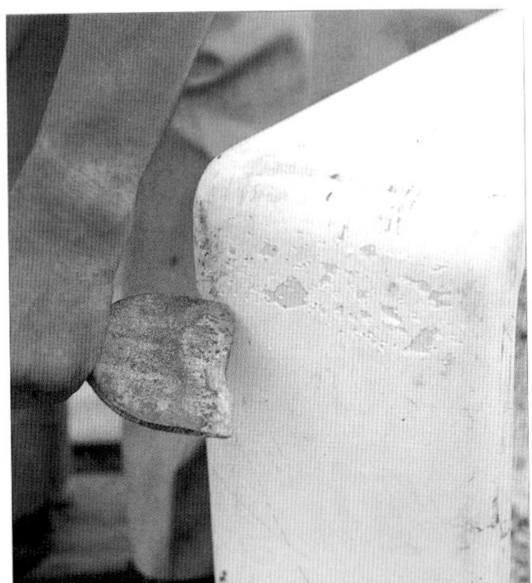

1 *The 'hypertufa' that you make must be able to stick to the surface, so scratch or chip the glaze to provide a 'key' for it to bond to.*

Marshall Cavendish

2 *To assist bonding, paint the sink with a PVA adhesive. You can buy it from hardware and DIY stores. Paint the outside, rim and an inch or so inside.*

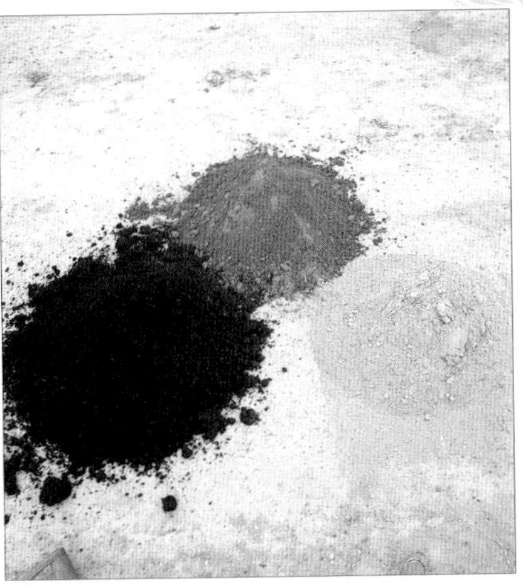

3 *To make the hypertufa, mix 1 part coarse sand, 1 part cement, and 2 parts moistened, sieved sphagnum peat (by volume).*

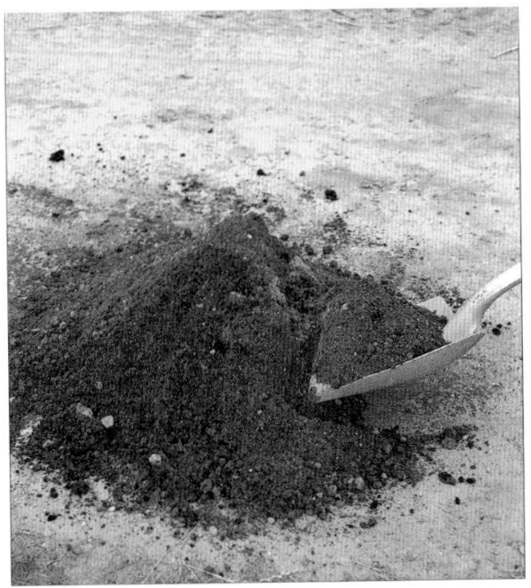

4 *Thoroughly mix the ingredients when they are dry, as they are not so easy to mix well when wet. Then add water until it assumes a doughy consistency.*

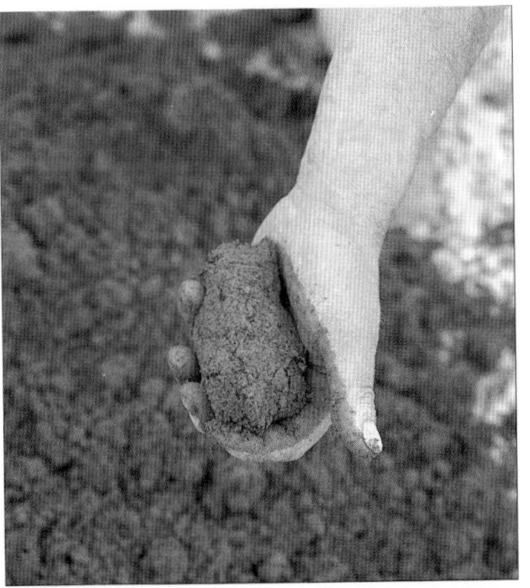

5 *Test the hypertufa for consistency by moulding some in the hand (use gloves to protect your hands). It should not be too wet but must not fall apart.*

6 *While the PVA is still tacky, press the hypertufa against the sink, a handful at a time. It should be about 12mm/½in thick when finished.*

7 *Extend the hypertufa over the rim and an inch or two down the inside – so that the glazed part is not exposed above the compost when the sink is filled.*

8 *The finished sink will look like this, but to weather it and encourage algae and mosses to grow, brush periodically with yogurt or liquid fertilizer.*

CHECKLIST

WHAT TO DO

BULBS
Examine stored dahlia tubers
Bring pots and bowls of bulbs indoors to flower as they become ready

HEDGES
Knock heavy snow off evergreen hedges

TREES AND SHRUBS
Plant deciduous trees, shrubs and hedges if the ground is not frozen

PONDS
If there is a prolonged freeze, make sure a small area of water is kept free of ice

LOOK AHEAD

PLACE ORDERS
Order catalogues, seeds and seedlings

SOW
Geraniums and begonias

MACHINERY
Service the mower and other machinery

WHAT TO SEE

BORDER PLANTS
Algerian iris (*Iris unguicularis*), *Cyclamen coum*

SHRUBS AND TREES
Autumn cherry (*Prunus subhirtella* 'Autumnalis'), Christmas box (*Sarcococca confusa*), heathers (*Erica* × *darleyensis*, *E. carnea*), laurustinus (*Viburnum tinus*), *Mahonia* 'Charity', *Viburnum* × *bodnantense*, *V. farreri* (syn. *V. fragrans*), winter jasmine, winter sweet (*Chimonanthus fragrans*), witch hazel

VISITORS

FRIENDS
Blue tits, great tits, greenfinches, robins

FOES
Fieldfares, redwings, woodpigeons, wood mice

EARLY WINTER

WEEK 4

WHAT TO DO

The next few weeks are often particularly cold, and apart from routine maintenance jobs like checking tree ties and repairing and maintaining fences, most gardening activity is best confined to armchair activities like planning your garden for the coming year and ordering seeds and plants. Do not be in too much of a hurry to sow summer bedding plants, even if you have a greenhouse.

Order catalogues and seeds

Most garden centres offer a wide range of seeds, including some of the more exotic kinds and some new varieties. You may wish to browse among the seed packets, which often contain more detailed sowing and growing information than catalogues can include (and generally there is an illustration of the plant to help if you do not know what it looks like).

Seed catalogues contain many more varieties, however, and often more unusual and newer kinds than garden centres can offer. If you want to order your seeds from catalogues and have not sent for them, do so without delay.

It is worth sending for several catalogues as different seedsmen often specialize in different kinds of plants. You may find something that catches your imagination.

When to sow

Although you can germinate almost all kinds of seeds easily in a warm place, such as an airing cupboard or on the window-sill of a heated room, the problem with sowing too early is the lack of light to keep the seedlings growing sturdily. There is also a limit to the number of plants that you can grow on a window-sill, and even then they will become drawn unless you turn the plants every day to even up the growth.

If you have a greenhouse, light is less of a problem if you keep the glass clean, but providing adequate heat can be expensive.

Seedlings need light and warmth to grow.

Although the seed packet may tell you that the seeds can be sown now, unless you can provide sufficient warmth and good light it is best, with a few exceptions, to delay sowing your seeds for another three or four weeks.

Many summer bedding plants, such as busy Lizzies, salvias, alyssum, and French and African marigolds, grow rapidly and flower young, so these can be left until mid spring for sowing (they will flower a week or two later than those sown earlier, but should continue for longer).

What to sow now

*Those summer bedding plants that require a long growing period before they flower, and especially those that are also slow to germinate, do benefit from an early start. Geraniums (pelargoniums), fibrous-rooted begonias (*B. semperflorens*) and seed-raised, tuberous-rooted begonias (such as the 'Non-stop' range) are best sown within the next couple of weeks if you want your plants to get off to a flying start when you plant them.*

Start them off in a propagator, in a greenhouse or in an airing cupboard. Once they have germinated, however, you must grow them in a very light but frost-free position.

LOOK AHEAD

Seedlings instead of seeds

Many seedsmen offer seedlings as well as seeds. Although more expensive than buying seeds, at least the tricky part – germination – has been done for you, and you can save on some costs if you would otherwise have had to heat a greenhouse or buy a propagator.

The range of seedlings is more limited than the range of seeds, but an adequate selection of basic bedding plants, such as ageratums, lobelias, busy Lizzies, petunias, nicotianas and pansies, is available.

Those that have fine seeds, or can be tricky to germinate, such as begonias and primroses, are well worth considering, even if you raise most other types from seed yourself. But bear in mind that you still require the space to grow them on in a light, frost-free place until planting out in late spring or early summer.

There are three basic types of seedlings by post. The cheapest and smallest come as trays of germinated seedlings ready for pricking out. Young individual seedlings in small plugs of compost are more expensive but easier to handle. 'Pot ready' plantlets are the largest and are ready for potting up into individual pots.

Peter McHoy

Petunia seedlings through the post.

The seedlings are not usually despatched until about mid spring, but orders for most types have to be sent in during the next three or four weeks.

WHAT TO SEE

With a name like Christmas box, it is surprising that* Sarcococca *is not better known and widely grown.

Several species are readily available, all of them unassuming plants that you may consider insignificant in comparison with most summer-flowering shrubs, but anything that flowers at this time of year and is very fragrant into the bargain certainly has to be worth growing.

Sarcococca confus *produces its clusters of small white but very fragrant flowers, nestling among evergreen leaves, from early to late winter.* S. hookeriana digyna *often starts to flower in late autumn. Both are good evergreens for a shady spot, provided the soil does not dry out.*

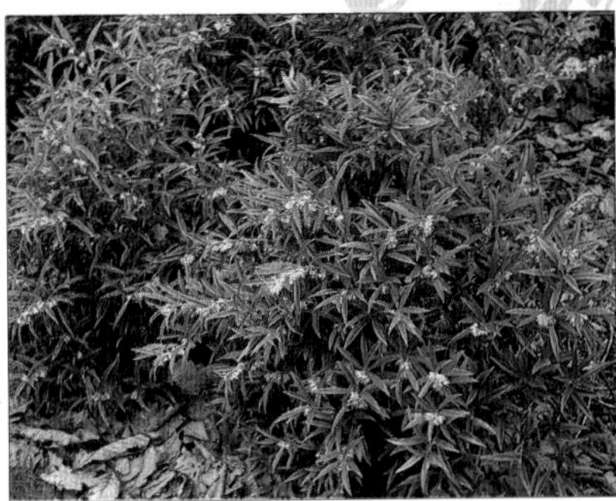
Eric Crichton

***Clumps of* Sarcococca hookeriana digyna.**

VISITORS

Visitors to the bird table are likely to include greenfinches, sparrow-sized birds that quite happily compete with the acrobatic tits on hanging bags of peanuts.

Greenfinches are seen throughout the year but in icy or snowy weather they can be depended on to bring flashes of green and yellow to the garden as they search for food in small groups. They will eat seeds and other scraps from the bird table, but they are especially fond of nuts, and will come close to the window for them.

Roger Tidman/NHPA

The greenfinch often visits bird tables.

SOW BORDER PERENNIALS

Border perennials are generally sown outdoors in early summer to flower the following year (some take several years to flower), but you can have them blooming in their first season by sowing in warmth now.

Plants to try include lupins, Korean chrysanthemums, Shasta daisies, some dwarf delphiniums and hollyhocks. They will put on an even better show in future years.

All Photos Peter McHoy

1 *Fill pots with a good seed compost. You will not require many plants, and pots will take up less space than seed trays on a window-sill or greenhouse bench.*

2 *Firm and level the compost using the base of another pot. Seed pans, which are shallower than ordinary pots, can be used, and these need less compost.*

3 *Many perennials, like these lupins, have quite large seeds. Space them out individually whenever possible, as this makes transplanting easier.*

4 *Cover the seeds with about twice their own depth of compost, unless otherwise advised on the packet, then firm gently. Do not forget to add a label.*

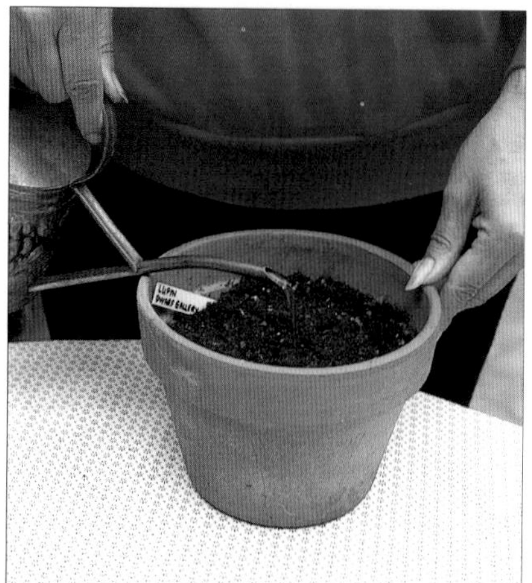

5 *Water thoroughly. If the seeds are large, you can use a small watering can, but if they are fine soak the pot in a bowl of water to let the moisture seep up.*

6 *Cover with glass to keep the compost moist, and stand the pot in a warm place until the seeds germinate. Keep seedlings in a very light position.*

7 *Pot up the seedlings individually as soon as they are large enough to handle, using potting compost. Grow them on in a greenhouse or cold frame.*

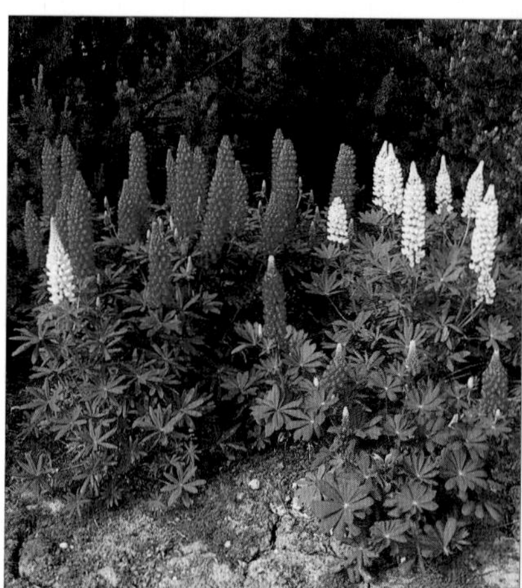

8 *Keep the plants well watered and fed and plant them in the border in late spring or early summer after hardening off. They may flower late in the first year.*

MAKE A MINI HERB GARDEN

Make yourself a mini herb garden for the patio and create a super feature that will act as a focal point as well as providing herbs.

A formal herb garden is often difficult to fit into a small garden, and plants in small containers seldom provide a generous supply for the kitchen. Here are two ideas for practical small-space herb gardens that you can prepare now.

Vana Haggerty

1 *Lift a few paving slabs from your patio to create a pretty herb feature like this one. Plant something tall, such as a bay, in the centre to provide height.*

2 *Carefully lift a number of slabs. You may have to break the first one but subsequent ones can generally be levered up (use a cold chisel if necessary).*

3 *Remove lumps of mortar and hardcore, then fork in a generous quantity of garden compost or a planting mix to improve the soil.*

4 *Most herbs are best planted in spring but for an instant effect plant a bay and some evergreen herbs, such as variegated sages and a prostrate rosemary.*

5 *A patio is a good weather-proof base from which to plant up and, later, pick your herbs. If you prefer not to lift paving, why not use a half-barrel?*

6 *Position the barrel before you fill it, and make sure there are good drainage holes. Place gravel or rubble in the bottom then fill with loam-based compost.*

7 *To give the herb garden height and proportion, and to provide winter interest, include an evergreen like bay or rosemary as a centrepiece.*

8 *Fill around the edges with smaller but bushy perennial herbs like marjoram and hyssop. Fill in the spaces with small herbs like parsley and chives.*

CHECKLIST

WHAT TO DO

BULBS
Bring pots and bowls of bulbs indoors to flower as they become ready

BEDS AND BORDERS
Clear leaves and debris, tidy plants
Refirm spring bedding plants after frost

TREES AND SHRUBS
Knock heavy snow off evergreens
Prune wisteria

COLD FRAMES
Ventilate on mild days, protect on cold nights

PONDS
Keep a small area of water free of ice

LOOK AHEAD

SOW
Geraniums and begonias

PREPARE FOR SOWING
Clean pots and seed trays

WHAT TO SEE

BORDER PLANTS
Cyclamen coum

SHRUBS AND TREES
Christmas box (*Sarcococca confusa*), heathers (*Erica* × *darleyensis*, *E. carnea*), laurustinus (*Viburnum tinus*), *Lonicera fragrantissima*, *L.* × *purpusii*, *L. standishii*, *Mahonia* 'Charity', *Viburnum* x *bodnantense*, *V. farreri* (*V. fragrans*), winter jasmine, winter sweet (*Chimonanthus fragrans*), witch hazel

VISITORS

FRIENDS
Blue tits, great tits, greenfinches, robins

FOES
Bullfinches, fieldfares, redwings, woodpigeons

MID WINTER
WEEK 1

WHAT TO DO

Mid winter is a time of contradictions. On bad days gardening is impossible and spring seems very distant. In the brief spells of mild weather a whole range of winter-flowering plants manage to put on a brave display, and the shoots of many spring-flowering bulbs will be giving a hint of better things to come. At this time it is best to forget about gardening outdoors if the ground is frozen, but make the best of warmer and brighter days to get those useful odd jobs done.

Tidy borders

Go round the beds and borders to pick up leaves and cut off any lingering stems and dead leaves on herbaceous plants, which can harbour slugs and other pests. Leave the old growth on anything that is slightly tender, however, such as agapanthus and red hot pokers, which may benefit from the extra protection.

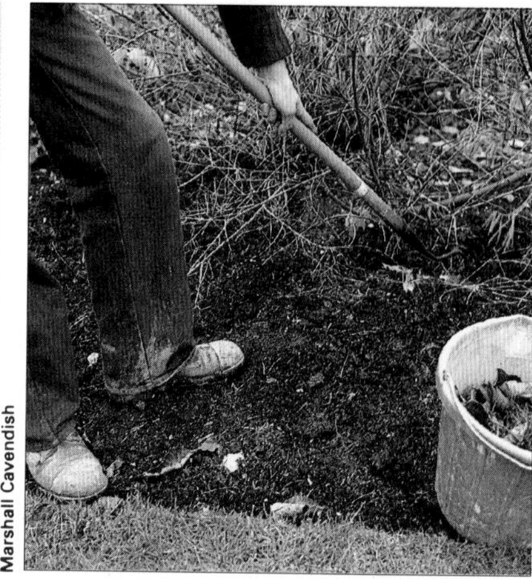

Marshall Cavendish

Now is the time to tidy up borders.

Check spring bedding plants

Spring-flowering biennials such as wallflowers and forget-me-nots may have been lifted by frost if they were planted late. Provided the ground is not frozen, go round and firm them in if necessary.

Winter prune wisteria

Wisteria is often pruned in stages, with the whippy summer growth being cut back to about 30cm/1ft in early autumn. Now is the time to cut the same shoots back to within two or three buds of the previous year's growth. The reason for this two-stage pruning is to concentrate food in the shoots, to assist the foundation of flower buds.

Very large wisterias may require additional summer pruning to control size, but this winter pruning will ensure that you get good flowers.

Andrew Lawson

Prune wisteria for good flowers next year.

Prevent snow damage

Heavy falls of snow can spoil the shape of evergreens, especially conifers. Snow can also spoil the taller heathers. Knock or brush off any snow that is bending branches with its weight.

Keep an eye on cold frames

Do not forget to check your cold frames periodically. Cuttings that are overwintering may require watering, and you will need to watch for pests such as slugs and diseases like botrytis, which can rapidly spread in the still, damp conditions of a closed frame.

Whenever possible, open the frame a little during the day to ventilate it, but on very cold nights be prepared to cover it with an old carpet or some similar form of insulation.

LOOK AHEAD

Sowing can soon begin in earnest, so if the weather is too unpleasant to garden outdoors take the opportunity to wash and clean old pots and seed trays.

Never be tempted to use old ones without cleaning them, as the remains of old compost are likely to contain disease spores that can be especially harmful to vulnerable young seedlings.

Wash the worst of the old compost off under a jet of water from a hose, then dip the pots and trays in a bucket of water containing a disinfectant. Use an old scrubbing brush to get off stubborn dirt and compost, then rinse them in clean water and leave them to dry.

Old labels can often be reused if they are washed and scrubbed. A household cleaner will usually remove the remains of the old writing from the surface.

If you think you require more pots, trays or labels, buy them now so that they are ready when you need them in the spring.

WHAT TO SEE

You can have fragrant honeysuckles in flower in mid winter! These are not the showy climbing kinds associated with summer, however, but shrubby plants that seldom exceed 1.8m/6ft and have small white flowers on bare stems (in mild areas the plants are actually semi-evergreen).

These winter-flowering honeysuckles have a restrained delicacy of flower and fragrance that makes them especially welcome on a winter's day. If you decide to plant one, position it near a path that you use regularly in the winter, not among other shrubs in some part of the garden you seldom use. These are subtle plants to be placed where you can admire their brave weather-defying display.

Eric Crichton

Lonicera × purpusii *in flower.*

Lonicera fragrantissima *is a twiggy shrub with sweetly scented, creamy-white, bell-shaped flowers from midwinter to early spring.* L. standishii *is very similar, and* L. × purpusii *is a hybrid between these two species.*

VISITORS

Bullfinches are bold and bright birds that can add a sudden splash of colour to the winter garden as they alight on trees and shrubs.

They often work over a tree or shrub in groups of a half a dozen or so, nipping off developing buds systematically, working from the tops of shoots to the bottom. The buds are protected by hard outer scales at this time of year, but they leave these and eat the more succulent centres.

On a frosty morning or after a fall of snow, you may notice the hard bud scales beneath the plant, a sure sign that bullfinches are in the area.

Bullfinches can do a lot of harm. By removing the developing buds, they can affect flowering, fruiting and growth. Apples, cherries, gooseberries, pears and plums are sometimes badly affected. Bird scarers and deterrents have only a marginal effect, and netting may be unacceptable in an ornamental area. If you do not mind a reduced crop, why not enjoy what are, after all, attractive and colourful birds?

They are also partial to flowering cherries, forsythia, lilac, viburnums and wisteria.

L. Campbell/NHPA

The handsome bullfinch can be a nuisance.

SOW BEGONIAS AND GERANIUMS

It is too early to sow most bedding plants, but geraniums and begonias need more time to reach flowering size so are best sown early.

Both need warmth to germinate, but they can be sown in pots indoors. Even if you have a greenhouse, it is more economical to germinate them indoors than to heat a greenhouse. You can grow them on in the greenhouse after pricking out.

1 *Use pots or seed pans rather than seed trays. They take up less space, and there are usually relatively few geranium seeds in a packet.*

All Photos Peter McHoy

2 *Use a seed compost and compress it first with the fingers to remove large air pockets, then with another pot to provide a level surface for sowing.*

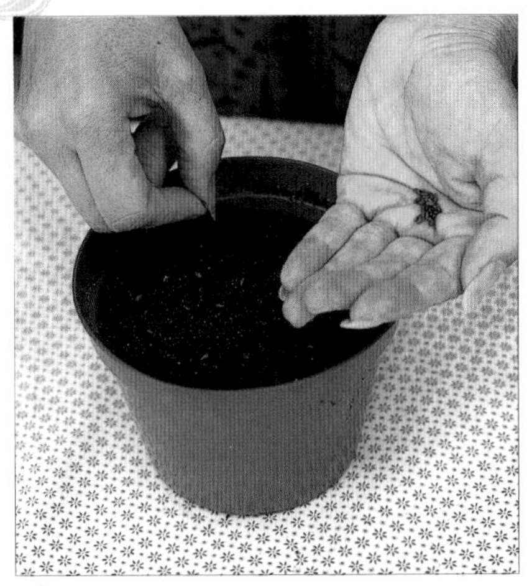

3 *Geranium seeds are large enough to be spaced individually. Make sure they are well spaced, and use a second pot rather than overcrowd them.*

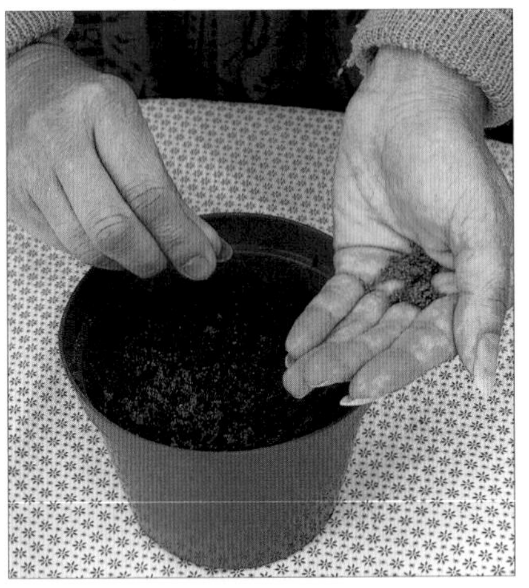

4 *Begonia seeds are very fine and you may find it helpful to mix them with a little sand to make spreading easier. Sprinkle them between finger and thumb.*

5 *Cover the geranium seeds with a sprinkling of sifted compost before watering. An old kitchen sieve is useful for spreading compost thinly and evenly.*

6 *Begonias are best left uncovered. Just press them lightly into the surface. To avoid washing them away when watering, stand the pot in a bowl to water.*

7 *To keep the seeds moist, cover the pots with small sheets of glass, or put them in polythene bags. Turn the covers daily to avoid condensation drips.*

8 *Stand the plants in a warm place (21-24°C/70-75°F). The airing cupboard is a good spot for the geraniums until they germinate, but keep the begonias in light.*

PLANT A WALL CLIMBER

Make the most of vertical space by clothing those bare walls with colourful climbers. Some of the self-clingers, such as the Boston ivy and Virginia creeper may be too rampant for what you want, but if you fix a trellis to the wall you can grow choice climbers like large-flowered clematis, fragrant summer jasmine, and interesting honeysuckles like **Lonicera × brownii,** ***the scarlet trumpet honeysuckle.***

1 *Large-flowered clematis are an ideal choice for a wall trellis, as they are less vigorous than the species and are easily kept compact with flowers low down.*

2 *Buy a trellis or make your own, but be sure to treat all wood with a plant-safe preservative. Measure the position on the wall, then drill and plug the wall.*

3 *Use scraps of wood (or cotton reels) to keep the trellis about 2.5cm/1in away from the wall so that the plant can twine behind it. Use rust-proof screws.*

4 *Dig the planting hole 30-45cm/12-18in away from the wall. This is very important, as the soil close to a wall is almost always too dry.*

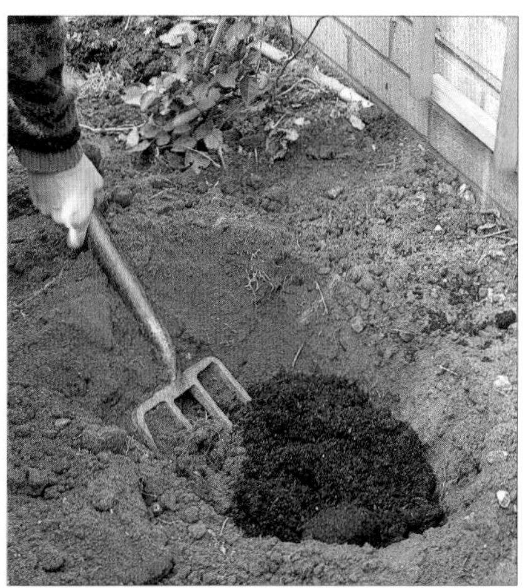

5 *Work a generous amount of garden compost or proprietary planting mix into the planting area. This can be the key to success.*

6 *Plant the root-ball at a slight angle so that the growth slopes towards the wall. Return the soil and firm it well, then water generously.*

7 *If the plant does not come with a cane, insert one at an angle to bridge the gap between the planting hole and the trellis support. Loosely tie the plant.*

8 *Tie as many shoots as possible to the trellis, using soft garden string or proprietary ties. Once established, they will twine themselves around the trellis.*

CHECKLIST

WHAT TO DO

BULBS
Bring pots of bulbs indoors to flower

TREES AND SHRUBS
Check tree ties

COLD FRAMES
Protect or ventilate as appropriate

LAWNS
Lay a new lawn with turf
Improve poor drainage

HOUSEPLANTS
Make a bottle garden

LOOK AHEAD

SOWING
Sow geraniums and begonias
Make your own seed-sowing compost

DAHLIAS AND CHRYSANTHEMUMS
Start dahlia tubers and chrysanthemum stools into growth if you want to take cuttings

FORCE RHUBARB
Cover rhubarb for early blanched stems

WHAT TO SEE

BORDER PLANTS
Cyclamen coum

SHRUBS AND TREES
Christmas box *(Sarcococca confusa)*, heathers, laurustinus *(Viburnum tinus)*, *Lonicera fragrantissima*, *L.* × *purpusii*, *L. standishii*, silk tassel bush (*Garrya elliptica*), *Viburnum* × *bodnantense*, *V. farreri*, winter jasmine

VISITORS

FRIENDS
Blue tits, coal tits, great tits, greenfinches

FOES
Bullfinches, woodpigeons

MID WINTER
WEEK 2

WHAT TO DO

With the garden looking bleak and the weather uninviting, this is a frustrating time for gardeners. But there are always some jobs that you can find to do. Energetic projects – improving the drainage, for instance – are better tackled in cold weather than when it is warm. If frozen ground makes even that impossible, why not make yourself a bottle garden, which will thrive whatever the weather?

Force rhubarb

If you have clumps of rhubarb in the garden, cover some now to provide a supply of forced stems that are always so much more succulent and appetizing than unblanched stems.

Andrew Lawson

To blanch rhubarb, force some in the dark.

Cover a crown with a box or old bucket filled with straw. Within a few weeks shoots should start to grow, and the blanched stems can be harvested once they are large enough to pull.

Check tree ties

Young trees can grow rapidly, so tree ties should be checked at least once a year to make sure they are not cutting into the stem. Most proprietary types are easy to adjust. Taking just a few minutes each year to do this small job can save your valuable specimen trees from permanent damage.

Lay a lawn with turf

Turf can be laid whenever the ground is not frozen or excessively wet. If the weather is unfavourable it will not harm the grass to leave it stacked for a few days, but it is better to arrange delivery when a favourable spell of weather is forecast.

In cold areas it is best to lay your turf in late winter. Prepare the ground thoroughly now to produce a good, flat, weed-free surface ready for turfing.

Turf laid in winter requires regular watering if the weather is dry, and after a period of prolonged heavy frosts it may need firming down.

Check apples in store

If you grow late apples to store, check them periodically and remove any that are rotten. Use up any that are just beginning to

Photos Horticultural

Check stored apples regularly for rot.

deteriorate. Rotting fruit will quickly affect the perfectly sound apples nearby.

Check garden frames

Cold frames need regular attention now. Ventilate them whenever possible on fine days, and give extra protection with something like an old blanket or carpet on very cold nights.

Keep compost in pots and trays almost dry, but always give the plants enough water to keep them growing. Pots of bulbs may be ready to bring indoors.

LOOK AHEAD

If you have been carefully overwintering dahlias and chrysanthemums, you can increase your stock easily by taking cuttings in late winter and early spring. Start the plants into growth now if you want to do this, as it will take several weeks for the shoots to grow large enough to use.

Start dahlia tubers into growth by planting them in trays of moist peat or ordinary seed or potting compost. Keep them moist, in a light place – such as a window-sill – where you can maintain a temperature of about 16°C/60°F, at least during the day.

The shoots can be used for cuttings when they have grown to about 5-8cm/2-3in long.

Chrysanthemum 'stools' (crowns with the top growth cut down) are usually kept in a frame or cold greenhouse or a warm, light place where the plants can be stimulated into growth. They do not need much heat, and 7°C/45°F is adequate. The new young shoots should have grown long enough to use as cuttings by late winter or early spring.

WHAT TO SEE

The silk tassel bush* (Garrya elliptica) *is the kind of plant that will give your garden a real touch of distinction. It is not brash and colourful, but its long silvery-grey catkins drip elegantly from the branches like silvery evergreen foliage.

The longest and best catkins are on male plants, and one of the best forms is a male clone called 'James Roof' (who was the garden director of the botanic garden near Berkeley in California where the plant was raised). On the ordinary male plants the catkins can be up to 30cm/12in long, but on this variety they are often a couple of inches longer.

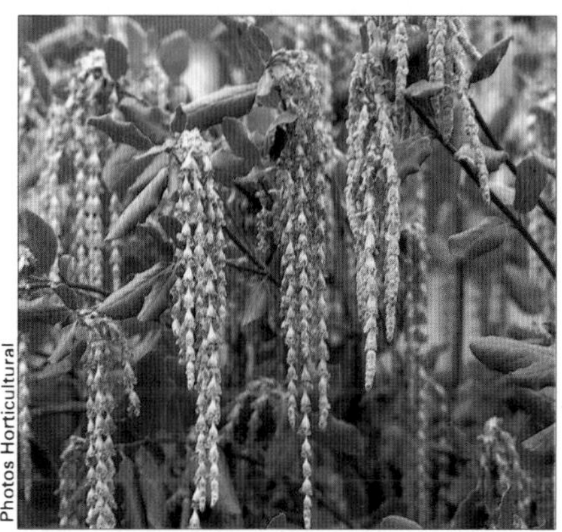
Photos Horticultural

Catkins of Garrya elliptica *are striking.*

Unfortunately the shrub is not totally hardy and it does best where the winters are mild. Elsewhere it should be grown as a wall shrub so that it receives some protection. It usually does well in coastal areas. Buy container-grown plants, as bare-root plants do not transplant well.

VISITORS

The common tits are with us all year, but when food is scarce in the winter they visit gardens more often and are not afraid to come to a bird table or perform their acrobatics on a bag of nuts or an upside-down coconut.

It is not uncommon to find blue tits, great tits and coal tits all feeding together in the winter if you put out bird food regularly.

The blue tit is a small, friendly bird that most people recognize immediately, with its pale yellow underparts and blue and white head. The coal tit is about the same size but has more sombre colouring, olive-brown above and buff beneath, and a distinctive black cap and throat that contrast starkly with the white cheeks.

The great tit is larger than the other two, cleanly coloured with a greenish back, black and white head and a band of black that runs along the yellowish underside from chin to tail.

E.A. Janes/NHPA

The coal tit has a white patch on its neck.

MAKING A BOTTLE GARDEN

The wide-necked bottles often sold for bottle gardens are easy to plant as you can usually insert your hand. Narrow-necked bottles are much more difficult to plant, but you will have a greater sense of achievement, and friends will be impressed.

Make sure you choose small specimens of plants that will not grow too large or too fast, as you do not want to have to replant frequently.

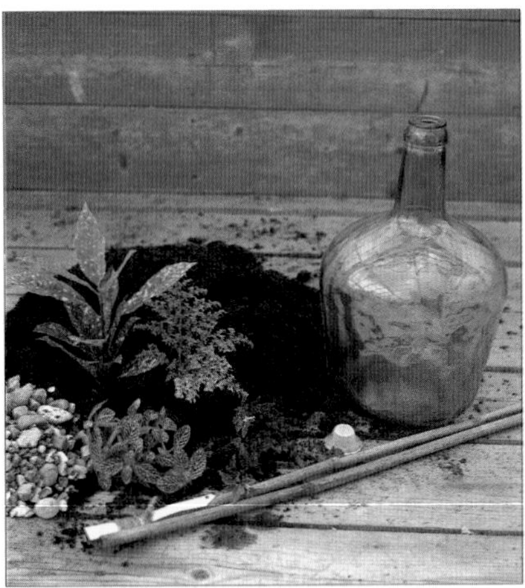

1 *You will need a peat-based compost, some pebbles or gravel, improvized tools and various bottle garden plants (sold by most garden centres).*

2 *Place a layer of gravel in the base before adding the compost. It is a good idea to add some horticultural charcoal (available from garden centres).*

3 *Make sure the peat-based compost is moist but not wet before adding enough to form a layer about 2.5-5cm/ 1-2in deep over the gravel.*

4 *Use an improvized tool to make a hole large enough to take the roots of the plant to be added. Here a label has been used as a small 'trowel'.*

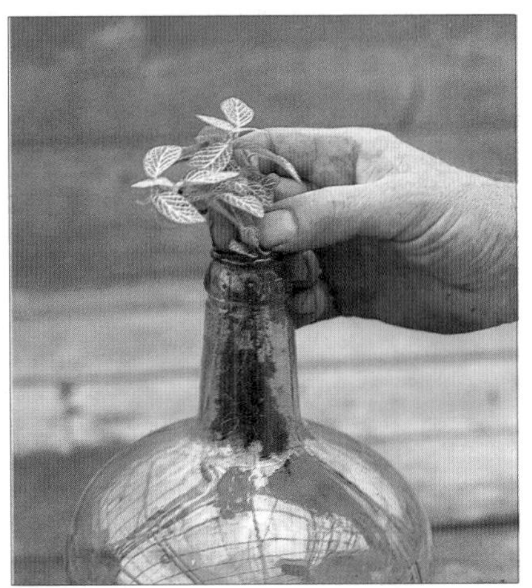

5 *For a small-necked bottle it will be necessary to remove most of the compost from the plant, but do this gently. Drop the plant onto the compost.*

6 *Use another cane to position the plant (try tying a small fork to the cane if necessary). Push compost around the roots with the improvized trowel.*

7 *Add a few more plants, but do not overcrowd them. Use a cane to adjust their positions and to tamp the compost around the roots.*

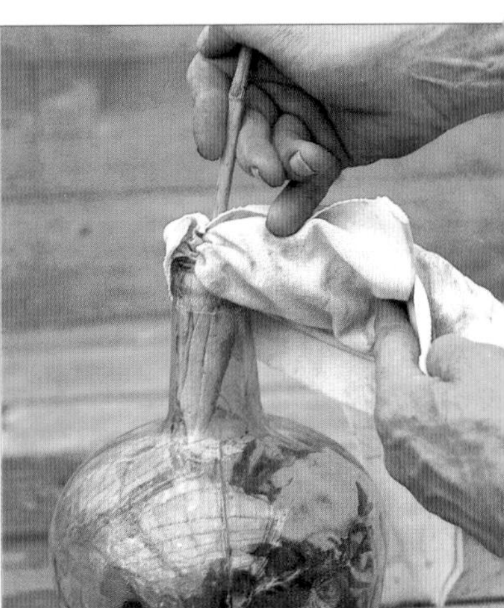

8 *Use a cloth to clean compost from the neck, then trickle water down the sides to clean them. Be careful not to overwater. You can add a stopper.*

IMPROVE POOR DRAINAGE

If parts of your garden often remain waterlogged, or if the lawn has rampant moss and turns into a lake after heavy rain, instal a drainage system. Some heavy digging is involved, but you can hire a jobbing gardener to excavate the trenches if necessary.

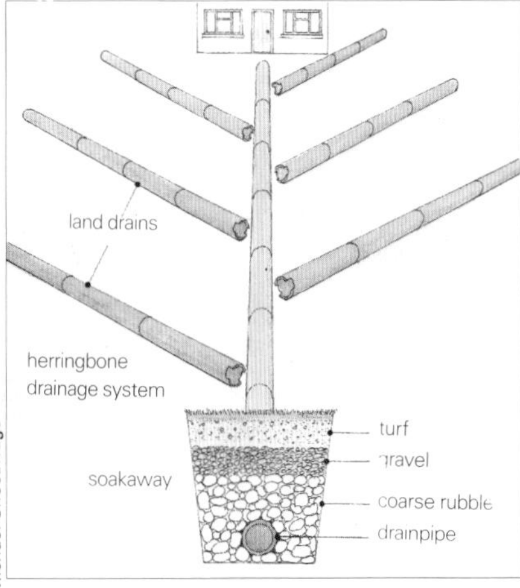

To improve a lawn you must remove the turf carefully before digging trenches. Plan the drains so that they drain to a soakaway or drainage ditch at a low point. Use a herringbone pattern.

1 *Clay or plastic land drains can be bought from a builder's merchant. Dig the trench with a slight fall, and bury drains at least 30cm/1ft deep.*

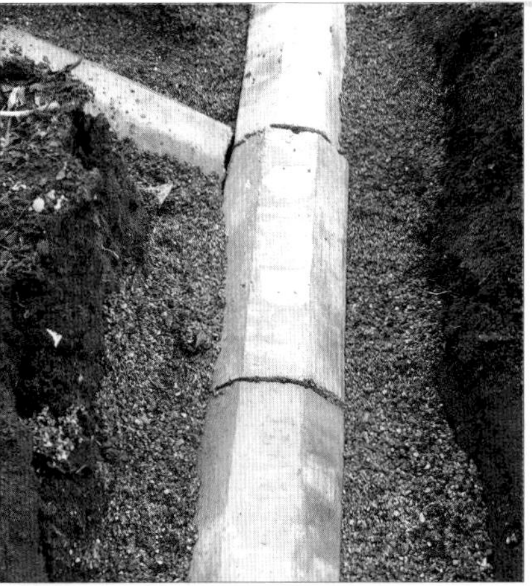

2 *To improve drainage further and prevent the drains becoming clogged with soil, pack coarse grit or fine gravel around and over the drains.*

3 *As joints are vulnerable to clogging, cover them with pieces of polythene before adding grit or gravel and returning the soil.*

4 *You will need to cut drains to ensure a good fit where they butt at side joints. Clay drains can be cut by scoring with a cold chisel and striking with firm blows.*

MAKE YOUR OWN COMPOST

Seed-sowing compost is expensive, so try making your own. Loam-based composts are difficult to make in small quantities. Peat- or peat substitute-based ones are quick and easy to make, and you can make just enough for one seed tray.

Buy a compost base (which contains the fertilizers). You can get multi-purpose or separate ones for seed-sowing and potting composts.

1 *Use all peat or a peat substitute, or a mix of three parts peat to one part sand, perlite or vermiculite, with an appropriate fertilizer.*

2 *Mix the ingredients together thoroughly on a clean and level surface. Leave the mixed compost for a day or two before using it.*

Michael Shoebridge

All photos Peter McHoy

CHECKLIST

WHAT TO DO

BULBS
Bring pots and bowls of bulbs indoors to flower as they become ready

BEDS AND BORDERS
Continue winter digging
Apply a decorative mulch

CLOCHES
Place cloches to warm soil before sowing

ROCK GARDEN
Refirm loose plants and replace dressing of stone chippings if necessary

CONTAINERS
Fix brackets and hooks

LOOK AHEAD

PLACE ORDERS
Order catalogues, seeds and seedlings

SOWING
Start sowing summer bedding if you have a heated greenhouse

FORCE RHUBARB
Cover rhubarb for early blanched stems

WHAT TO SEE

BORDER PLANTS
Cyclamen coum

SHRUBS AND TREES
Christmas box (*Sarcococca confusa*), Cornelian cherry (*Cornus mas*), heathers, laurustinus (*Viburnum tinus*), *Lonicera fragrantissima*, *L. × purpusii*, *L. standishii*, silk tassel bush (*Garrya elliptica*), *Viburnum × bodnantense*, *V. farreri*, winter jasmine

VISITORS

FRIENDS
Blue tits, great tits, greenfinches, robins

FOES
Bullfinches, woodpigeons, wireworms

MID WINTER
WEEK 3

WHAT TO DO

On fine days, this is the time to finish jobs like winter digging and tidying beds and borders. Good weather will also provide an opportunity to appreciate just how much there is in the garden.

Variegated evergreens can look beautiful in shafts of wintry sunshine, and there are almost sure to be a few winter-flowering plants to admire. Emerging bulbs will remind you that spring is not that far away.

Continue winter digging

Winter digging is good for the soil structure, if you can work in plenty of organic material such as garden compost. It also helps to control soil pests, such as wireworms and cutworms. Bringing them to the surface exposes them to the birds, and those that the birds miss may succumb to frosts if they are nearer to the surface.

Digging also brings new weed seeds to the surface, however, and ground dug earlier in the winter may now be showing signs of weed growth if there have been mild spells. Hoe now before the seedlings become too large.

Apply a decorative mulch

Most mulching is done in the spring, as this is when weeds are likely to need suppressing and conservation of soil moisture is important. There is a lot of exposed soil in the winter, however, and applying an attractive mulch now will do much to improve its appearance.

A good mulch improves the look of a bed.

Make sure the ground is moist, then apply a thick mulch of pulverized bark, coconut fibre or whatever other material is available and improves the appearance of the soil.

Check the rock garden

Rock plants wake quickly from winter sleep when sunny days arrive, so check to see whether they have been lifted from the soil by frost. Firm them back in if necessary. Make sure the soil or dressing of grit has not been washed away from the crowns.

Start sowing in the greenhouse

Indoors, where the light is poor, most seeds are best sown later, but if you have a greenhouse in which to grow them on, you can start to sow bedding plants such as antirrhinums, petunias, begonias and geraniums.

Check the seed packet and do not sow seeds earlier than recommended, otherwise the plants may become starved and drawn before it is warm enough to plant them outside.

LOOK AHEAD

If you have space to grow a few early vegetables, or some hardy annual flowers for cutting extra early, cloches will usually advance them by at least a couple of weeks over those sown in the open ground. It is too early to sow yet, but cloches should be in position several weeks beforehand to give the soil time to warm up.

If you want to germinate seeds early so that they get off to a quick start, tent cloches are adequate. If the crop has to grow with cloche protection for some

Collections/Patrick Johns

Rows of early lettuces under cloches.

time, or if the plants grow tall quickly, like broad beans, barn cloches (which have almost straight sides) will provide useful additional height.

If you do not want to buy cloches, many crops, such as carrots, can be sown in shallow troughs between ridges of soils about 10-15cm/4-6in high. Stretch a sheet of ordinary polythene across the tops of the ridges and hold it in place with bricks.

WHAT TO SEE

The Cornelian cherry* (Cornus mas) *has tiny flowers, but they make a real impact at this time of year when colour is still scarce. Individual flowers are only about 4mm/⅙ in across, but are bright yellow and are produced in profusion along the tree's bare branches.

The Cornelian cherry can make a tree more than 9m/30ft high, but usually it is seen as a large shrub and with pruning can be kept relatively compact. Before the

Eric Crichton

Cornelian cherry flowering in late winter.

Japanese witch hazels were introduced into Europe, C. mas *was a popular choice for a winter-flowering yellow, and it is still well worth a place in the garden.*

As the common name implies, it also has red, cherry-like fruits, which are edible. They are not, however, freely produced and are best regarded as a bonus.

There are variegated forms too. 'Aurea' has foliage prettily suffused yellow, 'Elegantissima' has yellow variegation but the leaves are also flushed pink, and 'Variegata' has leaves bordered creamy-white.

VISITORS

Wireworms are with us all year, but as soil pests they are often noticed during winter digging or when crops like potatoes are harvested.

They are tough-skinned, wiry-looking larvae up to 2.5cm/1in long. The colour varies between white and golden yellow. Unlike millepedes and centipedes, they have just three pairs of legs on the central body or thorax.

Wireworms are the larvae of various species of click beetle, but the adult form is unlikely to be troublesome. The wireworm, however, feeds on the roots of many plants. Among the ornamentals that are vulnerable are anemones, carnations, chrysanthemums, dahlias, gladioli and primulas. They also cause damage to corms and tubers, where they leave small holes which slugs and millipedes often enlarge.

Wireworms are particularly troublesome in ground that has until recently been grassland. The act of cultivating a new garden often helps to reduce the population, as birds will eat them after winter digging. If they are really troublesome, work a soil insecticide, such as bromophos, into the soil around vulnerable plants in spring.

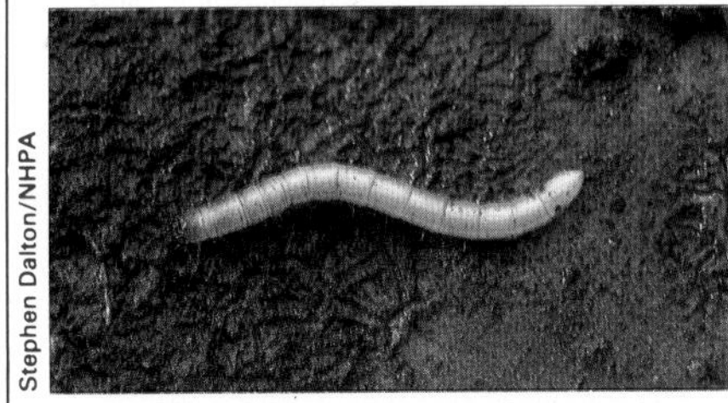

Stephen Dalton/NHPA

Wireworms are a pest on plant roots.

PLANT POPPY ANEMONES

The poppy anemone, a very popular florist's cut flower, is an easy plant to grow. The tubers are available in most garden centres. The De Caens are single, while the St Brigid type are double or semi-double; they will flower within three to six months of planting. They can be planted outside in early spring, but if you want earlier flowers for a succession of blooms, start some under glass now.

1 *The peculiar-looking tubers are often hard and dry when you buy them. If they are too dry they will not grow. Soak them overnight before planting.*

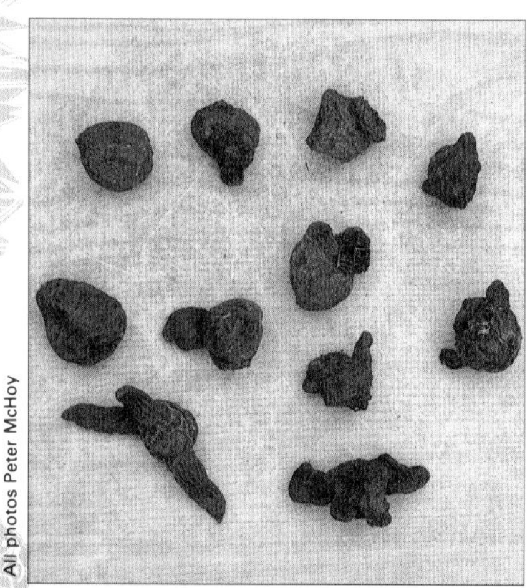

All photos Peter McHoy

2 *Plant them the right way up. The pointed side is the top, but this is sometimes difficult to determine as they can resemble large dried raisins.*

3 *If you want cut flowers and have space in a cool greenhouse or can cover them with cloches, plant directly into the ground, 5cm/2in deep.*

4 *You can start them off now in pots in a cold frame, and plant them out in the garden in spring. Plant about five in a 15cm/6in diameter pot.*

5 *In mild areas you can naturalize them in grass for a pretty spring display. Try them in a strip along the edge of the lawn, near a border.*

FIX WINDOW BOX BRACKETS AND BASKET SUPPORTS

Winter is a good time to do those jobs that usually seem a rush in spring and early summer when there are so many other tasks to be tackled. Fixing window box brackets or the hooks for hanging baskets is a useful task if there is no pressing sowing or planting to be done.

Always make sure window box brackets have a lip to prevent the box sliding off.

1 *This type of bracket is widely available and is ideal for normal sized proprietary window boxes if you want to fix them to the face of a house wall.*

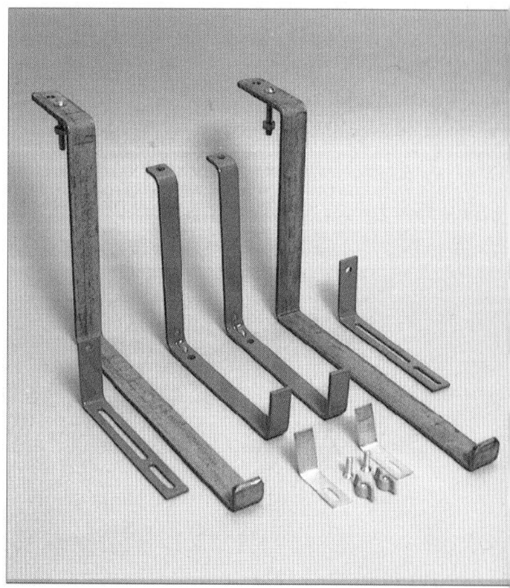

2 *If you want to hang the box over the top of a garden wall, choose a type with special fittings that can be adapted for this use, like those illustrated.*

FORCE RHUBARB

Forced rhubarb is one of the welcome sights of late winter and early spring, and if you have grown it yourself it is always much more welcome.

If you have a clump of rhubarb in the garden you can use that, otherwise you may be able to buy a root from a garden centre.

It is possible to force a clump in the garden by covering it with an old bucket, but pot some up for even earlier shoots.

1 *Lift an established root when the ground is not frozen, and remove excess soil before potting it up. 'Timperley Early' is very good for forcing.*

Marshall Cavendish

2 *Use a large pot, tub or plastic container to hold the root. Drainage holes are advisable, but are not essential if you are going to keep it indoors.*

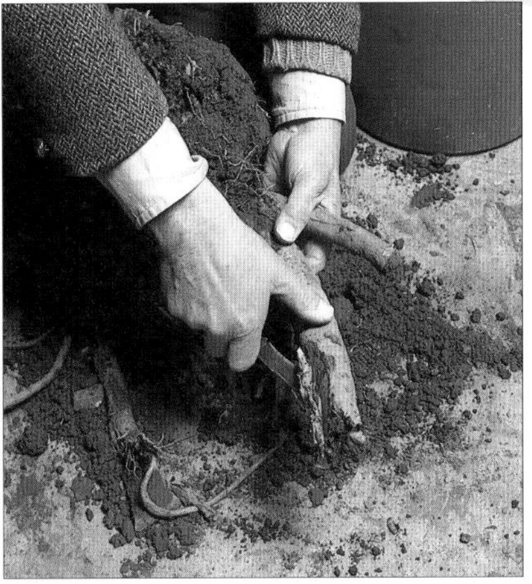

3 *You may need to trim off some of the larger roots with a sharp knife to ensure that the clump fits the container. This will not harm the plant.*

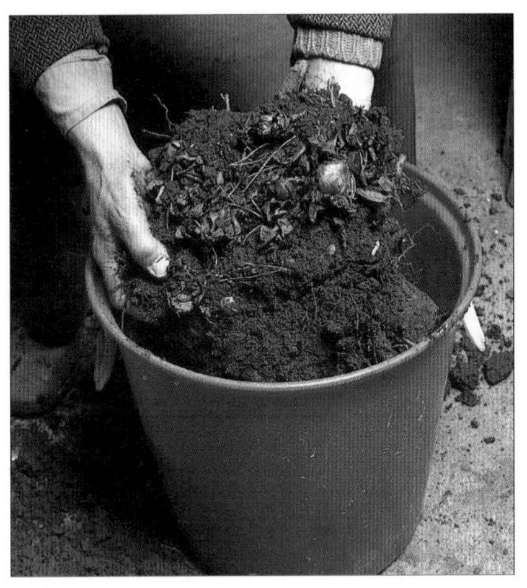

4 *Place the roots on a bed of garden soil and sprinkle soil around the crown. A potting compost is unnecessary, as the root contains all the food needed.*

5 *Water so that the soil is damp but not wet, and place the container in a dark place – under a greenhouse bench covered with black polythene, for instance.*

6 *After a few weeks the shoots will appear, and if kept in a warm, dark place you will soon have long, thin, pale pink stems of tasty rhubarb.*

7 *For an even easier method of forcing, simply place the lifted root in a black polythene bag. Tie the bag at the top, but make ventilation holes.*

Right and above: Peter McHoy

8 *Place the bag in a convenient place, such as a cupboard under the stairs, or under the sink. Check the bag now and then to see when the rhubarb is ready.*

CHECKLIST

WHAT TO DO

BEDS AND BORDERS
Plant Dutch irises

CLOCHES
Place cloches to warm the soil before sowing

CONTAINERS
Pot up lilies

LOOK AHEAD

PLACE ORDERS
Order bulbs, seeds and seedlings

SOW
Begonias, geraniums, pansies, petunias, sweet peas, tomatoes, verbena

POT PLANTS
Plant gloxinia tubers

MAKE A TRELLIS
For climbers you will plant in spring

WHAT TO SEE

BULBS AND BORDER PLANTS
Snowdrops, winter aconites (*Eranthis hyemalis*)

SHRUBS AND TREES
Christmas box (*Sarcococca confusa*), Cornelian cherry (*Cornus mas*), heathers, laurustinus (*Viburnum tinus*), *Lonicera fragrantissima*, *L. × purpusii*, *L. standishii*, silk tassel bush (*Garrya elliptica*), *Viburnum × bodnantense*, *V. farreri*, winter jasmine

HERBACEOUS
Helleborus niger, *H. orientalis*

VISITORS

FRIENDS
Blue tits, great tits, greenfinches, robins, ground beetles

FOES
Bullfinches, woodpigeons

MID WINTER

WEEK 4

WHAT TO DO

Snowdrops and winter aconites may give the illusion that winter is on its way out, but this can be one of the coldest months and the number of jobs that can be done outside is limited.

There are seeds to be sown, however, even if you do not have a greenhouse. It is also time to order summer-flowering bulbs that have to be planted in spring.

Seeds to sow

Pelargonium (geranium) seeds can be sown now if you can keep them on a light window-sill or have a heated greenhouse.

Other flower seeds that benefit from a long growing season and can be sown now include begonias, petunias and verbena. But unless you have enough space to grow them on in good light, it is better to buy your plants.

It is worth sowing some pansies indoors now. When they have germinated they can be grown in a cool position and eventually placed in a cold frame or cool greenhouse, as they do not require much warmth. Sowing now will provide plants to flower in early summer, bridging the gap between the winter-flowering type (which are often best in spring) and the main summer show.

Greenhouse jobs

If you have a heated greenhouse, sow tomato seeds now. Wait another few weeks before sowing outdoor varieties, otherwise they may become drawn and weak before they can be planted out.

Start dormant fuchsias into life by spraying them with water regularly to encourage a flush of vigorous new growth.

Most bedding plants can be sown if you have a propagator to provide some extra warmth and have the space and heat to keep them growing – otherwise it is best to wait for another month.

Sweet pea check

Check autumn-sown sweet peas regularly. Make sure slugs are not causing damage, and avoid too much heat if they are in a greenhouse. Even a cold frame may require ventilation on a sunny day. If the growing tips have not already been pinched out to encourage bushy growth, do this simple job now.

Don Wildridge

Sow pelargoniums if you have the space.

Ventilate sweet peas in the cold frame.

Sweet peas can be sown indoors or in a greenhouse now, and these will flower much earlier than those sown directly in the open ground later. They will need warmth for germination, but after that keep them in a cool, light place to encourage sturdy growth.

LOOK AHEAD

Spring-flowering bulbs tend to steal the limelight, but do not overlook the potential of summer-flowering types. Many bulb merchants offer an extensive range of common and unusual summer-flowering bulbs, corms and tubers, and some seedsmen also list a range of more popular types such as anemones, begonias, crocosmias, dahlias, gladioli, lilies, ranunculus, tigridias and other favourites.

Many of these can be planted from early spring to late spring, so order them now.

Garden centres and shops also sell the more common summer-flowering bulbs. Mail-order suppliers have a wider range and often offer a few unusual plants, such as the Peruvian daffodil (ismene), *flower of the west wind* (zephyranthes), *and the almost hardy orchid* Pleione formosana.

The autumn-flowering Nerine bowdenii *should be planted by mid spring, so make sure you order these truly outstanding plants in plenty of time.*

Why not order a few gloxinias at the same time? These will make really stunning pot plants for the window-sill *(see overleaf)**. Order half a dozen tubers and plant one every week or so to maintain a succession of these bright and beautiful flowers.*

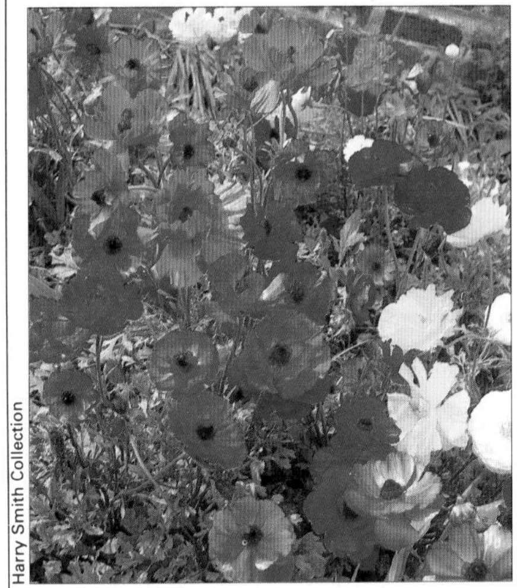

Harry Smith Collection

Persian buttercups (Ranunculus asiaticus).

WHAT TO SEE

Early bulbs, such as snowdrops and winter aconites, really help you feel that winter will soon be coming to an end – no matter how unpromising the weather may be.

The snowdrops most often seen are the common species Galanthus nivalis, *but there are dozens of other kinds, including one that flowers in autumn. A really early snowdrop is* G. caucasicus hiemalis. G.c. *'Early Form' can even be in bloom as early as Christmas.*

There is a double form of the common snowdrop, G. nivalis *'Flore Pleno', but look too for some of the singles with large or interesting flowers. 'Atkinsii' is an excellent variety with long, graceful flowers on long stems. 'S. Arnott' has exceptionally large flowers, while 'Lutescens' has yellow markings instead of green.*

VISITORS

There are not many beneficial insects to be found during the winter, so it is important to recognize those that you find while digging or tidying up garden debris.

Ground beetles, which can be found in almost every garden, are active all the year round. As they do not like strong sunlight and hunt mainly at night, they usually remain well hidden and are only noticed when they scurry away as soil is disturbed.

There are many kinds of ground beetle, but the violet ground beetle (Carabus violaceous), *which has violet margins to its wing cases, is one that most gardeners encounter.*

Ground beetles consume quantities of small insects. They help to control soil pests and should be encouraged. Relatives of the violet ground beetle prey upon furniture beetles and death watch beetles, so they really are a very useful group of insects.

M.I. Garwood/NHPA

The violet ground beetle eats insects.

MAKE A TRELLIS

If you have to buy the wood, a home-made trellis will not save you much money, but you can make it the size that suits you. If you have suitable wood already, it will be less expensive than buying a good trellis to support your climbing plants.

This is a project that even the most inexperienced woodworker can tackle. Winter is a good time to make a trellis, ready for you to plant out climbers in spring.

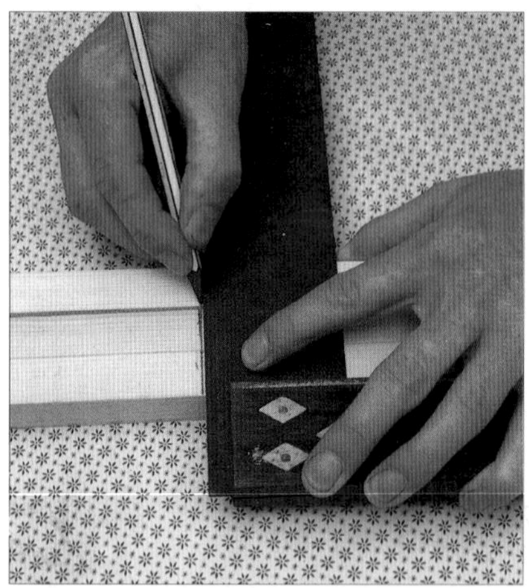

1 *Use softwood 20mm wide by 10mm deep. Timber is sold in 1.8m/6ft lengths, so make your trellis this height. Mark out and cut the cross-pieces.*

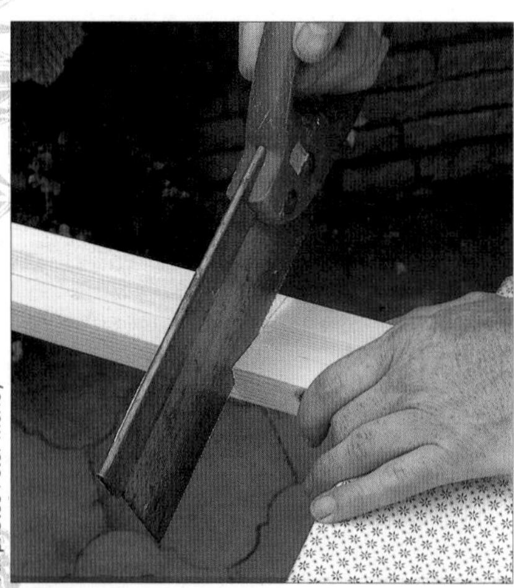

2 *A small tenon saw is fine for cutting these small pieces of wood. You can cut two or three pieces at once if you hold them firmly on a suitable support.*

All photos Peter McHoy

3 *Calculate the spacing for the horizontal pieces, trying to make the trellis pattern as square as possible. Mark these positions on the upright battens.*

4 *Use rustproof nails or staples to fix the pieces together, using your pencil lines as guides. Make sure the trellis is on a firm surface before you knock them in.*

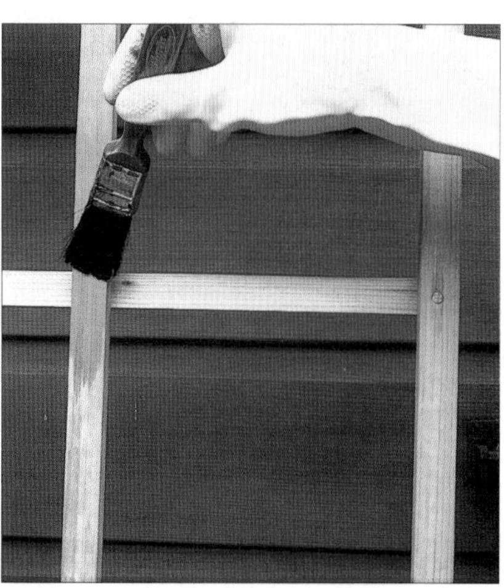

5 *Softwood will soon rot unless you use a wood preservative. Choose one safe for plants, and apply several coats, particularly on cut ends.*

GROW A GLOXINIA

Gloxinia tubers are available in the shops, and now is a good time to start them into growth. They make excellent showy greenhouse plants, but also flower well in the home. You can grow them on a window-sill. If you have a warm greenhouse, start them off there and bring them in once they begin to flower.

The huge trumpet-shaped flowers are available in a range of colours, often with contrasting rims.

1 *Plant in a peat-based compost with the top of the tuber level with the surface. The round side is the bottom and the slightly concave side the top.*

2 *Keep the tubers in a warm place (about 18°C/65°F). Within a few months you will have flowers like thi. For big flowers, limit the plant to one shoot*

POT UP SOME LILIES

Liven up your patio with tubs of exotic lilies this summer. You can plant them direct into tubs and other containers, but it is a good idea to get some off to an early start by planting them in ordinary pots now. Move them into outdoor containers to flower once these have been vacated by spring-flowering plants.

A mixture of loam, peat and leaf mould is ideal, but you can use potting compost.

1 *Place the bulbs deep in the pot and cover with 5cm/2in of compost. Many types produce roots on the stem above the bulb as well as below it.*

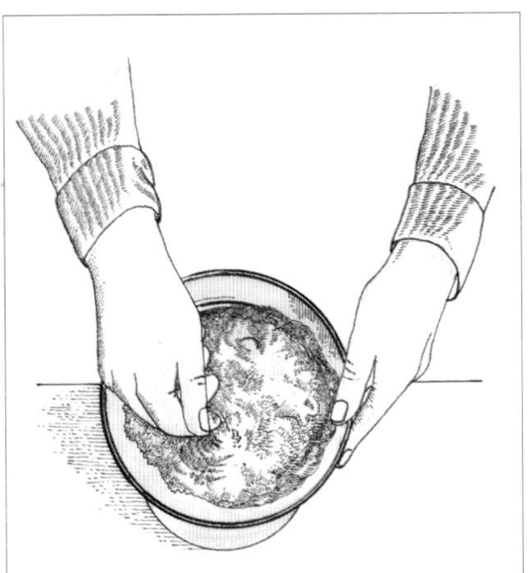

2 *As they grow, cover emerging shoots of stem-rooting types with compost. Grow plants in a light, cool greenhouse or a cold frame until ready to plant out.*

PLANT DUTCH IRISES

Dutch irises (which are a type and do not necessarily come from Holland) bring an extra splash of colour to the border in early summer. You can use them to fill a gap between the spring flowers and those of mid summer. If you have space, grow some of these popular florists' flowers to cut for the home. You can even plant some in pots to grow in the greenhouse or bring them on in a cold frame for an earlier display of flowers.

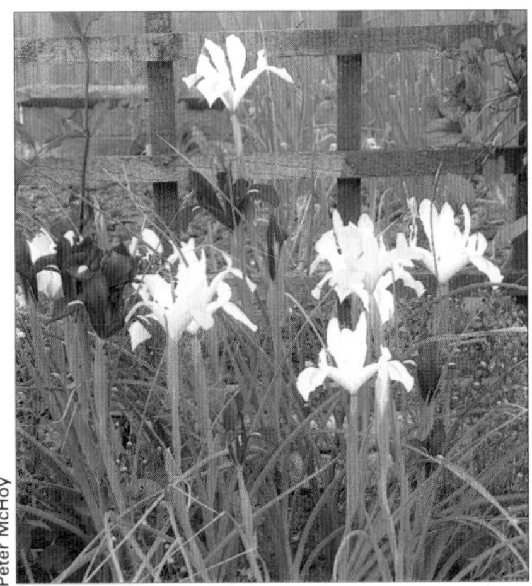

Peter McHoy

1 *If you did not plant Dutch irises in the autumn, plant them now if the ground is not frozen. You can buy them from garden centres and catalogues.*

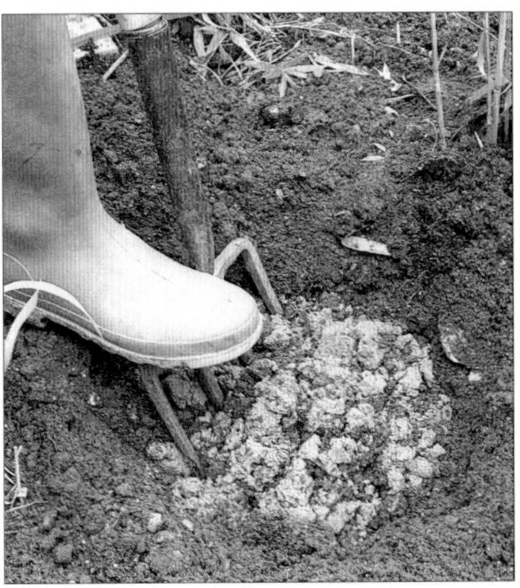

2 *Choose a position in full sun. If the bed is not naturally well-drained, dig the soil deeply and work in plenty of grit or coarse sand before planting.*

3 *Plant the bulbs about 10cm/4in deep and 10-15cm/4-6in apart. Close spacing produces a bolder show and hides the 'leggy' appearance of the stems.*

4 *Mark the area with small canes before you return the soil so that the shoots do not get hoed off, then mulch thickly to provide warmth and protection.*

5 *Put some Dutch iris bulbs in a large pot, using a loam-based compost, for a few early flowers. Keep the pot in a cool greenhouse or a cold frame.*

CHECKLIST

WHAT TO DO

BEDS AND BORDERS
Clear up leaves and debris, hoe off weeds

CLOCHES
Put in place to warm the soil before sowing
Protect early flowers for cutting

TREES AND SHRUBS
Prune and trim trees if necessary

LOOK AHEAD

SOW
Summer bedding plants that need a long growing season
Tomatoes for the greenhouse

PLANT
Lilies

PROPAGATE
Heathers by 'dropping'

WHAT TO SEE

BULBS AND BORDER PLANTS
Crocus chrysanthus hybrids, daffodils (early *cyclamineus* hybrids such as 'February Gold'), snowdrops, winter aconites (*Eranthis hyemalis*)

SHRUBS AND TREES
Cornelian cherry (*Cornus mas*), heathers, laurustinus (*Viburnum tinus*), silk tassel bush (*Garrya elliptica*), *Viburnum × bodnantense*, *V. farreri*, winter jasmine

HERBACEOUS
Helleborus niger, H. orientalis

VISITORS

FRIENDS
Blue tits, great tits, greenfinches, robins, common shrew, ground beetles

FOES
Bullfinches, woodpigeons.

LATE WINTER
WEEK 1

WHAT TO DO

Although the weather is still very wintery, and snow and ice are common deterrents to gardening, at last there are signs of change. Every week more flowers are in bloom, and even the real harbingers of spring, the daffodils, have well developed shoots. Very early varieties, such as 'Peeping Tom' and 'February Gold' may already be in flower. There may not be much to do in the garden, but there will be plenty to see from now on.

Garden hygiene

Reduce the pest and disease problem this year by taking a few simple steps towards good garden hygiene now. Many diseases, like black spot on roses and powdery mildew on gooseberries and blackcurrants, can overwinter on old leaves on the ground.

Aphids can overwinter as eggs, or as immature adults that hide in crevices on material that should perhaps be destroyed. Slugs and snails thrive in litter and debris that could be cleared away. All these, and many more, will quickly multiply once favourable weather conditions return in the spring.

Burn prunings, pick up and destroy leaves that have fallen around shrubs, and clear up leaves and rubbish from the bottom of hedges and fences. And keep those weeds down – they too may be maintaining a population of pests and diseases.

Ann Kelly/Garden Picture Library

A good bonfire will spruce up the garden.

Flowers for the home

Early bulbs start flowering about this time in many areas, but there will still be a dearth of blooms for some time. It is tempting to leave what flowers there are to bloom untouched in the garden, but it is worth cutting some for the home. Just two or three blooms and perhaps a sprig of early blossom can make a pretty arrangement full of promise.

A few shoots taken from the Cornelian cherry (Cornus mas) *and sprigs of heather will hardly be missed. Cut a few shoots of winter-flowering cherry* Prunus subhirtella *'Autumnalis', which almost always has a few flowers ready to open during the winter in mild spells and where there is enough protection.*

The blooms of many small

bulbs can be very attractive in flower arrangements. Snowdrops are one example, and a few early primroses will go well with them. Cover a few primroses, polyanthus, Lenten roses (Helleborus orientalis) *and bulbs with cloches to provide early and unblemished flowers for a good display in the home.*

LOOK AHEAD

Lilies are among the aristocrats of the garden, yet they are quite easy to grow if you can find a suitable spot in the garden. Try planting them in the shrub border, or in clumps among herbaceous plants. Some are great for containers, too, although they should be planted in the ground after flowering and are unattractive before they actually flower.

Gillian Beckett

Lilium *'Abendglut' – a stunning variety.*

Provided the soil is not frozen, lilies can be planted now. Most will grow in any reasonable garden soil (some dislike lime in the soil, but many will grow happily on alkaline soils). A pH of 6.5 is ideal, as this will suit most varieties of lily.

If the soil is heavy, work plenty of coarse sand or grit into the planting area. All soils will benefit from lots of leaf mould or garden compost added to the planting hole and used as a mulch around the plants.

If planting instructions are not on the packet, check in a good encyclopaedia. Stem-rooting types are generally planted more deeply than those that are just basal-rooting, and a few types are planted shallowly.

WHAT TO SEE

Crocus chrysanthus *hybrids are often the earliest crocuses, appearing in late winter when the weather is still cold. The large Dutch crocuses follow later, once spring really starts to make a tentative appearance.*

You can use C. chrysanthus *varieties to provide bright bowls of colour indoors. They must, though, be kept outside, perhaps in a cold frame, until the flower buds show colour. Never force them in heat indoors.*

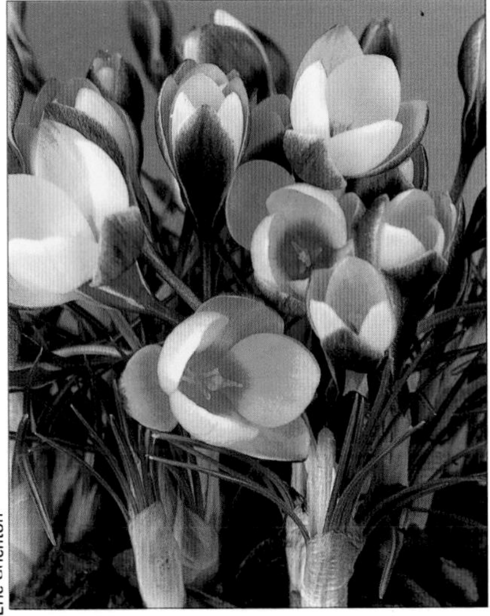

Eric Crichton

Crocus chrysanthus *'Zwanenburg'.*

In the garden they are most effective in small clumps in the rock garden or naturalized in short grass around a tree.

Good varieties to look for are 'Blue Bird' (blue outer petals with a white margin, creamy-white inside), 'E.A. Bowles' (old gold with a dark bronze throat), 'Ladykiller' (purple petals edged white, silvery-white inside) and the dainty white 'Snow White'. One of the earliest to flower is 'Zwanenburg', which is a bright golden yellow and its petals are bronzed on the outside.

VISITORS

Many small mammals remain largely inactive during the winter and seek food only during particularly mild spells. The common shrew, however, is a voracious eater and will forage throughout the year for insects and other small creatures. Although it eats some insects that are beneficial to the garden, it also devours pests such as snails and woodlice and can be happily regarded as a gardener's friend.

The combined length of the shrew's head and body is only about 7.5cm/3in, but the tail can add half as much again. It often stands on its hind legs, poking its long snout into the air to sample the odours of potential meals and to survey the possibilities with its tiny bead-like black eyes. Its soft, silky fur is yellowish-grey beneath and dark brown above (some have almost black fur).

Stephen Dalton/NHPA

A common shrew eating a slug.

TRIM TREES

Established trees require little pruning, other than removing any dead or diseased branches, or any that are growing in the wrong place and perhaps blocking the light. Occasionally, however, the shape of a developing or established tree can be greatly improved by a little judicious pruning, and late winter is a good time.

Never tackle major tree surgery – that is a job for the professionals.

Vana Haggerty

1 In a small garden, loss of space may be as much a problem as lack of light. If you remove some of the lower branches you will gain space and light.

2 Trees overhanging the lawn may encourage moss and make mowing difficult. Saw off offending branches. If need be, remove others for symmetry.

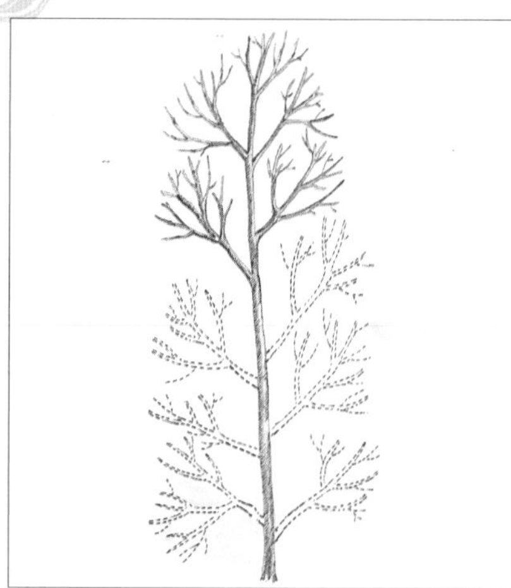

3 If a young tree is becoming bushy and failing to make a good head on a clear stem, prune off the lowest branches every two years, until the shape is right.

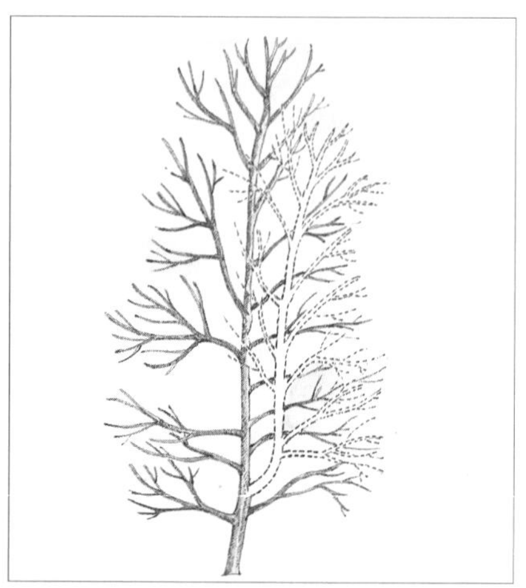

4 If a tree has formed a second leader, forming a narrow fork that is likely to split in a severe storm, remove it while it is still relatively young.

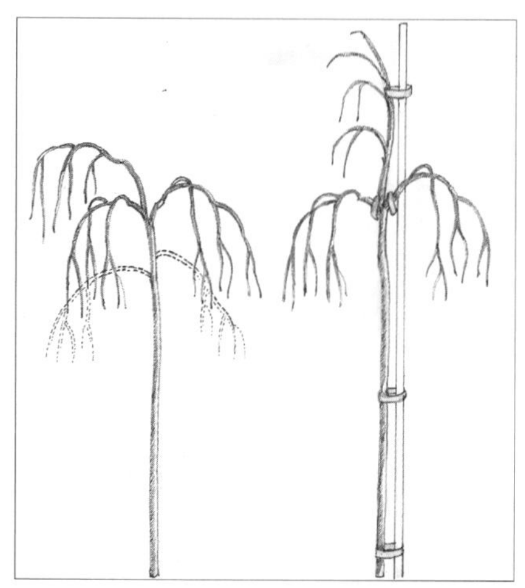

5 If your weeping tree lacks height, tie a suitable branch to a support to make it taller, and remove the lower weeping branches for the required appearance.

SOW TOMATOES

It is easy to raise your own tomatoes from seed. For a greenhouse, choose one like the old 'Alicante' or 'Ailsa Craig', or the newer 'Shirley'. 'Outdoor Girl' is popular as a staked variety for the garden, but for flavour and crop the bush-type 'Red Alert' is difficult to beat if you do not mind small tomatoes.

Sow now if you have a heated greenhouse to grow them in, but do not sow outdoor tomatoes yet.

All photos Peter McHoy

1 If you require a lot of plants, sow them in a seed tray or large pot. Space seeds so the plants do not become overcrowded. Cover with compost.

2 If relatively few plants are required, sow directly into small pots. Sprinkle three or four seeds in each one, then thin to just one if more germinate.

SOW BEDDING PLANTS

Sowing your own bedding plants can save money, and it is far more satisfying than buying them. You can also choose the varieties that you want to grow – if you buy plants from a garden centre the choice will be limited.

To sow now you need a heated propagator or a warm window-sill. You must also have somewhere light and frostproof, such as a light window-sill, to grow them on.

1 *Use a fibrous material, such as peat, moss or shredded bark, in the bottom of the seed tray to prevent the compost being washed through the holes.*

2 *Almost fill the tray with a good seed compost. Press it well down with the fingers, to ensure there are no large air pockets that will expose roots to drying air.*

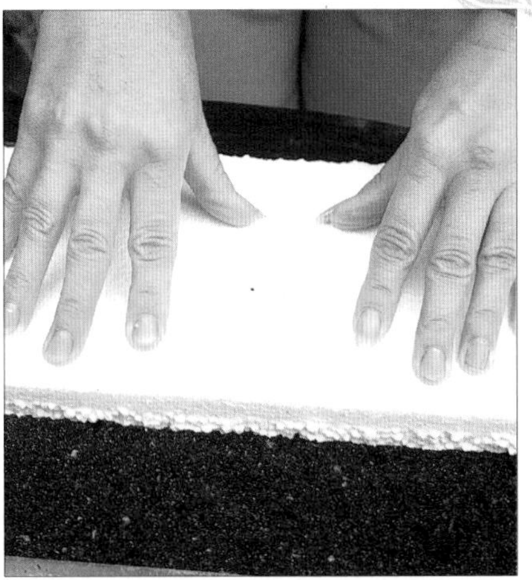

3 *Make sure the surface is level before sowing, or the seeds will run to one side when you water. Make yourself a 'firmer' from wood or polystyrene.*

4 *Fine seeds will have to be scattered, but large seeds, such as French and African marigolds, are best spaced to make thinning easier and less urgent.*

5 *Unless the packet instructs otherwise, cover thinly with compost. Remember to water and label. If you need just a few plants, save space by using a half-tray.*

'DROP' HEATHERS

'Dropping' is a useful way to get new plants from a straggly old heather. The new plants are not always as well-shaped as those raised from cuttings, but the method is dependable.

If the heather has previously been pruned to stimulate young growth the result will be even better, but unpruned plants also root readily. The new plants that form on the old one will be well rooted and ready to sever in the autumn.

1 *Provided the ground is not frozen, dig a hole deep enough to bury the whole heather plant, and work in plenty of moisture-retaining organic material.*

2 *Lift the old plant with as much root-ball as possible, and bury it so that only 2.5cm/1in of the shoot tips are exposed. Keep well watered all summer.*

CHECKLIST

WHAT TO DO

FENCES
Make repairs, apply preservative

CLOCHES
Place cloches to warm the soil before sowing

ROCK GARDEN
Refirm loose plants, apply stone chippings

SEEDLINGS
Prick out seedlings sown earlier indoors

PATHS
Apply a weedkiller to control weeds

LOOK AHEAD

SOW
Summer bedding plants if you have a greenhouse or sufficient window-sill space

SWEET PEAS
Prepare ground, check overwintering plants in cold frame or sow under glass now

CUTTINGS
Start fuchsias for spring cuttings

WHAT TO SEE

BULBS AND BORDERS
Crocus chrysanthus hybrids, early daffodils, snowdrops, winter aconites (*Eranthis hyemalis*)

SHRUBS AND TREES
Cornelian cherry (*Cornus mas*) heathers, laurustinus (*Viburnum tinus*), silk tassel bush (*Garry elliptica*), winter jasmine

HERBACEOUS
Helleborus niger, H. orientalis

VISITORS

FRIENDS
Blue tits, great tits, greenfinches, robins, starlings, common shrew

FOES
Bullfinches, woodpigeons, rabbits

LATE WINTER
WEEK 2

WHAT TO DO

On most days the garden will still seem to be in the harsh grip of winter, despite the increasing number of very early flowers that seem determined to bloom. For gardeners with a heated greenhouse, sowing and pricking out are now priority jobs. If you have to depend on a light window-sill for your seedlings, be patient; they are slow to develop.

Plan your sowing

The majority of summer bedding plants, and lots of pot plants, can be sown between now and late spring. Make yourself a timetable of what to sow when, using the instructions on the seed packets as a guide and taking into account the facilities that you have available. If you have a heated greenhouse, and especially if you have a propagator, too, an early start will produce more advanced specimens to plant out in early summer.

An airing cupboard can serve as a propagator indoors, but bear in mind how much space seedlings will need once they are pricked out. They must have good light, otherwise they will become drawn and weak. It may be better to sow some seeds late when you can soon move them into a cold frame without too much risk of frost damage.

Gillian Beckett

Make stone chippings an attractive feature.

Check the rock garden

Get the rock garden into good shape for the spring, when it will become one of the most colourful corners of the garden.

Because rock plants generally have a shallow root system, and there is often not much depth of soil above some of the rocks, heav frosts can push some of the plant partially out of the ground, especially if they were young ones planted in the autumn.

Choose a day when the ground is not frozen to firm them back into the soil. Firm well so that there are no large air pockets to expose the roots to drying air. If labels have also come adrift, replace these too.

Top up stone chippings if these have worn thin in places. If your rock garden is not dressed with fine gravel or stone chippings, consider doing it now. They make a much better background again which to admire your tiny rock treasures, and when the plants are not in flower the rock garden will be a more attractive feature.

Warm the soil

If you are planning to sow early vegetables or make an early start with hardy annuals for cutting, put your cloches or sheets of polythene into position now, so that the soil can warm up for a few weeks first.

LOOK AHEAD

Sweet peas have all the qualities of a popular plant: fragrance, beauty and a long flowering period. They are also tough and will give you a respectable display for the garden or for cutting, even if you simply sow them where they are to flower and do little else other than offer them support. These plants, however, will produce flower stems that are very inferior to those grown from good plants on well prepared ground.

Marshall Cavendish

Prepare the ground for sweet peas now.

If you want really super sweet peas this year, prepare the ground now. If you plan to grow them on the cordon system (each plant up an individual cane, in a row) take out a deep trench and fork over the bottom to ensure that there is a good depth of loose soil. Work in as much garden compost, rotted manure, or other organic material, as you can spare.

If you want early flowers but did not sow in the autumn, sow now in a greenhouse and move to a cold frame once they have germinated and are growing well.

Overwintered plants in the cold frame will still benefit from protection on cold nights – cover the frame with old blankets or pieces of carpet. Remove the insulation in the morning when the air has warmed up.

WHAT TO SEE

Winter aconites* (Eranthis hyemalis) *make an early appearance, along with the lesser celandine of hedgerows. From a distance they look somewhat similar, with pretty, bright yellow, buttercup blooms on ground-hugging plants.

Closer inspection reveals the true beauty of the winter aconite, however, with its big, yellow, cuplike flowers set off by a ruff of divided green leaves. It is a combination that manages to look good whether the plants are viewed against dark soil or naturalized in grass around a tree. Because they bloom so early it is not uncommon to see the yellow flowers poking defiantly through a cloak of snow.

Eric Crichton

Eranthis hyemalis *blooms early.*

Make a note to plant some yourself this autumn, but do not expect them to do well the first year after planting. They take a while to settle down, then bloom dependably, with the minimum of maintenance, for years.

E. cilicica *is similar but does not flower until early spring. There is also a hybrid between the two species:* E. × tubergenii, *and a particularly good variety of it called 'Guinea Gold'. These also flower in early spring.*

VISITORS

Starlings are quarrelsome, noisy birds that will often try to dominate the bird table. They can turn a quiet garden scene on a cold winter's day into a noisy bustle of activity within minutes.

In the autumn they can do some good for the gardener by searching the lawn for leatherjackets, and they eat lots of grubs of many kinds.

Although there is a resident population, the numbers are swollen in winter by migrants from the continent, which arrive in mid autumn and depart again in early spring. Those in northern Britain may have come from Russia and the Baltic States, those in southern Britain are more likely to be from places like Holland, Belgium and Germany.

The starling's winter plumage is often particularly bold, with the white speckles especially pronounced.

Laurie Campbell/NHPA

Note the starling's speckled winter plumage.

START FUCHSIAS INTO GROWTH FOR CUTTINGS

If you have been overwintering pot-grown fuchsias in a garage, greenhouse or cold but frost-free room, they will probably look like the one below. If you want to take cuttings in the spring, now is the time to stimulate them into growth.

If you do not want to take cuttings, wait a few more weeks before starting your fuchsias into growth.

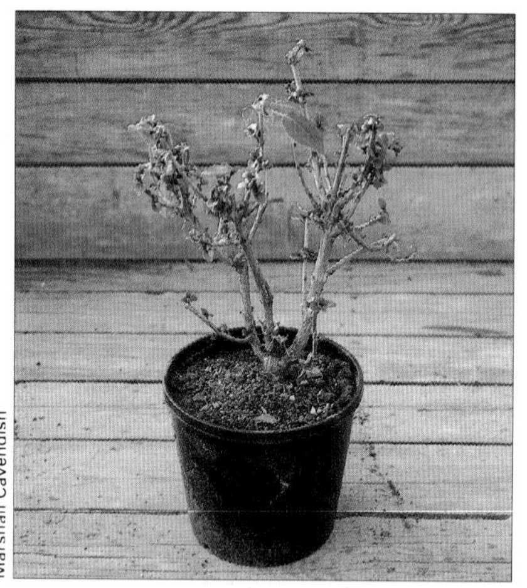

Marshall Cavendish

1 *Fuchsias kept in a cold but frost-free place have few leaves and look straggly. They soon improve if you stimulate them into growth.*

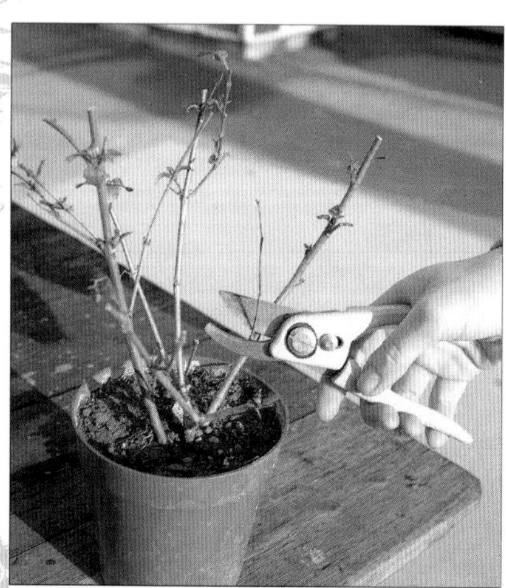

2 *Cut out weak shoots and lightly trim back main shoots. Put in a warm place (about 10°C/50°F) in good light and start to water. Mist with water occasionally.*

PRICK OUT EARLY-SOWN SEEDLINGS

Prick out seedlings sown a couple of weeks ago, such as geraniums and others with a long growing season, before they crowd each other.

Most bedding plants, such as antirrhinums and fibrous-rooted begonias, are best pricked out into seed trays, which take up less space. Geraniums (pelargoniums), however, benefit from the extra compost contained in individual pots.

Peter McHoy

1 *For pelargoniums, fill small pots with potting compost and firm it gently. Seed trays, which hold more plants, can be used for most other seedlings.*

2 *Loosen the compost with a dibber or transplanting tool, then lift the seedlings carefully, holding them by their leaves and not the stems.*

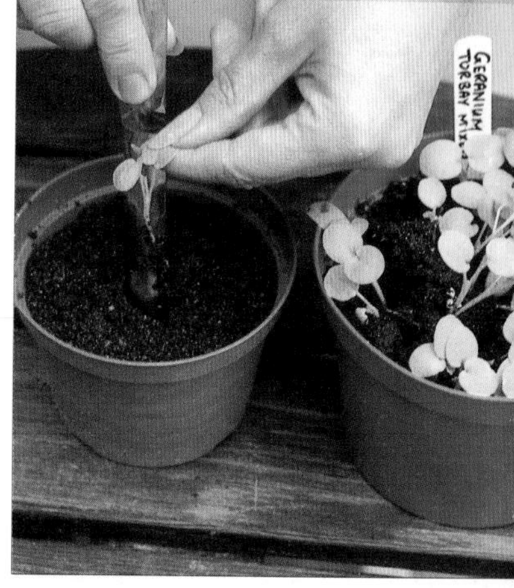

3 *Make a small hole in the centre of each pot with a transplanting tool, a dibber or even a pencil, deep enough to take the roots without damage.*

4 *Hold the seedling very gently by the seed leaves, then carefully firm the compost around the roots with a finger or a dibber.*

5 *Water the seedlings, which will help to settle compost around the roots, then keep in a warm, humid place out of direct sunlight for a few days.*

KILL PATH WEEDS

Weeds make paths look untidy and neglected. Hand weeding is tedious and a continuous job through spring and summer. However, a single application of a suitable weedkiller will keep paths and drives clear for a whole season.

Sodium chlorate is a traditional weedkiller but can seep sideways. Most modern path weedkillers do not 'creep' and are better at controlling moss.

Peter McHoy

1 *A sprinkler bar helps to distribute weedkillers evenly with the minimum of drift. Hold the head close to the ground, especially if it is windy.*

2 *Use a board, or sheets of polythene, to keep the weedkiller off plants in borders. This is particularly necessary if using an ordinary rose on the can.*

MAINTAIN YOUR FENCES

Garden fences are expensive to replace, so protect your investment with regular maintenance. Winter is the best time to mend fences. They are usually more accessible and, except for evergreens, nearby plants are less likely to be damaged.

The brackets and spurs mentioned below are available from DIY stores, good garden centres and from fencing contractors.

1 *If a wooden post has rotted at the base, you can buy a concrete post spur. Excavate a hole next to the old post, insert the spur and bolt it on.*

2 *Broken arris rails are common on closeboard fences. They are easily repaired with an arris bracket; just nail it into sound wood either side.*

3 *If the arris rail has rotted where it fits into the mortis, nail a special end bracket into a sound part of the arris rail and the fence post.*

4 *Refix loose feather-edged boards with rust-proof nails. If the old board has rotted, replace it with a new one from a fencing contractor.*

5 *Once the fence is sound, paint it from both sides with a preservative. Creosote is good but if you have plants in leaf, choose one safe for plants.*

CHECKLIST

WHAT TO DO

STORED BULBS
Check condition of bulbs and tubers

CLOCHES
Put in place to warm the soil before sowing

FRAMES AND GREENHOUSES
Clean and disinfect
Ventilate carefully, protect on cold nights

ROSES
Prune repeat-flowering climbers

DIGGING
Complete winter digging

LOOK AHEAD

SOW
Summer bedding plants if you have a greenhouse or sufficient window-sill space

CUTTINGS
Start fuchsias into growth if you want to take cuttings in spring
Take dahlia and chrysanthemum cuttings

WHAT TO SEE

BULBS
Crocus chrysanthus hybrids, early daffodils, snowdrops, winter aconites (*Eranthis hyemalis*)

SHRUBS AND TREES
Cornelian cherry (*Cornus mas*), *Daphne mezereum*, heathers, laurustinus (*Viburnum tinus*), winter jasmine

VISITORS

FRIENDS
Blue tits, greenfinches, robins, wrens

FOES
Bullfinches, woodpigeons, rabbits

LATE WINTER
WEEK 3

WHAT TO DO

The transition from winter to spring is seldom an easy one, and though the days are lengthening it can still be extremely cold. Regional differences are also very pronounced at this time of year. Do not be misled by a few fine days; keep your plants well protected.

Cold frame protection

Plants in cold frames and greenhouses can be more vulnerable now than in mid winter. Plants that have received some warmth and protection will already have started into growth and they can easily be damaged. Only tough plants should be kept in the cold frame, but even these should be protected by placing a blanket or old carpet over the top when very cold nights are forecast. Wind can also devastate young growth, so do not open the frame for ventilation if it exposes the plants to cold winds.

Modern hybrid primroses will be in the shops, already coming into flower. These make pretty short-term house plants, but do not plant them in the garden without first hardening them off in the cold frame for a few weeks.

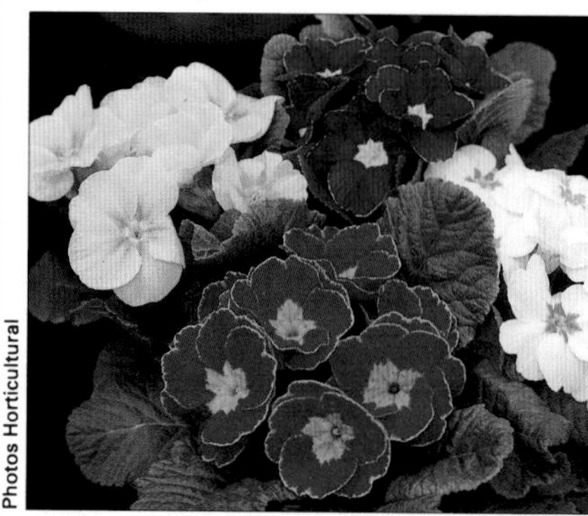

Photos Horticultural

Harden off primroses before planting out.

Check stored bulbs

Continue to check bulbs, corms and tubers to make sure they have not started to rot. Make sure that tubers have not dried out too much. Dahlia tubers that have become very dehydrated may be difficult to start into growth.

Those dahlia tubers not required for cuttings should be kept dormant in a frost-proof place until ready for planting in late spring, but if they have become very dry, stand them in a bucket of water overnight so that they become plump again. Dry them off thoroughly before returning to store.

First winter digging

Provided the ground is not frozen or waterlogged, finish winter digging as soon as possible. This will allow the ground to settle before you sow or plant. There is also time for weed seedlings to germinate so that you can hoe them off before you plant.

Continue sowing

Continue sowing summer bedding plants if you have a greenhouse. Do not sow quick-growing types such as alyssum and French marigolds yet, otherwise they will be too advanced in their growth by planting time. Sow only those that need early sowing.

LOOK AHEAD

Birds can devastate the earliest blooms of plants like crocuses, primroses and polyanthus. Yellow varieties are particularly prone to attack, and the house sparrow is often the main culprit.

They do not usually eat the petals, and the damage seems quite wanton. It is probably a displacement activity that they indulge in when they are not fully occupied with essential activities.

If birds are a regular problem in spring, be sure to get protection in place now before the flowers are damaged.

Harry Smith Collection

Crocuses are prone to attack from birds.

Netting and cages work well if the mesh is small enough, but these are not a practical solution for crocuses in grass or rock gardens, or polyanthus in beds of spring bedding. Black cotton criss-crossed between short, inconspicuous pegs is one of the most efficient deterrents. It does not always work, but black cotton is almost invisible against the soil and it does deter many birds.

WHAT TO SEE

Daphne mezereum *is one of those invaluable shrubs that bridges the gap between the winter-flowerers and the plentiful blooms of spring. It has many other desirable qualities: it is colourful, very fragrant and compact, seldom growing much more than 1.2m/4ft tall, with a spread of similar dimensions.*

The flowers are usually prolific, clustered along the bare stems, and sometimes there is a bonus of red berries in summer. Be careful, though, if you have small children, as the berries are poisonous.

The flowers vary from pale purple-pink to violet-red, and there is a white form ('Alba') with yellow berries. 'Grandiflora' has larger flowers, and blooms much earlier, often in the autumn.

Plant D. mezereum *in sun or partial shade, in well-drained soil with plenty of humus if possible. Grow it where you can appreciate its heavy scent as well as its bold colour. It is compact enough to be planted close to the front door, or near the garden gate, where visitors, too, can appreciate it on a cold winter's day.*

Eric Crichton

Daphne mezereum *brightens up a garden.*

VISITORS

The wren's subdued brown colouring and small size (hardly 10cm/4in long), together with its mouse-like way of creeping about under the cover of shrubs, make it easy to overlook. But its rounded appearance and tilted-up tail make it unmistakable when you do see it.

The wren is a common visitor to country gardens, but in large towns and cities you are only likely to see it if there are parks or large gardens in the area. It is one of the few insectivorous birds that remains with us all year, and as such can help the gardener by keeping down the number of grubs and insects.

Despite its small size, the wren has a surprisingly loud song – it is said that it can be heard about half a mile away – and it continues to sing right through the winter. It usually cocks its tail when it sings.

In very cold weather wrens roost together in holes or nest boxes (up to 46 wrens have been counted entering one nest box to roost!).

Melvin Grey/NHPA

Wrens keep down garden insects.

TAKE CHRYSANTHEMUM CUTTINGS

Large flowered types chrysanthemum that bloom in the garden in late autumn, and those taken into the greenhouse for later flowering, should have been lifted and the roots (stools) stored in boxes of compost in a cold frame or cool greenhouse. The best time to take cuttings of most garden varieties is any time during the next few weeks.

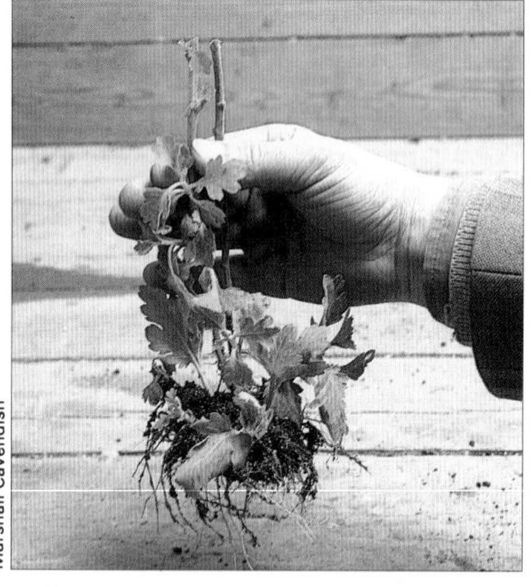

Marshall Cavendish

1 *If old crowns have not yet produced shoots, bring them into a warm place and keep just moist. When they have shoots like this you can take cuttings.*

2 *Choose healthy shoots about 6-8cm/2½-3in long, and cut them off about 12mm/½in above compost level. Use a sharp, clean knife for this.*

3 *Trim off lower leaves, and cut the base of the cutting cleanly below a leaf joint. Use a sharp knife and be careful not to crush the cuttings.*

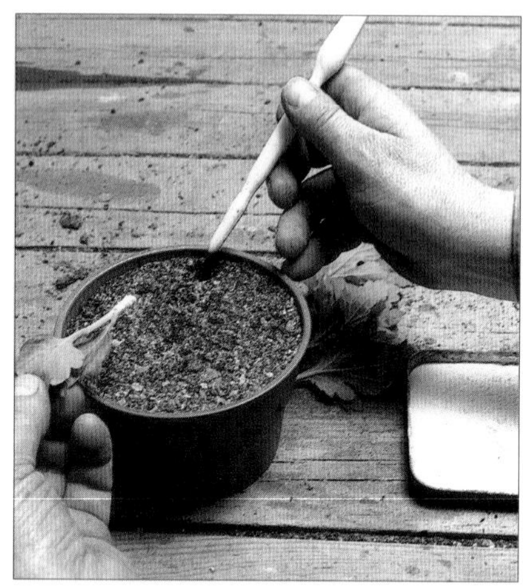

4 *Dip the moistened base into a hormone rooting powder. Insert in trays or pots of a rooting compost, peat/sand mix, or vermiculite.*

5 *Water the cuttings then cover with a polythene bag if you do not have a propagator. Stop the bag touching the cuttings, otherwise they may rot.*

PRUNE CLIMBING ROSES

If you have not already pruned your climbing roses, do so now before the new growth starts.

The best method of pruning depends on the type of climbing rose that you have. The advice given below is for repeat-flowering climbers that generally have large hybrid-tea type flowers. These include climbing forms of hybrid teas (such as 'Climbing Fragrant Cloud') and modern climbers such as 'Compassion' and 'Golden Showers'.

These climbers should be dead-headed during the summer. This is a form of summer pruning if you cut them back to the nearest leaf.

Start winter pruning by cutting out any dead or very weak shoots, and tie in strong ones.

Cut out any withered shoot tips then shorten flowered laterals to two or three buds.

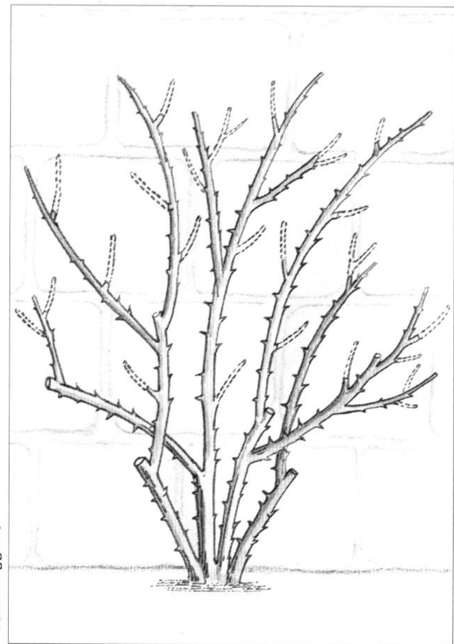

Vana Haggerty

Climbers do not require severe pruning. Cut out dead or weak shoots, then cut back lateral shoots that have flowered to two or three buds.

TAKE DAHLIA CUTTINGS

You can plant your old tubers in the ground in late spring. If you require just one or two extra plants they can be divided before planting, if each piece has some stem with an 'eye' (bud). Enthusiasts prefer to raise new plants from cuttings, however, and this is a good way to increase your stock.

If you have already started the tubers into growth take the cuttings now.

Marshall Cavendish

1 *Place the tubers in pots or trays of compost or a peat/sand mixture, and use shoots about 7.5cm/3in long for the cuttings. Cut them close to the tuber.*

2 *Carefully remove the lower leaves to give a length of clear stem to insert into the compost. Use a knife or pull them off with the fingers.*

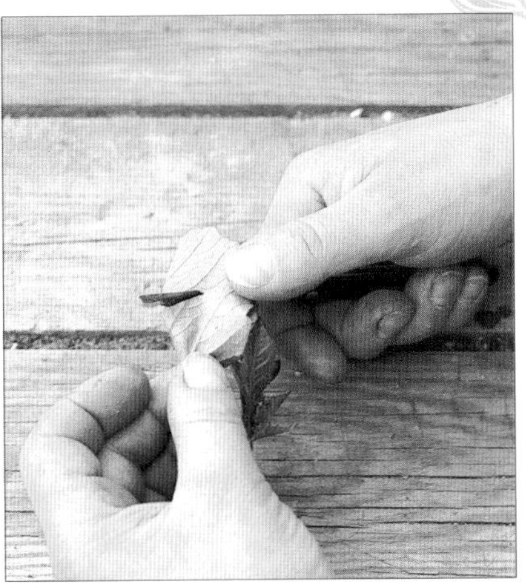

3 *Cut the largest leaves in half, and discard the top, to reduce transpiration (water loss). This is not essential but cuttings are less likely to wilt.*

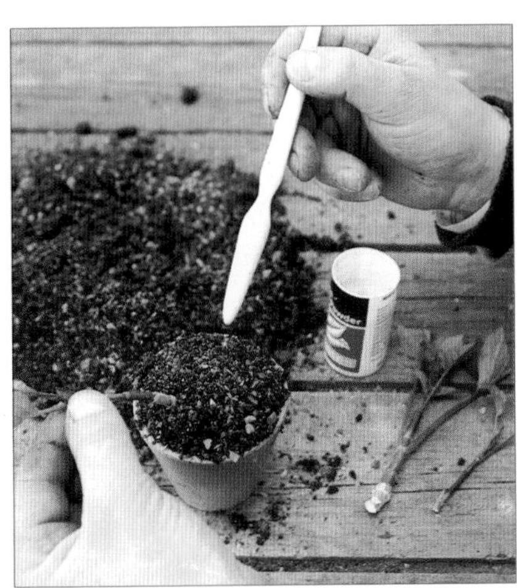

4 *Insert cuttings into small pots of rooting compost or a mix of peat and sand, or into vermiculite or perlite. Use a rooting hormone to speed rooting.*

5 *Water and label the pot, then place in a propagator if you have one. Otherwise, put a polythene bag over the top and keep in a warm, light place.*

CLEAN THE COLD FRAME AND GREENHOUSE

Fungus diseases thrive in the damp, still conditions found among crowded plants in cold frames and greenhouses in spring. Pests also spread rapidly among the succulent growth of seedlings once the temperature begins to rise. Reduce the risk by keeping your frame and greenhouse as clean and sterile as possible, paying particular attention to nooks and crannies.

1 *Remove the plants then scrub the wood-work or metal frame of your cold frame and greenhouse with a disinfectant. Clean the glass too.*

2 *Disease spores can lurk unseen in old pots and seed trays. Even if they look clean, scrub them in a bucket of disinfectant. Rinse and dry before use.*

CHECKLIST

WHAT TO DO

PLANTS
Remove winter protection from alpines
Trim summer heathers with shears
Prune hybrid tea and floribunda roses
Divide and transplant snowdrops
Plant trees and shrubs while still dormant
Prick out seedlings

LAWNS
Neaten edges with an edging strip

ROCK GARDEN
Add new plants, apply stone chippings

LOOK AHEAD

PLANT
Pot up gladioli corms for early flowering

PREPARE GROUND
For sowing hardy annuals later in month

PROTECT EARLY FLOWERS
Use black cotton to protect crocuses and other early flowers from bird damage

SOW
Summer bedding plants

WHAT TO SEE

BULBS AND BORDER PLANTS
Crocuses, daffodils, *Iris danfordiae*, *I. reticulata*, Lenten rose (*Helleborus orientalis*)

SHRUBS AND TREES
Camellias, *Chaenomeles japonica*, heathers, laurustinus (*Viburnum tinus*)

VISITORS

FRIENDS
Chaffinches, greenfinches, robins, wrens

FOES
Bullfinches, house sparrows

LATE WINTER

WEEK 4

WHAT TO DO

The increasing activity of birds, many preparing to nest, and perhaps the evening mating call of frogs, is a sure sign that winter is coming to an end. The number of plants in flower is increasing almost daily, and there are now plenty of jobs to be done in the garden whenever the weather is mild enough.

Trim summer heathers

Use a sharp pair of shears to clip over summer-flowering heathers. Remove old flowered growths, but be very careful not to cut into the base of the flowering spike. They do not shoot readily if you cut into old wood, but trimming them helps to keep most of the plants tidy and compact.

Transplant snowdrops

Unlike most bulbs, snowdrops are best transplanted 'in the green' (when the foliage is still on, just after flowering). Do not disturb them unnecessarily, but lift and divide the clumps if they are overcrowded or if you want to multiply your plants.

Remove protection from alpines

If you protected vulnerable alpines with sheets of glass or cloches, remove them now if the weather is not too wet and cold.

Peter McHoy

Weed spring bedding plants often.

Spruce up the spring beds

Spring bedding plants such as double daisies, pansies and wallflowers will now start to grow more strongly, but so will the weeds. Use the hoe or, if necessary, resort to hand weeding. Even though the spring bedding is not yet in flower, a background of weed-free soil will make your garden look so much neater and smarter.

Prick out seedlings

Never let seedlings become overcrowded before you prick them out into seed trays or individual pots.

Plant trees and shrubs

Plant bare-root trees and shrubs without delay, while they are still dormant. This is also a good time to plant container-grown plants.

Sow more bedding plants

Continue to sow bedding plants if you have a greenhouse. If you have to depend on a light window-sill do not sow quick-growers yet, such as French marigolds and sweet alyssum. Give the space to those that need more growing time, such as ageratums and bedding dahlias. If necessary, plants that flower quickly, such as French marigolds, can be sown in a cold frame later to ease the pressure on window-sill space.

LOOK AHEAD

Many hardy annuals, such as Californian poppies* (Eschscholzia californica), *candytuft, clarkia, cornflowers, godetia and pot marigolds* (calendulas), *can be sown outdoors during the next month. These are usually sown where they are to flower, but do not be in a hurry to sow them yet, even though the seed packet may suggest that you can. They will usually germinate better and grow more rapidly if you wait for a few weeks until the soil is warmer.

Californian poppies can be sown outdoors.

Now is the time to prepare the ground, however, so that weed seedlings have time to germinate before you sow. Direct-sown seeds have to compete with weed seedlings that are always present in the ground, and if these germinate more quickly than the plants you have sown, identification and thinning will be rather difficult.

Dig or fork the ground over now where hardy annuals are to be sown, then rake it level. Within a week or two you can start to hoe off weed seedlings. Rake the ground level again for sowing.

As you dig, be sure to remove any deep-rooted perennial weeds, or difficult ones such as couch grass and bindweed, which will be difficult to control after the annuals germinate.

WHAT TO SEE

Dwarf bulbous spring-flowering irises make a big impact for their small size. The first to flower is* Iris danfordiae, *with its bright, bold, yellow flowers that seem to burst into bloom almost as the shoots emerge. In mild areas these may already be over, but they are followed by the slightly later, blue-flowering* I. reticulata *and its varieties.

Iris reticulata *provides a spectacular show.*

I. danfordiae *is often in bloom when late snow still carpets the ground, yet its deep lemon flowers make a real show if you plant them densely enough for a bold display. They are slightly fragrant, too. As they are only about 10cm/4in high, grow them in window boxes and other containers if you want to appreciate the scent.*

I. reticulata, *with its purple-blue flowers splashed orange on the falls of the lower petals, is also slightly fragrant. It is at its best when left to form large clumps in the rock garden or at the front of a border. There are several good varieties, including 'Cantab' (cobalt blue with Cambridge blue falls), and 'Harmony' (deep blue with dark falls). All these plants are hardy.*

VISITORS

The birds that many of us loosely call sparrows may, in fact, be one of several species, so take a closer look at those that visit your garden.

House sparrows are the most common and, as their name suggests, they are happy to nest in or near houses. The female is all brown but the male has a bold, black bib and a grey crown.

Both sexes of the tree sparrow are very similar to a male house sparrow, but the black bib is much smaller, and there is a distinct brown 'cap'. There is also a small black cheek spot that should confirm the identification.

The so-called hedge sparrow, which is almost slate grey beneath and brown above, does not even belong to the sparrow family. Its other common names are hedge accentor and dunnock.

The male house sparrow has a grey crown.

GIVE YOUR LAWN A NEAT EDGE

A poor, broken down edge will mar even the best lawn. If you find the edges get broken down around flower beds, and constantly cutting them back with a spade or a half-moon edger is making your lawn smaller each year use a lawn edging.

Several kinds are available from garden centres, both plastic and metal, so you should be able to find one that you like.

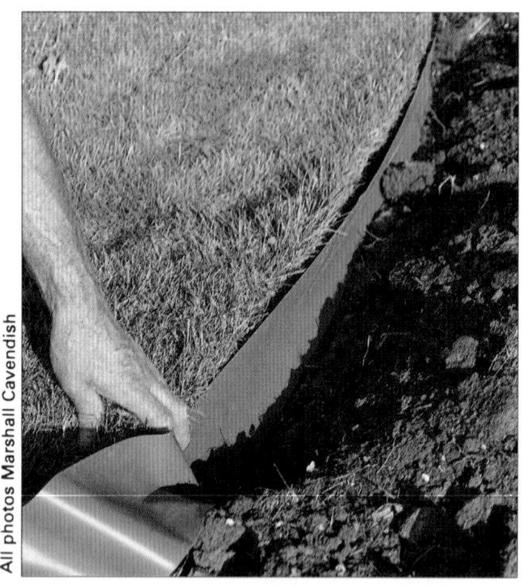

All photos Marshall Cavendish

1 *Start with a neat edge by cutting it back with a half-moon edger where it has been damaged. Make a slit deep enough to take the edging.*

2 *Make sure the top of the edging strip is not higher than the edge of the lawn, or it may damage the mower. Draw soil against it to hold it in place.*

PLANT UP A ROCK GARDEN

Whether you have just made a rock garden or need to replant parts of an existing one, now is a good time to plant your alpines. Most of them flower in spring, and many bloom while still young, so you will get quick results.

If there is a very cold spell and the ground is still frozen, wait for another week or two before planting. They will soon catch up once the better weather arrives.

1 *Alpines need good, free-draining soil. A loam-based potting compost with extra sand can be used, or mix 2 parts peat and 1½ of sharp sand with 3 parts soil.*

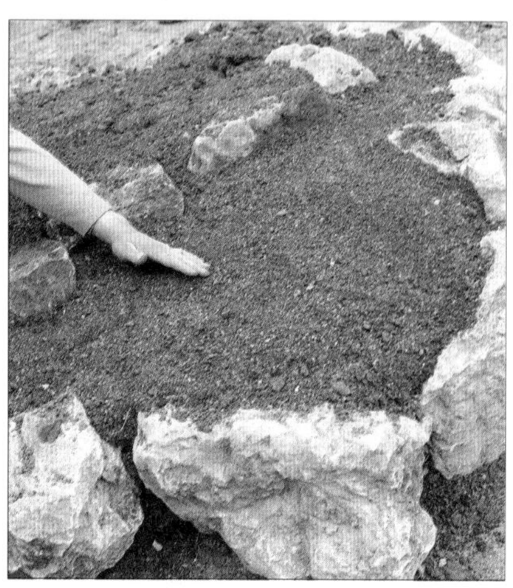

2 *Tread or press the compost down among the rocks to ensure that there are no large air pockets. Smooth the surface level before planting.*

3 *Choose a selection of plants with similar vigour so that more rampant kinds do not swamp restrained ones. Firm in well and water.*

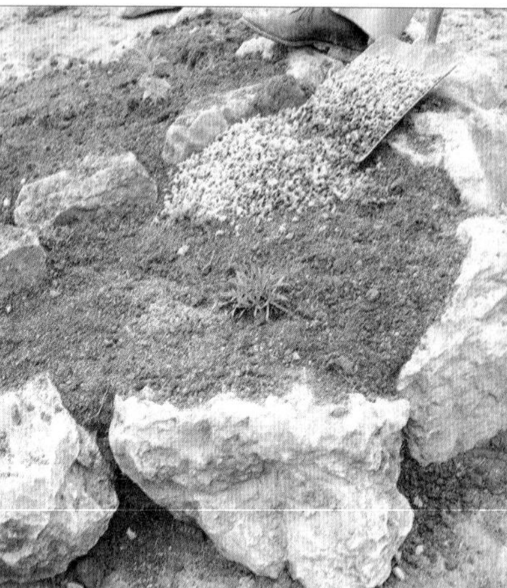

4 *The appearance of the bare soil around young plants can be improved with a dressing of fine stone chippings. These are on sale at garden centres.*

5 *For a professional finish, put some plants in crevices with their roots under the rocks, and let stone chippings cascade down between them.*

POT UP GLADIOLI

Gladioli corms should not be planted outdoors for another month in most areas, but you can obtain earlier flowers and extend the gladiolus season by starting some off in pots, if you have a greenhouse or cold frame.

They do not require much heat, but you must be able to protect them from frost. Once the main risk of frost has passed, you can plant them out in the garden.

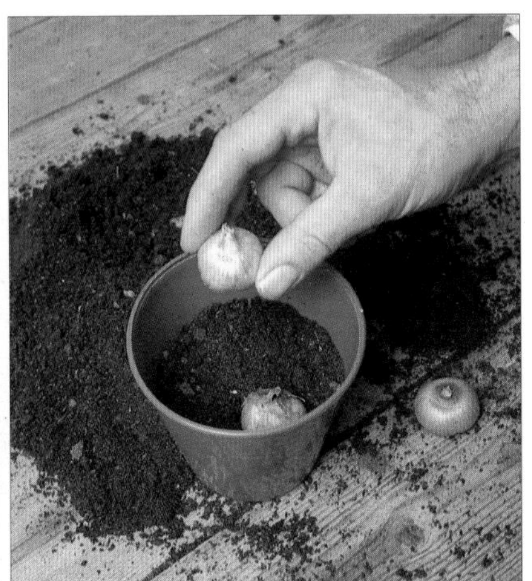

1 *Half fill a 12.5-15cm/5-6in pot with a peat-based or loam potting compost. Choose firm corms in good condition, and plant three in a pot of this size.*

2 *Top up the pot with more compost, firming it gently around the corms, then water well. Keep in a light place, ideally at a temperature of about 10°F/50°C.*

PRUNE HT AND FLORIBUNDA ROSES

Some rose enthusiasts prefer to prune their roses in the autumn, but most gardeners do the job in early spring. Make sure you finish pruning before the leaves start to grow.

Newly planted roses are pruned hard so that they form a strong root system and branch from the base, but established hybrid tea (large-flowered) and floribunda (cluster-flowered) roses need to be pruned only moderately.

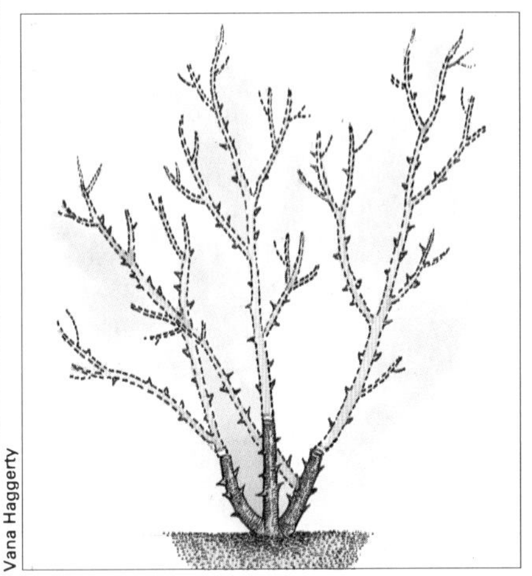

Vana Haggerty

1 *Prune hybrid tea roses planted in the autumn or more recently to within 10-15cm/4-6in of the ground, floribundas to about 15cm/6in from the base.*

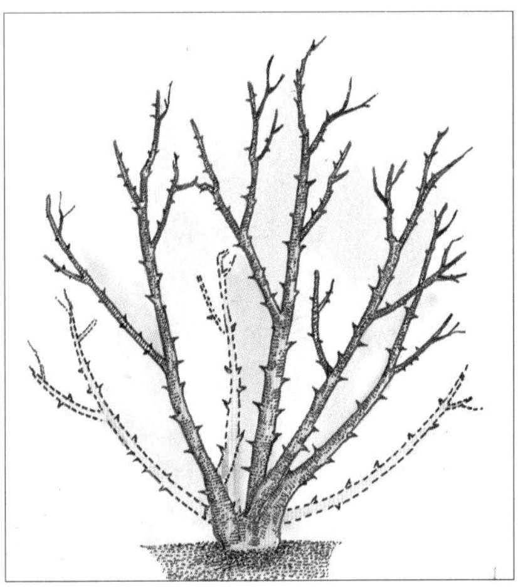

2 *Start pruning established roses by cutting out any very old shoots that flowered poorly last year. Cut out completely any dead or diseased shoots.*

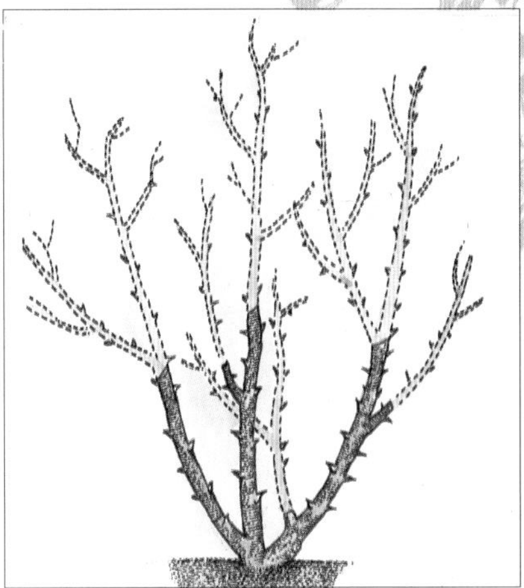

3 *Cut back all the remaining shoots on hybrid tea roses by about half. This encourages strong new shoots to grow from near the base.*

4 *If the remaining shoots look weak, cut these back harder. Leave them about one third of their original length before pruning, to encourage stronger new shoots.*

5 *Floribunda roses are pruned in a similar way. Leave a few shoots unpruned to flower early, and cut some old ones close to the ground.*

CHECKLIST

WHAT TO DO

ALPINES
Protect from slugs and snails

BOG GARDEN
Weed and thin out crowded plants

BORDER PLANTS
Lift and divide if necessary, insert supports

LAWNS
Start mowing, sow or lay a new lawn

ROSES
Finish pruning

SEEDLINGS
Prick out before they become crowded

LOOK AHEAD

PROPAGATE
Take cuttings from old pelargonium plants

PLANT
Pot up some gladioli corms for early flowering
Ranunculus tubers for an early summer show
Tuberous begonias in pots and trays for planting out later

SOW
Summer bedding plants indoors, beetroot, broad beans, carrots, parsnips, peas, radishes and turnips outdoors

WHAT TO SEE

BULBS AND BORDER PLANTS
Crocuses, daffodils, *Iris reticulata*, Lenten rose (*Helleborus orientalis*)

VISITORS

FRIENDS
Chaffinches, frogs, robins, wrens

FOES
Bullfinches, slugs and snails

LATE WINTER
WEEK 5

WHAT TO DO

In mild areas spring already seems well advanced, while in cold districts winter still appears to have an iron grip. But anywhere can experience fluctuations in the weather from day to day at this time of year. There is plenty to do in the garden now, but do not be in too much of a hurry to sow seeds outdoors. They may rot or be eaten before they germinate if you sow outdoors when it it still too cold.

Tidy the bog garden

Bog gardens can become so overgrown after a few years that controlling weeds and preventing cultivated plants from becoming overgrown can be difficult. This is an ideal time to tackle any thinning, dividing and weeding that has to be done, before lush new growth makes it tricky.

Derek Gould

Weed a bog garden before it becomes lush.

Prune roses

Finish pruning roses as soon as possible if not done already. See page 217 for how to prune hybrid tea and floribunda roses, page 212 for repeat-flowering climbers.

Start mowing

Regular mowing will be necessary from now on in most areas, but wait until the grass is dry. Keep the mower blade high initially – 5cm/2in is enough for the first cut when the grass will probably be long anyway.

Make sure blades are sharp and the mower is in good condition. Check the manual for servicing instructions, or have it serviced professionally.

Make a new lawn

This is a good time to sow or lay turf so that the grass can become established before the dry summer weather. If you have already prepared the ground, sow or lay the grass now, otherwise prepare and level the ground then allow it to settle for a couple of weeks.

Vegetables to sow now

If you have a vegetable garden, sow early varieties of carrots and beetroot, broad beans, parsnips, peas, turnips and radishes.

Control slugs and snails

Herbaceous plants such as delphiniums and hostas are at their most vulnerable to slug and snail damage as the new shoots and leaves appear. Alpines too are easily damaged at this time.

Use slug pellets around plants that are normally attacked, and

Harry Smith

Hostas are prone to slug damage.

replace them periodically. If you do not want to use slug pellets there are 'safe' alternatives. Just sprinkling coarse sand or grit around the plants may help.

LOOK AHEAD

Staking is always more successful if it is done early. With the exception of tall, spiky plants such as delphiniums (in which case putting the canes in now will look premature), border plants will look more natural if you insert the supports now so that they can grow through them.

If you have a supply of twiggy sticks of appropriate length, insert these among border plants that tend to get blown over or flop unattractively without support.

Should a supply of suitable natural supports not be available, there are plenty of proprietary ones that work well if you insert them early enough.

Sweet peas can be grown up netting, but canes are usually used, especially if long, straight stems for cutting are required. It is almost time to plant or sow sweet peas, so get the canes or netting in place now – then you can tie them in immediately.

If you want to grow columns of sweet peas at the back of a border, make cane wigwams or construct a tubular column of wire-netting fixed around four long canes.

WHAT TO SEE

Daffodils, in all their golden glory, epitomize spring for many people. There are earlier spring flowers, but none so bold and brash, or so universally planted. They also naturalize well and can be left undisturbed to flower prolifically for years.

If you are used to planting only one or two of the most popular varieties you may think that daffodils have a relatively brief flowering period. By choosing different types and varieties, however, you can have daffodils in bloom in the garden from late winter to mid spring. The exact flowering time of each variety varies from year to year, and is more advanced in a mild spring after a kind winter, but if you buy your bulbs from a good catalogue it will give you the relative flowering times of each variety. By planting varieties from, say, five flowering groups (very early, early, normal, late and very late) you will get the maximum display from your daffodils.

Neil Holmes

Golden daffodils herald spring.

Among the earliest trumpet daffodils to flower are 'Dutch Master' and 'Spellbinder', but earlier still are the dwarf cyclamineus 'Jack Snipe' and 'Peeping Tom', and the outstanding 'Tête-a-Tête', with two or more flowers on each stem.

VISITORS

Whether or not you like frogs, the way in which they seem to appear as if from nowhere at the appointed time in spring, in even the tiniest pond, is something to marvel at. Even a modest pond in a small garden can attract dozens of frogs on an early spring evening, and often many more. In shallow water, the surface can appear to be a seething mass of bodies.

You will know when they have arrived for mating by the incessant croaking, which can go on long into the night. If your pond attracts a large number of frogs, they may make enough noise to wake you at night.

Frogs can change their colour to suit their surroundings, rather like a chameleon, as the pigment cells of the skin expand or contract under the influence of varying intensities of light reflected from their surroundings.

The female is usually fatter than the male, which you can identify by black pads on the first fingers. These help him to hold his mate and are particularly pronounced at this time of year.

The common frog is the one that can be spotted almost everywhere, but in a few areas, the large edible frog can also sometimes be found.

Eric Crichton

A pond crowded with frogs spawning.

TAKE GERANIUM CUTTINGS

Geranium (pelargonium) cuttings are often taken in the autumn and overwintered as young plants. But if you decided to keep the old plants instead, use these to take cuttings as soon as the new shoots have started to grow.

Cuttings will produce more shapely and vigorous plants, and, of course, you will have more of them. If you do not have a greenhouse, a light window-sill will do.

Eric Crichton

1 *For a stunning display of geraniums like this, take cuttings from old plants now if you did not propagate them in the autumn.*

Marshall Cavendish

2 *Take cuttings about 7.5cm/3in long from shoots with healthy leaves. Trim off the lower leaves and stipules (small bract-like growths below each leaf stalk).*

3 *Fill a 13-15cm/5-6in pot with a seed compost or rooting mix. Dip the moistened tip of each cutting into a rooting hormone.*

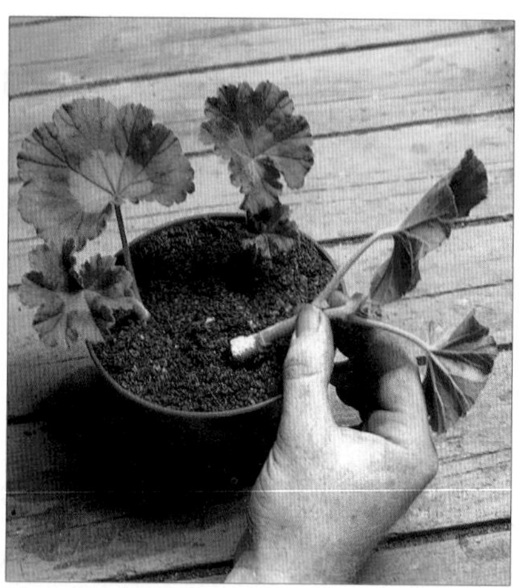

4 *Insert the cuttings around the edge of the pot, using a dibber or a finger to make the holes. Keep just moist in a warm place – a propagator is ideal.*

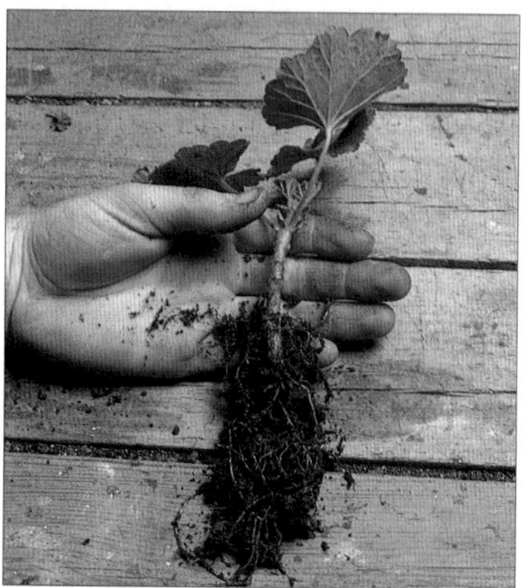

5 *Most cuttings will root within a few weeks. When they have a good root system like this, pot them up individually and plant out in early summer.*

START BEGONIA TUBERS

Tuberous-rooted begonias can be grown in pots in the greenhouse, in window boxes and hanging baskets, and even used for bedding in a sheltered spot. In all cases they are best started off in trays or pots in the greenhouse first. Those for greenhouse display can be put straight into larger pots to avoid having to move them later, but for outdoors use small pots.

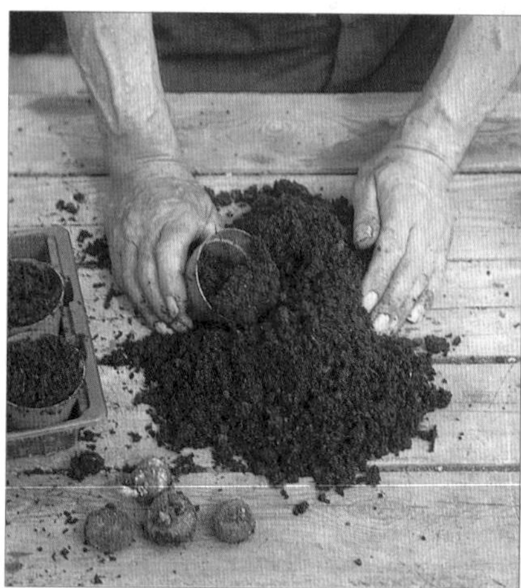

Marshall Cavendish

1 *Loosely fill the pots with a peat-based seed or multi-purpose compost, or a peat-substitute compost. Press the tuber into the compost, concave-side up.*

2 *Keep in a warm, light place, preferably in a greenhouse. Water sparingly until they have started to root. Plant out once there is no risk of frost.*

DIVIDE BORDER PLANTS

If you want to divide herbaceous border plants to propagate your stock, or simply to replant them because the clump has become too large, do it as soon as the shoots emerge.

The plant being divided here is* Sedum spectabile*, but the same method can be used for all border plants with a fibrous root system.

If it is frosty, wait until the weather improves.

1 *Lift the clump with a fork. It may be necessary to loosen the soil around the plant from all sides before you try to lift a very large clump.*

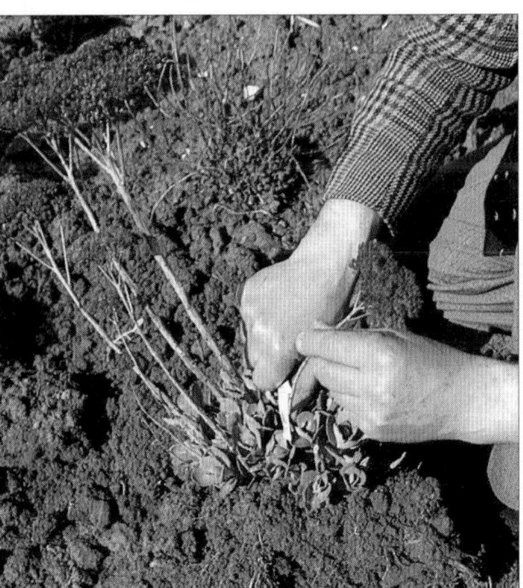

2 *If last year's stems have not been trimmed yet, do it now. If the clump is very large and heavy to move, knock off some of the soil from around the edge.*

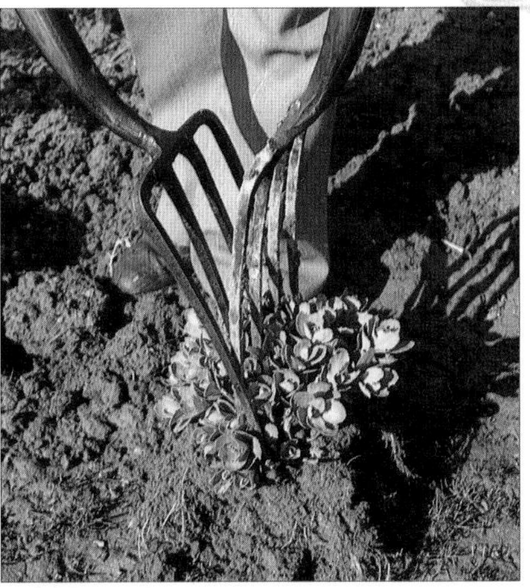

3 *Divide the clump into two or three large pieces initially. Prize them apart with two forks placed back-to-back to provide leverage.*

4 *If you want a few large clumps, replant them as they are. If you require a lot of plants or want to space them out more, separate into smaller pieces by hand.*

5 *Prepare the new ground by forking it over and removing any weeds. Rake in a balanced general fertilizer, then replant the divisions.*

PLANT RANUNCULUS

The double and semi-double forms of* Ranunculus asiaticus *are very different from the buttercups to which they are related. These highly desirable flowers, great for the front of a border or simply to grow as cut flowers, would be more widely grown if they were reliably hardy. The tubers have to be lifted for the winter in cold areas, but you can buy them now in most garden centres and shops that sell bulbs.

1 *Ranunculus tubers are arranged in claw-like clusters. They look unpromising but will produce bright and beautiful flowers in early summer.*

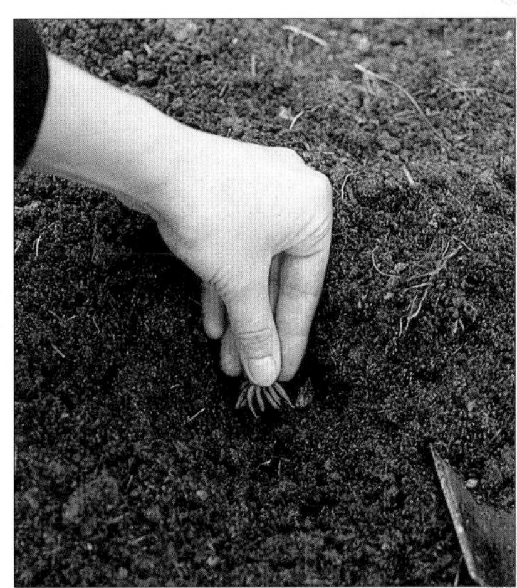

2 *Plant the tubers, claw downwards, about 15cm/6in apart and 5cm/2in deep, in a sunny position, or where they will receive sun for at least a few hours.*

INDEX